Praise for *In Letters of Blood and Fire*

"George Caffentzis's essays in this timely [...] promising analysis of the transmutations of capi [...] a rereading of the classic texts in light of our own times. They teach us the constant alertness that we must embrace at the frontline of value struggle. This teaching is so much more precious to us as we approach a renewed period of struggle capable of subverting the meaning of the current crisis and turning it into an opportunity for emancipation. An alertness that is essential, for our own safety and that of our communities, and that does not find comfort in false myths: capital's beast remains a beast, and there is no technology or privileged type of labour that will deliver us a world of social justice and peace."

—Massimo De Angelis, editor of *The Commoner: A Web Journal of Other Values* and author of *The Beginning of History: Value Struggles and Global Capital*

"George Caffentzis has been the philosopher of the anticapitalist movement from the American civil rights movement of the 1960s to the European autonomists of the 1970s, from the Nigerian workers of the oil boom of the 1980s to the *encuentros* of the Zapatistas in the 1990s, from the feminists of Wages for Housework to the struggle of the precariat for the commons. Trained as both an economist and a physicist he has taken fundamental categories such as money, time, work, energy, and value and rethought them in relation to both revolutionary Marxism and the dynamics of our changing movement. A historian of our own times, he carries the political wisdom of the twentieth century into the twenty-first. He is a lively and dogged polemicist; he dances circles around the pompous marxologist; with the passing of time his thought has grown in depth and increasingly tends to be expressed with pleasure and humor. The lever by which he overturns the world is light as a feather, and its fulcrum is as down-to-earth as the housewife, the student, the peasant, the worker. Here is capitalist critique and proletarian reasoning fit for our time. In one sense he is equally at home in Brooklyn, Maine, the UK, Italy, Nigeria, Greece, or Indonesia, and in another sense he is just as at home with Æsop and Diogenes of antiquity, the English empiricist philosophers of money in the mercantile epoch, or the various European philosophers of modernity who have held sway in U.S. Academia."

—Peter Linebaugh, author of *The Magna Carta Manifesto: Liberties and Commons for All*

"These essays reveal not only not only the blood and fire of twenty-first-century primitive accumulation but also the inescapable linkage of this savage and ongoing process to new forms of futuristic dispossession inscribed with robot ichor, silicon chips, and genomic code. George Caffentzis has for decades been creating a contemporary Marxism that is profoundly theorized, deeply historical, utterly original, compulsively readable and always connected to the fighting fronts of an ever-changing class struggle. Today his writings are integral to, and indispensable for an understanding of, the uprisings of a global proletariat that again explode across the planet."

—Nick Dyer-Witheford, author of *Cyber-Marx: Cycles and Circuits of Struggle in High-Technology Capitalism*

IN LETTERS OF BLOOD AND FIRE
WORK, MACHINES, AND THE CRISIS OF CAPITALISM

George Caffentzis

ISBN: 978-1-60486-335-2
LCCN: 2011939665

Cover and interior design: Antumbra Design/antumbradesign.org

10 9 8 7 6 5 4 3 2

PM Press
PO Box 23912
Oakland, CA 94623
www.pmpress.org

Common Notions
131 8th St. #4
Brooklyn, NY 11215
www.commonnotions.org

Autonomedia
PO Box 568 Williamsburg Station
Brooklyn, NY 11211-0568
www.autonomedia.org

Printed in the USA

Common Notions is an imprint that circulates both enduring and timely formulations of autonomy at the heart of movements beyond capitalism. The series traces a constellation of historical, critical, and visionary meditations on the organization of both domination and its refusal. Inspired by various traditions of autonomism in the United States and around the world, Common Notions aims to provide tools of militant research in our collective reading of struggles past, present, and to come.

Series Editor: Malav Kanuga
info@commonnotions.org | www.commonnotions.org

In the Common Notions series

Selma James, *Sex, Race, and Class—The Perspective of Winning: A Selection of Writings 1952-2011*

Silvia Federici, *Revolution at Point Zero: Housework, Reproduction, and Feminist Struggle*

George Caffentzis, *In Letters of Blood and Fire: Work, Machines, and the Crisis of Capitalism*

Strike Debt, *The Debt Resisters' Operations Manual*

ACKNOWLEDGMENTS

The essays contained in this volume, written over three decades and in three continents, are the product of much collective work, responding to the political problems faced by the anticapitalist movements in which I have participated. Over the years some of these texts have circulated in different forms, but I appreciate that Common Notions and PM Press have decided to make them available in a book, as the political ideas they articulate are still relevant to the present.

The decision to compile this volume came during a two-week session on the Commons I attended held at Blue Mountain Lake Center organized by Dara Greenwald, who though suffering from the disease that was to destroy her life was a powerful presence, inspiring us all to collaborate and engage in new projects. In this spirit, it was another participant, Malav Kanuga of Common Notions, who suggested that it was time for me to weave these essays together (many still unpublished then) into a cohesive theoretical work. For this and for the assistance he has given me to keep the project moving, I deeply thank him. I also want to thank Ramsey Kanaan of PM Press for joining the project and putting his expertise behind it.

Special thanks go the Midnight Notes Collective, my political "home" for more than thirty years. I thank in particular Michaela Brennan, Steven Colatrella, Dan Coughlin, Peter Linebaugh, Monty Neill, David Riker, Hans Widmer, and John Willshire-Carrera as those who I continue to learn from on a daily basis.

I thank also Silvia Federici, who with her love and wisdom has kept me healthy, sane, and as politically precise as possible. Aside from co-authoring "Mormons in Space," she has been involved in all my writings.

Finally, I want to thank my granddaughter Anna, for she is now turning my thoughts to the future. I hope she will find this book useful when she reads it decades from now.

"The Work/Energy Crisis and the Apocalypse" was originally published in *Midnight Notes* 2, no. 1 (1980), 1–29. This article was republished in *Midnight Oil: Work, Energy, War, 1973–1992* (Brooklyn: Autonomedia, 1992) [1980], 215–71.

"Mormons in Space" was originally published in *Midnight Notes* 2, no. 1 (1982), 3–12. An expanded version was published in *Semiotext(e) USA*, edited by Jim Fleming and Peter Lamborn Wilson (Brooklyn: Autonomedia/Semiotext(e)).

"The End of Work or the Renaissance of Slavery? A Critique of Rifkin and Negri" was originally published in *Common Sense: Journal of the Edinburgh Conference of Socialist Economists* 24 (December 1998). This article was revised and republished in *Revolutionary Writing: Common Sense Essays in Post-political Politics*, edited by Werner Bonefeld (Brooklyn: Autonomedia: 2003), 115–34.

"On Africa and Self-Reproducing Automata" was originally published in *The New Enclosures* (Brooklyn: Midnight Notes/Autonomedia, 1990), 35–41.

"Why Machines Cannot Create Value: Marx's Theory of Machines" was originally published in *Cutting Edge: Technology, Information, Capitalism and Social Revolution*, edited by Jim Davis, Thomas Hirschl, and Michael Stack (London: Verso, 1997), 29–56.

"Marx, Turing Machines, and the Labor of Thought" was originally published in *Maine Scholar* 11 (Autumn 2000): 97–112.

"Crystals and Analytic Engines: Historical and Conceptual Preliminaries to a New Theory of Machines" was originally published as "immaterial and affective labor: explored," in *ephemera: theory & politics in organization* 7, no. 1, (June 2007): 24–45, http://www.ephemeraweb.org.

"The Power of Money: Debt and Enclosure" was originally published in *Altreeragioni: Saggi e documenti* 4 (1995): 23–28.

"Notes on the Financial Crisis: From Meltdown to Deep Freeze" was originally published in *Uses of a Whirlwind: Movement, Movements, and Contemporary Radical Currents in the United States*, edited by Team Colors Collective (Oakland: AK Press, 2010), 273–82.

"On the Notion of a Crisis of Social Reproduction: A Theoretical Review" was originally published in *Donne, sviluppo e lavoro di riproduzione*, edited by Mariarosa Dalla Costa and Giovanna Della Costa (Milan: FrancoAngeli, 1996), 173–209. The English translation of the article was published in *Women, Development and Labor of Reproduction: Struggles and Movements*, edited by Mariarosa Dalla Costa and Giovanna Della Costa (Trenton, NJ: Africa World Press 1999), 153–87.

CONTENTS

INTRODUCTION

This selection of political essays I wrote between 1980 and 2010 in the United States, Europe, and Africa deals with the topics that appear in the book's subtitle, "Work, Machines, and the Crisis of Capitalism." I want to briefly describe here the setting of these pieces, their conceptual continuity, and the political aims that animate them.

The last thirty years often seemed to me to be an unrelenting period of chronic capitalist crisis, but the two terminal years illustrate the methodology that these essays reflect. They were moments that were declared to be crises by all the media of the time from Left to Right, the first being called the "energy" crisis and the second the "financial" crisis. But these descriptors are, to my mind, misnomers. An "energy crisis" implies that an abstract physical quantity (energy) is essentially implicated in the crisis, while a "financial crisis" implies it has been caused by an abstract social quantity (money). Such implications conveniently direct oppositional political thinking, strategy, and action down many dead ends. This is why I use scare quotes around "energy" and "financial": the whole point of these essays is to give comrades in the anticapitalist movements a way of speaking and thinking about capitalist crisis that rejects the fetishizing impulse redolent in these phrases and in the political terminology of our time (including much in the rhetoric of the Left). My political assumption here is that a better description of the system may offer up more effective ways of dismantling it.

Thus, in the book's first essay, "The Work/Energy Crisis and the Apocalypse," the "energy" crisis is renamed a work/energy crisis, for what was in crisis in 1980 was capital's control over *work* across the planet and in question was how *energy* commodities were to be used to impose once again the control that capital once had over the work process (the most important process within capitalism). In one of the last essays of the book, "Notes on the Financial Crisis," the "financial" crisis of 2010 is described as an outcome of class struggles being fought between workers and capitalists around the world, often in new territory that includes credit and debt.

From beginning to end, these essays present a continuous effort to apply Marxist categories that (to use Fanon's topological phrase) are "stretched," i.e., they are transformed without being "torn." They must be stretched because they take unwaged workers' (especially women's) struggles as basic to the understanding of capitalism and its crises; they refuse to accept a fetishism of machines as well as of commodities and money to provide an explanation of historical events; and they provide a space of possibility for anticapitalist movements.

The essays make sense of, and provide evidence for, the claim that workers can change the world. These essays, by refusing to pose the main problematic of anticapitalism as a technical one (whether it be climate change or the lack of high-tech food production), put the blockages squarely on the divisions and hierarchies—sexual, gendered, racial, ethnic, national, and legal—that capitalism is continuously creating and reproducing among workers, waged and unwaged.

Before going on to describe some of the novelties of the book, I should point out that these essays are not "mine" as such, since most of them were written with the help, inspiration, and discussion of comrades, most of whom were either members of the Midnight Notes Collective or politically close to it. They provided my essays with an immediate external audience and even came to constitute my interior "impartial spectator" (to borrow a conceptual persona from Adam Smith) to this day. More than a few words, then, about the Midnight Notes Collective are appropriate for an introduction of these essays. Midnight Notes (MN) was founded in 1979 in Boston and New York City and we saw ourselves as a bridge between the workers' movements of the past (and the wealth of knowledge produced by them, including but not exclusively Marxism) and the new social movements that were beginning to take on a major role in thwarting capital's plans.

One simplistic formula for defining our project then is "MN = social movements + working-class categories." In this project, we were deeply influenced by the Wages for Housework theorists like Mariarosa Dalla Costa, Silvia Federici, and Selma James, who in effect did exactly that (and more) for the feminist and for the waged workers' movements, especially Marxism.[1] By using categories such as wages, surplus value, and profits to describe reproductive work in the home, they preserved and transformed these very notions. Of course, the Marxist categories we used were also already "stretched" by other operaist thinkers and activists in Italy such as Mario Tronti, Ferruccio Gambino, Sergio Bologna, and Toni Negri among many others. Finally, we were also affected by the historians like E.P. Thompson and his comrades who studied the class struggle in the seventeenth

---

[1] Mariarosa Dalla Costa and Selma James, *The Power of Women and the Subversion of the Community* (Bristol: Falling Wall Press, 1972) and Silvia Federici, "Wages against Housework" in *Revolution at Point Zero: Housework, Reproduction, and Feminist Struggle* (Oakland: PM Press/Common Notions, 2012).

and eighteenth centuries when the wage had not yet become the dominant pole of analysis of class composition.

MN's first application of this methodology was with the anti–nuclear power movement in the late 1970s that proved to be a major force for blocking the diffusion of nuclear reactors in Europe and the United States. "The Work/Energy Crisis and the Apocalypse" came out of this effort. After that, up until about a decade ago, we applied similar logic to the anti–nuclear war, anti–capital punishment, anti-globalization, pro-Zapatista, and pro-commons movements. Though only a few of the essays in this book were published in *MN*, they were all affected by the political trajectory of the collective until the end of its active phase a few years ago.

Work and Its Refusal

I was blessed with a few enlightening epiphanies about capitalism in the early 1970s, undoubtedly generated by the power of the anticapitalist movements of the time. One was the insight in 1971 when I finally began living with, and seeing in everything around me, the work of men and women—frozen and inured, speaking, whispering, and even screaming. The second, in 1973, was the recognition stimulated by the Wages for Housework movement that much of the work in capitalism was unwaged reproductive labor done by women.[2] The third was in 1974, when I began to hear and see the refusal of work in the objects of everyday life. Ever since then, I have seen the world of objects as products of an intertwined struggle between work and its refusal and every person's actions as being either work for capital (or preparation for it) or its refusal. Rarely do I find these opposing forces in pure form or easily disentangled. Therefore, for me, the class struggle is not to be found only in the great strikes, workers' insurrections, and revolutionary charters. Its heart is the microstruggles between work and its refusal that eventually become the strikes, insurrections, and charters that are recorded in the history books.

A key element of this insight was to reinterpret the process of work in capitalism. Work is a manifold extending throughout human activities with much of it unwaged, invisible, and unrecognized. Any attempt to isolate work in a particular locale (a factory, field, or mine) distorts it, since work is also to be found in the home, in the transport of workers, and in prisons. As we learned from the Wages for Housework perspective, the worker and the working class are no longer to be identified with the waged workers who wear a watch and are "protected" by union contracts. Housewives, slaves, drug runners, sharecrop peasants, and prisoners are all part of the working class. Their work creates value on par with the work of waged workers throughout the history of capitalism and their refusal of this work can have as devastating consequences for capitalists as the strikes of waged workers.

I had to "stretch" (as Fanon said) the Marxist concepts of labor and labor-power to achieve this result. But along with this stretching of the notion of work is

---

[2] Although it is convenient, I am reluctant to use the phrase "capitalist society" because the phrase implies that the relations ruled by capital are the product of voluntary decisions.

also a widening of the area of the struggle against work. This vision of the manifold of work had an impact on me similar to the one the notion of universal gravitation had on many others centuries ago. Just as the fall of the apple and the movement of the moon were explained by a single force, I began to see the signs of responses to the struggle against work everywhere, from the shape and weight of bricks or door knobs to the design of Levittown in the late 1940s. The world of objects began to speak to me not only of labor, but of the negative power of its refusal. The formal strike was no longer to be the measure of the struggle against work; rather, it was the result of thousands of microrefusals in the course of a workday. The details of "counterplanning" from the shop floor to the kitchen began to reveal themselves in my eyes everywhere they settled.

In the essays in Part One, I applied this insight about work in a variety of ways: the analysis of the "energy crisis" as a *work*/energy crisis, space travel as housework (with Silvia Federici), computerization of production as the initiation of huge areas of slave-like work, time as conditioned by the work/refusal of work process, and cognitive workers being as vulnerable to the loss of their autonomy as the cottage industry workers of the seventeenth and eighteenth centuries.

Machines

The middle section of the book is devoted to an investigation on the nature of machines in capitalism. The essays herein were inspired by an ongoing debate concerning the view that the integration of science into the production process has created a system of machines that made capital's need for workers obsolete. This view has had influential proponents on both on the Left as well as on the Right, who argue that with increasing mechanization, capitalism did not need any more workers and that, indeed, the number of "superfluous" workers would explode in the beginning of the twenty-first century. I have been arguing against this view since the late 1970s in debates with political comrades like Toni Negri and Christian Marazzi.[3]

I believe that the critical experiment concerning this hypothesis was run in the 1990s with the application of structural adjustment throughout Africa, Asia, and South America; the so-called "collapse" of communism in the Soviet Union and Eastern Europe; and finally the complete triumph of Deng's economic counterrevolution in China. After all, the addition of two to three billion workers to the world labor market showed that capitalism's "lust for labor" has hardly been diminished by the introduction of computers, robots, and self-reproducing automata to the heat engines and levers and pulleys of the past in the production of commodities. The "superfluous worker" hypothesis has been quite decisively disconfirmed and most of the theorists who were disdainful of the labor theory of value have recently begun to recycle it.

Aside from their original inspiration, these machine essays open up two still-controversial claims. The first is that the new theory of machines introduced in the twentieth century—or, more accurately, a theory of a new machine along side

---

[3] Antonio Negri, *Marx Beyond Marx* (Brooklyn: Autonomedia, 1991) and Christian Marazzi, *The Violence of Financial Capitalism* (Los Angeles: Semiotext(e), 2010).

the simple machines of ancient Greek and Roman times (the lever, pulley, screw, wedge, inclined plane, and wheel and axle) theorized by Galileo in the seventeenth century and the heat engines theorized by Sadi Carnot in the nineteenth century—put the Marxist theory of capitalism into crisis. This "new" machine is the Turing machine, theorized by Alan Turing in the 1930s (although its prototype was implicit in Charles Babbage's analytic engine that was being worked on in the London of Marx's time).

Every basic machine type abstracts, analyzes, and measures a species of human work. Thus, the lever gives us the image of a certain kind of work that moves masses and in general transforms mechanical forces from one site to another (e.g., the arm), while the heat engine transforms heat energy into mechanical force that models the movement of the heart. The theory of Turing machines models computational labor (in fact, in the original expositions of the theory the "computer" was a clerical worker) and gives us a way of abstracting, analyzing, and measuring this labor (of the brain). Certainly, Marx was familiar with simple machines and heat engines, but he was unaware of the importance of Charles Babbage's work on the analytic engine, although he had read Babbage's texts on machinery in general, and they were contemporaries and fellow Londoners.

This gap in Marx's theory of machines is not fatal to his theory, but it is an important lacuna. A theory of Turing machines brings into focus the form of work that is increasingly important in the late twentieth and early twenty-first century as well as the limits to this form of work. As each machine type has its characteristic limits that reflect the limit of the application of labor it models, there is a limit to the possibility of transforming heat into work determined by the Second Law of thermodynamics. Hence the ratio between workers' caloric input and labor output (a ratio obsessively measured by Nazi scientists) could never reach 100 percent efficiency. Similarly, there are limits to the solution of certain problems (e.g., the halting problem cannot be solved since there cannot be a Turing machine that would determine whether any particular Turing machine will halt at some point in its operation) that are based upon the very nature of such machines. These Turing machine limits show that there are limits in the computational work process as well.

The second aspect of the theory of machines for capitalism that these essays deal with is the defense of the claim that machines do not create value. This is an important axiom of Marx's, but this claim can appear strange in this period of automated factories, robots, and drones. Aren't machines employed to increase the production of objects with fewer workers? Ideally, wouldn't it be possible to have machines that would not require workers' supervision producing commodities that have value?

My response to these retorts is in Part Two of this book. But the key, I argue, is to be found in the refusal of work I discussed above, for a necessary condition for there to be value-creating labor is that it can be refused. If a movement cannot be refused, then it becomes part of the value-transferring, not value-creating, part of the production process. A zombie assembly line factory (in the sense of a series of human beings who are under the total control of a sorcerer-boss) would show us an example of valueless production even though the products have value imposed on them due to the transfer of value from other areas of production that are actually value-creating.

Crisis and War

Part Three analyzes crisis and war using the categories of class struggle. In both Marxist thought and in bourgeois economics, the notion of crisis is usually reserved for the realm of commodity production or financial transactions when the transactions between money and commodities are in question and capitalists default on their loans. In these essays, however, the notion of crisis is stretched in two dimensions.

The first stretching introduces a notion of a crisis of social reproduction that includes traumatic changes to the form of social reproduction that indicate the inability to complete a cycle of reproduction. These phenomena range from war to famine to women's mass refusal of pregnancy, from Ares to Demeter to Lysistrata. Of course, there cannot be a crisis of social reproduction that does not have an impact on the sphere of commodity production, since the latter depends upon the former to provide the vital ingredient for all production of value, labor. But when the continuation of a mode of social reproduction is put in question, the class struggle is revealed with exceptional clarity. It shows, for example, war to be as essential to capitalist social reproduction as the decline of value production in response to a decline in the rate of profit.

The second stretching of the notion of crisis is in the class struggle analysis of debt and credit. In Marxism, the notion of class struggle between workers and capital has traditionally been reserved for the often-antagonistic relationship between wages and profits, while financial categories like interest, debt, and credit were determined by relations among capitalists. Workers' struggles were not seen as involved in the availability of credit and its interest rate. In analysis of the present crisis, however, it is essential to introduce class dynamics into the explanation of debt's onset, duration, and outcome.

Conclusion: The Title

The meaning of this book's subtitle is straightforward enough, but the title, "In Letters of Blood and Fire," needs an explanation. It is a quotation of a passage in the first volume of Marx's *Capital*, where he concludes his account of how the accumulation of capital originated. In a complex metaphor, Marx states that the only way to write about the history of the origins of capitalism in the sixteenth century is to recognize that if history were a book and if actions were its letters, then the actions comprising the chapter on original accumulation are "written . . . in letters of blood and fire." Images of this blood and fire can be readily found in numerous sixteenth- and seventeenth-century paintings of peasant cottages in flames, surrounded by soldiers holding bloody swords: the story of rural workers being driven from the common lands, forests, and waters is often hidden under a biblical titles like "The Slaughter of the Innocents."

Capitalism did not start as the result of the realization that trading commodities is a "win-win" exchange, but as a series of acts of violent expropriation and enslavement in many sites across the planet. This violence made it possible to accumulate the initial mass of laboring bodies required for the endangered ruling classes of Western Europe to begin a cycle of exploitation that has lasted to this day. Though the origin of capitalism required European working bodies and lands, the "lust for labor" (in Silvia Federici's phrase) was to drive this quest to the Americas in the form of conquistadors and "explorers."

Marx also wrote that workers would eventually become so accustomed to the rhythms and flows of capitalist life that they would come to consider them equivalent to forces of nature. They would go to work and leave it as "naturally" as the swimmer rises and falls with the tides. But in this assessment he was mistaken. Refusal of work and of capitalist relations has been an essential force shaping the history of capitalism as much as work itself. Only in a few souls is capitalism considered even "second nature." Everywhere that we examine capitalist regimes, we can see, from macroeconomic policies to the shape and weight of doors and the design of office chairs, a refusal of work mixed in with the overriding obsession with work that is the birthmark of capitalism. In fact, the very logic of capital requires this antinomy. That is why the annals of contemporary capitalism are *still* written in "letters" of blood and fire and why this will be so until its blessed end.

I
WORK/REFUSAL

THE WORK/ENERGY CRISIS AND THE APOCALYPSE

The litany of natural stuffs—petroleum, natural gas, uranium, coal, wood, water, sunlight—apprehension about their limits, joy in their abundance, and skepticism about their benefits, pass for the bulk of "analyses" of the "energy crisis" that "we" face. Whereas in the 1950s and 1960s, Nature was "under control" and the robots (e.g., Hal in *2001*) were rebelling, now it appears that Mother Nature is turning a new face. Instead of the obedient, invisible, and infinitely malleable material of social development, the terrestrial abode seems stingy and treacherously seductive. For the energy crisis is usually traced to two problems:

(a) The "limited" or "finite" amount of fossil and uranium fuels in the earth;
(b) The increasingly "surprising" discovery of interactions between the use of these fuels and their biological and social effects.

Although the analysts place different emphases on these two "problems," their "solutions" usually address both. Indeed, the "great energy debate" (at least what passes for it) is a confrontation between the anti-limitationists, who are anxious about the rapidly approaching abyss of zero-oil-coal-natural gas-uranium and are ready to introduce any "way out," however untried, and the collective interactionists, who argue that the "balance" or "fabric" of Nature is so intricate and fragile (to mix metaphors) that any of the schemes of the anti-limitationists would drive Mother Nature into a schizophrenic breakdown.

From this debate, one would presume that these are momentous times.

They are, but not in the way that is being implied. On the one side, the anti-limitationists cringe in terror at the prospect of a "day the earth stood still" repeated so often that "civilization" (sometimes with the proviso "as we know it") collapses into an age of social anarchy—starvation, rape, murder, and cannibalism ("What's new?" we might ask). On the other side stand the equally apocalyptic interactionists envisioning huge floods let loose by the CO_2 "hot house" effect, or the end of all biological life due to the depletion of the ozone layer causing a tidal wave of high-energy radiation to penetrate the chromosome linkages and break down the proteins, or a festering mutant jungle released by the radioactive wastes of nuclear reactors. Conclusion: either social anarchy or natural anarchy. "Take your choice," we're told. But must we choose? Are these our alternatives?

This debate, with its apocalyptic overtones, indicates a crucial crisis for capital and its attempt to carry through a major reorganization in the accumulation process to overcome it. The Apocalypse is no accident. Whenever the ongoing model of exploitation becomes untenable, capital has intimations of mortality *qua* the world's end. Every period of capitalist development has had its apocalypses. I'm not referring here to the microapocalypse of death: everybody dies, and even if everybody dies at the same time (I mean everybody), what's the problem? The earth becomes a cleared tape and why should the angels grieve?

I am talking about those functional apocalypses that mark every major change in capitalist development and thought. For the Apocalypse was approached at other times in the history of capital, when the class struggle reached a level that jeopardized capital's command.

In the seventeenth century, a pervasive premonition of apocalypse was voiced by the "philosophers," "astronomers," and "anatomists" (i.e., capital's planners) in the face of the revolutionary upheavals of the newly forming proletariat that was being introduced to the capitalist discipline of work. In this phase, questions of inertia, time, and order were paramount. The control mechanisms were manageable only by external forces. Capital's concern with its apocalyptic potentialities can be seen reflected in Newton's theory of the solar system: the planets revolve around the sun, but their revolutions continually deviate from the equilibrium path because of the random, irregular gravitational impulses they communicate to each other. Ptolemy's crystal suddenly looked like a mob that with this-and-that, slowly, imperceptibly, became unruly, though it was nominally dominated by the gravitational field of the sun. The deviations accumulated to a point where some planets would spin off into the stellar depths while the others would dive into the sun's inferno. Hence Newton's argument for the necessity of God's existence, whose function in the universe was to prevent this catastrophe by periodically returning the planets to their equilibrium orbits via a true miracle. The solar system was the "Big Watch" and God was not only the watchmaker but also the watch repairer. Otherwise the mechanism, however finely wrought, would snap and break through its blind obedience to the laws of inertia. God must intervene to create orderly time from chaotic mixtures of inertia and attraction. Given the universal identification of God with the state in the seventeenth century, it is not hard to decipher Newton's prescription for the state policy vis-à-vis the apocalypse portended by its "wandering stars," the proletariat. (A prescription Newton embodied in his job as the inquisitor and torturer of counterfeiters for the Royal Mint.)

In the Newtonian period, capital's main task is the regularization of time as a precondition for lengthening the working day. Medieval production time was circular and the pacing of work and "rest" fixed by "eternal" seasonal and diurnal dichotomies. Summer and days could not be stretched; winter and nights could not be shrunk at will. Newton and his fellow "century of genius" planners had to create a nonterrestrial work-time that would be the same in winter and summer, in the night as in the day, on earth as it is in heaven. Without this transformation of time, lengthening the working day would be impossible to imagine, much less impose "with fire and blood."

By contrast, the "revolutions" and organizational forms thrown up by the working class in the first half of the nineteenth century spelled the end of a period where profits could be created by stretching the working day to its limit. Capital had to "revolutionize" the technical and social conditions of production to turn the proletarian revolt against work into an intensively productive working day. Absolute time was no more of the essence, productive intensity was. Capital could no more complain that the working class was inert, unmotivated, or tending to rest. The class was on the move, scheming, energetic, and volatile. If the workhouse prison sealed from "the elements" was the first laboratory of work, the working class was clearly blowing out the sides of the container and destroying the experiment. The problem was no more how to confine workers as long as possible, but how to transform their energy and revolutionary heat into work. Not surprisingly, thermodynamics, "the study of energy, primarily with regard to heat and work," became the science after 1848.

Thermodynamics began with Sadi Carnot's attempt to determine the possibilities and limits of creating productive work out of heat and energy; when in confining it, it explodes. His leading idea was that if a mass is exploding, you should give it a way out in a way that it will push a piston and thus do work for you. Carnot's analysis focused upon an idealized version of Manchester's "demonic" steam engine, and attempted to determine the conditions under which the expansion/compression cycle of a gas would give a maximum amount of work. Carnot's cycle thus became a representation of the cycle of class struggle that was taking shape in the nineteenth century, putting the working class's wage demand at the center of the "business cycle."

Carnot's laws of thermodynamics grew out of his memoir and led, as Ariadne's threads, out of the "crisis labyrinth." For physics is not only about Nature and applied just to technology, its essential function is to provide models of capitalist work. The ultimate nature for capital is human nature, while the crucial element of technology is work. The First Law of thermodynamics, for example, did not simply recognize that though energy has many forms (not just "mechanical"), each could be transformed into the other without loss. Its consequences impinged on capital's conception of labor-power. A more general view of energy was imperative if the technical and social conditions of production were to be "revolutionized," for the old mode of production assumed a fixed limit on the forms of energy that could generate work. This new Law taught capital a generality and flexibility in its productive arrangements that it did not even experiment with in the First Industrial Revolution.

Like Darwin's discovery, Gustav Mayer's first enunciation of the law of the conservation of energy occurred in a typical nineteenth-century way—on an imperial voyage to the tropics. "A sailor fell ill of some lung disease. Mayer bled him, observed that venous blood was a brighter red in the tropics, much closer to arterial, and concluded that metabolism drew less oxygen from the blood in hot climates because maintenance of body temperature required less heat."[1] In Mayer's perspective, the sailor's body was the mediator of manifold forms of force that are "indestructible, variable, imponderable." Though the forms of force and energy would change their transformations, they conserved the basic quantity of production—energy. The concept of energy is thus defined on such a level of generality and abstractness that an enterprising spirit would see the possibility of producing work from novel, untoward sources.

While the infinite multiplicity of energetic forms inspired a tremendous optimism in capital's search for new workforces, thermodynamics laces this high with arsenic: the Second Law. An ominous version goes like this: a perpetual motion machine completely transforming the energy of the surroundings into work without loss is an impossibility. The Second Law, however, has even darker consequences than deflating capital's dream of getting work for free (having workers "living on air"). It states that in any work-energy process less and less energy becomes available for work. Entropy (the measure of work unavailability) increases. Clausius put it in cosmic form: "The energy of the universe is constant; the entropy of the universe increases to a maximum."[2]

The Second Law announced the apocalypse characteristic of a productivity-craving capital: heat death. Each cycle of work increases the unavailability of energy for work. As the efficiency of the heat engine depends on the distance between heat input and heat output, the Second Law predicts a slow, downhill leveling of heat-energy differences (on a cosmological scale), until there are no more flows of energy for work. "The world is living on its capital" and all around is the whisper of the impending silence.

This image of an undifferentiated, chaotic world had a twofold echo: in the rhetoricians of mass culture like Henry Adams ("the so-called modern world can only pervert and degrade the conceptions of the primitive instinct of art and feeling, and that our only chance is to accept the limited number of survivors—the one-in-a-thousand of born artists and poets—and to intensify the energy of feeling within that radiant centre"), and in the pragmatic thought of Frederick Taylor.[3] Henry Adams mourned over the loss of accumulated values that, at best, could only be "saved" in the leveling of social and cultural differences announced by "energy's

---

[1] Charles Gillespie, *The Edge of Objectivity* (Princeton: Princeton University Press, 1960), 376.

[2] Ibid.

[3] Quoted in Jacob Clavner Leventon, *The Mind and Art of Henry Adams* (Boston: Houghton Mifflin Co., 1957), 377.

dissipation" into a heat death apocalypse. Taylor instead saw in this apocalypse the essence of a project: productivity is efficiency. His answer to the Second Law (if not absolutely, relatively) is not "conservative," it is a "revolutionary" attempt to create a far more efficient organization of work and to perfect the intermeshing of worker with environment. Taylor attempted in practice what Carnot did in theory: test the limits of an efficient transformation of energy into work. In a typical American fashion, he turned to the man-machine. Once again, it seemed that the apocalypse could be averted if Action was taken. This time, however, it was not the action of God *qua* superstate, but capital's planning in its own self-conscious, scientific analysis: scientific management.

Newton's apocalypse and Clausius's apocalypse do not simply have analogical connections with capital's crisis in their respective periods. The theories from which their apocalypses derive from do not merely have contingent or ideological relations with the contemporary, ongoing organization of work. Capitalist crises stem from refusal of work. Thus, in times of crisis, new analyses of work, new schemes for overcoming resistances to it become imperative. Physics, in this context, does not have a separate content, but provides definite analyses of work and new plans for its organization. Its "models" may appear abstract, but they are directly related to the labor process.

Newton's parable of the transformation of working-class inertia into work and his appeal to God *qua* State to restore equilibrium under centripetal and centrifugal pressures is a general methodological scheme. The relation of thermodynamics to work is more explicit. The work of thermodynamics and the work of capital are no mere homonyms. Capital faces working-class resistance to work in continuously new ways as this resistance changes in its power and organization (though it may seem "impotent" and "chaotic"). Capital is concerned with physical work because the labor-process is the transformation of labor-power (energy, inertia) into labor (work). This is the "eternal necessity" of capital, and physics provides models for overcoming "resistances" and measuring rods of levels of crisis. The Apocalypse is an extreme measure of the failure of these models. Capital's problem in the nineteenth century changes from that of Newton's time in the same way the resistance of inert machines shifts into the chaotic energy of random microparticles. Essentially, however, it remains the same: what is the possibility, limit, and method of creating useful work ("order") out of the almost natural evasion, subversion, resistance, and covertness or the working class?

Capital's despair is always hypothetical, yet always virtually existent. This is the multiple function of the apocalypse. It serves not only as a parameter for the ongoing process of work organization and experimentation, it serves also as a reminder and a threat: a reminder, because capital's control is contingent and revolutionary potentialities exist at each instant; a threat, because it attempts to project the destruction of capital as the destruction of the universe (as in the heat death). As long as the "elements" of the working class are attached to the totality, the apocalypse is the extreme point where opposites meet in avoidance. It is capital's threat, if we go too far, to take us all down with it. If we annoy God too much, if we agitate too much, if we become too unavailable for work, then the "mutual destruction of the classes" is used as a club to bring us back into line. But must the molecule fear if the engine dies?

What of the "energy crisis" and its apocalypses? The first thing to note is that the term "energy crisis" is a misnomer. Energy is conserved and quantitatively immense, there can be no lack of it. The true cause of capital's crisis in the last decade is work, or more precisely, the struggle against it. The proper name for the crisis then is the "work crisis" or, better yet, the "work/energy crisis." The problem Capital faces is not the quantity of work per se, but the ratio of that work to the energy (or labor-power) that creates it. Capital is not just a product of work. Capital is the process of work-creation, i.e., the condition for transforming energy into work. Energy has within it a restless activity, an unpredictable microscopic elusiveness, antagonistic, indifferent as well as productive of the work that capital so desperately needs. Though the eternal cycle of capitalist reality is the transformation of energies into work, its problem is that unless certain quantitative levels are reached, the relationship expressed in the work/energy ratio collapses. If entropy increases, if the availability of the working class for work decreases, then the apocalypse threatens.

The forms that the apocalypse takes in this crisis are crucial. They signal both a warning and a specific threat, just as the heat death apocalypse inspired Taylorism and the Newtonian centripetal/centrifugal catastrophes dictated certain features of mercantilist state intervention. What do the anti-limitationists and interactionists allow for decoding the present crisis? The first step in the decoding must lie with "nature." It appears that Nature and its stuffs are an independent pole, given, and distinct from capital—it's "raw" material, as it were. From the exhaustion curves of oil or natural gas it appears that a black hole is absolutely devouring them. But for capital, Nature *qua* Nature is nonexistent. Nature too is a commodity. You never have oil, or natural gas, or even photons that do not take a commodity form. Their commodity reality is what is crucial. Even when you talk of the Earth or the solar system, you cannot speak of a noncapitalist reality. The energy problem is unequivocally a problem of capital and not of "nature" or "Nature and Man." Our problem is to see that capital's difficulties in planning and accumulating spring from its struggle against the refusal of work (the multidimensional subversion of the orderly transformation of energy into work). Thus, according to our decoding, through the noise of the apocalypse, we must see in the oil caverns, in the wisps of natural gas curling in subterranean abysses, something more familiar: the class struggle.

One's Apocalypse Is Another's Utopia

To decode the messages of the apocalypse we should see that both the anti-limitationists and the interactionists demand a complete change in the mode of production. They are "revolutionaries" because they fear something in the present mode that disintegrates capital's touch: a demand, an activity and a refusal that has not been encompassed.

The anti-limitationists focus on the "need" to end the oil-auto assembly line economy of the postwar era. Taking "the father of the H bomb," Edward Teller's "Energy: A Plan for Action" as indicative of their position, we see that by the beginning of the next century they envision a completely different world of production compared with the 1970s.[4] Consider some proportions. In 1973, electricity production demanded 25 percent of the total energy of the U.S., while transportation (excluding auto production) demanded 25 percent. There was a rough balance between these two sectors in the last decade.

Teller, on the contrary, envisions a radically new system where electricity would demand 50 percent of the total energy, with transportation reduced to 11 percent. (The "raw material" would come from a vast increase in Western coal strip mines and the use of nuclear reactors.) This would involve a complete reorganization of production and reproduction, though the number of workers necessary to supply the fuel and run the power plants would undergo relatively minor increases. Teller argues not only for a substantial increase in "energy" consumption, in line with the historical trend, but for a radical shift in the structure of work. What he has in mind is revealed by his "Manpower Requirements":

> No matter what popular opinion asks us to believe, technology will be crucial for human survival. Contrary to much of our current thinking, technology and its development is not antithetical to human values. Indeed, quite the opposite is true. Tool making and the social organization it implies are very deeply ingrained in our natures. This is, in fact, the primary attribute that distinguishes man from other animals. We must continue to adapt our technology, which is, in essence, our ability to shape nature more effectively in order to face the problems that this human race faces today. It is for this reason that the development and expansion of technical education is so important. It is only through the possession of high skills and the development of educational systems for the acquisition of these skills that human prosperity can be insured.[5]

Teller envisions a new "New Atlantis" with a priesthood of highly "skilled" scientist-technicians surrounded by an army of "craftsmen" who monitor, develop, and control the automated production processes with computer networks. This is a sample of how his vision would work:

> Computers have been introduced in central control stations to control interties for the purpose of optimizing the use of energy by drawing at any time on the cheapest available source of electricity. These computers are also beginning to be used to store and display data about the state of the major components of the generating plants and transmission lines. This will help the dispatcher to make the right decision, for instance, by accepting a local and temporary brownout, or even blackout, rather than permitting an overstrained system to break down.[6]

---

[4] Edward Teller, "Energy: A Plan for Action" in *Power & Security*, eds. Edward Teller, Hans Mark, and John S. Foster Jr., 1–82 (Lexington, MA: Lexington Books, 1976).

[5] Ibid.

[6] Ibid.

We have here a centralized neural society where the work process is integrated at the speed of light in reverberating feedback circuits modulated to prevent total breakdown. Capital finally finds its etymology. Teller spells the end of the ass-kicking truckers' songs, the lyric of the stoned highway at 3 a.m.; everything is concentrated now, controlled in the wires of an air-conditioned brain. The internal combustion engine, after all, has been an enormous source of "decentralization" of desires that cannot be tolerated, for it seems to lead to catastrophe.

Teller's apocalypse flashes the desolation of an oil-starved assembly line economy; his utopia is an electronic techno-nuclear model of capital allowing for a new leap in accumulation. Yet one's apocalypse is another's utopia. We see this when we turn to the interactionists, who argue that any step down Teller's path leads to human annihilation. The Odums, an ecologist and a social worker, serve as a precise counterpole to Teller for they are extremists even among interactionists.[7] They agree with Teller that the assembly line economy is over, but argue that the future holds no technological solution to declining "energy." They dismiss both the solar energy enthusiasts and the fusion freaks. In their view, "various schemes for harnessing solar energy turn out to be installations based mainly on fossil fuels, with their main energy flows not really supported by the sun." Their argument against the possibility of fusion power is certainly original: "Fusion could be disastrous to humanity either if it were so rich that it gave too much energy, or if it took all our capital and gave us no net energy." If it failed and all the energy eggs were in the fusion basket, disaster would follow; but if it were successful it would release such an intense energy flow that too much energy would be required "to maintain control as it is diluted to the intensity of the human system." The very price of success would guarantee disaster.

Thus "we" can neither remain with the present mode of production based upon dwindling reserves, nor can the path of "technological leap" save the system. They propose a new mode of production, a "steady-state and low-energy" economy, bringing the human race into a safe equilibrium with Nature. The price for survival, however, is not only the disco beat: "To become adapted to the steady state, people will have to give up their restlessness and their insistence on the large, the new and the different. But the young people who tried to form a low-energy subculture to avoid the excesses of the high-energy growth period will also have to change. More work will be expected from each individual in the low-energy society because there will be fewer machines."[8]

Examples of the Odums' steady-state utopia are rainforests, coral reefs, and the "uniformly cold bottom of the sea (near freezing)," as well as preindustrial India's agricultural villages. The common element in such systems is "a great diversity; intimate, highly organized symbiotic relationships; organisms with complex behavior programs by which they serve each other; well timed processing of

[7] Howard T. Odum and Elisabeth C. Odum, *Energy Basis for Man and Nature* (New York: McGraw-Hill, 1976).

[8] Ibid.

mineral cycles that do not lose critical materials; and highly productive conversions of inflowing energy."

"The Octopus's Garden in the Shade" becomes the solution to the energy crisis. Here are some features of the steady-state economy that more precisely describe the Odums' vision:

- Growth stimulating industries are eliminated.
- Less emphasis on transportation.
- Balanced governmental budgets.
- Miniaturization of technology to use less energy.
- Decrease in public and private choices and experiments.
- Urban construction will be replaced by separate and smaller houses.
- Farms use more land, less fuel, and more hand labor.
- Properties of high concentration of energy will decrease: crime, accidents, law enforcement, noise, central services, and taxes.

No more cities, no more travel, no more factories, no more power plants, and presumably no state. Just the quiet labor-intensive life on Jim Jones's farm (after they've seen Paree?). The necessary restructuring of employment to realize this utopia is obvious. Unemployment in the "growth and luxury industries" will "shift people to agriculture" with wages being steadily cut and unions taking on the role of employment transformers.

It all sounds so wholesome, a world apart from the nuclear-computer philosopher-kings of Teller! Spots on apples! Birds and Bees! Nature's watchful eye assures a fair day's work for a fair day's pay, instead of Teller's electronic-eyed cyclops monitoring our neural hook-ups tottering on the edge of breakdown. However, there is a coldness here, for all the coziness, reminiscent of the H-bomb's daddy— an anger, a fear that Teller and the Odums share. They offer opposite revolutions of production, apocalypses and utopias, but they agree on one thing: the present state of capital has had it, not only because it has lost its "energy" but because there is too much "chaos," uncontrolled behavior, too many demands and not enough work.

This commonality emerges sharply in what appear as marginal remarks upon the "youth" of the 1960s and 1970s. Both anti-limitationists and interactionists agree: they are lazy! So Teller complains of "an antiscientific trend among young people," while the Odums (in a passage quoted above) clearly expect the fuck-off young rebels to get down to work. Their deepest commonality however is that, like the apocalypticians of the past, they see their problem in Nature. On the one side, the raw limit of energetic stuffs, and on the other side, the "ecological" catastrophe induced by industrial development. They postulate a limit either on the natural "input" (fuel) or an "output" onto nature (pollution). But once again, we cannot read their fears and solutions straight, for in their text Nature is identified with Capital pure and simple. They never declare the obvious: capital is a relation of struggle. Once this translation is made, their sibylline visions can be deciphered and their ominous somberness dispelled. Their limits are not ours.

Decoding the Apocalypse

The decoded message of the Apocalypse reads: Work/Energy. Both sides of the "great energy debate" want to rebalance the ratio, but what unbalanced it in the first place? If the "energy crisis" began in 1973, the logical place to look is the period immediately before. What was happening to work/energy then? A capitalist catastrophe in commodity production and the reproduction of labor-power. Need we take out the old filmstrips? The ghetto riots, the Panthers, campus "unrest," SDS and the Weatherpersons, a strung out imperial army, DRUM in Detroit and the West Virginia wildcats, the welfare office sit-ins, the shooting of Andy Warhol, SCUM, the Stonewall blowout, Attica. Let Graphs #1 and #2 suffice.

The first deals with a historic transformation in the wage/profit relation, the second depicts the changed relation between defense and "social" expenditures. Both indicate that the late 1960s and early 1970s saw the inversion of long-term trends.

Graph #1

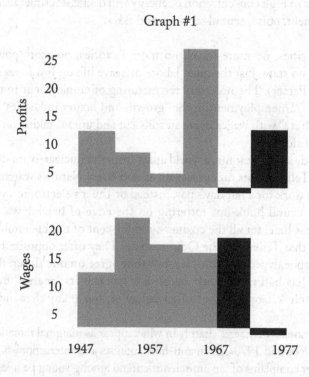

If we look, for example, at the two decades between 1947 and 1967 we see that in this period wages and profits intimated the fulfillment of an American Capitalist Dream: the class struggle can be bypassed, wages and profits can grow together, perhaps not at the same rate, but in a long-term growth equilibrium path. The Keynesian strategy of matching real wage increases with productivity increments seemed to succeed. To each his own, and thou wilt be satisfied. From 1967 through 1972 was the shocker: for the first considerable period there was a decline in profits. This decline appeared at the cost of increased wages. The bets were off. Once again, wages seemed antagonistic to profits as in the bad old days of Ricardo and Marx (lately exhumed by Sraffa). This period marked the end of the "social peace" worked out with the return of the vets from Europe and the Pacific into the plants. It was not, however, a period of wage "explosion" (as it could be characterized in Germany, Italy, and France). Rather, it involved mathematical inversion and the return to the zero-sum game of wage negotiation that seemed transcended by capital's game-theorists during World War II and immediately after.

Graph #2 deals with the state's function as the general guarantor of the average rate of profit. This requires that the state oversee the reproduction of the working class and provide for proportionate revenues.

Graph #2

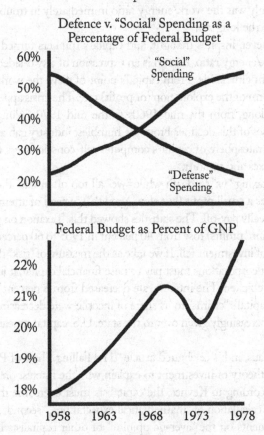

Defence v. "Social" Spending as a
Percentage of Federal Budget

"Social" Spending

"Defense" Spending

Federal Budget as Percent of GNP

1958   1963   1968   1973   1978

The bottom graph indicates the quantitative increase in the state's "share" of the total social value. It is not surprising that it should increase during the Vietnam War. What is surprising is that at the very moment the war was ongoing, the proportion of "defense" spending dropped dramatically.

"War" and "defense" are an essential, though unrecognized, part of the reproduction of labor-power, which can dictate the death of millions of workers. Auschwitz, Dachau, and Belsen were extermination factories whose product—the suffocation and cremation of millions of bodies—was an essential moment in Nazi capital's "labor policy." The reproduction of labor-power should not only be identified as the reproduction of "human bodies" and "beings," but also death. Moreover, "social welfare" spending by the state can be defense spending. Indeed, this second aspect was apparent in the late 1960s. Another war was being fought white-hot in the streets of the United States that needed immediate attention. Hence the precipitate increase in "social welfare" expenditure, i.e., "transfer" payments (but what is not a transfer payment in this system?) to deal with women, Blacks, youth, who were increasingly refusing the way they were being reproduced. This chart indicates that whether you call it "war" or "welfare," the process of ensuring a population accepting the large-scale wages, profits, and productivity relations as well as the microrelations of love, job, discipline, and quiet dying was in crisis. Not only was the work/energy ratio immediately in trouble, it was in more serious trouble over the long run.

Trouble, however, inspires thought, and capital's thinkers turned with new apprehension to the work/energy ratio. A ratio is an expression of a two-sided relation and can be looked upon from either side. From capital's point of view, the work/energy ratio is a more generalized form of the exploitation (or profit) rate. The crisis appears through these lenses as a decade-long, from the mid-1960s to the mid-1970s, plunge of profit rates. What were the causes of this decline? From the humblest industry gab and gripe sheets to the mathematical stratosphere of capital's computer self-consciousness the answer comes in reverberations: taxes and timidity.

The state is taxing "us" to death while "we" all too often take the "safe and secure path" that guarantees a small profit (but slow "growth") instead of attempting risky, long-term ventures that really pay-off. The statistics showed this. Taxation on profits (calculated on "current production" profits) rose from 40 percent in 1965 to 60 percent in 1974. At the same time, the risk of investment fell. If we take as the measure of "risk" the interest rate on debt and equity that corporations must pay to raise financial capital, it is clear that capital collectively became chicken. The interest rate decreased from 8 percent in 1966 to 4 percent in 1972–73. Capital's "claims" to its share of income were decreasing while what was claimed had to be increasingly given over to the state. U.S. capital appeared to be catching the "British disease."

W.D. Nordhaus, in his celebrated article "The Falling Share of Profits," appeals to Keynes's subjective theory of investment to explain why the interest on investment faced such a decline.[9] According to Keynes, the capitalists must overcome their "ignorance of the future" through calculation of "mathematical expectations," second-, third- (and even higher) order judgments on the "average opinion" of other capitalists in the investment market, and finally of "animal spirits," i.e., capital's "spontaneous urge to action rather than inaction." In agreement with this Keynesian existentialism, Nordhaus claims that the fall in profits was due to an extraordinary period of calm in capital's heart and mind:

> The answer seems to me to lie in the general dissipation of the fear of a
> new Great Depression. For many years after the Crash, investors justifiably

---

[9] William D. Nordhaus, "The Falling Share of Profits," *Brookings Institute Papers* (Brookings Institute, 1975).

worried about a repetition of those events. Even as late as March 1955 when the fear might have reasonably faded, the statement by Prof Galbraith that the Great Crash could repeat itself was sufficient to send the market into a temporary panic—or so he claims. Since that time, however, the memory of the bad old days has dimmed, and this freedom from fear may well provide a rationale for the post-war movement in the cost of capital.[10]

Presumably, in the different psychic "climate" prevailing in the post–World War II era, investors became more confident in the future, had a new sense of guaranteed horizons, the risk factor seemed reduced. Thus, (according to this theory of profits) the expected returns on investment fell. For if risk is high, the investor demands high profits, if the risk is low, s/he will settle for lower profits. What had brought about this freedom from fear, what psychoanalytical therapy had the capitalist mind undergone? Nordhaus does not explain, but to any therapist this much should be obvious: the healer must be paid his/her dues. In this case, the healer of capital's long-term fears was the state and the "dues," taxes. This is why the major structural transformation of the GNP was in the share of the state. The federal budget increased from 10 percent of GNP in 1940 to an average of 20 percent in the period between 1960 and the present. In other words, by investing in the reproduction of labor-power the state exorcised the trauma of the Depression (and its potentially revolutionary consequences), and the increased tax on corporate profits was its fee. Every step capital takes in feeling more secure leads to a loss of profit.

But why should capital fear, why is investment risky, and the future so obscure? Why, indeed, must capital have "animal spirits" in the first place? Is this a metaphysical truth? Not really, because there are risks of different sorts. Some are dealt with in an almost mathematical manner, e.g., in fair toss gambling or in predicting the weather. You calculate future probabilities from past data, lay down your money and wait for the outcome. Such risks are not what Keynes is talking about. There are also strategy-game risks, those you take when you depend upon (or reply to) the actions of another player in a game where all the players agree to and are governed by the same rules. Here you cannot simply go upon past behavior: any game with a rich enough set of rules and positions can present completely novel situations and this forces you to speculate on the strategy of your opponent, to read out his likely move. This involves a risk, but the risk is encompassed in the network of rules that bind you with your opponents and allies (who may be continually turning into each other). This risk, typical of the poker game, is also calculable, as Von Neumann showed. There is however a final risk that is not dependent upon mathematical expectations nor upon considerations of strategy, because your opponents are neither predictable nor in agreement about the rules. Here, you have no clear basis for judging their future behavior in response to your moves. This is a totally new kind of risk that requires "animal spirits," a "spontaneous optimism," an "urge to action" or, perhaps, a "will to power." This is the class struggle.

Keynes worried about capital's "state of confidence" during the Depression not because it involved a downturn in the business cycle, however steep. Such dips in

---

[10] Ibid.

capital's life are to be expected and capitalized upon. What concerned Keynes was the altogether novel "sixth sense" capitalists had to develop in their investment decisions after the revolutionary wave that followed World War I. This involved shifting attention from risks "outside" (market fluctuations, weather, mineral discoveries, etc.) to risks "inside" (working-class attitudes, training, work habits) the process of social production. The state had to intervene in Keynes's prescription because of the increasing realization that the working class was neither predictable nor "part of the game," but powerful enough to rip up the rules. The mixture of taxes and timidity are a direct consequence of Keynes's recommendations.

Since the New Deal, the state by careful use of collective bargaining, nuclear terror, FHA loans, had increasingly reduced the risks of investment. Hence the reduced interest on capital, for cooling capital's anxiety inevitably reduced the pay-off of its projects. The transformation of the composition of the federal budget from "defense" to "welfare" in the 1960s indicated, however, that not only would the State's "taking care" have an increased cost, but that the direction and nature of working-class insubordination was changing in new, unpredictable ways. The period between 1967 and 1972 showed that the cost of calmness was increasing to a point where the therapy was ruining the patient. Freud never wrote that therapy could create the anxiety it was reducing. While the interest on capital followed the historical post–World War II trend, capital began to confront the fact that this trend meant euthanasia. Moreover, confidence was diminishing in the effectiveness of the State's therapy when applied not to the traditional line workers, the veterans of Flint, Guam and McCarthy, but to altogether new subjects. Just what did those Blackpowerlonghaireddopesmokingflagrantqueerhousewifelesbians want!

Between the mid-1960s and mid-1970s, the tax-timidity syndrome intensified. The relation between state and individual capital proposed by Keynes was in crisis. Capital was in a knot, a double bind, and it attempted to cut it in October 1973. The relaunching of the profit rate depended upon capital taking the initiative, cutting out its most vulnerable areas and, most crucially, quit playing by its old rules.

The Keynesian Crisis

What was the relation between state and society during the "Keynesian" period? What distinguished U.S. Keynesian planning was its concern with the reproductive sector, because U.S. capital did not have an experienced working class whose production and reproduction had been bargained over for centuries. The waves of immigration and genocide barely gave any demographic and geographic constancy to rely on. The U.S. working class was inevitably "volatile" and "unstable," almost a "thing in itself."

The basic realization of U.S. Keynesian policy was that the enormous accumulation of fixed capital embodied in the assembly-line factories required a proportionate accumulation of capital in the working class ("human capital" as it was called later). Once capital reaches River Rouge dimensions, i.e., factories that appear to be a mile long packed with machines, the short-term disciplinary effect of unemployment is more than counterbalanced by the long-term loss in the productivity of workers.[11] And it was exactly in productivity that profit was to be found. The obsession of New Deal planners was that the long stretches of unemployment would sap the "work ethic" from the latest generation of factory operatives who had undergone the rigid education of the line in the 1920s (You can learn a line job in a day, but it takes years to learn a line-life!). This discipline could not be kept in "cold storage" until individual capitalists were ready for it, for it depreciated and could turn inside out explosively. Thus, the ultimate profitability of capital based on increasing the productivity of work made "mass unemployment" intolerable.

Not only must labor-power be produced, it must be reproduced. The housewife becomes the correlate of the line worker in the Keynesian equations. Standardly, the housewife is taken as the consumer, but the Depression planners were more concerned with her as the producer of a "very special article," the availability for work of a factory worker. This requires capital, the home. This was exactly the capital that was disintegrating during the Depression as more and more women left home, divorced and in general "gave up." The Keynesians saw that no high intensity line worker would work or return to work without an equally high-intensity reproduction process.

The assembly line is peculiarly vulnerable to individual variations of work pace: the rhythm must be kept off the job as on. Regular meals, regular fucks, regular shits are essential for the gearing of labor-power and capital in a stamping plant. Not only had unemployment to be "conquered," but the real wage, which the working class "defended" during the starkest years of the Depression and later forced up, could be capitalized upon. If wage increases could be used to capitalize the home, this would eventually increase the productivity of labor, and thus increase profit. Here we have the basis of a class deal: happy workers, happy capital, and a compromise! The Keynesian system is delicately balanced upon the symbiosis of home and factory and the use of the wage not only for working-class subsistence but as a form of investment for capital.

The dynamic equilibrium between home and line required a precise meshing of the variables of wage, factory work and housework. In the period from the late 1960s to the mid-1970s the mesh began to tear. Divorces, for example, accelerated with the wage, which revealed a new tension between the poles of the Keynesian synthesis, but "surely nothing that would be enough to cause a crisis." The trouble with the Keynesian equilibrium, however, is that it is supremely vulnerable to such lapses (perhaps more vulnerable than to a "small" nuclear war). They were "boom" years, but not for capital. Not only did the struggle in the factories, homes and streets force capital to pay more for factory work; increasingly, capital had to pay, through the state, directly for reproduction work that had previously come financed via the male, factory wage. Women and young people would no more "naturally" do what they used to do under the direction of husband and daddy. Thus, though there was an enormous increase of energy generated by the working class during that

---

[11] The Ford River Rouge complex in Dearborn, Michigan, completed in 1928, was the world's largest integrated factory.

period, it proved especially resistant to the transformation into work. There was a precipitous drop in the work/energy ratio; this was translated into a "profits crisis" and a subversion of the axioms of Keynesianism.

Prices and Values

Capital's response to this invasion of entropic energy was not a "strike," an "investment freeze" or the beginning of an era of "slow investment economies." Allowing for the recession of 1974, investment since 1973 (relative to GNP) has sustained and even surpassed the levels prevalent in the 1960s (for all the crocodile tears of the business journals). There has been, however, a shift in the composition of investment, which to many capitalists and workers appears as a lack of investment.

Why?

Simply because fewer people see it.

What everyone has seen, however, is the leap in the relative and absolute prices of "energy" commodities (in the form of oil, natural gas, coal, uranium as well as electricity). Inflation has directly attacked working-class income by reducing the "average" real wage, but the changed ratio of energy prices to other prices has an immense indirect effect on the composition of the working class and organization of exploitation.

From the post–World War II period until 1973, there was a rough equality between price increases in the industrial and energy sectors. In a major structural change between 1973 and the present, both price series went up, but the industrial price index rose by approximately 100 percent while the energy price index rose by more than 200 percent. Along with these price changes have gone parallel changes in the relative "sales" and "profits" of the two sectors.

These numbers are the hieroglyphics of capital's response to the struggles of the late 1960s and early 1970s. They spell the end of the assembly line—auto—home political economy, the end of the "blue collar" line worker/housewife nexus, the end of the delicate machine of Keynesian society. By giving primacy to the energy sector, capital can command an enormous amount of work because this command takes place away from the actual scene of exploitation. It almost feels ghost-like. It short-circuits the nodes of class power accumulated in the factories, mines and streets, for this reorganization centralizes the accumulation process, while at the same time it enormously decentralizes the exploitation process. By developing the energy sector, capital is able to exert its magnetic command and extract surplus from every "pore" of the social fabric; every coffee shop, every apartment, every sweatshop must pay for energy costs.

The very image of the worker seems to disintegrate before this recomposition of capital. The burly, "blue collared" line worker seems to blur in the oil crisis, diffracted into the female service worker and the abstracted computer programmer. The large concentrations of factory workers that proved so explosive are dispersed, the specific gravity of the worker's presence is dramatically reduced. And it all feels so different! Your wages go up, but they evaporate before you spend them; you confront your boss but he cries that "he has bills to pay"; and even more deeply, you don't see your exploitation any more. On the line, you could literally observe the crystallization of your labor-power into the commodity, you could see your life vanishing down the line, and you could feel the materialization of your alienation. But in the service industries, your surplus labor seems to be nonexistent, even "nonproductive"; it is just a paid form of "housework," cleaning bedpans, massaging jogger's muscles, scrambling eggs. In the "energy/information" sector, you seem to be engulfed by the immense fixed capital surrounding you. It feels as if you were not exploited at all, but a servant of the machine, even "privileged" to be part of the "brains of the system." These feelings disorient struggles. As the vast spatial migrations "to look for a job" disaggregate militant circles, the old bastions are isolated and appear archaic, almost comic.

Finally, these price indices summarize the beginning of a shift in the organization of reproduction. A "society" built on autos is not like a "society" built on computers, McDonald's, and nukes, where by "society" we mean the entire reproduction process. The new form of life dictated by the primacy of the energy/information sectors, like the struggles against it, is only starting to be formed.

The "rationality of the energy crisis" for capital as a response to (and an attack on) working-class struggles against the poles of Keynesian "auto-industrial" society will be shown below. However, an important objection to this account could be made immediately: if capital can, at will, change and manipulate energy and industrial prices on the basis of multinational corporate power, i.e., independent of the amount of work that goes into the production of commodities, then we must abandon work and surplus value (exploitation) as our basic analytical categories. Marx would be an honored but dead dog. We would have to accept the position of Sweezy and Marcuse that monopoly organization and technological development have made capital independent of the "law of value," (viz., that prices, profits, costs and the other numerology of accounting are rooted in (and explained by) the work-time gone into the production of the commodities and reproduction of the relevant workers). Capital, it would seem, can break its own rules, the class struggle is now to be played on a pure level of power, "will to domination," force against force and prices become part of the equation of violence, arbitrarily decided like the pulling of the trigger. We disagree with these "monopoly power" theorists; work and exploitation still remain the basic determinants of motion in capitalist development, whether you deal with computers and nukes or spades and cotton gins.

How, then, do we explain the apparent freedom the capitalists seem to have in setting oil prices independent of the labor that goes into the production of oil (i.e., its value)?

The divergence of prices and values is nothing new. On the contrary, it has always been an essential aspect of capitalist rule. Values (work time) must be transformed into prices and this transformation is never one-to-one. The essence of the transformation of values into prices is that though capital extracts surplus value locally, it does not let those who do the extracting command and expend this surplus value. The hand of capital is different than its mouth and its asshole. The transformation of value into prices is real, but it also causes illusions in the brains of both capitalists and workers (including you and me!). It all revolves around "mineness," the deepest pettiness in the Maya of the system: capital appears as little machines, packets of materials, little incidents of work, all connected to us—its little agents of complaint, excuse, and hassle. Each individual capitalist complains about "my" money, each individual worker cries about "my" job, each union official complains about "my" industry; tears flow everywhere, apparently about different things, so that capitalism's house is an eternal soap opera. "Mineness" is an essential illusion, though illusion all the same. Capital is social, as is work, and it is also as pitiless as Shiva to the complainers, whose blindness capital needs to feed itself. It no more rewards capitalists to the extent that they exploit than it rewards workers to the extent that they are exploited. There is no justice for anyone but itself.

The transformation of values into prices is ruled by capital's instinctual demand to "get its just recognition." The body of capital has many different limbs, organs, arteries and veins, nerve strands, sensors and processors, each with its organic composition, its own need to be fed-back. The needs, balances, proportions, and ratios they imply must be met—or else it would not survive to see its own illusions.

How much surplus value goes to a particular organ of capital is determined by its organic composition: the mixture of dead and living labor that is found there. Let's take three examples: a nuclear plant, an auto plant, and a local "greasy spoon" restaurant and bar. Each is a machine with different needs and different products. The bar needs Jack Daniels, while the nuke needs refined U235; the restaurant and bar needs an easy-talking bartender and a speed-freak grill man, the auto plant needs welding bonders and line workers. All these "needs" have histories derived from struggles. The nuke "needs" to have a "two man rule" in monitoring all vital operations; the auto plant "needs" guards at the gates and computers assessing the speed of flow to detect slowdowns; the restaurant "needs" dishwashers that can't speak English. The struggles are written in the machine; they create the need for redundancy, since struggles are noise that keeps the message the machines send out from being reliable and eternal.

Each of these mixtures of living and dead, animal and mineral, energy and work, can be measured in a mathematical proportion roughly corresponding to the ratio of the value of constant capital (the value of the means of production) and the value of labor-power (the value of the wages). A typical nuclear worker works with about \$300,000 worth of equipment, a typical autoworker mixes with about \$30,000 worth of other machines, while a typical restaurant-bar worker uses \$3,000 worth of "means of production." Yet, the wages of the typical autoworker and nuke plant worker are almost the same, while those of a restaurant-bar worker are officially half (although the inclusion of tips would increase it). Clearly, the differences in capital per employee swamp out the differences in wages, and we see a segmentation in the skeleton of capital delineated in the exponential powers of the organic composition: 10^3, 10^4, 10^5. Let us call these the Low, Average, and High sectors of capital and consider Graph #3.

There is much to say of these vertebrae of capital, but let us concentrate on the work/energy relation in each of these sections. In the Average section, there is an obvious relation between the energy put in, the work that comes out, and the profit

Graph #3	C/V	S	Type of Work
High	10^5	Transfer	Program Engineer
Average	10^4	Relative	Assembly Line
Low	10^3	Absolute	Clerical McDonald's Masseuse

obtained from it. It is clear to the autoworker that a speed-up increases the flow of cars off the line and GM's profits. There appears to be here a one-to-one relation between increased investment in machinery and the productivity and intensity of work. This is the range of relative surplus value. The worker can see his/her exploitation via the speed of the line. In the Low sector, the length of the workday becomes important. This is the area of absolute surplus value, where the work comes by storing the energy of the worker within the job as long as possible. The problem here is that the worker cannot see the surplus. The local restaurant might kill its employees with overwork and still look like it's making "no money." The boss may be as depressed as his/her workers and poring out his energy "for nothing," thus the tears of the small business types, the "hard-working" sector of capital. Finally, there is the High sector. There, enormous profits are made, but not off the workers who operate the nuke plants, per se. True, they earn their wages on the way from the parking lot to the control room, but the amount of surplus value "produced" in the ensuing eight hours is absolutely minuscule, though relatively enormous! Where do their profits come from?

Surplus value is transformed into the nuclear industry by the divergence of prices and values. As Marx points out, social capital needs an average rate of profit, while individual capitals must be rewarded differentially according to the amount invested in each organ. But each organ has a different amount of constant capital in it. Those organs with a high capital investment per worker need an above average amount of surplus value fed back into them, those with an average amount of investment per worker requires an average feedback, while those with a low amount of capital "need" only a low return.

"Equal weights and equal measures," says social capital over the lamentations of its Jobs in restaurants, sweatshops, and construction companies. "I only recognize myself," "I am I" booms capital out of the whirlwind, and the petty bosses slink away with their boils. This feedback justice is determined by prices. Commodity prices in the High industries are always greater than their values. Low industry commodity prices are always below their value. High industries "suck up" the surplus value produced at the bottom of the system through this price structure. The diversion of price and value makes it clear that extraction of surplus value and command over the expending of the surplus are different operations. The boss of Alice's restaurant can complain, but he must still pay his electricity and heating bills (though he tries hard to avoid it). Like Job, the petty boss recognizes a higher power he cannot deny, for though it hurts him he would be annihilated if it abandoned him. So he must pay this power tribute, however unjust it appears. He perhaps even glimmers on the deeper, larger schemes of the Savage God, though it crusheth him.

The Deduction of the "Energy Crisis": A Theoretical Interlude

The divergence of prices from values shows how there is a possibility of an energy price rise versus other prices without abandoning a work exploitation analysis of capitalism. By investing in the High sector to escape assembly-line insubordination, women's refusal of housework and urban insurrections, the High sector attracts higher commodity prices. But why did the profits crisis actually require an "energy crisis" and not simply the traditional tools of the capitalist cycle? Why was the profit-fall—unemployment—wage-rate-reduction—profit-rise sequence (i.e., the "old time religion" of capital), which retains the general physiognomy of the system, not adequate anymore?

The answers to these questions have many parts, but one thing is clear: the source of the crisis is in the breakdown of the Keynesian factory-home circuit that was the basis of the post–World War II political economy. Capital, like an amoeba, contracts in areas of acidity and expands in more nutritious and bland waters. In the profits crisis decade, the areas of acidity concentrated in two spots: (a) in the assembly line production, in "middle level" manufacturing and extraction industries, and (b) in the "home" where reproduction work is centered.[12] Capital experienced the crisis of profits both as a local and global irritant as well as a decline in its self worth and "castration" by the big-bad state (the tax-timidity syndrome).

A typical "common sense" response to the questions of this section is that the taxation timidity syndrome has brought on a chronic productivity crisis of which the energy crisis is one instance. From the winged words of corporation executives, from the pulpits of economic Poloniuses, the same evil is identified and decried: the collapse of productivity. But are the sermons total myths? Yes, myths indeed, in the narrow sense of "productivity."

If by "productivity" we mean (as econometricians do) "real" output per working hour, then capital had no productivity problem. On the contrary, the post–World War II period has seen a productivity boom, at least compared with the 1914–1947 period, which saw two wars and the Depression. Moreover, though both periods showed comparable increases in output per hour, the previous one showed a greater

---

[12] What of race? We agree with the Wages for Housework analysis: the essence of racial (as well as sexual) division is to be found in the hierarchy of wages, and it was indeed that hierarchy that the Black movement attacked most directly in the welfare women's movement, in the formation of Black factory unions and caucuses, in the youth gangs and "parties" of the ghetto streets. The explosion of Black women, men, and youth attacked the Keynesian model of accumulation at its heart, since the thrust was from the largely unwaged sector. See Mariarosa Dalla Costa and Selma James, *The Power of Women and the Subversion of the Community* (Bristol: Falling Wall Press, 1972), for the seminal work on this matter.

increase in the real wage and a reduction in the workweek. If the performance of the first period had been repeated in the second, the workweek would now be 27.8 hours and the average real wage would be substantially higher (see Graph #4).

Graph #4	Changes in Real Output Per Person Hour	Changes in Real Wages	Changes in Work Week
1914–1947	+107%	+103%	-31%
1947–1979	+91%	+66%	-11%

Further, in the energy crisis period (1973–1980), though output per work hour was rising slower than in the past, real wages lagged even behind this pace. But capital is not interested in output, per se; it is interested in its share. The relation between changes in real profit and changes in productivity shows the statistical anomaly of the 1965–1973 period. In the post–World War II period up to 1965, year-to-year changes in profits tended on the average to be twice as much as changes in productivity: but in 1965 they began to equalize. Only after 1973 did the ratio return to its historical position. This shows that the 1965–1973 period cut down the attractive power of profits and further disintegrated the profits-wages ratio. Somewhere, there was a leak. Everywhere, there was the search for the thief of profit. Youth, women, Blacks, the "collapse of the work ethic," were the likely suspects. Consider the sage words of Ford's Malcolm Denise in December of 1969:

> Nowadays employees are (1) less concerned about losing a job or staying with an employer; (2) less willing to put up with dirty and uncomfortable working conditions; (3) less likely to accept the unvarying pace and functions on moving assembly lines; (4) less willing to conform to rules or be amenable to higher authority. Furthermore, the traditional U.S. work ethic—the concept that hard work is a virtue and a duty—has undergone considerable erosion. . . . There is also, again especially among the younger employees, a growing reluctance to accept shop discipline. This is not just a shop phenomenon, rather it is a manifestation in our shops of a trend we see all about us among today's youth.[13]

The wind was full of such lamentations! "LSD will eat up the line!" "The feminists will wreck the family!" "The Blacks want everything!" . . . *ad nauseam*.

When output per hour collapsed in mining and began to slow down in auto, steel, and rubber, the volume on the capitalist dial was turned up a few notches. But the source of complaint was not output per hour but profit per work hour. The share

---

[13] Quoted in B.J. Widick, "Work in Auto Plants: Then and Now," in *Auto Work and Its Discontents* (Baltimore: John Hopkins University Press, 1976), 10.

of profits in productivity increases was in peril ... hence the need for a total change in the structure of prices and work, for this was not another statistic, but the basis of the relation between working class and capital. As our introduction pointed out, a satisfactory matching of productivity to profit has been the essence of capitalist strategy since the end of the nineteenth century. Any serious disturbance of this strategy puts into question a century of that capitalist wisdom embodied in the "Marginal Theory of Value and Distribution." Capitalism is a system of margins, accelerations, of changes, differentials; not flows, but flows of flows. Thus, the appearances, though obvious and bemoaned, did not tell the tale. Capital is abstract and its snapping is at first abstract as well, for the problem is not speed but lack of impulse. The 1965–1973 profits crisis stopped not the flow, but the flow of flows. To understand the strategy of accumulation that was put in jeopardy by the class struggle of that period, we must do some investigation of capital's mind, not so much psychoanalysis as theoretical eavesdropping.

"Marginal Theory," the economics we get in every introductory course, significantly appears on the scene at the very time of the explosion and slaughter of the Paris Commune. It claims that in order for individual firms to maximize profits and for the accumulation process to flow throughout capitalism, wages and profits must be correlated with the ever-increasing productivity of social labor. In other words, productivity increases achieved by new technological leaps, more "efficient" organization of work in factories, mines, and farms, more "scientific" planning of family, school, and health, had to be shared with the working class. Capital could not appropriate it all. A classic application of this strategy is the early Ford wage policy that combined relatively capital intensive, mass production techniques with bonuses for punctuality and a "clean family life." Without such schemes, the worker turnover rate, which was approaching 300 percent per year, would have interminably broken the continuity of the line (the very basis of its productivity). Nobody is born an autoworker; they must be made, and their production in the home must be planned. Ford understood the other side of Marginal Theory: not only must wages be used to "induce" workers to accept the discipline of the assembly line, but with higher wages the working class can become a dynamic consumer and push the system to higher levels of production (hence profitability, since a concentration of fixed capital such as River Rouge requires continuous utilization to pay off). Once wages are as dynamic as social productivity, the working class becomes a production agent integrated into the capitalist system through the consumer-goods market. Reproduction becomes a "dynamic force of production" instead of merely guaranteeing the subsistence of labor-power.

Marxists have criticized marginalist theory as a subjective mathematization of vulgar economics ideologically motivated to slay Marx. Bukharin calls this theory "the ideology of the bourgeoisie who has already been eliminated from the process of production."[14] In reality, it is the strategy of introducing the working class into the process of consumption. Marxists did not see that the legitimizing purposes of

---

[14] Nikolai Bukharin, *The Economic Theory of the Leisure Class* (New York: AMS Press, 1970), 31.

marginalist theory were tangential, and that its primary purpose was to provide a new strategy to capital, in front of a radically different class struggle. By the 1870s and the Paris Commune's volcano of desires, it became clear that the working class could not be taken as a separate, almost-natural species, with fixed needs that might or might not be satisfied depending on population growth. As Marx's 1867 "Value, Price and Profit" suggests, in this period, the struggle for the normal working day was slowly yielding in the most advanced sectors to the struggle for wage increases.

The class forces were entering into a new Constellation. To see this, let us get back to basics. The working day resolves itself into two magnitudes:

$$V\rule{2cm}{0.4pt}/\rule{2cm}{0.4pt}S$$

V represents the amount of social labor time necessary to reproduce the working class in its capitalist function, S is the surplus labor capital appropriates in the working day. This unpaid labor, the secret of capital, appears in many forms, not only in the factory but in the kitchen, the ghetto street, and the laboratory. Mathematically, the class struggle resolves itself for capital into the relation between V, S, and V+S. The object is the accumulation of surplus, S, and there are only two ways of increasing it: absolutely and relatively. Absolute surplus value is appropriated by lengthening the working day, V+S, without changing V. This was the type of surplus value developed in Newton's time. But capital's ability to generate absolute surplus value was undermined by the working-class struggles for a "normal" workday, i.e., the "ten-hour" and "eight-hour day" campaigns. Capital's response was relative surplus value, which is appropriated by reducing V relative to S while leaving V+S constant or even decreasing it. Relative surplus value is the type of production that is at the basis of thermodynamics' investigation of work/energy.

It can only be produced by constant revolutions in the forces and relations of production, requiring the application of science, memory, and skill at every linkage. Marx saw the turn to relative surplus value as the necessary tendency of capital:

> In machinery, objectified labour confronts living labour within the labour process itself as the power which rules it; a power which, as the appropriation of living labour, is the form of capital. The transformation of the means of labour into machinery, and of living labour into a mere living accessory of this machinery, as the means of its action, also posits the absorption of the labour process in its material character as a mere moment of the realization process of capital. The increase of the productive force of labour and the greatest possible negation of necessary labour is the necessary tendency of capital. . . . The transformation of the production process from the simple labor process into a scientific process, which subjugates the forces of nature and compels them to work in the service of human needs, appears as a quality of fixed capital. . . . Thus all powers of labor are transposed into the powers of capital.[15]

[15] Karl Marx, *Grundrisse: Foundations of the Critique of Political Economy* (Harmond-

The Marginal Theory reflects capitalist strategy in the era of relative surplus value. "Productivity" becomes a central political category, "efficiency" the battle slogan in the regulation of the class relation as the shibboleth of "unproductive" was hurled at the feudal landowners by the early bourgeoisie. Thus Jevons, the "father of Marginal Theory," saw it as a statistical thermodynamics accounting for the transformation of energies (in the form of desires, pleasures and utilities) into work. For him, the capitalist system is a gigantic social steam engine that turns the millions of separate energetic impulses of the working class into accumulated capitalist power. It took a relatively short time for this theory to enter into the curriculum of the capitalist manager. Its pedagogical function is immediately evident even in its abstract form (despite the eternal complaint of the "shirt sleeve" business economists against their theoretical colleagues), for it accustoms capital to a fluidity in productive arrangements: the expectation of constant change in productive relations (aimed at destroying nodules of working-class organization) and an appreciation of its own abstractness. At the same time, the theory taught a complementary lesson: the working class could no longer be merely resisted, repressed and killed when it struggled; it had to be allowed a dynamic function in the system of productive relations and the market. The struggle could and had to be used.

This theory showed capital how unions could be used instead of being outlawed and crushed whenever they appeared. For it maintains that unions cannot increase wages beyond the productivity of labor in the long run, because wages are ultimately controlled by supply and demand in labor market. At worst, unions are innocuous; at best, though they may hurt individual capitalists, unions, by bargaining over wage and working conditions, can spur changes in the organization of work and stimulate productivity.

Consider Böhm-Bawerk, the Austrian finance minister and discoverer of the "error in the Marxian system" (i.e., the deviation of prices from values). In 1914 he wrote:

> If the entrepreneur finds his hands tied by the price of labor, but not in regard to the physical equipment of his factory, and he desires to adopt the presently cheapest combination of factors of production, he will prefer a combination different from the one used before, one that will enable him to make savings in the now more costly factor of labor, just as, for example, an increase in the cost of land may cause the transition from extensive to intensive methods of cultivation.[16]

In other words, if unions force wages up, this will force the capitalist to reorganize production by making it less extensive and more intensive in time (for space becomes time when we go from land to work). Unions can force a transition from absolute to relative surplus value and become a factor in the development of capital, provided they are attuned to the system: don't agitate too much, don't desire

---

sworth: Penguin, 1973), 693, 700, 701.

[16] Eugen von Böhm-Bawerk, "Control or Economic Law," in *Shorter Classics of E. Von Böhm-Bawerk* (South Holland, IL: Libertarian Press, 1962), 192–93.

too much and, most important, "get down with us." Although the variety of tactics capital uses to attune the working class are barely mentioned in the textbooks and treatises, the "entrepreneur" should figure it out himself: sometimes head-bashing, sometimes prime ministerships. What was crucial was the strategy that was taught to generation upon generation of capitalists: one doesn't fight the class struggle any more with the tactics of Scrooge.

Such a century-old strategy is not abandoned easily. Even the so-called "Keynesian revolution" did not question the importance of linking wage and profit increases with productivity increases. Keynes saw that it was crucial for "collective capital," the state, to intervene and guarantee this correlation, should the individual capitalists refuse. Yet throughout the 1960s and 1970s, Marginal Theory was systematically attacked in debates on capital's theory. "Why," say the marginalist economists, "can't wages and profits grow and twine together like tendrils from the graves of dead lovers?"

Just as statistical surveys were proclaiming the long run success in linking real wages with productivity, there was increasing disquiet in the councils of the wise. By the early 1970s, it was obvious that profits and wages were again antagonistic, as in the days of absolute surplus value. Profits were not gathering a normal share of productivity increases and, even more ominously, the institutions of bargaining essential for the equilibrium (the unions and social democratic parties) were subverted or bypassed by the struggle. Welfare struggles, ghetto revolts, wildcats, factory occupations, and a "breakdown" in discipline from the army to the university (reflecting a "disorder" in family and sexual relationships) all moved outside the orbit of union-management corridors and club house crap tables. Though the absolute content of these struggles took seemingly opposite poles:

> *The End of Work—Pay for All the Work We Do*
> *Make Love not War—Love Is Work*
> *Freedom Now—No More Free Work*

Capital was more concerned with their "nonnegotiability," their "unreasonableness." Capitalism lives on the future yet the immediate quality of these demands spelled "No future, we want it now!" What might have appeared as slight statistical shifts had the nature of auguries from the tangled guts of data charts and computer printouts. Productivity was no more guaranteed by the new class forces, who sniffed the astronomical level of accumulation achieved and were demanding it all and now.

As in the epistemology of pragmatism, irritation leads to thought, and these demands rubbed capital's managers raw. Lucky for capital, the needed thought had already risen to consciousness. Piero Sraffa had developed a system that suggested a strategy radically different from the Marginalist. Like all genuine capitalist responses to working-class struggles, Sraffa's took up the class's demands, but with a twist of its intent. Just as early capital took the Diggers' anti-landowner slogan, "Those who don't work should not eat," and turned it against them, the new capitalist strategy takes the working class's refusal of work and relativizes it to itself.

Sraffa's strategy begins with capital's perception of the crisis as an inability to link, in a balanced way, wage and profit growth with productivity changes. Sraffa argues that wages and profits must be considered antagonistic magnitudes, i.e., one is the inverse of the other. In Marginal Theory, on the contrary, the wage is a payment for the use of a certain "factor of production" labor, to its owner—the worker; while profits are payments for the use of invested capital (in the form of machines, raw materials or money) to its owner, the capitalist, i.e., wages and profits are theoretically independent of each other. The Marginal Theory begins with the individual firm, and each factor, labor and capital, contributes to the firm's production and is presumably rewarded accordingly: "a fair day's work for a fair day's pay" and "a good tool is worth its hire."

Sraffa, instead, considers the capitalist machine as a whole, with its total inputs and outputs, its food, and its shit. He has the total output cut in two: wages and profits. The wage is part of the total value appropriated by the whole working class. His image is that the capitalist machine (a complex intermeshing of material and work flows, transfers, creations, and interruptions) stops at every period and drops out a total product, then capitalists and workers struggle over how much each gets. No more "to each his own," now it is *lex talionis*, dog packs and wolf packs warring over the carrion. But there is a limit as to how little workers can get. They must receive enough of the total product to subsist and reproduce themselves. The wage, then, must be divided into two parts: the subsistence wage and the surplus wage.

We have up to this point regarded wages as constituting the necessary subsistence of the workers and thus entering the system on the same footing as the fuel for the engines or the feed for the cattle. We must now take into account the other aspect of wages since, besides the ever-present element of subsistence, they may include a share of the surplus product. In view of the double character of the wage it would be appropriate when we come to consider the division of the surplus between capitalists and workers to separate the two component parts of the wage and regard only the "surplus" part as a variable.[17]

The "subsistence" part of the wage is reminiscent of the classical notion of the wage (e.g., Ricardo's "natural price of labor . . . that price which is necessary to enable the laborers, one with the other, to subsist and to perpetuate their race, without either increase or diminution").[18] By its nature, the subsistence wage is not proportional to the amount of work done, though it is fixed by the constraints of the particular productive system and the presumably fixed (quasi-biological) needs of the "race of workers." The necessity of a subsistence wage reflects a problematic truth individual capitalists try to elude, but capital as a whole cannot: in order to work, you must remain alive even though you are not working. This is the final "externality" of capitalist production. It is the pollution of nonwork eternally produced by work that somebody must "clean up."

---

[17] Piero Sraffa, *Production of Commodities by Means of Commodities* (Cambridge: Cambridge University Press, 1960), 9.

[18] David Ricardo, *Principles of Political Economy and Taxation* (New York: Macmillan Co., 1914), 80.

Classical economic theory led to "the iron law of wages," but discovered that iron can melt under intense heat. Thus, Marginal Theory conceded that the wage can be a variable as long as its variability is ruled by the productivity of labor. For Sraffa, on the contrary, the variable part of the wage arises from the existence of a total surplus, produced by the production apparatus as a whole, beyond mere subsistence. Sraffa argues that the "race of workers" struggles with capital to appropriate part of this surplus independent of its productivity. This "surplus wage" is a sort of "political wage," for it is not determinable within the system of technical relations of production. With Sraffa, Böhm-Bawerk's confidence that the "free" market of labor will in the long run determine the wage is exploded. Sraffa's framework describes a world where the working class has effectively broken the tie with productivity and the relationship between wages and profits is strictly antagonistic. With Sraffa, capital conceptualizes a situation where the quantity of the total machine's production is no longer proportional to the amount of work squeezed out of the working class: the wage becomes independent of work. It spells the end of the Marginalists' attempt to justify profit as a "fair reward" for capital's contribution to the production process. Nothing is due capital, everything must be fought for. We reach here that situation of great class tension anticipated by Marx in the last century:

> Real wealth manifests itself, rather—and large industry reveals this in the monstrous disproportion between the labour time applied, and its product, as well as in the qualitative imbalance between labour, reduced to a pure abstraction, and the power of the production process it superintends. Labour no longer appears so much to be included within the production process; rather, the human being comes to relate more as a watchman and regulator to the production process itself.[19]

When the productivity of labor increases beyond certain limits, Marx argues, any attempt to use "labor time" as the measure of wealth fails and "exchange-value ceases to be the measure of use-value." Capital finds itself in its deepest contradiction: on the one side, then, it calls to life all the powers of science and nature, as of social combination and of social intercourse, in order to make the creation of wealth independent (relatively) of the labor time employed in it. On the other side, it wants to use labor time as the measuring rod for the giant social forces thereby created, and to confine them within the limits required to maintain the already created value as value.[20] When working-class struggle pushes capital to a point where necessary work time approaches zero, Sraffa's system can be profitably applied.

What can determine the wage in such a situation if not productivity? Sraffa turns to the old discussion of the Corn Laws, i.e., to the manipulation of the

---

[19] Marx, *Grundrisse*, 705.

[20] Ibid., 706.

wage by control of the relative prices of commodities. He argues that prices are fixed by the wage rate; at the same time, given commodity production, the wage rate can also be determined by exchange relations between commodities. As long as capital has the power to relate prices it has the power to control how much of the (surplus) "political" wage the working class will appropriate. But not just any commodity will do.

Sraffa distinguishes between two types of commodities: basic versus nonbasic. Basic commodities enter into the production of all commodities, while nonbasic ones do not.

Nonbasic products have no part in the determination of the system. Their role is purely passive. If an invention were to reduce by half the quantity of each of the means of production which are required to produce a unit of a "luxury" commodity of this type, the commodity itself would be halved in price, but there would be no further consequences; the price relations of the other products and the rate of profit would remain unaffected. But if such a change occurred in the production of a basic commodity that does enter the means of production, all prices would be affected and the rate of profits changed.[21]

In other words, if one wanted to influence the wage (and hence the profit) rate, it would make no sense to change the price of Pennsylvanian cuckoo clocks or even of stereos and TVs, i.e., the "consumer durables" that have proven so crucial to the development of the system in the past. A Sraffa-type strategy must employ energy commodities (e.g., oil and electricity) since they enter directly or indirectly into the whole spectrum of production from fertilizers to computers. "Energy" commodities are basic commodities. Thus, any attempt to affect the wage-profit relation in a period when marginalist theory is inoperative must involve price changes of basic commodities. This excursion into Sraffa's theory explains why the profits crisis of the 1965–1972 required an energy crisis. Only with price changes of the energy commodities can the average real wage be reduced and investment moved from lower organically composed industries to the High industries. Such price changes dispose of both global and local irritants affecting the profit rate, since they reduce the general wage (whether paid on the job or through welfare checks, pensions, unemployment checks), and at the same time, reduce the share of value that goes to the Average and Low industries. Energy plays a central role both in the wage commodity "bundle" (heating, food, etc.) and in the production of "capital" goods. To change its relative price is inevitably to affect the average rate of profit, instead of cyclically returning to a predetermined profit rate. The profits crisis heralded not another fluctuation around a given "long run" average rate of profit, but a fall in the average that could not be dealt with on the basis of the Keynesian wage-inflation cycle that coordinates real wages and productivity via the "money illusion." No "State Bank induced" inflation or "monopoly capital" pass-along of wage increases would deal with the surprising totality and novelty of working-class struggle. The essential mechanism

---

[21] Sraffa, *Production of Commodities*, 7–8.

to reshape the system had to be an energy price transformation that would effect the profits crisis both globally, in the realm of social reproduction, and locally, in the closedown of insubordinate factories.

The Manifold of Work: Reproduction

Sraffa's distinction between basic and nonbasic commodities is essential to our explanation of the energy crisis as a response to working-class attack on capitalist accumulation in the late 1960s and early 1970s. However, there is one crucial flaw in Sraffa's theory. Capital does not produce things, "commodity bundles," "finite pies," or physical shit, but values, work. It is a system for the exploitation of time, life, and energy. Though we have reached the period when all the "powers of science and of nature, as of social combination and of social intercourse" are integral to the process of production, capital has in no way gone beyond its measuring rod—work-time—as Sraffa suggests. The "law of value" has not been repealed; on the contrary, it rules with the greatest rigor. Similarly, the relation between capital and the working class is not a "pure power relation" (like that between De Sade's aristocrats and their subjects), but one in which work remains the basis of capital's power. What is transformed by the change in basic commodity prices is work from the Low sector to the High sector.

For the energy price rise strategy to succeed, an enormous amount of work must be produced and extracted from the Low sectors in order to be transformed to capital available for the High sector. In order to finance the new capitalist "utopia" of "high-tech," venture-capital-demanding industries in the energy, computer, and genetic engineering areas, another capitalist "utopia" must be created: a world of "labor-intensive," low waged, distracted, and diffracted production. The price rise would be reduced to paper unless it imposed a qualitative increase in shit work. This is the crisis within the crisis. Can energy price hikes be backed up with the requisite work? In this juncture, as always in capital's history, *a leap in technology is financed out of the skins of the most technologically starved workers.*[22]

Those in the antinuke movement with the slogan "Nukes destroy, Solar employs" are wrong. A nuclear society requires an enormous increase in work, not in the plants or the fuel cycle, of course, but in the capitalist environment. Utilities might invest in nuclear plants and the engineers and guards necessary to run them, but the investment does not guarantee a given "return." For profit to be made out of such a "high-tech" investment, it must be transferred from "low-tech" exploitation. As always, "Accumulation of wealth at one pole is . . . at the same time accumulation of misery, agony of toil, slavery, ignorance, brutality, mental degradation, at the opposite pole."[23] The resolution of the energy crisis requires the destruction of the old type of line worker and the creation of a new figure of exploitation. Where is this work to be extracted from? Or rather, from whom?

---

[22] For a development of this analysis on a planetary scale, see "On Africa and Self-Reproducing Automata," 127 in this volume.

[23] Karl Marx, *Capital: Volume I: A Critique of Political Economy* (London: Penguin, 1976), 799.

Capitalist development feeds on the energy of the working class, on its revolutionary disgust. Ironically, capital's answer was provided by the struggle itself. If the profits crisis had its epicenter in the fission and explosion of line workers and housewives, then its resolution had to use these energies against themselves. Such is the capitalist dance called the dialectic. To the men who said, "Take this job and shove it," capital responded by closing auto and steel plants; to the women who said, "Hit the road, Jack," capital responded with the "service sector" job. The increasing refusal to accept the Oedipal wage relation by women and youth forced a complete reorganization of the wage and the structure of work. The Oedipal wage is the wage paid to the male worker for his reproduction, which also, though in a hidden and distorted manner, is to reproduce his wife and children, and which gives him real power over them. The structure of the nuclear family is buried in this wage, the whole complex of power relationships between men and women is summed up in a number. But it is another example of the illusory nature of the wage. The energies released by women's revolt against unpaid labor in the home have been the basis of the enormous expansion of a low organic composition sector which has provided the work necessary for the energy price transformation. Women's revolt, while revealing their exploitation through the Oedipal wage, opened a new path for capitalist development.

The wage, economists say, is "the price of labor," but what is this price about? Five dollars an hour, $200 a week, $10,000 a year, $400,000 a life . . . what does the money per time really pay? Does any amount pay for your lifetime? Not really; it merely pays the time it takes to make you:

> The value of labor-power is determined, as in the case of every other commodity, by the labor-time necessary for the production, and consequently also the reproduction of this special article. In so far as it has value, it represents no more than a definite quantity of the average labor of society objectified in it . . . the value of labor power is the value of the means of subsistence necessary for the maintenance of its owner.[24]

So says Marx, but here he's wrong, for the production of labor-power does not "reduce" to a bundle of commodities, the means of subsistence. Labor is also necessary to produce this "special article," that must be included in the value of labor-power. It is the essential microwork, largely feminine, unpaid and thus invisible. Housework, from raw to cooked, washing, fucking, cooling tempers, picking up after the trash, lipstick, thermostat, giving birth, kids, teaching them not to shit in the hall, curing the common cold, watching the cancer grow, even lyric poems for your schizophrenia . . . sure Marx points out that there is a "historical and moral element" in the quantity of the means of subsistence, but his servant girl and Jenny seemed to come for free.

Why the microinvisibility and virtual character of housework? Simply because, as long as capital didn't have to pay for it, it could repress the demands of the

---

[24] Ibid., 274.

female house workers and have the sexual poles of the working class at each other's throats. Only when women refuse to do this work does capital begin to recognize it and pay for it; only when women struggle against this work does it become a commodity, for the primary way capital recognizes itself is in the mirror of the commodity form, and the necessary condition for something to be a commodity is that it satisfies a desire "real or fancied."

However, something cannot be desired if it is there, being *qua* being, pure facticity, if it is natural. Something cannot be a commodity unless someone lacks it. But what is lacked can be made to be lacking. Capital creates commodities by making what is natural unnatural, as in the case of land. But there is a complementary operation of making what is unnatural natural. These two operations have been applied to work. Regular waged work is desired by capital. It needed it, wanted it and can be denied it by a struggle: hence it is unnatural, a commodity, paid. The case of housework is qualitatively different: not only has housework been imposed on women, it has been transformed into a natural attribute of our female physique and personality—an internal need, an aspiration, supposedly coming from the depth of our female character. Housework had to be transformed into a natural attribute rather than be recognized as a social contract because, from the beginning of capital's scheme for women, this work was destined to be unwaged.[25]

When women refuse to do "what's natural," then their services become commodities for capital and whole industries are born. Similarly, at the moment black lung disease began to become "unnatural for a coal miner," when the miners' struggle refused the "constant concomitance" between their job and slow suffocation, the respirator industry "took off." And so, capital develops both from our death and our refusal of it. The revolutions of desires that lay behind the tides of capital's technological "creative destruction" are rooted in the refusal of the working class to just be. This is the dialectical harmonic that joins class struggle with capitalist development. This general correlation applies to this crisis as well.

At the very moment when Nature "refuses to give its gifts in abundance," the "Nature" within society—the woman—refuses its place. The fights, the visits to the therapist, the affairs, the divorce, the welfare line, and the service sector job meet the oil price hikes. The destruction of Oedipus is not just a psychoanalytic comedy, it is out of the revolt of the women and children and the wandering of the men that capital must create commodities in order to generate the work, and surplus value, essential for this period. A dangerous and even desperate ploy? Perhaps. But these are "apocalyptic" times.

Take jogging for instance. Men now know that the wife, or even mommy, will not necessarily be around after the open heart surgery, and that the cost of a private nurse would be prohibitive, especially given that the very requirements of a steady job over a few decades (which would make the private nurse possible) call for a care-and-feeding that only the now nonexistent family can provide. So you jog, you "take care of yourself." The same is true of women, as there is no insurance, no steady man's job with fringes, no regular wage coming. Part time jobs just don't provide. So

---

[25] Federici, "Wages against Housework."

you jog. Even the kids jog from the start since they've learned the facts of life early. At the end of the day, you invest your hour around the park, reproducing yourself since no one else will do it for you for free any more. But around this twilight act revolve whole industries, new health technologies, new clothing for jogging in the rain, new sneakers, massage specialists, health clubs, etc.

Indeed, as the death fear mounts, as you know that Colonus does not wait, but the leukemia, the I.V. and the oxygen tent remain, a new industry around death develops: death nurses guiding you through the "five stages" calmly, for it is all pre-planned and researched, massaged with a cocktail of morphine and whisky on the tray. As the family evaporates, the most explosive industry is that of the body. Not accidently, we see that independent of the ups and downs of the business cycles, "health services" have nearly doubled in employment in the crisis to fill up the vacuum. There are approximately four million women and about one million male workers in this industry. The scene is obvious: your former wife, mother or sister is doing something that she used to do for free, but now she gets paid for it. What was natural before is problematic now and you wonder if anybody will answer as you press the button beside your bed.

Unfortunately for capital, labor-power needs a body: it "presupposes the living individual," and so capital must keep us alive in order to make us work (and die) in its monitors. But there is nothing automatic about living. Work must be done to carry it on, and when the women of the family stop their work somebody must pick it up. Take the question of food . . . certainly its price has a crucial impact on the wage, but an equally important factor is brought in by the question, "Raw or cooked food?" Who is to cook it, serve it, and talk to you while you eat it? Mama? Increasingly, it is the teenaged girl at McDonald's who takes your order, now that approximately half the meals in the United States are eaten outside "the home."

The "service economy" becomes the counterpole of the "energy/information" economy and it's the growth sector of the crisis. This sector is but an extension and socialization of women's work in the home. In the Keynesian period, the "institutions of the state"—schools, hospitals, jails, and army—were supplements to the home. They would take over when the "woman" failed, or finished off and standardized her work. . . .Yet, at the hub, women's work in the home remained the fundamental producer of subsistence for the male worker. But with the work/energy crisis, the center can no longer hold. Increasingly, the invisible work previously crystallized in the assembly lines appears *qua* work in the service sector. The Oedipal wage gets disaggregated. The "external" agencies and industries expand and become replacements instead of aids for the home. Women's struggle against housework has forced a reanalysis of the wage and the reproductive work done in the home. Whereas before it was hidden in the male wage, now it takes on a separate status. The invisibility of housework, veiled by the wage, is nothing new. For the wage is designed to obscure:

> The wage-form thus extinguishes every trace of the division of the working day into necessary labor and surplus labor, into paid and unpaid labor. All

labor appears as paid labor. Under the corvee system it is different. There the labor of the serf for himself and his compulsory labor for the lord of the land are demarcated very clearly both in space and time. In slave labor, even that part of the working-day in which the slave is only replacing the value of his own means of subsistence, in which, therefore, in fact, he works for himself alone, appears as labour for his master. All his labour appears as unpaid labour. In wage labour, on the contrary, even surplus-labor, or unpaid labor, appears as paid. In the one case, the property-relation conceals the slave's labour for himself; here the money-relation conceals the uncompensated labor of the wage-laborer.[26]

The slave's revolt has forced the master to recognize the slave's labor-power as alien to him and has forced him to buy it, to pay for it. But in the wage, another form of exploitation is again hidden. Mirrors don't all lie in the same way. Formal slavery is not the same as waged work. There are forms of work organization that are impossible under slavery, types of rhythms that are not sustainable. Capital learned that the whip and chain are not the most profitable forms of work control. The slave is "inert," "invisible," "opaque," and he must be pushed around to get anything from him. It is capital's great discovery that "freeing" labor-power actually leads to greater levels of exploitation, and its occasional returns to slavery (Nazi Germany, Jim Jones, Southwest immigration) have reconfirmed this truth. The free laborers "freedom" gives capital a new dimension of movement while the slave sticks, is mechanically dependent upon the production process, is a machine among the machines and must be cared for when it breaks down.

Women's labor has had a formal status intermediate between the slave and the waged worker, for she is technically free but actually unpaid. In some ways, her status is worse than the slave's, for she was "the slave of the worker," instead of the master. But her revolt, while destroying the old system, creates the possibility of a new source of exploitation (as well as the possibility of capitalist catastrophe). For with the explosion of the service sector's extensions of housework, capital reopens a forgotten page in its history: absolute surplus value production.

Since housework has always been a "labor intensive," low-tech form of work, the service sector is low on fixed capital. (Sexual technology, e.g., has barely recovered the level of ancient Egypt in recent years, and though billions have gone into the research of better methods of conception, there has been next to no official research on the biochemical roots of pleasure, sexual or otherwise.) Hence the "low productivity" of the services, a fact used by some economists to explain the breakdown of the economy-wide productivity trends in the crisis. If relative surplus value productivity is not the source of exploitation, then capital must have recourse to time and the length of the workday, i.e., absolute surplus value.

There is a major problem in extracting relative surplus value from housework: although it can be industrialized, there are bottlenecks and anachronisms limiting its productivity. Take prostitution: though there are all sorts of tricks to make the john

---

[26] Marx, *Capital: Volume I*, 680.

come faster, there must be some time-consuming contact and an immediate struggle over time (hence the pimp). In fact, the reproductive effect of many services seems to necessitate some minimum amount of time (like the limits imposed on agriculture by the seasons). Theoretically, these too can be disposed of in the same way that agriculture can be completely detached from seasonal cycles, but this would require a history of struggles that have not yet taken place. Hence service work, because of its unit-by-unit character, largely allows only absolute surplus value production.

This development of absolute surplus value work is not statistically evident because much of this work is "part time." This does not imply that working part time reduces a woman's working day. On the contrary, it means that an enormous part of the total housework women still do remains unpaid. In this transition period, capital is still interested in getting as much unpaid work as possible out of women both via the job and what remains at home. Thus we have women in the 1970s (in the midst of a jungle of microcomputers, genetic technology, and fission reactors) with work schedules that would make Manchester operatives nervous: 6:30 get the kids and hubby ready, 9:00 on the "part time" job, 2:00 off the job and go to pick up kids, 5:00 make dinner, 8:00 school-time for Mommy to up-grade employment someday, 12:00 fuck and sleep (?). There is an enormous amount of surplus value in this schedule, though the energy to do it comes from the desire to get "from under the thumb" of hubby.

Housework then is externalized and waged. Surplus value is extracted directly from the labor time of the woman on the job, in addition to her reproduction work being extracted from the male workers on the assembly line. With the growth of the service sector in the crisis, the "human capital" experiments of the Kennedy and Johnson administrations were either abandoned or curtailed, for the indirect method of capitalizing on housework was too uncertain. The State's idea in the 1960s was that by investing in the home (via welfare, food stamps, etc.) women would do a proper level of housework with their children. Increasingly in the 1970s, however, the state was not willing to wait for the growing productivity of labor-power due to the human capital investment to produce the relative surplus value that would give a proper return to the investment.

As long as there was faith in the future, capital was willing to wait, sometimes a generation, to pick the fruits of the house workers' labors. However, the profit crisis showed that the future was in short order, it was no longer guaranteed. Thus, the surplus value of the housework had to be realized immediately, sucked up just at the moment of its exuding, rather than the next day in the reproduced line worker or the next generation in the new cohort of workers entering the labor marker. It is at this point that the energy crisis enters. Big Mother Nature is now used to squeeze little Mother dry. If Big Momma is stingy and has turned cold, capital turns to little momma: "Help me out or we'll all go down together."

As women refuse this deal, as they demand "too much" for their work, as they refuse to do it properly and efficiently, the energy crisis collapses. As this final veil falls, capital is faced with a working class untorn by the poles of sexual powers. An apocalypse indeed.

The Manifold of Work: Anti-entropy qua Information

The female service worker meets her complement in the computer programmer and technician in the energy crisis. For while the most archaic forms of exploitation are resurrected by the energy price rise, at the opposite pole there is an intensification in the development of the instrumentalities of information and control. Why the rise of the computation industry at the peak of the energy crisis? In order to understand this development we must turn again to the work/energy crisis of the late 1960s and early 1970s.

The overflowing of working-class energy imposed an energy crisis on a number of counts. First, energy prices, which are basic, have allowed capital to tip the wage/profit ratio in its direction and increase the average rate of profit. Second, these prices are the vehicle for the reorganization of the organic composition of capital, making the realization of profits insensitive to "immediate" factory worker's struggles. Third, the price transformation has made it possible to directly extract surplus value from the reproduction work. But this was still not enough. The mere fact that women were increasingly employed in the Low sector of the economy did not guarantee that this would turn into profit, into capital. The mere fact that auto plants are closed does not mean that cars and trucks are no longer produced; they are just made with fewer workers. Finally, the mere fact of investment in the high-tech areas does not mean that this investment will pay off, for the high organic composition sector is very sensitive to breakdown, indeed, catastrophic ones. Thus the energy crisis imposes a new premium on information, control and communication (transfer). The enormous decentralization of employment in the service industry has required new methods of transferring surplus value from one end of the system to the other. The expulsion of the mass factory worker reintroduces the drive toward robotization. Finally, the concentration of productive capital in complex machines requires an intensification of self-policing and conservation of capital.

To better understand the simultaneous rise of the information processing industry with the service industry, we must descend into the volcanic heart of capital: the work process. Work kills, and that is a problem, for capital needs to be able to reproduce the work process. Production is linear, but it must go around. There must be a mechanism of "eternal return" in the work process that will bring it back into the initial position (so that it can be done again). Work kills, but in each death there must be the seeds of its rebirth, a cycle of production and reproduction. As Mengele discovered, you can work a human to death in a few minutes, but you won't be able to do anything with the scraps except perhaps art deco lampshades and inefficient fertilizer. Capital then must plan the reproduction of the work process on a continuing basis. As in Carnot's cycle, though only one stage accomplishes the thrust, the others are essential, to restore the engine to a position where work can be done again.

To do without the reproductive part of the cycle is capitalist suicide. Moreover, as the example of the early post-Columbian silver mines and the Nazi work camps show, there is no "instinct for survival," only conditions and thresholds. Capital can only approach the thresholds of survival with the utmost caution: suicide always beckons at the margin of survival. The pleasure of a suicide that would rob the capitalist of his value becomes attractive to a worker when s/he can do nothing else.

To ensure the reproduction of production, however, it is not enough to reproduce the worker. Capital too must be preserved. Constant capital is an essential part of the production process, which must be protected from workers' corrosive energies. Capital's drive to self-preservation and self-reproduction appears in the classical personality of the little capitalist: "the capitalist taking good care that the work is done in a proper manner, and that the means of production are used with intelligence, so that there is no unnecessary waste of raw material, and no wear and tear of the implements beyond what is necessarily caused by the work."[27]

The microcapitalist is so concerned about his fixed capital because there is a constant threat of the worker who does the work "unintelligently," "sloppily," and is, above all, wasteful. Workers cannot only kill themselves in times of frustrated struggles, they can always kill capital in its most embodied and vulnerable form: the machine. To control this most basic form of class struggle, it is not enough to bring the cycle back to the initial state; it is all-important to bring about this return without "waste," "wear and tear," "loss of work," and "depreciation." Not only is work "expenditure" of energy that must be "reproduced," this expenditure must be controlled so that the amount of work required to reproduce the initial state is not excessive. This problem becomes agonizing when the constant capital reaches certain critical points of concentration, if the possibilities of rapid depreciation are not thwarted, investment in constant capital is the source of an enormous dis-accumulation. This poses an exact limit on the energy price strategy. If the Low sector work is transformed into High sector capital and it becomes so concentrated and vulnerable that it can be immediately depreciated, the whole strategy collapses. Protecting constant capital is a primary function of the information/computation industry.

We have already seen the game that can wreck the "energy crisis" strategy in the case of the nuclear industry. Consider Three Mile Island. To make up for the late start-up of the plant, its managers ordered it to be run at higher than normal capacity (for nuclear plants) from the beginning. Workers were often assigned to overtime and the intensity of "getting rid of the bugs" was beginning to wear. Then, at 4:00 a.m. on an early spring morning, a near meltdown occurred. Thus, in the process of producing a few million dollars of extra profit in its first few months of operation, Met Edison is suddenly faced with the need of shelling out almost a billion dollars just to get half of Three Mile Island operating again, and that with some difficulty. Here we have a situation where the amount of work needed to bring the nuclear plant back to the initial state, pre-4:00 a.m. March 28, 1979, will be many times the work produced by the plant in the first place. In fact, given the general work environment in central Pennsylvania, including the surrounding class composition, one might say that in no way will the plant be brought back to its initial state. In Three Mile Island, we see that the energy crisis response to the class

---

[27] In the original publication, the footnote said, "A free copy of *Midnight Notes* to the Marxologist who can spot this quote." The offer still stands!

struggle is far from stable. Indeed, it introduces a novel form of class confrontation, or rather recalls the ancient "strife between workman and machine."

The Accident becomes a central category of the political economy of the energy crisis, but what is an accident anyway? Accidents are work situations in which the amount of work that goes into reproducing the initial state (of the work process) becomes extraordinary. Accidents demonstrate the mortality of the work process. But as the Kemeny Commission report, "Accident at Three Mile Island," noted:

> The major factor that turned this incident in to a serious accident was inappropriate operator action, many factors contributed to the action of the operators, such as deficiencies in their training, lack of clarity in their operating procedures, failure of organizations to learn the proper lessons from previous incidents, and deficiencies in the design of the control room. . . .The control room, through which the operation of the TMI-2 plant is carried out, is lacking in many ways. The control panel is huge, with hundreds of alarms, and there are some key indicators placed in locations where the operators cannot see them. During the first few minutes of the accident, more than 100 alarms went off, and there was no system of suppressing the unimportant signals so that operators could concentrate on the significant alarms. Information was not presented in a clear and sufficiently understandable form; for example, although the pressure and temperature within the reactor coolant system were shown, there was no direct indication that the combination of pressure and temperature meant that the cooling water was turning into steam.[28]

Here, Kemeny, a coauthor of the computer language BASIC, issues the latest edition of the old capitalist wail: "Workers are stupid, if only we knew how stupid they are, if only we knew!" Machines break down, that's bound to happen, they depreciate after all, but such breakdowns are only "incidents"; what turns an incident into an accident is that the worker cannot or does not control the breakdown to bring the machine back to its initial state with no appreciable cost. The accident need not have happened. What stops accidents is immediately available knowledge, information and foresight, and, most important, communication. Consider the following:

> A senior engineer of the Babcock and Wilcox Company (suppliers of the nuclear steam system) noted in an earlier accident, bearing strong similarities to the one at Three Mile Island, that operators had mistakenly turned off the emergency cooling system. He pointed out that we were lucky that the circumstances under which this error was committed did not lead to a serious accident and warned that under other circumstances (like those that would later exist at Three Mile Island), a very serious accident could result. He urged, in the strongest terms, that clear instructions be passed on to the

---

[28] John G. Kemeny, Chairman, *Report of the President's Commission on the Accident at Three Mile Island* (Washington, DC: U.S. Government Printing Office, 1979), 11–12.

operators. This memorandum was written 13 months before the accident at Three Mile Island, but no new instructions resulted from it.[29]

"If only we had told them, if only we made the new information part of our commands," goes the lachrymose bitching. But it is just bitching, as Kemeny knows, for though any particular accident, by definition, can be avoided, accidents in general are unavoidable. It is in the fact that not every process is reversible that time itself has a direction. There is a deep relation between accidents, information, time, and work. Marx described this relation in the following way: the means of production created no new value; at best, their value is transferred and preserved in the product. Machines merely wear out or transfer their energy to the new form produced. The work process therefore has two components: (a) production of "fresh value" (both surplus value and the reproduction of variable capital), and (b) the transfer and preservation of the value of the means of production. As Marx points out, work must do both (a) and (b) at the same time, though for different reasons.

On one hand, then, by virtue of its general character as an expenditure of human labor-power in the abstract, spinning adds new value to the values of the cotton and the spindle; on the other hand, by virtue of its special character as a concrete, useful process, the same labor of spinning both transfers the values of the means of production to the product, and preserves them in the product. Hence, a simultaneous twofold result.[30]

There are no machines that create value out of nothing, no perpetual motion machines; further, the value incorporated in the machines is continually wearing out, being transformed into a new use-value in which the old exchange-value reappears. All the devices of the capitalist magicians end up as corpses, as not even the most ingenious thought can add a cubit to capital's stature:

> The technical conditions of the labor-process may be revolutionized to such an extent that where formerly ten men using ten implements of small value worked up a relatively small quantity of raw material, one man may now, with the aid of one expensive machine, work up a hundred times as much raw material. . . . Such a revolution, however, alters only the quantitative relation between the constant and the variable capital, or the proportions in which the total capital is split up into its constant and variable constituents; it has not in the least degree affected the essential difference between the two.[31]

The work process not only must expand and be reproducible, it must conserve old while creating new work. Computerization of a production process creates no new value. However, it makes it possible to make the variable part smaller while guarding against the too rapid exhaustion of constant capital. It is the mechanization of the "little capitalist" mentality. No elements of the production cycle must be

---

[29] Kemeny, *Report*, 10.

[30] Marx, *Capital: Volume I*, 309.

[31] Ibid., 319.

wasted, neither the time of the workers nor the time of the machines. Capital must make the cycle smooth, efficient, and as close to "reversible" as possible, for it determines, in part, the rate of profit:

> If surplus-value is a given factor, the profit rate can be increased only by reducing the value of the constant capital required for the production of the commodities in question. In so far as the constant capital is involved in production, all that matters is its use-value, it is not its exchange-value ... the assistance that a machine gives to three labourers, say, depends not on its value, but on its use-value as a machine. At one stage of technical development a bad machine may be expensive and at another a good machine may be cheap.[32]

Concurrently, each aspect of work has its peculiar repulsion. As far as the process of preserving and conserving the value of the means of production is concerned, the tactic of refusal is obvious. As constant capital increases with the development of industrialization, the gap between the value of the means of production and the part of the value used up during a unit cycle of production widens appreciably (think of the difference between an atomic power plant and a cotton gin). This leaves an enormous amount of capital hostage to the workers who have access to the machines. This intensifies with every new leap in the organic composition of capital, which is why slave labor cannot be incorporated in a highly capital-intensive process. For the gap between variable and constant capital would grow so enormous, i.e., the balance between the value of the slave and the value the slave could destroy would become so precarious, the slightest gesture of revolt would force capital's retreat. Capital, however, has organized the work process of "free laborers" in such a way that the hostage drama is rarely played out (one remarkable example to the contrary was the Flint "sit-down," or, better, "live-in" in 1936.)

There is an enormous amount of work involved in ensuring that the value of the means of production is slowly, efficiently and carefully transferred to the product. Not only must a full-fledged hostage drama be averted daily (for a Gdansk move is always beckoning); the invisible instants of revolt that continually pulsate through the work process, wearing out the constant capital beyond "what is warranted," must also be constantly thwarted. Thus Kemeny's lament beseeches "more care," "more policing," "better training," "better information display systems," "emergency planning." In a word, greater "efficiency," in the wearing out of enormously concentrated, volatile, perhaps "critical," pieces of constant capital.

Eternal vigilance is necessary to attain the circularity of a perfect production process. But a work process is never completely reproducible. There is always some little "blow-out," some little "fuck up," that makes returning the system to its initial state a work process also. Capital always dreams of a perpetual motion machine,

---

[32] Karl Marx, *Capital: Volume III: A Critique of Political Economy* (London: Penguin, 1981), 173.

work from energy without loss. But time is asymmetric, the future is not going to be like the past. Through our refusals, our insubordination, all the plans come to nothing, all the machines wear out, break down. Capital's contradiction is that the very agents that create the "fuck up" possess the energies it needs. Only *we* are in perpetual motion: eternally energetic, crafty, obedient, cowardly, insolent, revolting, but always in a motion that is the only source of work, development, surplus.

A parallel deduction of the need for a tremendous development of an "information" industry during the crisis arises from thermodynamics, the late nineteenth-century science discussed in the Introduction. The paradox that has troubled capitalist science since the First and Second Laws of thermodynamics is that though energy is conserved, the energy available for work in a system diminishes. Energy comes in ordered grades, thus what is essential is not its quantity per se but its structure. Some types of energy can easily be turned into work while others cannot. The amount of raw energy in the waters of a calm lake might be enormously greater than that of a slight wind blowing above it, but the wind can more easily be turned into work. The measure of the unavailability of energy for work is entropy that, within a closed system, increases to a maximum (the Second Law of thermodynamics). This Law enshrines capitalist pessimism, for it announces that the work creating process degrades energy invested in any and every system, including the human.

If we take a system as made up of millions of microparticles, the Second Law can be rephrased as the constant tendency for an ordered structure of microparticles to turn into a disordered chaos. In any system there is a constant "shuffling" of microparticles due to their eternal random motion eventually breakdown of any highly ordered structure. Schrodinger gave a telling example of such "shuffling" on the human plane.[33] Imagine an unruly mob that assaults a library of computer tapes for the fun of it and, while not taking away or destroying the tapes, simply rips them off from their assigned places to play games with them. At the end of the party, the tapes are conserved but their order is totally destroyed. Further, the work of recreating that pre-riot order is as real as the work of making new tapes and can be even greater.

The problem, according to this branch of capitalist science, is that Nature spontaneously loves Chaos; it is a perpetual upsetting of plans and orders and a wearing down of accumulated work, just like the lazy, anarchic, drunken, and riotous workers of the past. (If God is not on the side of the working class, certainly Nature is its darling.) Systems that apparently upgrade energy are eventually doomed; systems like the steam engine, or capitalism that transform energy into work ("upgraded" energy) are continually threatened with disaster, with accidents and the catastrophes of entropy invasion.

The Second Law shows a deep connection between time and accidents. Time is one-directional because work processes are not reversible, as there is always a positive amount of work necessary to return the system to its origin. However smoothly the fit is made between piston and cylinder, however carefully the emergency cooling systems are calibrated to switch on beyond a threshold temperature, there is always friction,

---

[33] Erwin Schrodinger, one of the founders of quantum mechanics, in 1944 drew the connection between genetics and information in his book *What Is Life?* (Cambridge: Cambridge University Press, 1944).

and stuck valves. Accidents will happen that turn reversibly planned processes (potentially having an eternal return) into irreversible vectors leading to higher entropic states. They create time as flow to death, for time, as capital knows it, is not just flow but the dissolution of what has been accumulated: the death of dead labor.

The "unruly mob" of molecular agents causing the wearing down of low entropy (highly ordered structures) into high entropy (disorganized fields) continually creeps in to create the conditions of the Grand Accident. Nuclear engineers may be right when they claim that the probability that a reactor core may become critical by itself is infinitesimal; but the probability of a stoned engineer, of a forgotten open valve, a sudden breeze shifting a candle's flame, are conditions that create the entropy for the Meltdown. That the molecules will win is the secret thought of capital. "Time is on their side.... Time is them," they whisper through the boardroom. But something can be done, something that will allow them to hold on: information. If enough information is gathered and communicated rapidly, then time can be slowed down, perhaps indefinitely. Thus the cruciality of machines that can store and compute information at light speed.

Information about the location of low entropy systems is an essential part of the production process. As the parable of Maxwell's demon shows, a machine with "intelligence" or "information" can thwart for a time the operation of the Second Law. When Clark Maxwell suggested the parable, he intimated the possibility of perpetual-work machines based not upon some complex and ultimately foolish contraption, but on the application of thought and categorization. His demon works like a sorting machine in the midst of an eternal shuffle (see Graph #5).

Graph #5

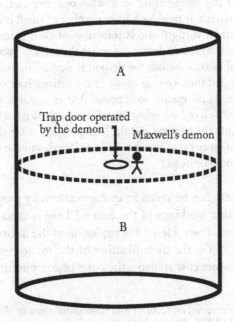

A

Trap door operated
by the demon

Maxwell's demon

B

Consider a perfect gas at an equilibrium temperature in compartment A. The particles of that gas are not all moving at the same velocity, though their average velocity remains constant. Some are moving faster than the average, some slower. Consider further an empty compartment B next to the volume of gas A connected by a small gate and a gate-keeper. This gate-keeper is smart: s/he opens the gate only to the faster than average molecules. Within a short time, the empty compartment is filled with molecules whose average velocity is higher than before, while the original compartment is filled with molecules whose average velocity is lower than before.

Thus A is cooler than before, while B is hotter; if the two compartments were connected by a heat engine, we could create work out of the temperature difference. At the end of the process, the demon can create a new division between fast and slow molecules. Thus we have a recipe for a perpetual motion machine: just combine a steam engine with a sorting-intelligent machine! If you could only identify the irresponsible workers, if you could only identify the faulty parts, if you could just pick out the microacts of carelessness, then you would have a new cycle that could possibly go on forever, recycling, upgrading, and reusing the used-up energy for work.

This scheme has a hitch, however: the demon must be able to know which of the molecules impinging on the gate are faster than the average and which slower. "Time can be turned back, if we know enough," capital pleads with the grim reaper . . . but the reaper replies, "You must work to know and work is death." Information is not free. True, it reduces entropy, but the process of its accumulation, retrieval, and communication is a work process as well that is filled with entropic menaces which eventually triumph. The question is, "How soon?" As Weiner put it:

> In the long run, the Maxwell demon is itself subject to a random motion corresponding to the temperature of its environment, and, as Leibniz says of some of his monads, it receives a large number of small impressions, until it falls into a "certain vertigo" and is incapable of clear perceptions. In fact, it ceases to act as a Maxwell demon. Nevertheless, there may be a quite appreciable interval of time before the demon is deconditioned, and this time may be so prolonged that we may speak of the active phase of the demon as metastable. There is no reason to suppose that metastable demons do not exist. . . . We may well regard living organisms, such as Man himself [*sic*], in this light. Certainly the enzyme and the living organism are alike metastable: the stable state of an enzyme is to be deconditioned, and the stable state of a living organism is to be dead.[34]

The work process can be saved from degradation by proper information decelerating the inexorable workings of the Second Law, if areas of low entropy can be found. But the search costs. Hence the explosion of the information industry, the emphasis on programming, the dissemination of the microcomputer, and the crucial importance of another cost statistic: the costs of computation. One of the most

---

[34] Norbert Weiner, *Cybernetics; or, Control and Communication in the Animal and the Machine* (Cambridge, MA: MIT Press, 1965), 58–59.

important developments in the crisis is the dramatic inversion of the energy price rises relative to the costs of computation.

This opens up the hope that the increase of entropy can be indefinitely held off, and a perfect circularity in the work/energy "interface" approached. Thus while the feminine service worker is to provide the emotional surplus labor necessary for accumulation in the high-tech sector, the computer programmer is to be the eternally vigilant Charon, identifying the stable worker, the stable situation, the stable machine, separating the quick from the dead.

Hence the concern of programming industry ideologists with the uncodable, the deliberately unidentifiable and uncategorizable: the Zen and criminal aspects of the struggle. At this point, the very success of the strategy of the energy crisis makes quite crucial the ability to select, with a high level of certainty, the different gradations of entropy in the labor-power of the working class. Deception, conning, cheating, and lying (i.e., all the self-reflexive moves of the slave) become problematic. Consider the polygraph tests given to more and more workers. They attempt to find out who is the low entropic worker via interrogation coupled with the detection of sweat production and blood pressure. But increasingly, workers with training in meditational processes are beating the machines and sailing to positions of responsibility in, of all things, programming. Again, and always, the problem capital faces with the new Maxwell's demons of the crisis is: "Who will select the selectors?"

The Manifold of Work: Anti-entropy qua Shit

Entropy can be reduced by information, i.e., by locating pockets of low entropy and incorporating them into the work process; the inevitable reduction in the availability for work can be held at bay. The more the information and the less the cost of creating it and communicating it, the more the stalling of Time. But this process can be reversed, i.e., the increasing entropy within a work process can be localized and expelled. Every production process shits; the question is, "Where is it going to be put?" If this shit, i.e., the material, social, physiological, radioactive, psychological waste that cannot be reswallowed and recycled, is allowed to remain in the vicinity of the production process, each new cycle of production will intensify the entropic rise exponentially. The reproduction of the machine cycle will be clogged by the leftover shit, and the costs of returning to the initial state will be so overwhelming that it will outpace the work produced by the thrust stage of the cycle. The network will fall into negativity, and needless to say, profit will be in jeopardy.

This aspect of capital's struggle against entropy involves the possibility of ejecting areas of high entropy into the surrounding environment without effecting the net work production: not only must waste be controlled and accidents prevented (the job of the computer controllers), if waste must be created, if little murders must be condoned, then it is crucial that the shit be localized and expelled. The corpses must be buried or burned. We have the final aspects of work: the passive work of absorbing capital's wastes. For in addition to the work of producing, reproducing, informing, and controlling, there is the immense work of absorbing, and imbibing capital's shit. Not only is capital concerned with transferring as much of the value of the means of production to the commodity product without waste and accident, but the work process necessarily also intensifies the entropy of its local and global workers. Marx comments on this aspect of work:

> If we consider capitalist production in the narrow sense and ignore the process of circulation and the excesses of competition, is extremely sparing with the realized labour that is objectified in commodities. Yet it squanders human beings, living labour, more readily than does any other mode of production, squandering not only blood and flesh, but also nerve and brain as well. . . . Since the whole of the economizing we are discussing here arises from the social character of labor, it is in fact precisely this directly social character of labour that produces the waste of the workers' life and health.[35]

Capital is more finicky than a cat when it comes to shitting. The whole debate on the location of nuclear plants is an example of this sensitivity, for there are complex considerations arising from the class composition to be found in any particular location. Will they riot if there is an accident, will they get nervous about the transport and spillage of used uranium, will they get "hysterical" when cancer rumors and chromosome damage reports begin seeping in, are they desperate enough to take the tax write-offs but not so desperate that they won't care and will explode anyway? Certainly it was no accident that Three Mile Island was located in the center of the heartland of patriarchy in the United States, surrounded by phallic silos, bearded Amish Jobs, and state employees.

At the same time, when capital discovers high entropic sinks in the production process, the expulsion is swift and violent. Need we refer to the execution of workers throughout capitalist development? Why is capital murdering its own labor-power? Why the Auschwitzes and Chiles? Quite simply because certain types of labor-power become too entropic for production, they become living shit for capital that must be eliminated. Of course, the direct slaughter of workers is just the most dramatic event in the never-ending struggle of capital to beat the odds. The endless string of methods to identity high entropic workers, "weed" them out, "blacklist" them, jail them, starve them, and kill them gag us now, it is too much past midnight! But if there is an institution for localizing, expelling and exterminating entropy, the "criminal justice system" is the one. Its function: to rid the production process of the "elements" that are completely unavailable for work.

There is, however, the work not only of locating high-entropy, and the work of expelling it, there is finally the job of absorbing it. Consider the "jumper." The disintegrating, entropic aspect of the reactor core of a nuclear plant is the radiation that does not go into the production of heat but "escapes." One of the main jobs of the nuclear worker is to absorb this entropy.

There are nuclear workers whose job is just that: to suffer the shit out of the reactor. This is the part-time jumper hired to be sent into areas dense with radioactivity

---

[35] Marx, *Capital: Volume III*, 182.

and absorb the full "quota" for radioactivity (absorbed by a regular worker in a year) within a few minutes. He picks up his $100 after twisting a valve and disappears, perhaps to return in a few months, perhaps to discover a suspicious lump ten years later. The "jumper" is an extreme figure, an ideal type; but certainly the proliferation of chemical and radioactive dumpsites across the country has made "fallers" of us all. It is apparent that the "squandering of human lives" does not occur only within the gates of the nuclear plant or chemical factory, but is as "social" as the labor that produces the radioactive electricity and poisons.

As we are dealing with the asshole of capital, we inevitably must deal with all that is most foul, decaying, and frightening: corpses, cancer, executions, slavery, and the Gilmorean joke. It is at the lowest level of the institutional hierarchy, at the bottom of our fear as to what they are doing to us, that the basic profit level is guaranteed. It is not because of any melancholic humors that we have wandered here; it is exactly in these dumps of matter, body, and nerve that you find the famous "bottom line." It's all in the physics: the efficiency of a heat engine is not only proportional to the work it produces, but is inversely proportional to the entropy it creates. The less the entropy, the greater the "efficiency": hence the greater the work/energy ratio, the greater the profit.

Prisons are as integral to the production process as the gas that makes the engines go, as the caress that sends one off to the plant, as the printout that tells you of your fuck up. For if there were no dumps of labor-power and constant capital, no way of eliminating entropic contamination, the system would stop. Of course, the capitalist idea is not to end the shit but to control it, dumping it in isolated, unobjectionable places, on unobjecting or invisible populations. Thus with the energy crisis comes the death penalty.

This is the last element of the profits crisis and the last reason for the energy crisis response. As the working class through the 1960s and 1970s has increasingly refused to be the dump of capitalist shit, the collective sewer of its entropic wastes, some antagonistic compulsion was in order. Energy price rises immediately put this refusal to absorb the shit on the defensive, for the high cost of energy seems to justify the need for entropy control and for expelling highly concentrated entropy deposits from the production process. Thus the explicit and implicit anti-nuclear movement meets its response: nuclear plants can only pass once energy prices go up. But once Teller's system of nukes and coal electrification is introduced, then the intensification of the mechanisms of control and information in the production process are inevitably realized. Finally, only with such increased prices (imposed by the very investment in this High sector), can the "need" for accepting the disintegrating excretions of the plants be forced down the throats of the surrounding populations. The rate payers of Three Mile Island are financing the repair of the plant with increased electricity bills, and the state's increasing pressure to open up the radioactivity dump sites throughout the country is felt by all.

The End of the Apocalypse

We began with the end of world, the Apocalypse. With all their noise, the capitalist prophets have suggested the problem of energy as the cause of the impending catastrophe: either too little energy (the anti-limitationists) or too much of it (the interactionists). Even the "revival" of "nuclear holocaust" thinking of the unthinkable takes energy as the trigger of the Bomb, for invariably it is seen as the most pressing Natural scarcity. The scenarios of nuclear war obsessively turn to the Gulf of Hormuz, for there appears here an inevitable source of international antagonism. According to the anti-limitationists, the only way to move in the face of fundamental scarcity is to prepare for the possibility of a military confrontation. On the other side, the inter-actionists warn that if we want to escape the threat of nuclear war, we must retreat to a "clean," "stable-state" economy autarchic enough to remove the need for such a confrontation. Both sides accept the "problem" as a collection of "natural brute facts."

While the facts might be brute enough, they are not "natural." Whenever capital announces a new apocalypse, we must see that the culprit is not Nature, the Bomb, or some autonomous bureaucratic drive to "exterminism." Capital's Apocalypse is the inverse image of the struggle against it, as it reaches critical proportions. You don't fight shadows with shadows, and you don't walk about "delicately and nonprovoca-tively" for fear of setting off the irrational Beast. At the root of all the missiles, bombs, atomic power plants, all the "idols of the theater" that capital displays so provocatively, is the struggle against capitalist accumulation, against a life dominated by work and exploitation. This struggle is the source of the current Apocalyptic Rumors and this struggle can end them. What ended the Bomb Apocalyptics in the early 1960s? It was by no means the rhetorical battle between pro- and anti-bomb movements. Capital had to demote the Bomb because the class movements in the early 1960s made it clear that they would not be intimidated by all this nuclear rattling. The riots in Watts, the revival of wildcats in coal, the refusal to accept Civil Defense regimentation even after the exercise of the Cuban crisis, made it clear to the Kennedy and Johnson administra-tions that the Bomb had begun to loose its hold. The grip of terror could not constrict the new class movements, their desires, and disgusts.

The same holds for the present. The Four Horsemen of the Apocalypse, "given a fourth of the earth, to kill with the sword and with famine and with pestilence and by wild beasts," can only be stopped by the development of the very struggles that unleashed them. Any "solutions" to the energy crisis that attempt to bypass the struggle—whether Teller's electronuclear path ringed with missile silos or the Odums' "alternativist" path of agricultural homeostasis and defensivism—merely repropose the crisis. As we have shown, capital cannot do with either Teller or the Odums alone. The seemingly opposing utopias of High and Low organic composition necessarily complement each other; indeed, they potentiate each other.

Capital has turned the world upside down to deal with the struggle against work, against the muscle, heart, nerve, and asshole of capital.

Against the four levels of work:

- the relative exploitation of the factory;
- the absolute exploitation of the housework;
- the reduction of entropy via smoothing of the work process with the detec-tion of low entropic pools;
- the reduction of entropy via the expulsion of high entropic wastes.

We have seen the corresponding levels of struggle:

- refusal of "productivity deals" on the assembly lines;
- disintegration of the family and the reproductive apparatus that keys workers into the production process;
- refusal to accept the entropy sorters of capital, e.g., in the education system and through the intensification of "crime";
- refusal to passively absorb the expulsion of capital's shit into the biosocial process of reproduction, e.g., the struggle against prisons and radioactive dumps.

All these forms of refusal directly caused the profits crisis and the subsequent "Energy Crisis" restoration of profitability. These struggles, however, remain intractable whatever the total "apocalyptic" attack that capital has confronted them with. As Polish workers have shown, the only way to confront the missiles is to demand more and juicier sausages: "Only those who strike eat meat."

MORMONS IN SPACE

(With Silvia Federici)

Space is but Time congealed. An arrangement of Work/Life in integrated sequences. The Earth is another Matter however. So why this urge to get out of Earth? To simultaneously destroy it and transcend it?

Is this capital's nasty little secret: the destruction of the final recalcitrant Body? The in-itself of capitalist functionality, the residue of a billion years of noncapitalist formation . . . why should there be Mountains here, Rivers there and an Ocean exactly here after all?

Why, indeed, space shuttles, space colonies mixed with such a density of bombs, bombs and still more bombs . . . to destroy the Earth n-times over as if to assure not the least roach existence? Why the simultaneous attempt to recode the chromosomes and the neural system?

Why, if not to define a truly capitalist BEING, in a purely capitalist plasm and a final purely capitalist sequence of work events? Weightless, formless neurosystems unwebbed and ready for infinite rewebbing.

Why, if not a search for a being unprogrammed by millennia, shifting at the bottom of a ton of oxygen, lugging all this weight around, this gravity against work?

Space is ultimately the obstacle of Time. . . . Bergson got it wrong. . . . Lukács, too. . . . capitalism is not the spatialization of Time but rather the temporalization of Space, the dissolving of distance, of the Just-Thereness of where we come from.

"Outer space" is not Space as we know it, but a final merging with the relations of time. It is lusted for not because of the minerals on Mars—no more than the gold and silver in the rivers of the Caribbean isles were—but what they can do to you on Mars when they get you there.

This is why the working class is so archaic, such a malfunctioning machine. The early Hobbesians were only partly right: Humans are not Machines, but only poor copies of

*them. Their desires are too limited and then again too wide. They have a desperation for a
housework built on a million years of noncapitalist pleasures and pains and a revulsion of
their own archaicness that is too arbitrary.*

*The Lebensraum of Hitler was really an Arbeitsraum that required an immense
destruction of "leben" to achieve and then finally failed. So, too, with porcelain tiles
glued on, computers in a soap opera of "You don't understand me": the return of the space
shuttle is heralded with a desperation that you wonder at this desire for a biologically
pure realm, freed from the seasonal, diurnal and lunar cycles, airless, weightless, and
open to infinite reductions.*

*This has always been capital's fatal attraction: its indifference to Space. The Here-
Now disappears when the essential problem is not what I need, desire, and want now but
what another needs, desires, or wants of what I need, desire, or want. The Here vanishes
in an abstracted There-Here-There.*

*You can see capital looking down from its space stations. . . . "Those poor, slightly
crazed machines! Their needs have been so thoughtlessly defined, their sexuality is incon-
siderate, and their desires are fixed by biochemical cycles so local that they make you want
to cry! When will we finally be able to rid ourselves of these Bodies?"*

In trying to define the Zeitgeist breathing through the New Right today, one
is confronted with a seemingly undecipherable puzzle. On one hand, these are the
spokesmen for a scientific and technological revolution that a few years ago would
have smacked of science fiction: gene-splicing, DNA computers, time-compression
techniques, space colonies. At the same time, the circles of the New Right have witnessed a revival of religious tendencies and moral conservatism that one would have
thought were buried once and for all with "our" Puritan Founding Fathers. Falwell's
Moral Majority is the most vocal of this return to the values of Calvin and Cotton
Mather, but not the only one by far. Wherever you turn, God-fearing, Satan-minded
groups, determined to reshape the country on the model of the Puritan colonies, are
sprawling like mushrooms: Christian Voice, Pro-Family Forum, National Prayer
Campaign, Eagle Forum, Right to Life Commission, Fund to Restore an Educated
Electorate, Institute for Christian Economics. Seen in its general contours, then, the
body of the New Right seems to stretch in two opposite directions, attempting at
once a bold leap into the past and an equally bold leap into the future.

The puzzle increases when we realize that these are not separate sects, but
in various ways involve the same people and the same money. Despite a few petty
squabbles and a few pathetic contortions to keep up the "pluralism" facade, the hand
that sends the shuttle into orbit or recombines mice and rabbits is the same hand
that fretfully pushes for gays to be sent to the stake and draws a big cross not just
through the twentieth, but the nineteenth and eighteenth centuries, too.

The extent to which the Moral Majority and Co. and the science futurologists are one soul, one mission, is best seen, if not in the lives of their individual
spokesmen (though the image of the "electronic minister" and of a President who in
the same breath blesses God and calls for stepped up nerve-gas production and the

neutron bomb are good evidence of this marriage), then in the harmony of intent they display when confronted with the "key issues" of the time. When it comes to economic and political matters, all shreds of difference drop off and both souls of the New Right pull money and resources toward their common goals. Free-market, laissez-faire economics (for business, of course), the militarization of the country (what is called "building a strong military defense"), bolstering "internal security" (i.e., giving the FBI and CIA free rein to police our daily life), cutting all social spending except that devoted to building prisons and ensuring that millions will fill them: in a word, asserting U.S. capital's ownership of the world and setting "America" to work at the minimum wage (or below) are goals for which all the New Right would swear on the Bible.

A clue to understanding the double soul of the New Right is to realize that its mixture of reactionary social policies and scientific boldness is not a novelty in the history of capitalism. If we look at the beginning of capital—the sixteenth and seventeenth centuries to which the Moral Majority would so happily return—we see a similar situation in the countries of the "take off." Just as Galileo was pointing his telescope to the moon, and Francis Bacon was laying the foundations of scientific rationality, women and gays were burnt on the stake by the thousands throughout Europe, with the universal blessing of the modernizing [sic] European intelligentsia.

A sudden craze? An inexplicable fall into barbarism? In reality, the witch hunt was part and parcel of that attempt at "human perfectibility" that is commonly acknowledged as the dream of the fathers of modern rationalism. The thrust of the emerging capitalist class toward the domination and exploitation of nature would have remained a dead letter without the concomitant creation of a new type of individual whose behavior would be as regular, predictable, and controllable as that of the newly discovered natural laws. To achieve this purpose, a magical conception of the world had to be destroyed that made the Indians in the overseas colonies believe that it was a sacrilege to mine the earth and that assured the proletariat in the heart of Europe that people could fly, be in two places at the same time, divine the future, or to believe that on some "unlucky days" all enter-prise had to be carefully avoided. The witch hunt, moreover, ensured the control over the main source of labor, the woman's body, by criminalizing abortion and all forms of contraception as a crime against the state. Finally, the witch hunt was functional to the reorganization of family life, which is to say the restructuring of reproduction that accompanied the reorganization of work on a capitalistic basis. On the stake died the adulteress, the woman of "ill repute," the lesbian, the woman who lived alone or lacked "maternal spirit" or had illegitimate children. On the stake ended many beggars who had impudently launched their curses against the refusal of some ale and bread. In the "transition" to capitalism, it was primarily the woman, especially the woman in rebellion, (destined to depend on a man for her survival) who became pauperized. The fathers of modern rationalism approved; some even complained that the state did not go far enough. Notoriously, Bodin insisted that the witches should not be "mercifully" strangled before being given to the flames.

That we find a similar situation prevailing in the United States today is an indication of the depth of capital's crisis. When uncertain of its foundations, capital always—in its beginning (and we would hope, in its end)—returns to its bases. At present, this means attempting a bold technological leap that on one side (at the developing pole of production) concentrates capital and automates work to an unprecedented degree and, on the other, consigns millions of workers to either wagelessness (unemployment) or to employment in intensive-labor types of jobs, paid at minimum rates, on the model of the much acclaimed "workforce." This involves, however, a reorganization of the process whereby labor is reproduced—a project in which women are expected to play a most crucial role.

Today, the institutionalization of repression and self-discipline along the line of the Moral Majority and the New Christian Right is required for both ends of the working-class spectrum: for those who are destined to temporary, part-time subsistence level of wages (accompanied by long hours of work or a perennial quest for jobs), as well as for those who are elected to a "meaningful wage," working with the most sophisticated equipment capital's technologists are now able to produce. That the holy trinity of God/Work/Family is always crucial in times of repression is a well-tested truth capital has never forgotten. What could be more productive than a life of isolation, in which the only relations we have with each other are relations of reciprocal discipline? Daddy controls Mommy, Mommy teaches the children that life is hard and survival is problematic, neighbors get together to keep the neighborhood "clean," sociality shrinks to those occasions that help us find or keep a job. And if life is pain, there is always God, in whose name you can even justify nuclear war against the infidels who, like the rebellious Sodomites, deserve to be wiped out from the face of the earth (even if a few of the righteous get wiped out, too). You can even justify a nuclear war that will wipe out yourself, too: after all, what's the big deal about life if you have already accepted to bargain cancer for a wage, renounced all your desires, and postponed your fulfillment to another world?

Let us not be mistaken. Weinberger needs Jerry Falwell. From Wall Street to the Army, all of capital's utopias are predicated on an infinitesimal micropolitics at the level of the body, curbing our animal spirits, and redefining the meaning of that famous Pursuit of Happiness that (so far at least) has been the biggest of all constitutional lies. Jerry Falwell is even more needed for the development of the high-tech (computer, information, energy, genetic) worker who—unlike those at the lower echelons of the working class—cannot be run by the stick (in case God failed); for the damage he can do (should he slip in his duty) is infinitely greater, because the machines he works with are infinitely more costly.

The launch of today's high-tech industry needs a technological leap in the human machine—a big evolutionary step creating a new type of worker to match capital's investment needs. What are the faculties of this new being, as advocated by our futurologists? A look at the debate on space colonies is revealing in this respect. All agree, first of all, that the main impediment today to the development of human colonies in space is biosocial rather than technological: you may be able to glue together the space shuttle's tiles, but gluing the right space worker-technician is a project that even the present genetic breakthroughs are far from having solved. The space colony needs individuals who can:

- endure social isolation and sensory deprivation for long periods of time without breaking down
- perform "perfectly" in an extremely hostile/alien and artificial environment and under enormous stress
- achieve a superb control of their bodily functions (consider: it takes an hour to shit in space!) and psychological reactions (anger, hate, indecisiveness), our all-too-human frailties that can be disastrous in the fragile, vulnerable world of life in space
- demonstrate total obedience, conformity, and receptivity to commands, for there can be little tolerance for social deviations and disagreements when the most minute act of sabotage can have catastrophic consequences to the very costly, complex, and powerful equipment entrusted in their hands

Indeed, not only will the space technician have a quasi-religious relation to his machine but he himself must become more and more machine-like, achieving a perfect symbiosis with his computer which, in the long nights of space, is often his only and always his most reliable guide, his companion, his buddy, his friend.

The space worker, then, must be a highly ascetic type, pure in body and soul, perfect in his performance, obedient like a well-wound clock, and extremely fetishistic in his mental modes. Where is this gem most likely bred? In a fundamentalist type religious sect. To put it in the words of biologist Garrett Hardin:

> What group would be most suitable to this most recent Brave New World (the space colony)? Probably a religious group. There must be unity of thought and the acceptance of discipline. But the colonists couldn't be a bunch of Unitarians or Quakers, for these people regard the individual conscience as the best guide to action. Space colonies' existence would require something more like the Hutterites or the Mormons for its inhabitants . . . integration could not be risked on this delicate vessel, for fear of sabotage and terrorism. Only "purification" would do.[1]

Not surprisingly, the first space shuttle astronauts were greeted by Elder Neal Maxwell at the Mormon Tabernacle a few days after landing. "We honor tonight men who have seen God in all his majesty and power," he said and the 6,000-member congregation responded, "Amen."

The fight between creationism and evolutionism is just an internal capitalist squabble about the most adequate means of control. Until our social biologists and genetic engineers—the heroes of today's scientific breakthrough—have found the means to create a perfect robot, the whip will do, particularly in an age still infected

---

[1] Stewart Brand, ed., *Space Colonies* (New York: Penguin, 1977), 54.

with the anarchic ideologies of the '60s, when a lot of bad germs have already been implanted in children and parents alike.

Moreover, the asceticism, self-control, the flight from the earth and the body which is the substance of puritan teaching, is the best soil in which capital's scientific and economic plans can flourish. Indeed, in its attempt to relocate itself on safer shores, capital is embracing the dream of all religion today more consciously than ever: the overcoming of all physical boundaries, the reduction of the individual human being to an angel-like creature, all soul and will. In the creation of the electronic/space worker, the priest of scientific exploration-exploitation of the universe, capital is fighting once again its historic battle against matter, attempting to break at once both the boundaries of the earth and the boundaries of "human nature" which, in its present form, present irreducible limits that must be overcome.

The thrust to the organization of industries in space and the dematerialization of the body go together. The former cannot be accomplished without the remolding of a whole nexus of needs, wishes, and desires that are the product of billions of years of material evolution on the planet and which up to now have been the material conditions of biosocial reproduction—the blues, the greens, the nipple, the balls, the hair of the anus, the texture of oranges and beef and carrots, the wind and sea smell, the daylight, the need for physical contact, SEX!!!

The dangers of sexuality are emblematic of the obstacles capital encounters in the attempt to create a totally self-controlled being capable of spending nights and nights alone, talking just to his computer with his mind focused on nothing but the screen. Can you afford to be horny or lonely in space? Can you afford to be jealous or have a marital breakdown?

The right attitude in this respect is indicated by a report on the South Pole Station in Antarctica, ostensibly set up to study meteorological, astronomical, and geographical conditions at the pole, but in reality a big center for human experimentation: the study of human beings in conditions approaching that of space (isolation for many months, lack of sensuous contact, etc.). The report states:

> As for sexual relations . . . all candidates were warned of the "dangers" of sexual liaisons under the supercharged conditions here. Celibacy was the best course . . . Men think of nothing but sex for the first few weeks, then it is submerged until nearly the end of the winter. [One worker reported,] "You just basically put it out of your mind. You are working all the time; there is no privacy."[2]

Celibacy, AIDS, abstinence: the last steps in a long process of capital's project to decrease the sensuous-sexual content of our lives and encounters with people, substituting the mental image for the physical touch. Centuries of capitalist discipline have gone a long way toward producing individuals who shrink from others

---

[2] Robert Reinhold, "Strife and Despair at South Pole Illuminate Psychology of Isolation," *New York Times*, January 12, 1982.

for fear of touch. (See the way we live our social spaces: on buses and trains, each passenger is closed in its own space, its own body, keeping well-defined invisible boundaries; each person is its own castle.) This physical as well as emotional isolation from each other is the essence of capitalist cooperation. But it—as well as the dematerialization of all forms of our life—finds culmination in the inhabitant of the future space colony whose success depends on his ability to become a pure, totally purified angel: a being who does not fuck, does not require the sensuous stimulations which are our daily nourishment on earth, but can live by solely feeding on its self-sufficient, self-centered will power.

Increasing the abstractness of the enemy body, reducing the person you destroy to a blip on a video machine: this is another essential element of death production that is likely to be the central product of space industrialization. Indeed, electronic war can become so abstract that unless your image is put into the video screen, you're likely to forget that you can be destroyed yourself. The abstractness of the object of aggression is the essence of the lesson taught to fundamentalist youth who from an early age are told that all "deviants" are the same—perfectly interchangeable—as equal expressions of the abstract powers of evil.

Communism = Homosexuality = Drugs = Promiscuousness = Subversion = Terrorism = . . . = Satan. From this point of view, all questions of "who," "what," "where," and "when" become irrelevant: a good practice for a politics of repression, and an excellent one for a policy of massive nuclear destruction, which requires building a type of being who can accept the destruction of millions of bodies as an unpleasant, perhaps, but nevertheless necessary goal to cleanse the earth from all social deviation and struggle—a pollution much worse in the eyes of the fundamentalist than strontium-90.

To achieve this, a strategy of systematic isolation is necessary, breaking all bonds between ourselves and others and distancing ourselves even from our own body. The electronic church completely dematerializes the healer, who becomes a cool image duplicated on thousands of screens or a "personal" comment in a letter written by a computer. One's main "feedback" with the preacher is the monetary one: you send your money and he begins to pray for you. If you fall back on the payments, the prayers begin to lose their fervor until they end with the "final notice."

With the electronic preacher, social relations become so abstract that they are virtually substituted by an image: the radio-TV sermon serves the same function as the home computer for the high-tech family: reproducing for you, in a purified-disembodied form, the relations/experiences of which you have been deprived in day-to-day life. They substitute dangerous—because unpredictable—human encounters with a gadget-produced sociality that can be turned off and shut down at will. It goes directly to the soul without passing through the body: clean, efficient, infinitely available at all hours of day and night. (In fact it can be recorded and replayed whenever you want—time, too, not only space, is won!!!)

To live with the machine is to become like a machine: a desexualized angel moving in the interstices of the engine, perfectly integrating work-space and life space as in the astronauts' pod, infinitely weightless because purified of the force of gravity and of all human desires/temptations, the ancient refusal of work finally negated. Capital's old dream of "human perfectibility" that loomed so prominent in the sixteenth and seventeenth-century utopias, from Bacon to Descartes, seems ready at hand. Not only can we now answer the famous Puritan question, "What do the angels do in heaven?" but we even know how they feel. According to Wally Schirra:

> Feeling weightless . . . I don't know, it's so many things together. A feeling of pride, of healthy solitude, of dignified freedom from everything that's dirty, sticky. You feel exquisitely comfortable, that's the word for it, exquisitely. . . . You feel comfortable and you feel you have so much energy, such an urge to do things, such an ability to do things. And you work well, yes, you think well, you move well, without sweat, without difficulty, as if the biblical curse *In the sweat of thy face and in sorrow* no longer exists. As if you've been born again.[3]

How petty life on earth seems from such heights. . . . No wonder capital is so careless with our earthly home, so eager to destroy it—the big bang of nuclear explosion—destroying in one second millions of tons of matter—the perfect embodiment of the victory of the spirit over the earth-matter—as creative as the first act of God! Big Bang Big Phallus reduced to its pure, power-hungry essence, fucking this rotting Earth in its god-like aspiration to be free from all constraints. Faust in an angel/astronaut/space worker face, a superman who does not need any-body, neither his own nor another's, to have his will not just on earth but in the universe as well.

A society of angels, ruled by God, and motivated by purely spiritual-religious-patriotic concerns. The adventure of space colonization will not be a "New America" in the sense of being the dumping ground of castaways, misfits, and slaves. The need for total identification with the work-project, total obedience, total self-discipline and self-control, is so high that, according to NASA, even the old forms of reward should be immediately ruled out: "High monetary incentive should not be used for space colonization recruiting because it attracts the wrong people. Furthermore, it would be unhealthy for the community as well as for the individuals concerned to make efforts to retain 'misfits' in the extraterrestrial community. It would be healthier to return them to Earth, even though this might seem more 'expensive.'"[4]

Work without a wage. It is the essential capitalist utopia where work and repression are their own rewards, and all the refusers are cast out into the cold stellar night. In space, capital finally reaches this limit.

---

[3] A quote from Walter M. Schirra Jr. during a television broadcast from space in the Apollo 7 in October 1968.

[4] Richard D. Johnson and Charles H. Holbrow, eds., *Space Settlements: A Design Study* (Washington, DC: NASA, Scientific and Technical Information Office, 1977), 31.

THE END OF WORK OR THE RENAISSANCE
OF SLAVERY?
A CRITIQUE OF RIFKIN AND NEGRI

Introduction

In the last few years, a discussion of work has emerged in the United States reminiscent of the mid-1970s, but with a number of twists. In the earlier period, books like *Where Have All the Robots Gone?*, *False Promises*, and *Work in America*, and phrases like "blue collar blues," "zerowork" and "the refusal of work" revealed a crisis of the assembly line worker that expressed itself most dramatically in wildcat strikes in U.S. auto factories in 1973 and 1974.[5] These strikes were aimed at negating the correlation between wages and productivity that had been the basis of the "deal" auto capital struck with the auto unions in the 1940s. As Peter Linebaugh and Bruno Ramirez wrote of the Dodge Truck plant wildcat involving 6,000 workers in Warren, Michigan, June 10–14, 1974: "Demands were not formulated until the third day of the strike. They asked for 'everything.' One worker said, 'I just don't want to work.' The separation between income and productivity, enforced by the struggle, could not have been clearer."[6]

---

[5] Harold L. Sheppard and Neal Q. Herrick, *Where Have All the Robots Gone? Worker Dissatisfaction in the 70s* (New York: The Free Press, 1972); Stanley Aronowitz, *False Promises: The Shaping of American Working Class Consciousness* (New York: McGraw-Hill, 1972); Special Task Force to the Secretary of Health, Education, and Welfare, *Work in America* (Cambridge, MA: MIT Press, 1973); Peter Linebaugh and Bruno Ramirez, "Crisis in the Auto Sector," in *Midnight Oil: Work, Energy, War, 1973–1992*, ed. Midnight Notes Collective (Brooklyn: Autonomedia, 1992), 143–68.

[2] Linebaugh and Ramirez, "Crisis," 160.

But this clarity was met with an even stronger clarity by the auto capitalists' decades-long campaign to reassert control over the work process in their plants and assembly lines. These capitalists did not hesitate to destroy these very plants and assembly lines in order to save themselves. "Rust belt" and "runaway plant" became the phrases of the business press when describing auto and other kinds of factory production in the 1980s; these phrases flowed almost seamlessly into "globalization" and "robotization" in the 1990s. The unprecedented result of this campaign was that full time weekly "real" wages in the U.S. manufacturing industry had fallen almost 20 percent while the work time had actually increased. But in the mid-1990s, books like *The End of Work*, *The Labor of Dionysius*, and *The Jobless Future*, and phrases like "downsizing" and "worker displacement" revived themes associated with the crisis of work at a time when the power relation between workers and capital is the inverse of the 1970s.[1] Whereas in the 1970s workers were refusing work, in the 1990s capitalists presumably are refusing workers! These books and phrases are misleading in claiming that "scientifically based technological change in the midst of sharpened internationalization of production means that there are too many workers for too few jobs, and even fewer of them are well paid,"[2] or that "technological innovations and market-directed forces . . . are moving us to the edge of a near workerless world,"[3] or, even more abstractly, that the "law of labor-value, which tried to make sense of our history in the name of the centrality of proletarian labor and its quantitative reduction in step with capitalist development, is completely bankrupt."[4]

Jobs and the Manifold of Work

A "jobless future" and a "workerless world" are the key phrases of this literature, but before we can examine the cogency of these phrases for the present and near future, it is worthwhile to reflect for a minute on the notions of job and work that they imply. "Job" is the easier of the two. It has a rather unsavory etymological past. In seventeenth and eighteenth-century England (and even today), "job" as a verb suggested deceiving or cheating while as a noun it evoked the scent of the world of petty crime and confidence games. In this context, a "jobless future" would be a boon to humanity. But by the mid-twentieth century, "job" had become the primary word used in American English to refer to a unit of formal waged employment with some fixed, contractually agreed upon length of tenure. To have a job on the docks

---

[3] Jeremy Rifkin, *The End of Work: The Decline of the Global Labor Force and the Dawn of the Post-Market Era* (New York: G.P. Putnam's Sons, 1995); Michael Hardt and Antonio Negri, *The Labor of Dionysus* (Minneapolis: University of Minnesota Press, 1994); and Stanley Aronowitz and William De Fazio, *The Jobless Future* (Minneapolis: University of Minnesota Press, 1994). Also phrases like "downsizing" in New York Times, *The Downsizing of America* (New York: Times Books/Random House, 1996).

[4] Aronowitz and De Fazio, *Jobless Future*, xii.

[5] Rifkin, *End of Work*, xvi

[6] Hardt and Negri, *Labor of Dionysus*, 10.

differs significantly from working on the docks, for one can be working somewhere without having a job there. The job, therefore, rose from the nether world of political economy to become its holy grail.

The mystic power of the word "job" does not come from its association with work, however. Indeed, "to do a job" or "to job" were phrases describing a "crooked" way to refuse to work and gain an income. "Jobs, Jobs, Jobs," became the shibboleth of late twentieth-century U.S. politicians because the "job" emphasized the wage and other contractual aspects of work in capitalism crucial to the physical and mental survival of the electorate. Hence, a "jobless future" would be hell for a capitalist humanity, since it implies a future without wages and contracts between workers and capitalists. Although its salience is unmistakable, the job marks off, often quite conventionally and even with dissemblance, a part of the work process, but there is no one-to-one correlation between jobs and work. The same work process can be broken down into one, two, or many jobs. Consequently, "work" and its apparent semantic cognate "labor" seem to have a greater claim to reality. Therefore, the "end of work" denotes a more radical transformation than a "jobless future," because there were many periods in human history when societies were "jobless"—e.g., slave societies and subsistence-producing peasant communities—but there were none, Eden excepted, that were workless.

Before one can speak of the end of work, however, one should recognize that there has been a conceptual revolution in the last political generation concerning the meaning of work. For a long period of time, perhaps coincident with the formulation of the collective bargaining regimes in the 1930s and their collapse in the 1970s, "work" was synonymous with "the job," i.e., formal waged work. But since then, a vast manifold of work was discovered.[5] This manifold includes informal, "off the books" work, which has a wage but could not be officially deemed contractual because it violates the legal or tax codes. This dimension of the manifold tapers into the great region of purely criminal activity that in many nations and neighborhoods rivals in quantity and value the total formal job-related activity. Even more important has been the feminist "discovery" of housework in all its modalities that are crucial for social reproduction (e.g., sexuality, biological reproduction, child care, enculturation, therapeutic energy, subsistence farming, hunting and gathering, and anti-entropic production). Housework is the great Other in capitalist societies, for it stubbornly remains unwaged and even largely unrecognized in national statistics, even though it is increasingly recognized as crucial for capitalist development. Finally, there is ur-level of capitalist hell that collects all the coerced labor of this so-called "post-slavery" era: prison labor, military labor, "sex slavery," indentured servitude, child labor. By synthesizing all these forms of work, we are forced to recognize an intersecting and self-reflective manifold of energetic investments that dwarf the "formal world of work" in spatio-temporal and value terms. This vast emerging

---

[7] See "The Work/Energy Crisis and the Apocalypse," 11 and "On the Notion of a Crisis of Social Reproduction: A Theoretic Review, 252 in this volume.

Presence as well as the inverse manifold of its refusal has transformed the understanding of work profoundly, even though many seem not to have noticed. It certainly puts the jejune distinctions between work and labor (Arendt), between biopower and capitalism (Foucault), and between labor and communicative action (Habermas) into question while forcing a remarkable expansion of class analysis and an enrichment of revolutionary theory beyond the problematics of planning for the factory system of the future. Most importantly for our discussion, this Manifold of Work problematizes the discussion of work and its supposed end at the hands of technological change.

The End of Work

Unfortunately, the notion of work that used in the "end of work" literature is often antediluvian and forgetful of work's capitalistic meaning. This is most clearly seen in Rifkin's central argument in *The End of Work*. He is anxious to refute those who argue that the new technological revolution involving the application of genetic engineering to agriculture, of robotization to manufacturing, and of computerization of service industries will lead to new employment opportunities if there is a well-trained workforce available to respond to the challenges of the "information age." His refutation is simple.

> In the past, when a technological revolution threatened the wholesale loss of jobs in an economic sector, a new sector emerged to absorb the surplus labor. Earlier in the century, the fledgling manufacturing sector was able to absorb many of the millions of farmhands and farm owners who were displaced by the rapid mechanization of agriculture. Between the mid-1950s and the early 1980s, the fast-growing service sector was able to re-employ many of the blue collar workers displaced by automation. Today, however, as all these sectors fall victim to rapid restructuring and automation, no "significant" new sector has developed to absorb the millions who are being displaced.[6]

Consequently, there will be a huge unemployment problem when the last service worker is replaced by the latest ATM, virtual office machine, or heretofore unconceived application of computer technology. Where will he/she find a job? There is no going back to agriculture or manufacturing and no going forward to a new sector beyond services. Rifkin applies this scenario to a global context and foresees not millions of unemployed people on the planet in the near future, but billions.

The formal logic of the argument appears impeccable, but are its empirical premises and theoretical presuppositions correct? I argue that they are not, for Rifkin's technological determinism does not take into account the dynamics of employment and technological change in the capitalist era. Let us begin with a categorical problem in Rifkin's stage theory of employment. He uncritically uses terms like

---

[8] Rifkin, *End of Work*, 35.

"agriculture," "manufacturing," and, especially, "services" to differentiate the three developmental stages of a capitalist economy as indicated in the passage quote above and in many other parts of *The End of Work*. One cannot fault Rifkin for making an idiosyncratic choice here, since major statistical agencies like the U.S. Bureau of Labor Statistics also employ these categories to disaggregate employment, production, and productivity in the last few decades. The core metaphors that helped shape this trichotomy are rooted in a distinction between material goods (produced on the farm or off) and immaterial services, and in the spatial distinction between farm, factory, and everywhere else (office, school, store, warehouse, road, etc.) This trichotomy allows for a rough and ready economic typology, with "the service industry" generally functioning as something of a fuzzy default category.

But it is one thing to use a category *ex post facto* and another is to use a category in a projective way (either into the past or the future). Rifkin's somewhat Hegelian scheme sees technological change as the autonomous moving spirit that transforms one stage to another until it comes to a catastrophic halt in the present "service" stage of history. Yet when we look at capitalistic societies in the past, this neat series is hardly accurate. For example, was seventeenth and eighteenth-century England agricultural? The "service industry" in the form of household servants in the larger agricultural estates at that time was quite substantial, but these servants often worked as artisans (manufacturing) and as farm hands (agriculture). Moreover, with the rise of cottage industry, agricultural workers or small farmers also doubled or tripled as manufacturing workers on the farm. Finally, throughout the history of capitalism, we find a complex shifting of workers among these three categories. Instead of a simple move from agricultural to manufacturing, and manufacturing to service, we find all six possible transitions among these three categories.

The vast literature on the "development of underdevelopment" and on the many periods of capitalist "deindustrialization" abundantly illustrates these transitions which were clearly caused not by some autonomous technological spirit, but by historically concrete and ever varied class struggles and power relations. A machine introduced by capitalists to undermine industrial workers' power can lead to these workers losing their employment and becoming "service workers" or becoming "agricultural workers" according to a complex conjuncture of forces and possibilities. There is no evidence from the total history of capitalism that there is only a linear progression that ends with the last service worker.

Rifkin's schema is further undermined, if we examine its future projection. After a look at the wide variety of applications of computer technology in the service industry (from voice recognition, to expert systems, to digital synthesizers), Rifkin ominously concludes: "In the future, advanced parallel computing machines, high-tech robotics, and integrated electronic networks spanning the globe are going to subsume more and more of the economic process, leaving less and less room for direct hands-on human participation in making, moving, selling, and servicing."[7] But here the very defaulting function of the category of service makes

---

[9] Ibid., 162.

its future projection problematic for Rifkin, since it will not stay in a single place in logical space in order to be reduced to degree zero by technological change. Let us consider one of the standard definitions of what constitutes service work: the modification of either a human being (giving a haircut or a massage) or an object (repairing an automobile or a computer). How can we possibly project such a category into the future? Since there are no limitations on the type of modification in question, there is no way one can say that "advanced parallel computing machines, high-tech robotics, and integrated electronic networks spanning the globe" will be able to simulate and replace its possible realizations. Indeed, the service work of the future might very well be perversely defined (at least with respect to the constructors of these machines) as modifications to humans and objects that are not simulatable and replaceable by machines![8] Just as today there is a growth in the sale of "organic," non–genetically engineered agricultural produce, and "handmade" garments made from nonsynthetic fibers, so too in the future there might be an interest in having a human play Bach (even if the synthesized version is technically more correct) or dance (even though a digitalized hologram might give a better performance according to the critics). I would be surprised if such service industries do not arise. Could they "absorb" many workers displaced from agricultural or manufacturing work? That I do not know, but then again, neither does Rifkin.

Rifkin's inability to project his categorical schema either into the past or into the future reveals an even deeper problem: his inability to adequately explain why technological change takes place in the first place. At the beginning of *The End of Work*, Rifkin rejects what he calls "the trickle-down-technology argument"—i.e., the view that technological change in one branch of industry, though causing unemployment there, eventually leads to increased employment throughout the rest of the economy—by appealing to Marx's *Capital* and *Grundrisse*. Rifkin's view of Marx can be surveyed in this extended passage:

> Karl Marx argued that producers continually attempt to reduce labor costs and gain greater control over the means of production by substituting capital equipment for workers wherever and whenever possible. . . . Marx predicted that the increasing automation of production would eventually eliminate the worker altogether. The German philosopher looked ahead to what he euphemistically referred to as the "last . . . metamorphosis of labor," when "an automatic system of machinery" finally replaced human beings in the economic process. . . . Marx believed that the ongoing effort by producers to continue to replace human labor with machines would prove self-defeating in the end . . . [as] there would be fewer and fewer consumers with sufficient purchasing power to buy their products.[9]

---

[10] This "perverse" definition is reminiscent of Cantor's diagonal method that has proven so fruitful in mathematical research in this century. The trick of this method is to assume that there is a list that exhausts all items of a particular class K and then to define a member of K that is not on the list by using special properties of the list itself.

[11] Rifkin, *End of Work*, 16–17.

This use of Marx is part of a new and widely noted trend among social policy analysts on the U.S. Left, broadly considered. But this revival of Marx's thought is often as selective as is the use of Smith and Ricardo on the Right.[10] In Rifkin's case, he definitely gets the broad sweep of Marx's views on technology right, but with some notable omissions. The first omission is of workers' struggles for higher wages, for reduced work, for better conditions of work, and for a form of life that absolutely refuses forced labor. These struggles are the prime reasons why capitalists are so interested in introducing machinery as weapons in the class war. If workers were docile "factors of production," the urgency for technological change would be much reduced. The second omission is Marx's Ricardian recognition that every worker permanently replaced by a machine reduces the total surplus value (and hence the total profit) available to the capitalist class as a whole. Since the capitalist class depends upon profits, technological change can be as dangerous to it as to the workers. Hence, the capitalist class faces a permanent contradiction it must finesse: (a) the desire to eliminate recalcitrant, demanding workers from production, (b) the desire to exploit the largest mass of workers possible. Marx comments on this eternal tension in *Theories of Surplus Value*:

> The one tendency throws the labourers on to the streets and makes a part of the population redundant, and then absorbs them again and extends wage-slavery absolutely, so that the lot of the worker is always fluctuating but he never escapes from it. The worker, therefore, justifiably regards the development of the productive power of his own labour as hostile to himself; the capitalist, on the other hand, always treats him as an element to be eliminated from production.[11]

Capital's problem with technological change is not the loss of consumers, but the loss of profits.

Marx's most developed discussion of this story is to be found in Part III of the third volume of *Capital*: "The Law of the Falling Tendency of the Rate of Profit." There, he recognizes that a tendency toward the total replacement of humans by an "automatic system of machinery" must continually be met by "counteracting causes" or else the average rate of profit will actually fall. These counteracting causes either increase the mass of surplus value (e.g., raising the intensity and duration of the working day), or decrease the mass of variable capital (e.g., depress wages below their value, expand foreign trade), or decrease the mass of constant capital (e.g., increasing the productivity of labor in the capital goods industry, expand foreign trade) or some

---

[12] For example, in much of the current discussion of free trade, a low wage level is considered by many to be a Ricardian "comparative advantage." But such a reading is a distortion of Ricardo's views and an invitation to justify repressing workers' struggles. The sources of comparative advantage for Ricardo are quasi-permanent features of the physical and cultural environment of a country, not economic variables like wages, profits, or rents.

[13] Karl Marx, *Theories of Surplus Value, Part II* (Moscow: Progress Publishers, 1968), 573.

combination or these disjunctive possibilities.[12] Contemporary U.S. capitalism appears to be applying the maximal synthesis of these counteracting causes while the European capitals are being more selective. There is no inevitable capitalist strategy in the drive to overcome workers' struggles and prevent a dramatic decline in the rate of profit. These struggles can lead to many futures—from the reintroduction of slavery, to a dramatic increase in the workday, to the negotiated reduction of the waged workday, to the end of capitalism—depending on the class forces in the field.

But there is one outcome that definitely cannot be included in the menu of possible futures as long as capitalism is viable: Rifkin's vision of "the high-tech revolution lead[ing] to the realization of the age-old utopian dream of substituting machines for human labor, finally freeing humanity to journey into a post-market era."[13] Capitalism requires the stuff of profit, interest, and rent which can only be created by a huge mass of surplus labor, but the total replacement of human work by machines would mean the end of profit, interest and rent. Although Rifkin seems to agree with much of Marx's analysis of the dynamics of capitalism, Marx's fatal conclusion is carefully kept out of the sanguine scenario presented at the last part of his book. Rifkin lays out a future that would combine a drastic reduction in the workday along with a "new social contract" that would provide financial incentives (from "social" or "shadow" wages to tax benefits) for working in "the third sector"—the independent, "nonprofit" or volunteer sector between "the public and private" sectors. This sector can become the "service industry" of the twenty-first century, since it "offers the only viable means for constructively channeling the surplus labor cast off by the global market."[14] That is, it absorbs workers who do not produce surplus value, and provides them with a wage for non-surplus-value-creating work.

In other words, Rifkin's vision of the "safe haven" for humanity is a form of capitalism where most workers are not producing profits, interest or rent. He contrasts this vision with a future where "civilization . . . continue[s] to disintegrate into a state of increasing destitution and lawlessness from which there may be no easy return."[15] But how viable is Rifkin's social Chimera with its techno-capitalist head, its ample, woolly third-sector body, and its tiny surplus-value-producing tail? There are proportions that must be respected even when dealing with futuristic Chimeras, and Rifkin's cannot exist simply because the head, however technologically sophisticated, cannot be nourished by such a tiny tail. The capitalism resulting from Rifkin's "new social contract" is impossible, for it is by definition a capitalism without profits, interest, and rents. Why would capitalists agree to such a deal after they trumpeted throughout the Cold War that they would rather blow up half the planet than give up a tenth of their income?

This "impossibility proof" is so obvious that one cannot help but asking why Rifkin invoked Marx so directly at the beginning of *The End of Work* only to completely exorcise him at the end? Is he avoiding reference to the unpleasantness of

---

[14] Marx, *Capital: Volume III*, 339–48.

[15] Rifkin, *End of Work*, 56.

[16] Ibid., 292.

[17] Ibid., 291.

world war, revolution and nuclear annihilation that his earlier reflections stirred up? Is he trying to coax, with veiled Marxian threats, the techno-capitalist class into an act of suicide camouflaged as a new lease on life? Answers to such questions would require a political analysis of the type of rhetoric Rifkin and his circle employ. I forgo this effort. But it is worth pointing out that Rifkin's chimerical strategy is not totally mistaken. After all, he is looking for a new sector for the expansion of capitalist relations. He mistakenly chose the "nonprofit," volunteer sector, for if this sector is truly "nonprofit" and voluntary, it cannot be a serious basis for a new sector of employment in capitalism. (And there is no way to get out of capitalism via a massive fraud, however tempting that might be).

But Rifkin's intuition is correct, for the Manifold of Work extends far beyond the dimension of formal waged work and this nonwaged work does produce surplus value in abundance. If it is more directly and efficiently exploited, this work can become the source of a new area of surplus value creating employment through the expansion of forced labor, the extension of direct capitalist relations into the region of labor reproduction and finally the potentiation of micro- and criminal enterprises. That is why "neoliberalism," "neoslavery," "Grameenism," and the "drug war" are the more appropriate shibboleths of the Third Industrial Revolution rather than the "nonprofit" third sector touted by Rifkin, for they can activate the "counteracting causes" to the precipitous decline in the rate of profit computerization, robotization, and genetic engineering provoke.

Negri and the End of the Law of Value

Rifkin can, perhaps, be indulged in his half-baked use of Marx's thought. After all, he did not come out of the Marxist tradition and his previous references to Marx's work were few and largely in passing. But the themes Rifkin so clearly presented in *The End of Work* can be found in a number of Marxist, post-Marxist, and postmodern Marxist writers, often in much more obscure and sibylline versions. One of the primary figures in this area is Antonio Negri, who developed arguments supporting conclusions very similar to Rifkin's in the 1970s but without the latter's Marxist naiveté. Published in 1994, *The Labors of Dionysius* (with Michael Hardt), continued a discourse definitively begun in *Marx Beyond Marx*[16] and continued in *Communists Like Us*.[17] In this section, I will show how Negri's more sophisticated and Marxist analysis of contemporary capitalism is as problematic as Rifkin's. It is hard to discern Negri's similarity to Rifkin, simply because Negri's work is rigorously anti-empirical—rarely does a fact or factoid float through his prose—while Rifkin's

---

[18] Antonio Negri, *Marx Beyond Marx* (Brooklyn: Autonomedia, 1991).

[19] Felix Guattari and Antonio Negri, *Communists Like Us* (New York: Semiotext(e), 1990), originally published in 1985; republished as *New Lines of Alliance, New Spaces of Liberty* (Brooklyn: Minor Compositions/Autonomedia, 2010). This is not the place to discuss Negri's political and juridical life since the 1970s. For more of this see Yann Moulier's Introduction to *The Politics of Subversion* (Negri, 1989). Negri voluntarily returned to Italy from exile in France in July 1997 and was in prison in Rome until his release in 2003.

The End of Work is replete with statistics and journalistic set pieces on high-tech. Negri does not deign to write plainly of an era of "the end of work." He expresses an equivalent proposition, however, in his theoretical rejection of the classical Labor Theory or Law of Value with hypostasized verbs. In the late twentieth century, according to Negri, the Law is "completely bankrupt," or it "no longer operates," or "the Law of Value dies."[18]

This is equivalent to Rifkin's more empirical claims, but the equivalence can only be established after a vertiginous theoretical reduction. Negri's version of the classic labor theory of value has as its "principal task . . . the investigation of the social and economic laws that govern the deployment of labor-power among the different sectors of social production and thus to bring to light the capitalist processes of valorization,"[19] or it is "an expression of the relation between concrete labor and amounts of money needed to secure an existence"[20] or it is a measure of "the determinate proportionality between necessary labor and surplus labor."[21] The Law of Value was alive in the nineteenth century, but just like Nietzsche's God, it began to die then. It took a bit longer for the Law to be formally issued a death certificate, however. The bankruptcy, inoperativeness, and death of the Law of Value simply mean that the fundamental variables of capitalist life—profits, interest, rents, wages, and prices—are no longer determined by labor-time. Negri argues, as does Rifkin, that capitalism has entered into a period that Marx, in his most visionary mode, described the "Fragment on Machines" in the *Grundrisse*.[22] Let me choose just one of the many oft-quoted passages in this vision:

> The development of heavy industry means that the basis upon which it rests—the appropriation of the labour time of others—ceases to constitute or to create wealth; and at the same time direct labour as such ceases to be the basis of production, since it is transformed more and more into a supervisory and regulating activity; and also because the product ceases to be made by individual direct labour, and results more for the combination of social activity . . . on the one hand, once the productive forces of the means of labour have reached the level of an automatic process, the prerequisite is the subordination of the natural forces to the intelligence of society, while on the other hand individual labour in its direct form is transformed into social labour. In this way the other basis of this mode of production vanishes.[23]

The development of "automatic processes" in genetic engineering, computer programming and robotization since the 1960s have convinced both Negri

---

[20] Hardt and Negri, *Labor of Dionysius*, 10; Guattari and Negri, *Communists Like Us*, 21; Negri, *Marx Beyond Marx*, 172.

[21] Hardt and Negri, *Labor of Dionysus*, 8.

[22] Guattari and Negri, *Communists Like Us*, 21.

[23] Negri, *Marx Beyond Marx*, 172.

[24] Ibid., 140–41; Rifkin, *End of Work*, 16–17.

[25] Marx, *Grundrisse*, 382.

and Rifkin that the dominant features of contemporary capitalism are matched point-for-point by Marx's vision in 1857–1858. The major difference between Negri's work and Rifkin's *The End of Work* is that while Rifkin emphasizes the consequences of these "automatic processes" for the unemployment of masses of workers Negri emphasizes the new workers that are centrally involved in "the intelligence of society" and "social labor." Whereas Rifkin argues that these new "knowledge workers" (e.g., research scientists, design engineers, software analysts, financial and tax consultants, architects, marketing specialists, film producers and editors, lawyers, investment bankers) can never be a numerically large sector and hence are no solution to the problems created by this phase of capitalist development, Negri takes them as the key to the transformation to communism beyond "real socialism."

It is important to note a terminological difference between Negri and Rifkin, because Negri has over the years termed Rifkin's "knowledge workers" first in the 1970s to be "social workers," and later in the 1990s he baptized them as "cyborgs" à la Donna Haraway.[24] Although singularly infelicitous in its English translation, the term "social worker" directly comes out of the pages of the *Grundrisse*. When looking for a descriptive phrase that would contrast the new workers in the "information and knowledge sector" to the "mass workers" of assembly line era, many of Marx's sentences deeply influenced Negri. For instance, "In this transformation, it is neither the direct human labour he himself performs, nor the time during which he works, but rather the appropriation of his own general productive power, his understanding of nature and his mastery over it by virtue of his presence as a social body—it is, in a word, the development of the social individual which appears as the great foundation-stone of production and of wealth."[25] The social worker is the subject of "techno-scientific labor" and s/he steps out of the pages of the *Grundrisse* as a late twentieth-century cyborg, i.e., "a hybrid of machine and organism that continually crosses the boundaries between material and immaterial labor."[26] The old mass worker's labor-time on the assembly line was roughly correlated to (exchange-value and use-value) productivity and s/he was alienated from the factory system, the social cyborg's labor-time is independent of its productivity but it is thoroughly integrated into the terrain of production.

Rifkin sees the "knowledge class" of "symbolic analysts" as fundamentally identified with capital and explains the new interest in intellectual property rights

---

[26] Donna Haraway, *Simians, Cyborgs, and Women: The Reinvention of Nature* (New York: Routledge, 1991), 149–81.

[27] Marx, *Grundrisse*, 705.

[28] Hardt and Negri, *Labor of Dionysius*, 280, 1. Negri often describes the work of the social worker cyborg as "immaterial." But an analysis of Turing machine theory shows that there is no fundamental difference between what is standardly called material labor (e.g., weaving or digging) and immaterial labor (e.g., constructing a software program). Consequently, one must look to other aspects of the labor situation to locate its value creating properties. See "Why Machines Cannot Create Value: Marx's Theory of Machines," 139 in this volume.

as a sign that the elite capitalists have recognized the importance of the knowledge class and are willing to share their wealth with it. Knowledge workers are "fast becoming the new aristocracy."[27] Negri has a rather different reading of this class's present and future. The existence of social cyborgs not only is evidence that the dialectic of capitalist development has been "broken," according to Negri, but capital simply cannot "buy it out," because "the social worker has begun to produce a subjectivity that one can no longer grasp in the terms of capitalist development understood as an accomplished dialectical movement."[28] In order words, techno-scientific labor cannot be controlled by capital via its system of wages and work discipline rounded out with the promise of entrance into the top levels of managerial, financial, and political power for the "best." Not only is the social working cyborg beyond the bounds of capital's time honored techniques of control, it is also in the vanguard of the communist revolution. Why? Let us first hear and then interpret Negri's words:

> Cooperation, or the association of [cyborg] producers, is posed independently of the organization capacity of capital; the cooperation and subjectivity of labor have found a point of contact outside of the machinations of capital. Capital becomes merely an apparatus of capture, a phantasm, an idol. Around it move radically autonomous processes of self-valorization that not only constitute an alternative basis of potential development but also actually represent a new constituent foundation.[29]

Negri claims that the cyborg workers have escaped capital's gravitational field into a region where their work and life is actually producing the fundamental social and productive relations appropriate to a communism. These relations are characterized by "self-valorization"—i.e., instead of determining the value of labor-power and work on the basis of its exchange-value for the capitalist, the workers value their labor-power for its capacity to determine their autonomous development—arises from the period when techno-scientific labor becomes paradigmatic.[30] In effect, Negri's notion of "self-valorization" is similar to the "class for itself" or "class consciousness" of more traditional Marxism; but self-valorization distinguishes the cyborg from the politics of the mass worker and marks the arrival of the true communist revolution ironically percolating in the World Wide Net rather than in the (old and new) haunts of the mass workers, peasants and ghetto dwellers of the planet.

The clash between Negri's picture of the anticapitalist cyborg and Rifkin's image of the procapitalist knowledge worker can make for an inviting theme. But just

---

[27] Rifkin, *End of Work*, 175.

[28] Hardt and Negri, *Labor of Dionysius*, 282.

[29] Ibid.

[30] Negri, *Marx Beyond Marx*, 162–63; George Caffentzis, "A Review Article on Antonio Negri's *Marx Beyond Marx: Lessons on the Grundrisse*," *New German Critique* 41 (Spring–Summer 1987), 186–92.

as Rifkin's knowledge worker (as the last profit-making employee) is built upon a faulty conception of capitalist development, so too is Negri's cyborg. Consequently, it is more useful to consider and critique the common basis of both these views. Negri bases his version of "the social worker" on Marx's *Grundrisse* just as Rifkin does for his knowledge worker, but we should remember that the "Fragment on Machines" was not Marx's last word on machines in capitalism. Marx continued work for another decade and filled Volumes I, II, and III of *Capital* with new observations. This is not the place to review these developments in depth. It should be pointed out that in Volume I, Marx recognized not only the great powers machinery threw into the production process; he also emphasized machines' lack of value creativity analogous to the thermodynamical limits on availability of work in a given energy field, but even more crucial for our project is the part of *Capital* III where Marx revisited the terrain of the "Fragment on Machines."[31] In these passages, he recognized that in any era where capitalism approaches the stage of "automatic processes," the system as a whole must face a dramatic acceleration of the tendency for rate of profit to fall. He asked, "How is it that this fall is not greater and more rapid?" His answer was that there are built-in processes in capitalist activity that resist this tendency and therefore the system's technological finale. These are to be found directly in the Chapter XIV on "counteracting causes" and indirectly in Part II on the formation of the average rate of profit. I mentioned the critical consequences of "counteracting causes" in my discussion of Rifkin, and they apply to Negri as well. Negri imperiously denies "the social and economic laws that govern the deployment of labor-power among the different sectors of social production" and rejects the view that labor-time is crucial to "the capitalist processes of valorization." But capital and capitalists are still devoutly interested in both. That is why there is such a drive to send capital to low-waged areas and why there is so much resistance to the reduction of the waged workday. For the computerization and robotization of factories and offices in Western Europe, North America, and Japan has been accompanied by a process of "globalization" and "new enclosures."

Capitalists have been fighting as fiercely to have the right to put assembly zones and brothels in the least mechanized parts of the world as to have the right to patent life forms. Instead of a decline, there has been a great expansion of factory production throughout many regions of the planet. Indeed, much of the profit of global corporations and much of the interest received by international banks has been created out of this low-tech, factory, and sexual work.[32] In order to get workers for these factories and brothels, a vast new enclosure has been taking place throughout Africa, Asia, and the Americas. The very capital that owns "the ethereal information machines which supplant industrial production" is also involved in the enclosure of lands throughout the planet, provoking famine, disease, low-intensity war, and collective misery in the process.[33]

---

[31] Caffentzis, "Why Machines Cannot Create Value: Marx's Theory of Machines," 139 in this volume.

[32] Silvia Federici, "War, Globalization, and Reproduction," *Peace and Change* 25, no. 2 (April 2000): 153–65.

[33] See "On Africa and Self-Reproducing Automata," 127 in this volume; George

Why is capital worried about communal land tenure in Africa, for example, if the true source of productivity is to be found in the cyborgs of the planet? One answer is simply that these factories, lands, and brothels in the Third World are locales of "the counteracting causes" to the tendency of the falling rate of profit. They increase the total pool of surplus labor, help depress wages, cheapen the elements of constant capital, and tremendously expand the labor market and make possible the development of high-tech industries that directly employ only a few knowledge workers or cyborgs. But another complementary answer can be gleaned from Part II of *Capital*, volume III, "Conversion of Profit into Average Profit," which shows the existence of a sort of capitalist self-valuation. In order for there to be an average rate of profit throughout the capitalist system, branches of industry that employ very little labor but a lot of machinery must be able to have the right to call on the pool of value that high-labor, low-tech branches create. If there were no such branches or no such right, then the average rate of profit would be so low in the high-tech, low-labor industries that all investment would stop and the system would terminate. Consequently, "new enclosures" in the countryside must accompany the rise of "automatic processes" in industry, the computer requires the sweatshop, and the cyborg's existence is premised on the slave.

Negri is correct in connecting the rise of the new workers in the high-tech fields with self-valuation, but it has more to do with capitalist self-valuation—i.e., the right of "dead labor" to demand a proportionate share of "living labor"—rather than workers' self-valuation. Indeed, capital's self-valuation is premised on the planetary proletariat's degradation. One can easily dismiss Negri's analysis as being profoundly Eurocentric in its neglect of the value-creating labor of billions of people on the planet. Indeed, he is Eurocentric in a rather archaic way. He would do well, at least, to look to the new global capitalist multiculturalism and the ideologies it has spawned, instead of to the rather small circle of postmodern thinkers that constitute his immediate horizon, in order to begin to appreciate the class struggles of today, even from a capitalist perspective.[34] But the charge of Eurocentrism is a bit too general. His adherence to one of the axioms of the Marxist-Leninism—the revolutionary subject in any era is synthesized from the most "productive" elements of the class—better accounts for Negri's methodological oblivion of the planetary proletariat. It is true that Negri has nothing but scorn for the metaphysics of dialectical materialism and for the history of "real socialism," but on the choice of the revolutionary subject he is Leninist to the core. Negri makes so much of computer programmers and their ilk because of their purported productivity. Since the General Intelligence is productive, then these intellectual workers are its ideal (and hence revolutionary) representatives, even though they have not yet launched a concrete

Caffentzis, "On the Fundamental Implications of the Debt Crisis for Social Reproduction in Africa," in *Paying the Price: Women and The Politics of International Economic Strategy*, eds. Mariarosa Dalla Costa and Giovanna F. Dalla Costa (London: Zed Books, 1995).

[34] Silvia Federici, "The God That Never Failed: The Origins and Crises of Western Civilization," in *Enduring Western Civilization: The Construction of the Concept of Western Civilization and Its "Others,"* ed. Silvia Federici (Westport, CT: Praeger, 1995).

struggle against capitalist accumulation *qua* "social workers" or "cyborgs." But this methodological identity between revolution and production has proven false time and again in history. Leninists and Leninist parties in the past have often paid for this mistake with their lives. Mao's political development clearly shows that it took the massacre of Communist workers in the cities and many near mortal experiences in the countryside before he recognized that the Taoist principle—the seemingly weakest and least productive can be the most powerful in a struggle—was more accurate than the Leninist. Negri's choice of revolutionary subject in this period—the masters of the ethereal machines—is as questionable as the industrial worker bias of Leninists in the past. Indeed, the failure of *The Labor of Dionysius*, which was published in the United States in June of 1994, to address the revolutionary struggles of the indigenous peoples of the planet, especially the Zapatistas in Mexico, is a definite sign that Negri's revolutionary geography needs expansion.

Conclusion

Negri and Rifkin are major participants in the "end of work" discourse of the 1990s, although they occupy two ends of the rhetorical spectrum. Rifkin is empirical and pessimistic in his assessment of the "end of work" while Negri is aprioristic and optimistic. However, both seem to invoke technological determinism by claiming that there is only one way for capitalism to develop. They, and most others who operate this discourse, forget that capitalism is constrained (and protected) by proportionalities and contradictory tendencies. The system is not going to go out of business through the simple-minded addition of more high-tech machines, techniques, and workers come what may, for Marx's ironic dictum, "The *true barrier* of capitalist production is *capital itself*," is truer than ever. It might be an old and miserable truth, but still to this day profit, interest, wages, and labor in certain proportions are particular but necessary conditions for the existence of capitalism.[35] Capital cannot will itself into oblivion, but neither can it be tricked or cursed out of existence. Rifkin tries to trick the system into believing that a viable way out of the unemployment crises he foresees is to abandon profit-creating sectors of the economy. He reassuringly says that all will be well if the capitalists are in control of automated agriculture, manufacturing, and service industries and nearly everyone else is working in a nonprofit third sector that makes no claim on hegemony. But this scenario can hardly to pass the eagle eyes of the capitalist press much less those of the boardroom without ridicule. So it cannot succeed. Negri tries philosophical cursing instead. He calls late twentieth-century capitalism "merely an apparatus of capture, a phantasm, an idol" ontologically.[36] I appreciate Negri's desire to put a curse on this system of decimation, humiliation and misery, but I question his "merely." As the highest organs of capitalist intelligence (like the Ford Foundation) have shown, capital is as impervious to these ontological curses as the conquistadors were to the theological curses of the Aztec priests. Indeed, capital revels in its phantom-like

---

[35] Marx, *Capital: Volume III*, 358.

[36] Hardt and Negri, *Labor of Dionysius*, 282.

character. Its main concern is with the duration of the phantasm, not its ontological status. The "end of work" literature of the 1990s, therefore, is not only theoretically and empirically disconfirmed. It also creates a failed politics because it ultimately tries to convince both friend and foe that, behind everyone's back, capitalism has ended. It's motto is not the Third International's "Don't worry, capital will collapse by itself sooner or later"; rather it is, "Capitalism has always already ended at the high-tech end of the system, just wake up to it." But such an anticapitalist version of Nietzsche's motto "God is dead" is hardly inspiring when millions are still being slaughtered in the many names of both God and Capital.

THREE TEMPORAL DIMENSIONS OF CLASS STRUGGLE

Time past and time future
What might have been and what has been
Point to one end, which is always present.
—T.S. Eliot, "Burnt Norton"

So beat it, Bo, while your feet are mates;
Take a look at the whole United States;
There's a little fire and the pipe at night;
And up again when the morning's bright;
With nothin' but road and sky in sight,
And nothin' to do but go.
—H.H. Knibbs, "Nothing to Do but Go"

Introduction

Time is of the essence in capitalism. After all, "Time is money," as Poor Richard said, and money is what capitalism is about. If Poor Richard is right, then by contrapositive reasoning, Anti-capitalism is Anti-time.

But what could that possibly mean? If to negate capitalism, one must negate time, then rational people should forget about the effort or even the effort of the thought of the effort. Doesn't this piece of logic immediately demonstrate the irrationality of struggles against capitalism (even though struggles *within* it might be perfectly rational)?

Not necessarily, since the monopolistic conception of time in, say, Kant's philosophy has been rejected long ago. We now know that time is not a given. Like its constituents, who/which have their stories, concepts of time themselves have a complex and contradictory "history" and "genealogy." In fact, there are many different times in capitalism. In the course of a day, a unit of capital itself proceeds along many different temporal dimensions simultaneously. In what follows, I will examine three ways in which the time essential to capitalism can be *and has* been stolen, broken, and transcended in the course of class struggle that is in essence a struggle over time in its many dimensions.

After a discussion of the first two more well-known temporal dimensions of class struggle, I will concentrate on the third which requires using primitive accumulation—i.e., the creation of the working class instead of the commodity—and primitive *dis*accumulation—i.e., the creation of noncapitalist forms of social coordination within capitalism—as the starting points of an analysis of class struggle. One of the most attractive aspects of this approach is that it reveals a number of struggles often seen as "cultural" or "superstructural" (e.g., indigenous people's struggles, struggles over intellectual property, and environmental struggles) to be class struggles.

Three Forms of Time and Time-Breaking in Capitalism

The times in capitalism that I will discuss here are the linear, the circular, and the tensed forms.

Linear Time

This is the time constituted by temporal lengths and ratios among these lengths. It is the most well known dimension of time in capitalism and appears as work-time in the factory, farm, and office (that also absorbs the work of labor reproduction in the home). This kind of time is initially measured by village church clocks, Taylorist time-watches and satellite-monitored computer stroke counters. The length of the workday, the workweek, and the work year is a crucial quantity for the health of capitalism. So too are the ratios between segments of the work unit. There is a direct struggle over labor time in production (a linear structure)—e.g., over the length of the working day, the real and nominal wage rate, and the rate of profit.

In the first volume of *Capital*, Marx claimed that value and surplus value should be measured in temporal units. To do this, he conceptualized the workday and its division into necessary and surplus labor time. These quantities, however, were not ultimately measurable by the time-watch because they depended upon the operation of the whole capitalist productive system over a cycle, since the value of a commodity was measurable by the "socially necessary labor time" involved in the production of a commodity. That is not a "crystallized substance," but is a "field quantity." The socially necessary labor time required for the production of a commodity involves the labor required for the production of inputs (labor-power and means of production). It is only when the average labor time required for typical commodity in all the branches of industry are determined can the labor time be defined (just as the temperature of a gas is not determinable in a nonequilibrium state). This can only be accomplished when the formation of the average rate of profit is completed.

The working class has historically refused its total submission to capital's dictates of its value and its life and has always struggled over the length of the working day. In every capitalist enterprise, there have been struggles over "wages and hours." Sometimes they are obvious, at times these struggles are impossible to observe "unless you are there." Capital's initial impulse in its eternal effort to increase the rate of profit is to increase the working day (without increasing wages), what Marx called "absolute surplus value." When the working class successfully challenges this type of accumulation and significantly reduces the working day, capital responds with an effort to intensify the work rhythms in the shrunken workday and/or make the time more productive (through investment in machinery or new work methods), i.e., the relative surplus value response. Marx tells this story in Chapters 8 through 16 of the first volume of *Capital*.

The working class has expressed its "refusal of work" against the intensification of the workday, especially in the mass assembly line factories of the "industrial age." The many techniques of working-class opposition (from wildcat strikes to organized slow-downs on the line) have been the collective response to the relative surplus value "solution" to the reduction of the working day. This refusal of work has been the stimulus of an enormous effort of surveillance and "industrial psychology" (quality circles, total quality control, etc.) to undermine the anti-work cooperation of workers.

There is a direction in these struggles, if one examines them over a long period. They indicate a stark difference between "the realm of freedom and of necessity," and a struggle of the working class to (mostly) incrementally increase its freedom from capital (though never its autonomy). As Marx put it in the third volume of *Capital* the "true realm of freedom can flourish only upon that realm of necessity as its basis," and the realm of necessity is that of labor "under the compulsion of necessity and external utility."[1] The historic progress of working-class emancipation can be measured in "the shortening of the work day [which] is its fundamental premise."

This linear notion of time has found its most frequent application in the managerial and workers' analyses of class struggle from the Taylorist methods to make the application of labor-power more intense to the manifold of methods workers use to shorten and relax the work process. This is indeed simultaneously a titanic and a microscopic struggle that is often seen on picket lines, in strikes and lockouts, but it quickly becomes invisible and corpuscular throughout the social metabolism. For example, in the thousand and one sly ways workers use machines in factories and offices for their own amusement and enrichment in antagonism to the profit of their bosses. Much of the analysis of the labor process is an account of the multiple ways in which time is "stolen" (either by capitalists or workers).

Circular Time of Reproduction

There are circular structures of time in capitalism, e.g., turnover time and circulation time (which characterizes the kind of social "speed up" typical of capitalism and resistances to it). Marx spends much of the second volume of *Capital* discussing it. Millions of these cycles are begun and completed in the course of a day in any contemporary city.

This time is rooted in an ordinal aspect of capital. Just as wages are normally paid *after* the labor-power purchased is put to work, so too there is an order to the

---

[1] Marx, *Capital: Volume I*, 958–59.

fundamental stages in the process of capital accumulation. The most elementary form is the cycle of money-commodity-money, M-C-M. It is a necessary order. It cannot be M-M-C, for one must buy before one sells. That is, M-C, the buying stage, precedes the selling stage, C-M. There must be the possibility of there being a profit as well, so the ideal process is M-C-M where M > M. Finally, the cycle is organized in a reproductive cycle, so that the original capital M is used to become the basis of a new cycle of "simple reproduction":

$$M-C-M' \rightarrow M-C-M' \rightarrow M-C-M' \rightarrow \ldots$$

or of "expanded reproduction":

$$M-C-M' \rightarrow M'-C'-M'' \rightarrow M''-C''-M''' \rightarrow \ldots$$

$$\text{Where } M<M'<M''<M'''<\ldots.$$

This cycle actually requires a productive aspect to become truly capitalist, i.e., the commodity C must have the possibility of being produced under capitalist circumstances. C can be the product of L, labor-power applied, and the means of production, Mp (raw material, factory structures, machines and energy). This is the basis of Marx's "complete cycle":

$$
\begin{array}{c}
L \\
M-C \ldots P \ldots C-M \\
Mp
\end{array}
$$

It should be clear that these complete cycles are multifarious throughout the capitalist system, e.g., one capitalist's means of production is another's "end product" commodity. It should also be recognized that labor-power L is a commodity of a special type. It is the source of surplus value and at the same time it must be produced through a combination of largely unwaged labor (especially women's) and through a set of commodities (a relatively large set in areas where the wage is high enough to command consumption commodities and various kinds of "services," e.g., formal education).

The most important element in these cycles is, of course, the dash! This is where the cycle is vulnerable and can be broken. The majority of economic crises appear as breaks in the last dash, i.e., selling. For the capitalist finds him/herself as having already invested, often on the basis of loans, in the production of a commodity and, after the commodity is produced, either the capitalist cannot sell the commodity or it must be sold below "cost." A single capitalist in such a situation is simply bankrupt, but if this happens across many interlinked cycles a crisis looms. For a capitalist A who cannot sell, cannot buy from capitalist B, which leads to B not being able to sell to C, etc. The complex interdependency of branches of industry, in a systemic crisis, leads to an unpredictable set of failures leading to incomplete cycles and a crisis of systemic reproduction. This intracapitalist struggle in a period of global linkages creates easily observable mayhem. However, these interconnections and their failures, determined by the organic chemistry of capital, are not the whole story. The dashes can be broken by interclass action.

The clearest example of this capacity is in the *boycott*. For the capitalist buys with the intent to sell, while the working class buys with the intent to "consume." Therefore, beyond a certain wage level, working-class consumption is volatile. It can have a wide spectrum of objects, but it can also be selectively withdrawn. Consequently, the working class as an agent in the commodity market can politically affect the composition of capitalism. True, this type of transformation is limited; since it can, at best, redistribute value within and across the branches of industry. It cannot halt this mechanism, since it depends upon it. However, boycotts and other forms of class-oriented purchases have been used effectively to shape social reproduction in a favorable way (selectively "punishing" parts of capital that have unacceptable labor policies).

Another example of class struggle in the social reproduction cycle is the M-L segment. The capitalist goes out with his/her money M to the labor market to find specific grades and quantities of labor-power L. But this does not mean that the L on offer is satisfactory. For the decisions involved in creating certain quantities and qualities of L are not determined by M. L requires a production process that involves many laborers (especially women) whose interests and desires are not directed by capital. This is the region of demography and education that is often left to the "cultural" aspects of capitalism, which is often shorthand for "of secondary interest." But demography and education (considered in their broadest meaning) form the foundation of the *sine qua non* (and yet the most peculiar) commodity in capitalism.

Thus, capitalists require certain quantities of labor-power at a given wage levels in predetermined sites and times. This presents a formidable coordination problem that was not first invented in the "just in time" production processes of the 1980s and 1990s (although these processes depend upon the successful functioning of this coordination mechanism to an extraordinary extent!) These variables must be brought together throughout the history of capitalism even though there are many forces that can undermine a successful coordination. For example, there is the question of place. The capitalist might mark the spot where labor-power is needed, but that does not mean that workers will be there to offer it. Often capitalists must use state power (or their own private police forces) to physically and/or psychically fix workers to a site of production. The problem with workers is that they are bipedal, i.e., they can walk (or run) from sites of production, if the conditions of employment are unacceptable or if attractive alternative paths to subsistence are available (independent of the labor market).

Then there is the question of time. Workers can *delay* the sale of their labor-power collectively. When this delay is organized then it is called the *strike*. Strikes, however, are not expressions of a total rejection of exchanging labor-power for money. The end of a strike is the return to M-L (the capitalist's version of) and L-M (the worker's version of) the labor-power-money exchange, but on a more (or less) favorable basis for the workers. That is why strikes are always so disappointing from a revolutionary perspective, for they are powerful exertions of class power only to repropose a return to the reproduction of capital. They are ruptures in the reproduction process that are meant to be healed *later*.

More crucial than the gaps of the reproduction process caused by the uncontrolled mobility of workers and their ability to collectively delay the sale of their labor-power is the quantity of labor-power available. Marx claims that there are demographic "laws" appropriate to capitalism.[2] This might be so, but the crucial question point is that these are "laws" for a system that is constructed on all levels through struggle. Thus, the "optimal" population in a capitalism might be determined with respect to a given profit level, but why is it that such a quantity of workers available is often less (or more) than the "optimum"? This happens because the ultimate decisions to produce workers generationally are neither the capitalists' nor their state's. Workers, men and especially women, must decide whether they are going to reproduce. Only in the rarest of instances has capital taken on the challenge of directly "breeding" workers, e.g., in the United States after 1808 when the slave trade was outlawed, the slave owners attempted to have their slaves breed new slaves. In many cases, capital has found itself with fewer (or more) workers than would satisfy its "optimum" requirements. Why? As Silvia Federici has pointed out in *Caliban and the Witch*, Marx and most of the Marxist tradition have not taken demography as part of class struggle:

> Marx never acknowledged that procreation could become a terrain of exploitation and by the same token a terrain of resistance. He never imagined that women could refuse to reproduce, or that such a refusal can become part of the class struggle. . . . Nor did he imagine that men and women might have different interests with respect to child-making, an activity he treated as a gender-neutral, undifferentiated process.[3]

Thus, the quantity of L is not given by the mechanical operation of the labor market. Behind the institutions of that market (from the employment office, to the temp company, to the "want" ads, the interviews and drug tests) is another, largely female, force with desires that are not the capitalists.' Capital had to gain some control of this netherworld where its most precious commodity is produced and, as Federici has insightfully shown, that is one of the driving motives of the witch hunt of the sixteenth and seventeenth centuries.

Tensed Time: Beginnings-Middles-Ends

There is a third, tensed structure of time that is crucial in understanding class struggle: Beginning-Middle-End (or precapitalist, capitalist, and postcapitalist).

---

[2] Marx, *Capital: Volume I*, 783–84.

[3] Silvia Federici, *Caliban and the Witch: Women, the Body and Primitive Accumulation* (Brooklyn: Autonomedia, 2004), 91.

This kind of tensed time directly relates to the class struggle, for there is a struggle to prevent the establishment of the preconditions of capitalism and to transcend these conditions once they are established as well. It is not exactly a "class struggle" for it is an attempt to either deny the presuppositions of class existence or to transcend them.

Self-conscious capitalist ideologists, of course, do not recognize this structure and the struggles it intimates, since they are continuously engaged in an effort to posit only capitalism itself in the continuous past (as always already) and as the continuous future (always will be), i.e., as not having had a beginning and a coming end. It is a process of "eternalization" characteristic of any idea that has been transformed in the course of historical struggles into a totality.

A classic example of this process is Adam Smith's identification of the beginnings of capitalism with the "very slow and gradual" workings of an "original principle of human nature": "the propensity to truck, barter, and exchange one thing for another."[4] This propensity is, according to him, "common to all men" and is "the necessary consequence of the faculties of reason and speech." In other words, if one finds a being without these propensities, he/she/it is not likely to be human. So the conditions of capitalism seem to merge with the conditions of human existence and the lineaments of human history.

In fact, those who, like Smith, discuss the beginning of capitalism seem committed to shrouding it in myth or presenting it from "the standpoint of the nursery tale as the one thing fit for all age-groups and all stages of development."[5] But capitalism has a beginning . . . in fact, as we shall see, many beginnings. In the Marxist analysis, it is posed as the "secret of primitive (or original) accumulation": *primitive accumulation's dirty little "secret," however, is that the conditions for capitalism's existence were not, are not, and will not be eternally present.*

The logical key to primitive accumulation is the process of depriving people of noncapitalist access to the means of subsistence (metonymically described as the "enclosure of the commons") whenever and wherever this access arises. Certainly, resistance to capitalism arose before capitalism became established (e.g., in the struggle against enclosures in late feudal Europe and in the indigenous American's struggles against The Conquest). It continues to the present when workers appropriate "new commons" (from the "digital commons" to the "genetic code" to the expropriation of colonial settlers at the end of anticolonial struggles to the formation of social security systems) and capital's attempts to deny this access (in their latest incarnations they often are organized under the rubric of "neoliberalism"). Consequently, capitalism is born and dies (as well as accumulates and depreciates) diurnally throughout the field of class struggle and the monolithic "stages" of history dissolve into the present. Just as slavery is always on the agenda of the masters, as Pierre Dockes argues, so too is the commons (in the sense of a collective access to the means of subsistence and production) on the agenda of the workers.

---

[4] Adam Smith, *Wealth of Nations* (Amherst, NY: Prometheus Books, 1991 [1776]), 19.
[5] Marx, *Capital: Volume I*, 874.

Marx understood, at least propagandistically, the beginning (and end) of capitalism from a stadial point of view and not as a process that has many starting (and ending) points. For him, "the capitalist era dates from the sixteenth century"[6] and its ending is going to be less "protracted, violent and difficult" since that transformation will involve the "expropriation of a few usurpers by the mass of the people."[7] However, I argue that, in another sense, capitalism has not yet completely begun, since many of the older commons still exist and have made it possible for people to resist their total dependence on the labor market.

The class struggle understood in a tensed structure is constructed by two basic actions—*prevention and commonization*—that are antagonistic to capital's eternalization of itself. Both actions are relational, one outside the capitalist circle attempting to bar absorption to the inside, one inside going out and attempting to bar a return. One prevents the loss of, the other expands, the commons. One prevents absorption into capitalist time and the other exits from it.

Prevention arises from a struggle to defend a precapitalist commons that already provides tools and wealth for subsistence. This type of commons offers the possibility of refusing entrance into capitalist relations. Prevention is the *ur*-class struggle that aborts the formation of the working class. Those who are fated to be workers conduct this struggle in order to stop their metamorphosis. (The many legends of demonic possession and vampiric assault in the beginning of colonization in South America and Africa are powerful oblique expressions of this struggle.[8] It is a struggle against primitive accumulation with a long "history." Many of the struggles of the last 10,000 years or so (since the beginning of the agricultural era) are largely efforts to resist the expanding circle of capitalist relations, since all the basics for the creation of capitalism were already in existence by then. There is a difficulty in seeing this struggle at times because it does not express itself as a class struggle, and it has often been dismissed by practitioners of standard conceptions of class struggle as reactionary or irrelevant.[9]

But these are not "backward-looking" struggles, they are "outward-looking" ones. What is at stake in them are the remaining commons of the precapitalist period that still provide an enormous noncommodified wealth to workers and nonworkers alike. Neoliberal economists have attempted to devise a way of measuring the "value" of the various commons that are based upon "nature" at the very moment when there is a systematic effort launched by agencies like the World Bank and the large multinational construction companies to commodify them. Hence ground

---

[6] Ibid., 876.

[7] Ibid., 930.

[8] See Luise White, *Speaking with Vampires: Rumor and History in Colonial Africa* (Berkeley: University of California Press, 2000) and Michael T. Taussig, *The Devil and Commodity Fetishism in South America* (Chapel Hill: University of North Carolina Press, 1980).

[9] See Midnight Notes Collective, "The Hammer and . . . or the Sickle: From the Zapatista Uprising to the Battle of Seattle" in *Auroras of the Zapatistas: Local and Global Struggles in the Fourth World War* (Brooklyn: Autonomedia, 2001).

water (often thousands of years old) is increasingly being "privatized" and commodified throughout the planet as its value is being computed.

It should be clear that the access to precapitalist forms of subsistence is not an all-or-nothing affair. For even when one is a waged worker, his/her ability to access a precapitalist source of subsistence is an enormous power against capital. For example, when factory workers have access to an agricultural village either directly or indirectly through family ties, then their strikes can be longer because they have access to food or land to grow food. So the barriers between the various commons and the capitalist realm are not absolute for workers.

There is a continual crossing of these lines in an individual's life. In fact, much of our oft-lamented confused sense of self, our fragmentation and alienation, reflect this continual transgression of the barriers between age-old commons (human and not) and capital. In this sense, the memory of dignity, collective autonomy, and "moral economy" arises from the fact that one is continually employing different antagonistic logics diurnally. I suppose this is one way of understanding what Joyce was reflecting in *Ulysses*, i.e., the copresence of precapitalist presences in the midst of a modern, though peripheral, city busily reproducing capital.

But this copresence is not a given. Neoliberalism is an open admission of capital's totalitarian urge to "commodify, commodify!" Its articulation has been a helpful reminder to those who have forgotten during the long hiatus of Keynesianism and socialism exactly what capitalism is all about. Now that the "Cold War" has ended, a truly "Hot War" has begun under the banner of the complete triumph of privatization (with an appropriate religious expression in certain Christian fundamentalist sects like the New Life Church, whose members apparently like "the benefits, risks, and maybe above all, the excitement of a free-market society," according to their leader, Pastor Ted).[10] Capital cannot escape its fate of continually trying to transcend its limits, both quantitative and qualitative, even when its overall survival is not best serviced. But this drive is hardly doomed to succeed. For it not only is facing the precapitalist commons that often present themselves as irreducible even to the fire and blood of capital's bombers and death squads, but also the continually creation of new postcapitalist commons.

When I refer to the "postcapitalist commoning," I am not *either* reverting to the stadial framework of classical Marxism (whatever Marx's actual views were) of a communist future, preceded by a series of forms of production that included primitive communism, the Asiatic mode, ancient slavery, feudalism, and capitalism *or* echoing Hardt and Negri's notion of "exodus" from capitalism.[11] For the commoning process I refer to involves the ongoing transformation of the commodified forms of life into a commons. This is not a process that is all-or-nothing nor is it a utopian vision of a "future" life. On the contrary, it recognizes that much of the commons

---

[10] Jeff Sharlet, "Inside America's Most Powerful Megachurch," *Harper's* 310, no. 1860 (May 2005): 47.

[11] Karl Marx, *Pre-capitalist Economic Formations* (New York: International Publishers, 1964) and Michael Hardt and Antonio Negri, *Empire* (Cambridge, MA: Harvard University Press, 2000).

is already operating, often extensively, under capitalism and the issue is the self-organized expansion of that area of life that is common. That is, the class struggle in this temporal dimension is not only a matter of *preventing* enclosures (and thus an entrance into capital's time) but to actually *expanding* the commons into new areas of social life (and so exiting capital's time). This expansive commonizing process is not an ideal safely ensconced in the future perfect. It is time future in the present or it is nothing.

There are a large number of examples of the creation of a commons out of capitalist terrain where time future becomes time present. I will only give one example in this paper, rooted in a technology that was once central to the development of capitalism: the heat engine. (I believe that it will have some helpful insights to the often referred to "new commons" that is forming around the technology of the Turing machine.) The commons I will discuss relates to the establishment of "Hobohemia" in the late nineteenth and early twentieth centuries.[12] The "hobo" residents of Hobohemia were migratory "white" male workers in North America of that period who used the railroads and railroad property as their commons. Although they were individually nomadic in the sense that they did not travel in the boxcars of freight trains in large permanently defined groups (as Eastern European, Chinese, and Mexican workers often did), they were quite collective in their reproduction, since an essential part of hobo life was "the jungle," i.e., a site "located in close proximity to a railroad division point, where trains are made up or where trains stop to change crews and engines."[13] Hoboes would congregate in the jungles when they were on the road. They were places where they could cook their "Mulligan stew," clean themselves and their clothes, sleep in relative safety, share their knowledge about the whereabouts of the railroad police or of jobs, and persuade their mates about their politics.

Although some jungles were temporary others were continuously in existence, even though the turnover of residents was quite high. They dotted the rail arteries of the nation and provided nodal points for the practical communalization of the railway system. The jungles were in general hospitable and democratic (although they rarely challenged the color and gender lines that divided the working class then as now).[14]

They were run on the basis of a number of "unwritten Jungle laws" that banned acts like making fire by night in jungles subject to raids, wasting food or destroying it after eating, leaving pots or other utensils dirty after using, and so forth. These rules were strictly enforced internally by the hobo rule-makers themselves just as they would defend the jungle from external invasion by police, vigilantes, and the Ku Klux Klan.

---

[12] Nels Anderson, *The Hobo: The Sociology of the Homeless Man* (Chicago: University of Chicago Press, 1923). Also, Todd Depastino, *Citizen Hobo: How a Century of Homelessness Shaped America* (Chicago: University of Chicago Press, 2003).

[13] Anderson, *The Hobo*, 16.

[14] Depastino, *Citizen Hobo*, 81–85.

Jungle committees would deal with infractions of the rules and prescribe punishments. For example, on one occasion mentioned by Nels Anderson, an ex-hobo sociologist, a "hi-jack" was caught in the act of robbing some "bo" who was sleeping; a committee was immediately formed and a chairman selected to decide on what should be done. The committee decided that the hi-jack should be whipped, but "no one steps forward; everybody declines to apply the strap or stick"![15] After a confused hiatus, a young fellow agreed to fight the hi-jack, and a boxing match is arranged, where the hi-jack is eventually knocked out. When he came to, he was kicked out of the jungle. "By eleven o'clock [at night] the excitement is over. Different men announce that they were headed for so and so and that the freight starts at such a time. To this someone replies that he is going that way too so they start off together."[16]

Through the complex organization of movement, information exchange, and reproduction nodes, the hoboes created a nationwide network that used the private property of the railroad companies as their commons. True, they expressed many different political ideals—with the Industrial Workers of the World (IWW) perhaps defining the predominant one—but their actual achievement was to show that the railroads and their land could be communalized. This was no mean feat, since they had to confront an industry which owned the most important transport modality for the continental economy at the time and that had just reached its peak of expansion marked by the laying of the 254,037th mile of rail in 1916.[17] Along with the tracks, another measure of the railroad companies' power were the enormous land concessions granted to them by the government from the Civil War on that made them the arbiters of the economic direction of the nation west of the Mississippi. Howard Zinn estimates that the federal government gave the railroad companies about 100 million acres during the Civil War alone.[18]

The main "economic" purpose of the communalization of the railroad territory and the freight trains was not immediately revolutionary. Hoboes rode the rails usually to follow the harvest, to go to a distant job contracted for, say, at one of the employment agencies on West Madison Street, Chicago (called the "main stem"), or, ironically enough, to go to a rumored railroad construction site, for track laying was a standard job for a hobo. But the hoboes' national presence was huge, since hundreds of thousands of men passed through one or another region of Hobohemia (the rails, the jungle, or the main stem) in the course of a year. Moreover, there is no doubt many a hobo's politics was anticapitalist, and the rails could not only bring workers for a harvest or a building boom, they also could bring a swarm of supporters to a "free speech" fight or a general strike. Consequently, they constituted a communal challenge to the heart of U.S. capital. The hobo commons of freight trains

---

[15] Anderson, *The Hobo*, 24.

[16] Ibid., 25.

[17] William Greenleaf, *American Economic Development Since 1860* (New York: Harper and Row, 1968), 79.

[18] Howard Zinn, *A People's History of the United States*. (New York: HarperCollins, 2003), 238.

and the railroad territory had to be enclosed, since, after all, the hoboes were recommunalizing the communal land of the indigenous Americans that had been first conquered and nationalized by the federal government and then privatized through land grants to railroad companies.

The path of enclosure was complex, involving raw repression and technological and ideological transformations.[19] The repression was obvious in the period of the Palmer raids. First, the IWW became the object of governmental harassment and the physical elimination of its leadership. Second, a tremendous number of railroad "trespassers" were killed and injured in the course of those years, e.g., 2,553 were killed in 1919 and another 2,166 in 1920, often with assistance of the railroad policemen's guns.[20] Third, the increase in the antiradical activities of the KKK and other more local death squads of the 1920s were often directed against the hobo jungles.

Along with this antihobo violence came a technological change in the modality of transport: as the highway system expanded and the rails declined, the automobile and truck were beginning to replace the passenger and freight train as the dominant form of transport. The movement of labor-power over the highway generated a completely different relationship to class struggle than the rails undermining Hobohemia.

Ideologically, the hoboes were attacked as examples of deviant "white men" who had become "homeless" and without the restraints of "home," hence they were dangerous to capital. The federal government, especially with the New Deal, saw the "problem of the hobo" as resolvable by the creation of "suburbia as the nation's dominant residential form."[21] By World War II, the effort to transform the railways into a commons had been definitely defeated.

The hoboes' story of an anticapitalist commons founded on a distinctly capitalist terrain is not unique. The history of the capitalist era has been filled with such efforts by all sectors of the working class, alone and in collaboration. The recent political interest in the communities of the eighteenth-century pirates of the Atlantic and Caribbean is motivated, I believe, by the desire to know about an anticapitalist struggle of largely male workers founding itself as a commons on the terrain of the highest level of the organic composition of capital which, in the case of the pirates, took the form of an ocean-going ship.[22] A similar interest is directed at the various movements trying to found an anticapitalist commons on the terrain of communicating Turing machines, whether they call themselves and their practices "free software," "creative commons," "peer-to-peer," "file-sharing." These constitute efforts to enlarge the commons from a terrain that is already organized and owned by capital. They speak to a future possibility that is actually present, even though it is inevitably

---

[19] Depastino, *Citizen Hobo*, 171–94.

[20] Anderson, *The Hobo*, 161–62.

[21] Depastino, *Citizen Hobo*, 219.

[22] Marcus Rediker, *Villains of All Nations: Atlantic Pirates in the Golden Age* (Boston: Beacon Press, 2004).

"distorted" by the terrain it commonizes. The free software movement, for example, has much to learn from the experiences of the hoboes and pirates.

Conclusion

The three dimensions of time sketched above can be useful in analyzing class struggle. At the very least, this approach makes it clear that there are many ways in which capital structures time. At the same time, there is very little hope in transcending capitalism, if time is not reappropriated in *all* the different ways capital organizes it. A politics that merely deals with time in the linear aspect, e.g., a "bread and butter" wages and hours politics, will miss the importance of the circular and tensed aspects to time. A similar point can be made about an overemphasis of the other kinds of time. All the different temporal modalities need to be simultaneously addressed in any political effort to go beyond a capitalist form of life and social coordination.

A CRITIQUE OF "COGNITIVE CAPITALISM"

> But since money itself is an omnipresent means, the various elements of our existence are thus placed in an all-embracing teleological nexus in which no element is either the first or last. Furthermore, since it measures all objects with merciless objectivity, and since its standard of value so measured determines their relationship, a web of objective and personal aspects of life emerges which is similar to the natural cosmos with its continuous cohesion and strict causality
> —Georg Simmel, *The Philosophy of Money*

Introduction

The last few years have witnessed both a major capitalist crisis (that is far from over) and a crisis of traditional Marxist explanations of capitalist crisis. That is why the development of the work of "post-operaist" or "Autonomous Marxists" like Hardt, Negri, Vercellone, Boutang, Virno, and Marazzi, has proven so attractive. They present a collection of new concepts or new approaches to old ones (e.g., cognitive capitalism, the General Intellect, immaterial labor, affective labor, biopower, common, Empire, multitude, rent, capture, singularity, formal and real subsumption, living knowledge) appropriate to conditions of post-post-Keynesian, post-post-Fordist capitalism, with a chance of providing a theory that might, finally, "grip the masses" or, in their terminology, "the multitude."

So much rides, then, upon the post-operaists' description of contemporary capitalism as "cognitive capitalism," or perhaps some of its cognates like "the informatization of production," "the knowledge economy," "informational capitalism." It and these cognates are meant to describe a novel form of capitalism on the verge of collapse because the very forces of production and class struggle that brought it into existence far outpace the relations of production it offers. In other words, "the time is ripe for (cognitive) revolution." However, in their laudable political effort to liberate the revolutionary energies of our time by portraying the hegemony of a new and inherently unstable capitalism, the theorists of cognitive capitalism dismiss the range and complexity of the forces in the field on both sides of the class line that make capitalism more unstable and, at the same time, potentially more enduring.

In this chapter, I "test" the strength of the concept of "cognitive capitalism" (and its cognates) and find it (them) inadequate to the task of fully characterizing contemporary capitalism. I argue that there is no direct formula connecting capitalism, knowledge-production, and political liberation, as the theorists of "cognitive capitalism" affirm. In the conclusion, I point to an alternative conception that escapes the strictures I bring against their "cognitivist" analyses.

The Genealogy of Cognitive Capitalism:
Capitalism = Rationality: Weber, Simmel, Hayek . . . sans Keynes with Marx in the Middle

In order to test the concept of cognitive capitalism, it is important to clarify what concept we are speaking about. Before the development of the concept of cognitive capitalism by Carlo Vercellone and other post-operaist or Autonomous Marxist thinkers, there was an already highly developed notion of a knowledge economy and knowledge production in the academic, popular business, and OECD–World Bank literature.[1] It is important to distinguish between these two traditions and discern their overlap and difference.

Indeed, there has been a long tradition connecting capitalism with cognition, rationality and the abstract quantitative spirit. Already in the period between the late nineteenth century and pre–World War I period, a series of economists and sociologists in particular, German neo-Kantians like Georg Simmel and Max Weber, looked at capitalism as a "form of life" characterized by the spirit of rationality, calculation, and abstractness. Their work was part of a widespread lamentation on the sterility of existence in modern capitalism where formal structures take predominance over "life"—here also we have the seeds of the critique of bureaucracy that was so influential in the mid-twentieth century.

Simmel, for example, rooted capitalism in the inversion of means/ends polarity and the application of a quantitative value system based on the exchange of equal-for-equal to all forms of life. As we see in the epigraph, Simmel both praised and despaired of the soul-eviscerating, totalitarian form of life (or "second nature") that such a rational capitalism promotes.[2] For Weber, capitalism was permeated with the "spirit" of rationality that leads to his famous "iron cage" image, i.e., capitalism drives humanity into a rational deployment of free labor, a rational form of accounting, and a rational form of industry responding to the market, but also to a soulless life world.[3] True, this spirit operationalized only an instrumental rationality, but it was a rationality all the same that was superior to all previous economic forms as well as to its contemporary rivals (including socialism). It seemed inevitable.

Decades later, Hayek further developed these cognitive approaches to capitalism by his famous equation of the market with an epistemological tool providing information about the commodities up for sale.[4] In his view, any other effort to organize

---

[1] See Edu-factory Collective, *Towards a Global Autonomous University: Cognitive Labor, the Production of Knowledge, and Exodus from the Education Factory* (Brooklyn: Autonomedia, 2009).

[2] Georg Simmel, *The Philosophy of Money*, 2nd ed. (London: Routledge, 2002).

[3] Max Weber, *The Protestant Ethic and the "Spirit" of Capitalism* (London: Penguin Books, 2002).

[4] Friedrich A. Hayek, *Individualism and the Economic Order* (London: Routledge and Kegan Paul, 1949), 77–91.

distribution would be continually dogged by a lack of measure leading to a system based on arbitrary, noneconomic, and inevitably corrupt choices. This approach led to his critique of socialism and his questioning of its long-term viability.[5]

Not every bourgeois commentator on capitalism came to the same conclusion concerning the rational and cognitive character of capitalism. Keynes questioned the rationality of capitalism on a wide variety of contexts, e.g., from his remarks concerning "animal spirits," to the game-like character of most investment and the gaming-like behavior of most investors, to the "bandwagon" effects of a stock market that comes down to betting on what the average bets of the bettors will be. His overall attitude is that capitalism was purely instrumental and he gave "one cheer" for it in the way that his fellow Bloomsburyian E.M. Forster gave "two cheers" for democracy. In fact, Keynes humorously expressed his attitude in his 1928 essay, "Economic Prospects of Our Grandchildren," arguing that once the accumulation process leads to the "solution" of the problem of scarcity (roughly in the early twenty-first century, i.e., now) humanity can finally assess the true value of the money-motive. It is then that "The love of money as a possession—as distinguished from the love of money as a means to the enjoyments and realities of life—will be recognized for what it is, a somewhat disgusting morbidity, one of those semi-criminal, semi-pathological propensities which one hands over with a shudder to the specialists in mental disease."[6]

In a word, the phrase "cognitive capitalism" was redundant for Weber, Simmel, and Hayek (but not for Keynes). Though they undoubtedly had an important impact on cognitive capitalism theorists of the early twenty-first century, clearly the most important influence is Karl Marx. On the one side, Marx recognized with Weber, Simmel, and Hayek that all capitalist epochs had a "cognitive" aspect because the basic mechanisms of the system—even those he emphasized like the exchange process, the labor time measure of value, the importance of reducing turnover time, the transformation of surplus value into profit, rent and interest—create "concrete abstractions" that stimulate the development of an instrumental rationality. Indeed, Marx, for all his criticisms of the absurdity and barbarity of the system, was the original "immaterialist" and "cognitivist" as far as capitalism is concerned, since he argued that capitalists are not interested in things, but they definitely want to *know* their quantitative *value* and value is hardly a material stuff!

The Autonomist Marxist adherents of the theory of "cognitive capitalism" like Vercellone, however, are not particularly interested in Marx's general equation of capitalism with some form of quantitative (but fetishized) rationality as was Alfred Sohn-Rethel.[7] They place their emphasis on Marx as the student of the knowledge-capitalism relation and of the terrain where political economy and epistemology merge. In so doing, they revalue Marx's collection of midnight notes, the *Grundrisse*, for it is there, they

---

[5] David Ramsay Steele, *From Marx to Mises: Post-Capitalist Society and the Challenge of Economic Calculation* (La Salle, IL: Open Court, 1992), 119–22.

[6] John Maynard Keynes, *Essays in Persuasion*, vol. 9 of *The Collected Writings of John Maynard Keynes* (London: Macmillan, 1972), 329.

[7] Alfred Sohn-Rethel, *Intellectual and Manual Labour: A Critique of Epistemology* (London: Macmillan, 1978).

claim, that the basis for a political theory about the capitalist crisis generated by the application of knowledge to production and (potentially) leading to the liberation of workers from exploitation is laid out.

Marx's well-known argument in the "Fragment on Machines" in the *Grundrisse* is that with the advent of large-scale industry a phase of capitalist development is inaugurated in which science becomes the main force of production, technology takes over the labor process and machines are substituted for human labor (with the consequent fall of the rate of profit). The worker is reduced to being an attendant to the machine but at the same time the use of labor time to measure wealth is proving to be increasingly irrational.[8]

The "Fragment on Machines" has been extremely influential on the Autonomist Marxists' conception of immaterial labor and cognitive capitalism, in their potential for fostering a transition to a different society, and exodus from capital. There is a general belief (prominent especially in the recent writings of Negri and Hardt) that we are in a stage in which capitalism is an obstacle to the further development of the productive forces, in which the historic contradiction between forces and relations of production is coming to a head, and that cognitive labor is the crucial element in the extremization of the contradiction.

Marxology, however, has not been the only force driving the development of a theory of cognitive capitalism. The epochal changes that followed the capitalist crisis of the mid-1970s—a crisis clearly produced in great part by the cycle of struggles made by industrial workers worldwide—were crucial. It was the restructuring of the world economy in response to these struggles—deindustrialization, globalization, and the computer/information revolution—that triggered the idea of Cognitive Capitalism. The geniality of the Autonomist Marxist theorists is to have turned the defeat of the industrial working class in the 1970s into a victory, by reading the deindustrialization of production, at least in the global North, as a response to and concretization of the refusal of the factory. In this perspective, cognitive capitalism is the step workers have forced capitalists to take by refusing the assembly line, causing a productivity crisis, and demonstrating that a whole industrial regime of life had to come to an end.

The OECD and World Bank

The "promotion" of knowledge from the rank of an exogenous independent variable to that of an endogenous variable dependent on input, on the allocation of resources, is an important step.
—Fritz Machlup (1962)

There is nothing new under the sun. This is true of an economic approach to knowledge and cognition and hence to "cognitive capitalism." Even though terms like "knowledge economy" began, by the mid-1990s, to be widely used by economists and sociologists as well as by the main capitalist planning institutions like the World Bank to define the new reality emerging from the economic restructuring

---

[8] Marx, *Grundrisse*, 704–11.

responding to the crisis of the 1970s, economic theorists like Fritz Machlup had already developed the categories that would transform knowledge into a commodity and an industrial sector in the early 1960s. Indeed, Machlup argued in 1962 that by 1958 more than 30 percent of the waged work force was constituted by "knowledge-producing persons."[9]

What adds complexity to this already complex genealogical picture is the fact that bourgeois economists and their antagonists, the post-operaists or Autonomist Marxists, both use the term "cognitive" and its cognates ("knowledge" and "information") as adjectives to mark off a specific (indeed the latest) period in capitalism's history. "Cognitive" is used in the same way that "industrial" appears in phrases like "industrial capitalism" or "industry-based development," etc. The implication being that though knowledge and cognition were important in previous eras of capitalism, its latest phase should be properly baptized by terms like "cognitive" or "knowledge."

What is it that has changed in capitalism that justifies the use of such terms? Is "knowledge" *qua* adjective functioning like "industry" in the past? Semantically, the notions of a "knowledge-based economy," "knowledge-related jobs," and "knowledge-based industries" began to be used with increasing frequency in the 1990s (although Robert Reich's term "symbolic analysis" that he introduced in *The Work of Nations* would have been a more accurate phrase).[10] Already by 1994, the World Bank was pointing to new trends like "the emerging role of knowledge as a major driver of economic development."[11] This development seems to coincide with the "discovery" of the "new economy" in that first post–Cold War decade.

Beginning in this period, slogans like "Knowledge has become the most important factor in economic development" or "Today, economic growth is as much a process of knowledge accumulation as of capital accumulation" became shibboleths.[12] Certainly, the evidence that the World Bank, at least, used to justify these claims and more generally to prepare us for a new, epistemic characterization of capitalism begs more questions than it answers. For example, consider (1) the OECD has determined that the knowledge-based industry sector between 1985 and 1997 saw major increases in their share of total value added (51 to 59 percent in Germany, 45 to 51 percent in the UK, and from 34 to 42 percent in Finland) and (2) firms in the OECD devote at least one third of their investment to "knowledge-based intangibles." [13]

The problem with this "evidence" is the ambiguity of what is being measured: "the knowledge-based industry sector" and the "knowledge-based intangibles." What characterizes them as well as knowledge-jobs, knowledge-work, and

---

[9] Fritz Machlup, *The Production and Distribution of Knowledge in the United States* (Princeton: Princeton University Press, 1962), 393.

[10] Robert Reich, *The Work of Nations* (New York: Random House, 1992).

[11] World Bank, *Higher Education: The Lessons of Experience. Development in Practice Series* (Washington, DC: World Bank, 1994).

[12] World Bank, *Constructing Knowledge Societies: New Challenges for Tertiary Education* (Washington, DC: World Bank, 2002), 7.

[13] Organization for Economic Cooperation and Development, *Education Policy Analysis: Education and Skill* (Paris: OECD, 2001).

finally the knowledge economy? The OECD and the World Bank defined the "the knowledge-based industry sector" as including "high and medium-high technology industries; communication services; finance, insurance, and other business services; and community, social, and personal services"[14] while "knowledge-based intangibles" include "training, R&D, patents, licensing, design, and marketing."[15]

There is an extraordinary fuzziness in the terminology describing such serious matters. The knowledge-based industries and intangibles are no more connected with knowledge than non-knowledge-based industries and tangibles. They prompt an excess of questions over answers. How does reproducing labor-power and constant capital, computing, communicating, or speculating make a firm, a job or an industrial sector "knowledge-based"? What makes an "intangible" non-knowledge-based, e.g., are "surveillance services" knowledge-based but "guard-services" non-knowledge-based? Are non-knowledge-based industries ignorance-based? What brings together banks, pornographic film companies, software design firms, communication corporations, airplane manufacturers under the knowledge-based industry sector rubric that excludes auto companies, real estate firms, restaurants, mines, and farms? Are the former more dependent on knowledge than the latter, do the former create significantly more knowledge than the latter, and/or do the workers in the former know more than those in the latter? Finally, and most pointedly, why did the World Bank launch structural adjustment programs during the 1990s in African countries that defunded their educational systems when, it had presumably recognized that knowledge and a knowledgeable workforce was the most decisive "input" for any contemporary economy that hopes to survive in the global market?[16]

Cognitive Capitalism from an Anticapitalist Perspective

a. From Knowledge Economy to Cognitive Capitalism

The term "Cognitive Capitalism" seems to be of more recent origin than the "knowledge economy," since the books and articles presenting it date from the "dot-com" crash in 2000–2001. The books that Vercellone and Boutang write with "Cognitive Capitalism" in the title were published in 2007 and the first references to a "cognitive capitalism" research program were from the year 2000 or so.[17] In speaking of the Autonomist Marxist theory of cognitive capitalism, I refer to a theory that in many ways has been collectively elaborated by scholar-activists centered mostly in France and Italy, including Negri, Hardt, Boutang, and Virno. However, one author stands out—Carlo Vercellone, who in his work has stated the major outlines of the

---

[14] World Bank, *Constructing Knowledge Societies*, 22.

[15] Ibid., 9.

[16] Silvia Federici et al., *A Thousand Flowers: Social Struggles Against Structural Adjustment in African Universities* (Trenton, NJ: Africa World Press, 2000).

[17] Yan Moulier Boutang, "Cognitive Capitalism and Entrepreneurship: Decline in Industrial Entrepreneurship and the Rising of Collective Intelligence" (paper presented at the Conference on Capitalism and Entrepreneurship at Cornell University, September 28–29, 2007), 11.

theory and has been responsible for many of its key insights. I will therefore concentrate on his work for my comments on the theory of cognitive capitalism with due qualifications and occasional references to the other theorists.

While recognizing the pitfalls of self-defined genealogies, it is useful to listen to Vercellone's efforts to place the notion of cognitive capitalism with respect to other theories of contemporary society and economy. He claims that "the hypothesis of cognitive capitalism develops from a critique of the political economy of the new theories of the knowledge-based economy" and then explains:

> The critical perspective on apologetic accounts of neoliberal inspiration is inscribed in two terms which compose the very concept of cognitive capitalism: i) the notion of 'capitalism' defines the enduring element in the change of the structural invariants of the capitalist mode of production: in particular, the driving role of profit and wage relation or, more precisely, the different forms of dependent labour on which the extraction of surplus labour is founded; ii) the term 'cognitive' emphasizes the new nature of the conflictual relation of capital and labour, and of the forms of property on which the accumulation of capital rests.[18]

One can appreciate the need for such a hypothesis in the turn of the millennium when the atmosphere was full of "new economy" rhetoric that pumped up the dot-com bubble, when procapitalist ideologists were proclaiming the arrival of an era of endless growth due to the fast approaching "singularity" (when presumably machines would outpace human intelligence), driven by exponentially increasing computing power.[19] This was the time when the day trader *qua* dot-com millionaire was being pointed to as the model of the worker in the twenty-first century. The "Capitalism" side of "Cognitive Capitalism" soberly reminded everyone that for all the changes in technology and psychology, capitalism was still capitalism and that workers' labor would have to be exploited in order for the system to exist and so, inevitably, the struggle between capital and labor would continue, and perhaps intensify.

b. Back to the Future

> Man educated at the expense of much labor and time . . . may be compared
> to one of those expensive machines.
> —Adam Smith, *The Wealth of Nations*

What makes this era's capitalism more "cognitive" than any other? The answer for Vercellone lies in a new periodization of the history of capitalism using the concepts found in Marx's unpublished "Results of the Immediate Process

---

[18] Carlo Vercellone, "From Formal Subsumption to General Intellect: Elements for a Marxist Reading to the Thesis of Cognitive Capitalism," *Historical Materialism* 15 (2007): 14.

[19] E.g., Ray Kurzweil, *The Age of Spiritual Machines: When Computers Exceed Human Intelligence* (New York: Penguin, 2000).

of Production"—real and formal subsumption of labor under capital—as well as terms from the first volume of *Capital*, such as absolute and relative surplus value. "Subsumption" itself is a technical term derived from formal logic and refers to the inclusion of one logically defined class by another or even the minor premise of a syllogism which functions as mediating element in the larger argument. But Marx used this logical relation in his critique of political economy to distinguish two different ways that capital can subsume labor in the immediate process of production.

The formal subsumption of labor under capital is "viz., the takeover by capital of a mode of labor developed before the emergence of capitalist relations."[20] He claimed that with such modes, "surplus-value can be created only by lengthening the working day, i.e., by increasing absolute surplus-value."[21] For Vercellone, the model of such formal subsumption of labor under capital is the "putting-out system" (or *Verlagssystem*) in the sixteenth to eighteenth centuries when mercantile and financial capital were dominant.

For Marx, the real subsumption of labor under capital happens when:

> The general features of the formal subsumption remain, viz., the direct subordination of the labour process to capital, irrespective the state of its technological development. But on this foundation there now arises a technologically and otherwise specific mode of production which transforms the nature of the labour process and its actual conditions. . . . The real subsumption of labour under capital is developed in all the forms evolved by relative as opposed to absolute surplus-value.[22]

This form of subsumption induces the direct application of science and technology to the production process. This period includes the Ford-Smith-Taylor-Mancunian (Manchester) model of production, i.e., from the nineteenth century to the crisis of the assembly-line worker of the 1960s and early 1970s. But Vercellone is also critical of those who find in the "Toyotist"/"just-in-time" labor regime a new "post-Fordist" period, because it is still "bound to a factory-inspired vision of the new capitalism seen as a further development of the Fordist-industrial logic of the real subsumption of labour by capital." This model, however, does not show "the tendential crisis of some of the more structural invariants of the long-period dynamic that opened with the first industrial revolution."[23] An example of such a "structural invariant" would be the capitalist's insistence on intervening in the labor process whether via a Tayloristic time-motion study in the "Fordist" model or via labor-management networking and the formation of "quality circles" in the "post-Fordist" model. In other words, "Fordism" and "post-Fordism" are not as different as the "post-Fordists" avow. Vercellone claims that a better way of periodizing is to

---

[20] Marx, *Capital: Volume I*, 1021.

[21] Ibid., 1021.

[22] Ibid., 1034–35.

[23] Vercellone, "From Formal Subsumption," 14.

fold in many "post-Fordist" features to the previous stage of real subsumption and baptize the third stage of capitalism to be "cognitive capitalism."

The supporters of cognitive capitalism are making a bold claim that is attractive in the midst of what is clearly a historic crisis of capitalism, and when the standard Marxism of our time shows itself to be both politically and conceptually ineffective. They are asking us to take a new view of class struggle (that pits a parasitic capitalist against a collective, globally socialized knowledge worker) and to reinvestigate the possibility of a direct transition from capitalism to communism without state socialism as mediator. It is vital, then, that we assess the claims and hypotheses that Vercellone and other supporters of cognitive capitalism provide.

The novelties of this "cognitive" stage of capitalism, Vercellone claims, are many. But a key feature is that capitalists have been driven out of the zone of the labor process and have returned to a formal subsumption of labor, although labor-time no longer is a measure of value. Vercellone argues that the ever-intensifying capitalist drive for relative surplus value accumulation that applied ever more scientific and technological knowledge to production, and was typical of the second stage of capitalism, is a thing of the past. Cognitive capitalism involves a return to a formal subsumption of labor under capital (in the sense that capital returns to a position external to the production process) but with two qualifications. Strictly speaking, formal subsumption ought to involve precapitalist forms of labor and absolute surplus value accumulation but (a) instead of a return to precapitalist forms of labor we find new forms of labor that are not under capital's immediate control, and (b) instead of a return to absolute surplus value accumulation, we have a form of labor that cannot be temporally measured (and hence the categories of relative and absolute surplus value are inoperable in this era).

Consider the claim that capital is no longer an organizer of production and that "the subsumption of labour is once again formal in the sense that it is based essentially on the relation of monetary dependence of the wage-labourer inside the process of circulation."[24] Admittedly, Vercellone is rather abstract on this central point, but according to him capital apparently loses its control of the labor process due to "the new qualitative preponderance of living knowledge, incorporated and mobilized by labour over dead knowledge, incorporated in fixed capital (and the firm organization)."[25] The new knowledge-driven labor is no longer dependent upon machines and other forms of fixed capital (e.g., office buildings, fiber optic networks, and management personnel). In fact, the tipping point for such a development was when "the share of intangible capital (R&D, education, health) incorporated essentially in people, exceeded that of material capital held in stock and became the principal factor of growth."[26] This is reminiscent of the long period in the U.S. history when

---

[24] Ibid., 31.

[25] Ibid., 6–7.

[26] Carlo Vercellone, "Cognitive Capitalism and Models for the Regulation of Wages," in *Towards*

the share of capital invested in slaves was larger than the value of the national stock of constant capital. He writes:

> In so far as the organization of labour becomes increasingly autonomous, white collar offices either disappear or become the avatar of times past. In this framework, control over labour no longer takes on the Taylorist role of direct allocation of tasks; it is mostly replaced by indirect mechanisms based on the imperative to deliver, the prescription of subjectivity and a pure and simple coercion linked to the precarisation of the wage relation.[27]

This is a "back to the future" model of the autonomous and creative worker that tips its hat to Paolo Virno's characterization of contemporary work as a virtuoso communicative performance.[28] As the category of immaterial labor—i.e., labor producing immaterial affects (affective labor) and knowledges (cognitive labor)—expands to tendentially dominate production, the nature of work inevitably changes. It can no longer be supervised or measured in the way that labor-producing material products can. Consequently, Vercellone suggests, it is in the nature of things that the capitalist employer treats such immaterial workers carefully and from the "outside"—similar to the way that record and film industry bosses deal with their "artists." This is especially true of cognitive labor, the embodiment of "living knowledge." Instead of the factory, the production of contemporary cognitive capitalism has as its model the putting-out system where the merchant provides the wages, inputs, and at times the machines and receives the product in return. In fact, there is a deep relationship between an increasing workers' autonomy in the production process and capital's tendency to "indirect forms of domination of production and of the mechanisms of surplus appropriation realized by means of the sphere of monetary and financial circulation."[29]

The second qualification has to do with the intimate relation Marx drew between formal subsumption and absolute surplus value. Since absolute surplus value is based on a time measure of value, it is entirely inappropriate when dealing with knowledge work. In that case, there is no relation between this cognitive capitalist subsumption and absolute surplus value. In fact, this lack of relation constitutes a crisis of the law of value because a contradiction opens up between the knowledge-value of a production process's product and its time-value that capital insists on using even though it becomes, to paraphrase Marx, an increasingly "'wretched base' of the measure of wealth and norm of its distribution."[30]

---

a Global Autonomous University: Cognitive Labor, The Production of Knowledge, and Exodus from the Education Factory, ed. the Edu-factory Collective (Brooklyn: Autonomedia, 2009), 120.

[27] Carlo Vercellone, "The New Articulation of Wages, Rent and Profit in Cognitive Capitalism" (paper presented at the conference, "The Art of Rent," Queen Mary University School of Business and Management, London, 2008), 6.

[28] Paolo Virno, *A Grammar of the Multitude* (New York: Semiotext(e), 2004), 61–63.

[29] Vercellone, "From Formal Subsumption," 22.

[30] Ibid., 30.

c. The Return of Rent

The next theoretical innovation with respect to Marx is Vercellone's reconfiguration of the relation between profit and rent. His thesis is that since "the law of value-labour time is in crisis and cooperation of labour appears to become increasing autonomous from the managerial functions of capital, the very frontiers between rent and profit begin to disintegrate."[31] The key idea here is that since capital has retreated from organizing production (at least in the areas where the "cognitive" powers of labor are crucial), it, in effect, "leases" the means of production to the workers and receives a rent in return. I presume that, for example, a genetic laboratory owned by Merck is surreptitiously "leased out" to the scientific and technological workers who pay their "rent" to Merck management and stockholders by turning over to Merck Inc. the knowledge of the pharmacological powers of substances on certain genetic configurations that they research. Merck can then turn this knowledge into drug patents it can lease out to pharmacological firms throughout the world. "We are witnessing the return of a mercantilist and financial logic that is reminiscent of pre-capitalism."[32]

This is a very different model from that of "productivist" capital that takes charge of each instant of the labor process to efficiently exude the greatest amount of production possible from a given worker. This concern for efficiency—from the smallest movement of a ditch digger to the color of the walls in a corporate headquarters office—is typical of the period of relative surplus value (from the nineteenth century to the 1970s) when capital really subsumed labor. At that time, profit was the dominant form of revenue and it was sharply distinguished from rent. Indeed, from Ricardians to the neoclassical economists, the rentier and the rent-seeker was taken to task as a parasitic tumor on the body of capital. Rentiers were so cancerous to the system that Keynes at one time called for their euthanasia.[33]

However, Marx in his more prescient moments in the third volume of *Capital*, argues Vercellone, saw the "becoming rent of profit": a situation that he noted in the rise of the joint stock company that increasingly distinguished between owning capital and "performing capital" in which the former extracts surplus value "whilst no longer exercising any function in the organization of labor" while the latter "becomes increasingly embodied in the figure of the manager, where the functions of leadership and exploitation of labour take on the false appearance of a wage labourer practicing conceptual and organizational tasks in production."[34] But Marx went beyond Keynes's anathema on the rentiers (the owners of capital) in recognizing that even the performing capitalist's role as manager is bound for extinction once s/he is "confronted with a productive cooperation that is capable of organizing itself

---

[31] Vercellone, "The New Articulation," 2.

[32] Ibid., 2.

[33] John Maynard Keynes, The General Theory of Employment, Interest, and Money (New York and London: Harcourt Brace Jovanovich, 1964).

[34] Vercellone, "The New Articulation," 5.

autonomously from capital."[35] But this productive cooperation fostered by a diffused intellectuality generated by mass education and an increased level of training displaces performing capitalists, increasingly making them superfluous to the production process.

With the estrangement of the performing capitalist from the production process, s/he finds a role as a "middleman" between production and the market. By "capturing" the results of the production process autonomously run by workers, the new capitalist prepares it for the market both legally and through advertising. It is only due to the stranglehold the capitalist "middleman" has on the production process (given the present relations of production, i.e., intellectual property law) that s/he has any claim to revenue from production. This is the reason why income from licensing the use of knowledge that is privatized by patents, copyrights, and trademarks has become so important to contemporary capitalism. For example, Secretary of Commerce Gary Locke claimed in a recent speech that "50 percent of our exports *depend* on some form of intellectual property like software or complex technology."[36]

This situation completely parallels the stranglehold aristocratic landowners had on agricultural production for centuries that the Physiocrats decried when they called for taxing the land (cf. Marx's *Theories of Surplus Value*). The answer to their critique came with the French Revolution and the slide of the guillotine onto the aristocracy's neck. And in the case of knowledge, Vercellone, Hardt, Negri, and Boutang's call for breaking the fetters of archaic relations of production on the forces of production has been heard. Will its answer be long in coming?

Coda

Cognitive labor in the era of cognitive capitalism appears in Vercellone as a crucial element in the "transition"—a theme that has become more and more prominent in Autonomist Marxist writing. Not accidentally, Autonomist Marxists refuse to take a gloomy view of precarity and precarization and all the concomitant changes in the work relation that are often condemned as generators of economic insecurity like flexibilization or casualization. Though recognizing the hardship consequent to the lack of an income, on the one hand, Autonomist Marxists see precarization in more positive terms, insofar as they read it both as the product of a struggle against the regimentation of work—a condition, they argue, to which no one wishes to return. On the other, they interpret it as expression of the fact

---

[35] Ibid., 2.

[36] Gary Locke, "National Export Initiative Remarks," last modified February 4, 2010, http://www.commerce.gov/news/secretary-speeches/2010/02/04/national-exports-initiative-remarks. NB: This statement must be taken with a grain of salt, since only about 5 percent of U.S. exports are in the form of licenses and royalties (i.e., arising from *direct* intellectual property income), not a small matter, but then again, not a major amount. Moreover, U.S. exports that depend on some form of intellectual property (however *this* is defined) like jet aircraft are by no means costless to reproduce even after the design, testing, and manufacturing work for the patented prototype is completed (i.e., the reproduction of intellectual property is not always costless in practice). Undoubtedly, however, revenue from renting intellectual property is an important source of corporate income.

that with the cognitivization of labor, areas of production become, in a way, zones liberated from immediate capitalist supervision and organization ("no management zones"), thereby becoming terrains of autonomy and self-organization.

It is easy to understand why such a theory has been so successful. It not only offers an optimistic view of contemporary life where the exodus from capitalism has already begun, but also a means of self-understanding to the vast population of "knowledge workers"—students, programmers, "creative" designers, architects, artists—who constitute a large segment of the workforce in the metropolitan areas of the world. To them, Autonomist Marxists offer the self-definition of the "cognitariat" as the new subject of capitalist production, the one on whom the "transition" beyond capitalism depends. It is important to restate here that Vercellone's views are now not unique. They have, so to speak, "gone viral" and now in different forms are a central component of most Autonomous Marxist theories.

A Critique of Cognitive Capitalism

> The rule and criterion of Truth is to have made it.
> —Giambattista Vico (1710)

Vercellone and his colleagues are to be praised for their efforts to both reintroduce Marxist analysis and anticapitalist revolution into contemporary political discourse. However, there is much to criticize in their theory of cognitive capitalism from a political and conceptual perspective. In this section, I will present a series of semantic, historical, and Marxist challenges to this theory, in the spirit of convivial dialogue leading to a stronger practice on both counts.

a. Who Knows What? (Semantics)

> Garbage in, garbage out.
> —Anonymous

One of the most important, but confusing aspects of the writing of the adherents of cognitive capitalism is in their use of the terms "knowledge" and "cognitive." Vercellone frequently introduces these notions as arising from a radical critique of the "apologetic vision of the actual mutation entailed by the neoliberal theories of [a] knowledge-based economy." He argues that "the term 'cognitive' emphasizes the changed nature of the capital-labour relation and the forms of property upon which the accumulation of capital depends."[37] This self-description of a concept by one of its creators is weighty evidence in any effort of semantic clarification. By Vercellone's own admission, the chief critique that he moves against the knowledge-based economy theorists is their *apologetic* conclusions. He does not question the

---

[37] Carlo Vercellone, "The Hypothesis of Cognitive Capitalism" (paper presented at the Historical Materialism annual conference, London, November 4–5, 2005), 2.

notion of a knowledge-based economy, even though it waits on the answer to the vexed question: "what is knowledge?" Additionally, the term "cognitive" (instead of "industrial," I presume) is meant to *emphasize* the novel aspects of class struggle in a knowledge-based economy (that pits *living* against *dead* knowledge) as well as the newer forms of appropriation (e.g., licenses, royalties and rents based on copyright and patents instead of ownership of products).

On both counts, the issue is knowledge. The problem is that this problematic notion is not problematized. This lack of reflection on the meaning of "knowledge" is mirrored in the writing of their bourgeois opponents. What, indeed, is knowledge? Both the anticapitalist theorists of cognitive capitalism and the neoliberal theorists of the knowledge-based economy depend upon *the lack of definition of knowledge* that circulates in the sphere of intellectual property law, for the simple reason that this sphere makes it possible to speak of intellectual commodities without referring to knowledge or cognition at all. We can copyright a cookbook titled *Tasty Italian Sauces* whose recipes are perfectly wretched and we can patent a mousetrap that actually traps no mice!—i.e., the form of property that is discussed by anticapitalist and neoliberal theorists I have referred to has nothing *directly* to do with "knowledge" or "cognition." That is why theorists like Vercellone can use these terms so blithely. Otherwise, we would find their texts wrestling with some rather thorny philosophical issues, e.g., is truth a necessary condition of knowledge? What is a true proposition? Is induction a knowledge-producing process? Is any scientific theory ever completely falsified or confirmed? Are mathematical propositions necessarily true? Is scientific knowledge the paradigm of all knowledge; if not, what, if anything, is?

These questions can be sidestepped because what is crucial is the *commodification* of intellectual, computational, mental, digital (choose, for the moment, whatever adjective you wish) labor's products *not* their status as knowledge or cognition. In fact, one can have a whole branch of industry of a "knowledge-based" economy or "cognitive" capitalism that produces propositions that are scientifically designed to be attractively deceptive, i.e., the advertising industry. Consequently, we have to be careful in interpreting theories of either sort, for they do not invoke a reprise of the older battles between ideology and science or between a false, fetishized, capitalist thought and the true proletarian perspective. Neither Vercellone et al. nor World Bank reps like Robert Solow are interested in such Cold War battles. The scene dramatically shifted in the 1990s and the issue of globalized production built on a new communication infrastructure (completed by the internet) has put both anticapitalists and neoliberals on a path to an "end of ideology" in the old sense.

This simple observation that much of this debate is operating under a misnomer, does not completely invalidate the insights of Vercellone et al. There is no doubt that however one measures it, the production of intellectual property commodities and—if one buys into the neologism—"intellectual property-intensive industries" [IPII] are important aspects of contemporary capitalist economy in the United States. It is certainly true that immaterial labor, defined as labor producing immaterial products, seems to be an important way of characterizing the division of labor. They need to be studied and politically assessed.[38] But it puts under some stress Vercellone's vision of the struggle between workers and capital on the cognitive level that he introduces into the irenic fairy tale of the knowledge economy told by Reich, Kurzweil, or the World Bank. For Vercellone sees this new dimension of struggle as including: (a) "the time directly dedicated to the production of high-tech commodities becomes every more insignificant, these commodities should be distributed for free" and (b) "the traditional opposition between dead labour and living labour, inherent to Industrial Capitalism, gives way to a new form of antagonism: that between the dead knowledge of capital and the living knowledge of labour."[39]

The first site of struggle is a bit confused because though propositions in a text or images on a surface can be easily *re*-produced at insignificant cost, the production of the propositions or images might take decades and at not an insignificant cost. So there are two kinds of struggle here. (A) The one we are most familiar with is the battle between record corporations and free downloaders who are dramatically reducing the profits of the companies by appropriating songs, texts, still images, and motion pictures off the net "for free." (B) The second one is that between the workers producing the texts or images who are making claims of their own as to how to produce and how much they will appropriate the value of the intellectual commodity produced and their corporate employer that claims the commodity to be its property and demands its "due" as profit.

These are very different struggles in dealing with intellectual property. A motion picture might take five years to make, involve hundreds of technicians, actors, artists, producers, and directors and cost millions of dollars, but it takes only a couple of minutes to download a film from the net literally for free! Within that five years, there will be struggles "on the set" over the work, how it is done, who gets the money, how much time it takes to do a particular animation, etc., while within that couple of minutes there will be the effort by the film company to electronically harass and threaten the determined "free" downloader. These are different struggles involving different agents—corporations like Sony, "artists," and audiences—allied as well as in conflict with each other.

For sure, however, it is not the case that "the time of labor directly dedicated to the production of high-tech commodities becomes ever more insignificant."[40] After all, the duration and cost of shooting films, an archetypal high-tech commodity product of "immaterial labor," are not insignificant. It still takes between sixty and ninety-six hours to shoot a forty-five minute television action-adventure show while the average "feature film" costs about $100 million.[41] Moreover, it

[38] George Caffentzis, "Immeasurable Value? An Essay on Marx's Legacy," in *Reading Negri*, eds. Pierre Lamarche, Max Rosenkrantz, and David Sherman (Chicago: Open Court, 2011), 101–24.

[39] Vercellone, "The Hypothesis," 10.

[40] Ibid., 10.

[41] Larry Wild, "Film Production," http://www3.northern.edu/wild/th100/flmprod.htm.

is not clear that there is any noticeable tendency for a reduction of either time or cost to insignificance. What is tending to zero is the time and cost of *re-producing* a film or television show. It is this contradiction between the cost of production and the cost of reproduction that poses serious problems for capital, of course—see the declining profits of media corporations—but it also creates conflicts between actors and musicians and their audiences, i.e., between im-material workers and other workers. What applies to film and song making also applies to science, for it is clear that in certain fields the cost of producing new knowledge is dramatically increasing (the need for near speed of light cyclotrons for subatomic physics) even though the cost of reproducing "old knowledge" (in the form of scientific journal articles) is dramatically decreasing.

The second place that Vercellone et al. face a problem, once we realize that the use of "knowledge" is an honorific misnomer in this discourse, is with the struggle between dead and living knowledge. This struggle parallels Marx's old dis-tinction in *Capital* (and in the "Results of the Immediate Process of Production," an unpublished manuscript Marx wrote while drafting *Capital*) between, on the one side, dead, past, passive, barren, objectified labor and living, present, active, creative, subjective labor. These binaries are basic to the metaphorical life of Marxism. Vercellone and others have extended them to the realm of knowledge by contrasting living with dead knowledge. What does this contrast mean? It does not echo Wordsworth's romantic call to an original form of wisdom compared to the dull, lifeless knowledge of books in his poem, "The Tables Turned":

> Books! 'tis a dull and endless strife:
> Come, hear the woodland linnet,
> How sweet his music! on my life,
> There's more of wisdom in it. . . .

But there is an echo of "the tables turned" theme in the account given by Vercellone and other theorists of living knowledge. For just as Marx pointed out in the mid-nineteenth century that the huge agglomerations of capital in the form of machinery, factory buildings, titanic iron ships, locomotives seem to dwarf the workers and make them appear insignificant, it is only the workers who create the value capitalists ultimately desire, so too a similar turning of the tables occurs on the plane of knowledge in the early twenty-first century.

The "intelligent" machines of the contemporary economy—the computer-communication-information net, the laboratories, the film production studios, the automated factories—that seem to be displacing human intelligence are, ac-cording to Vercellone and others, similarly dead capital and in order for them to be part of a process that can create value for capital they must be coupled with the living knowledge of cognitive workers; i.e., the net, the studios, the factories, and the laboratories are all crystallizations of dead, objectified knowledge and they await the vivifying, subjective action of a worker's living knowledge. The worker, as Marx himself put it, is the one "in whose brain exists the accumulated knowledge of society."[42] Though it looks like the machines are eliminating the humans in this period of capitalism (as envisioned in many a science fiction novel and film), a new "humanism" arises from these antihumanist Marxists claiming the renewed indispensable importance of knowledge embodied in humans.

My critique of this position is complex because there is an element in it that I agree with and have defended in many different venues, viz., that machines—whether simple machines, heat engines or Turing machines—cannot produce value.[43] I, like Vercellone and the other cognitive capitalist theorists, affirm the importance of living human labor in the creation of value. My points of criticism, however, are threefold:

(1) The living labor that is being exploited in Intellectual Property-Intensive Industries (IPIIs) is not necessarily either knowledge or productive of knowledge. What is crucial is that it can create exchange-value, irrespective of its epistemic value; so, for example, a commodity to have a value must "satisfy human needs of whatever kind. The nature of these needs, whether they arise, for example, from the stomach, or the imagination, makes no difference."[44] There is so much fraud, fallacy and fancy in this area of production (think of the work of derivative dealers!) that to call the labor-power in action there "knowledge work" or "living knowledge" is to stretch the semantic tolerance of even a postmodern cultural theorist! But once I get past my verbal squeamishness, I completely agree with Vercellone, Hardt, and Negri that capitalism still needs to transform labor-power (including the powers to know, to imagine, to create) into labor in order to create value that it can later "capture."

(2) The claim that living knowledge creates value, but (unlike the living labor of the past) it is measureless and uncontrollable is problematic, because the process of creating propositions, objects, ideas, and forms and other so-called "immaterial" products that could be transformed into intellectual property is a process in time that can be (*and is*) measured. Although the techniques used to control labor-time and to impose speed-ups differ from the assembly lines, workers in IPIIs are routinely given task-specific contracts with temporal deadlines. There is now a growing literature on the issue of the measurement and management of what Vercellone calls "living knowledge" in many different fields and the empirical results.[45] We should remember two things concerning this immeasurability claim, one general (A) and the other specific to the measurement of work (B):

(A) Claims of immeasurability are often simply a product of the limits of the tools and/or concepts of measurement. What can't be measured in time t does not

---

[42] Quoted in Vercellone, "From Formal Subsumption," 31.

[43] E.g., "Why Machines Cannot Create Value," 139 in this volume.

[44] Marx, *Capital I*, 125.

[45] See Massimo De Angelis and David Harvie, "Cognitive Capitalism and the Rat Race: How Capital Measures Immaterial Labour in British Universities," *Historical Materialism* 17, no. 3 (2009): 3–30.

mean that it cannot be measured at time $t+1$. This should be clear in the main measuring discipline, mathematics:

> one can look at the development of the notion of number as the continual confrontation with the "immeasurable" that is then integrated into a enlarged domain of number. The vocabulary of mathematics is littered with terms like "*imaginary* number," "*complex* number," "*transcendental* number," "a cardinal number of an *uncountable* set" that are semantic fossils of this transformation of the immeasurable into measurable.[46]

The most dramatic conversion of the immeasurable into the measured was in transfinite set theory in the late nineteenth century, when even infinity, the paradigm case of the immeasurable, was shown to have a measure and number (i.e., a cardinality).

(B) Consequently, when the cognitive capitalism theorists claim that in a society where cooperation, interactivity, and autonomy are primary features of the work process, it is not possible for the value created by labor to be "measured on the basis of labour time directly dedicated to production,"[47] I can only reply that this has been a characteristic of all sorts of commodities—material or immaterial, high-tech and low-tech, from ones that Dr. Johnson can kick to Berkeleyan ones that exist only when they are perceived—since the beginning of capitalism. As Marx pointed out, and as has been repeated in a thousand Marxism 101 courses, clock-time and labor-time are by no means the same. The value of a commodity is dependent on "the socially necessary labor-time [that] is the labour-time required to produce any use-value under the conditions of production normal for a given society and with the average degree of skill and intensity of labor prevalent in that society."[48] Socially necessary labor-time (SNLT) is not determined by the clock-time of labor directly employed in production. It is affected in a thousand different ways that cannot be measured "locally." For example, the value of the fabric produced by the English hand-loom weaver, once power looms were introduced, was cut by one half. So why should it be surprising that the clock-time of production has a tangential relation to the labor-time value of a commodity (which includes, e.g., the fact that the distinction between the work-day and the rest seems to be unwavering). The mechanisms for determining value through SNLT might appear useless by Hardt and Negri, but they are still operative in the actual functioning of capitalist production from Google to the sweatshops.

(3) The amount of reproductive labor that goes into the production of labor-power (from a mother's nursing to graduate seminars in postcolonial theory) can account for the value of the labor-power in the industries that have a high

---

[46] Caffentzis, "Immeasurable Value?," 115, emphasis added.

[47] Vercellone, "From Formal Subsumption," 30.

[48] Marx, *Capital: Volume I*, 129.

capital-to-labor ratio.[49] Indeed, there is a struggle as to who will bear the costs of that reproductive labor and suffer the consequences of the autonomy and insubordination it implies. As Ure said of the skilled workmen of the manufacturing period: "By the infirmity of human nature it happens the more skillful the workman, the more self-willed and intractable he is apt to become, and of course the less fit a component of a mechanical system in which . . . he may do great damage to the whole."[50] This increased training of the contemporary worker (the "diffuse intellectuality" of those in the IPIIs, as Vercellone would phrase it) adds additional value to the average labor-time, similar to the constant capital transferred to the product. Just as the skilled workmen in the period of manufactures, here too one finds the autonomy ("self-willed and intractable") of the contemporary worker in IPIIs . . . as well as his/her vulnerability.

b. "If We're So Smart, Why Aren't We Free?" (History)

A surprising feature of Vercellone's and other cognitive capitalism theorists' perspective has been its "back to the future" character. It presents a vision antithetical to the *Matrix* image of a world controlled by machines with the human worker "step[ping] to the side of the production process instead of being its chief actor" and playing the role of "watchman and regulator to the production process."[51] In the theory of cognitive capitalism, cognitive workers' living knowledge is still essential to the production of wealth while the capitalists, since the 1970s mass worker revolts, have been literally chased out of their role as supervisors of production in the knowledge-based industrial sectors. We have reached the stage that Marx discussed in *Capital* III where:

> Capitalist production has itself brought it about that the work of supervision is readily available, quite independent of the ownership of capital,. It has therefore become superfluous for this work of supervision to be performed by the capitalist. . . . Co-operative factories provide the proof that the capitalist has become just as superfluous as a functionary in production as he himself, from his superior vantage-point, finds the large landowner.[52]

Vercellone then notes an ingenious historical parallel between the contemporary forms of production and the putting-out system (or domestic industry, or cottage industry, or the *Verlagssystem*) of the sixteenth through eighteenth centuries. The key similarity is the autonomy of the workers from their bosses in both periods. Moreover, one can find further parallels in the erasure of the divisions of work/

---

[49] Here I am *not* referring to "affective labor"; see Silvia Federici's *Revolution at Point Zero* (Oakland: PM Press/Common Notions, 2012).

[50] Quoted in Marx, *Capital: Volume I*, 490.

[51] Marx, *Grundrisse*, 705.

[52] Marx, *Capital: Volume III*, 511.

nonwork and production/reproduction, since in the putting-out system the work is done at home (hence terms like "cottage" and "domestic" are used to describe it as well).

But if there is indeed a parallelism between these two forms of production, a careful examination of the catastrophe of the domestic-industry workers will be especially important for their contemporary equivalents. Let us examine, then, this parallel in some more detail to note a fatal problem for workers inscribed in the history of the putting-out system and, perhaps, for the contemporary cognitariat.

The putting-out system is so called because the merchant "puts out" to the worker (or, more correctly, to his family) the raw materials to be worked, he often leases out to the worker the machines to be used in the production process as well. He would then come to pick up the finished goods and pay the cottager for the "pieces" he, actually his family, produced (after docking him for the wasted raw materials or damage to the leased machines and tools owned by the putter-out). Though his ownership of the raw materials and tools/machines projected the merchant capitalist into the process of production, he did not supervise it. As Peter Kriedte put it, "When [the merchant] advanced credit for the acquisition of raw materials and/or provided raw materials, in some cases even the tools . . . the merchant thus intruded into the production sphere without, however, taking full control of it. The *Verleger* assumed control of the product; the small producer, on the other hand, kept control of the work process."[53] The delicate balance between control of the product and control of the work process completely unraveled when "the instruments of production became the property of the putter-out as well. In this case, capital dominated the sphere of production almost completely. The direct producers no longer manufactured commodities that they sold as their property; they merely sold their labour power for piece-wages (which included the upkeep of the workshops which were also their homes)."[54]

Thus, the image that Vercellone paints of the parallelism between contemporary cognitive workers and the protoindustrial cottage-industry workers of the sixteenth to eighteenth centuries should be taken either as a grain of salt or as a seed of truth. Vercellone sees in the old putting-out system a place where the direct producers were autonomous from the capitalist and need only meet him at the end of the labor process, i.e., at the point of "capture." However, the historical accounts of the putting-out system show the merchant capitalist deeply involved in the planning and organizing of the work process. At times, he was so involved that the so-called legally autonomous worker virtually became a piece-worker with, at best, "the semblance of power over the instruments of production."[55] The

[53] Peter Kriedte, *Peasants, Landlords and Merchant Capitalists: Europe and the World Economy 1500–1800* (Cambridge: Cambridge University Press, 1983), 138.

[54] Jürgen Schlumbohm, "Relations of Production—Productive Forces—Crises," in *Industrialization before Industrialization: Rural Industry in the Genesis of Capitalism*, ed. Peter Kriedte, Hans Medick, and Jürgen Schlumbohm (Cambridge: Cambridge University Press, 1981), 102.

[55] Ibid., 103.

connection was so close that Marx, in fact, identified piece wages as the "basis for modern 'domestic labor.'"[56]

This tendency of piece-wages to organize payment in the putting-out system is very important, especially if we run Vercellone's parallel in the other way and see the contemporary cognitariat as the domestic industry laborers of our time. For piece wages are, of course, an obscured and fetishized form of time-wages, but they also have a number of very important characteristics that Marx noted long ago, as if seeing in a vision the twenty-first century's cognitariat's plight.

First, "since the quality and intensity of the work are here controlled by the very form of the wage, superintendence of labour becomes to a great extent superfluous."[57] This describes the famous "autonomy" of the knowledge worker, who because s/he is not working by the clock can work "at his/her pace." But, of course, this pace is ultimately constrained by the demands of the piece-work schedule (whether it be the fifty phone calls to make from home in the evening or the six "ideas" to create while "vacationing"). Consequently, the capitalists save superintendence costs via the action at a distance that the piecework wage system provides ... a bitter autonomy indeed.

Second, piece-wages "form the basis ... for a hierarchically organized system of exploitation and oppression.'"[58] In this passage, Marx describes the cooperative work that is so touted by the theorists of cognitive capitalism in a somewhat different light. He argues that the piece-wage system gives rise to what we call subcontracting and what in his time was called "subletting of labor." This form of labor is standard in the world of the computer programmers, artists and designers, "social entrepreneurs," etc. In a way, domestic industry involves a capitalist subletting of labor, with the artisan's and his family's hands as the items to be sublet. But in the nineteenth century, sometimes these "middlemen" subletters were capitalists who organized the subcontracting and got their profits from "the difference between the price of labour which the capitalist pays, and the part of that price they actually allow the worker to receive"; this was appropriately enough called the "sweating system."[59] Sometimes capitalists hire "important workers .. . at a price for which this man himself undertakes the enlisting and payment of his assistants." The result here, however, is that "the exploitation of the worker by capital takes place through the medium of the exploitation of one worker by another."[60] In both cases, of course, the middleman and the "important worker" mediator must generate a level of cooperation that could guarantee a profit for them and their ultimate boss.

Third, the twenty-first century cognitariat's ideology or "subjectivity" that is generated by piecework is similar to the one that was found among the piece

---

[56] Marx, *Capital: Volume I*, 695.

[57] Ibid.

[58] Ibid.

[59] Ibid.

[60] Ibid.

workers of the past (including those in domestic industry). Marx connected the latter's subjectivity with the form of the wage: "But the wider scope that piece-wages give to individuality, and with it the worker's sense of liberty, independence and self-control, and also the competition of workers with each other."[61] This sense of "autonomy" that is touted as being basic to the cognitariat can also be expressed as a divisive individualism and competitiveness that is a well-known aspect of the "subjectivities" created in the IPIIs.

These parallels between the putting-out system workers and the so-call cognitariat brings us to ask: how did the struggle between worker and capital in the putting-out system proceed and how were the workers defeated and transformed into wage workers in the factories of the nineteenth and twentieth centuries? Historians of the *Verlagssystem* analyze the struggle between merchant capitalists and the direct producers on at least two levels: (1) over the materials (and sometimes the tools) that are worked on, (2) the withdrawal of labor in the boom periods, i.e., the infamous "backward bending labor supply curve."

Level (1) was a perennial issue in the putting-out system, for the *Verleger*, as the putter-out was called in German, had to "protect himself against the fraudulent use of the raw materials he was distributing to the families which were part of his network."[62] Whenever wages in the class relationship are paid before work is completed or constant capital is entrusted into the hands of the unpoliced workers, a chronic guerilla war frequently follows over the work paid for or the fate of the constant capital. The *Verleger*'s need to keep a constant surveillance over the materials put out put an inevitable limit as to the number of "cottages" he could employ. This limit was especially problematic, of course, during the boom part of the cycle. The different strategies employed by the *Verleger* and the often rural domestic industry workers are part of the wider struggle in the European countryside that took place in the period of the sixteenth through eighteenth centuries under the rubric of "protoindustrialization," including the struggle against enclosure.[63]

Level (2) was an even greater arena of struggle, since it expressed a basic clash of values and put a stranglehold on the expansion of capitalism in Europe. The *Verleger* was driven by the capitalist ethos (or even religion) to "accumulate, accumulate," while the families involved the domestic industries throughout Europe were still committed to a subsistence form of life, where the artisan work was a supplement to other forms of rural labor.[64] This clash of values was most clearly seen during the "boom" portion of the proto-industrial business cycle. As Kriedte writes: "the proto-industrial family had a propensity to reduce its output precisely in periods of boom; this was because as the return per unit

---

[61] Marx, *Capital: Volume I*, 697.

[62] Kriedte, *Peasants*, 142.

[63] See Herbert Kisch, *From Domestic Manufacture to Industrial Revolution: The Case of the Rhineland Textile Districts* (New York: Oxford University Press, 1989).

[64] Fernand Braudel, *The Wheels of Commerce* (New York: Harper & Row, 1982), 304–6.

rose, its subsistence needs could be satisfied with a smaller labour effort."[65] This sort of behavior has often been described in the economics literature by "the backward-bending supply of labor" curve [BBSLC], i.e., this curve describes a situation where there comes a point when an increase in wages leads to a reduction in the hours worked. This "paradoxical" behavior was conditional, of course, on the extent of capital's penetration in the sphere of production and whether it had "subjected the labourers to its interests by way of suppression or consumer incentives."[66] So, for example, if domestic workers had less and less access to land (common or freehold) for subsistence purposes, they were more dependent on the vagaries of the economic cycle and hence less able to cut back on the labor offered by the *Verleger*.

Indeed, the BBSLC was a fundamental constraint on capitalist development in Europe that was broken by both the "blood and fire" of primitive accumulation (which reduced the land available for subsistence agriculture) and the rise of the factory system that both increased the centralization of the workers and allowed for the technological transformation of production. The leader in responding to the resistance to the putting-out system (and to the power for the artisans in the manufacturing centers) was the textile industry in Britain beginning in the last half of the eighteenth century.[67] What in effect, happened was the substitution of new and expensive machinery for the traditional equipment, the centralization of workers in the urban factories and the use of slave labor in Brazil, the Caribbean and the American South for the cotton inputs to production. Eric Hobsbawm wrote of this development, "The most modern centre of production thus preserved and extended the most primitive form of exploitation."[68] Although it was barbaric, the form of capitalist slavery that marked the Atlantic slave trade was no more "primitive" than the technologically refined Nazi death camps.

In conclusion, we should apply our excursus on the putting-out system to our meditation on the fate of the cognitariat of the beginning twenty-first century. For if Vercellone's parallel between the cognitariat and the workers of the putting-out system is more a seed of truth than a grain of salt, then we should prepare for a similar outcome for a set of workers who claim that they cannot be replaced and that the value of their work is immeasurable. If the experience of the domestic industry workers of the past is any guide, one should then expect (in the words of cognitive capitalism theorists) a counterattack on a number of sides: (a) an internationalization of the sources of "living knowledge," (b) the substitution of machinery (dead knowledge) for the workers' "living knowledge," (c) the creation of new techniques of centralization of cognitive workers, (d) the development of new systems of measurement of cognitive labor, (e) the development of new methods of payment.

---

[65] Kriedte, *Peasants*, 142.

[66] Schlumbohm, "Relations of Production," 100.

[67] Kriedte, *Peasants*, 142–45.

[68] Quoted in Kriedte, *Peasants*, 145.

It does not take too much imagination to see this scenario being played in the present crisis. For example, the "knowledge workers" in education (actual or perspective) in Europe and North America are facing unprecedented cut-backs and deficits, lay-offs of faculty and staff, etc. from kindergartens to graduate schools and are being told that they and their children must face competition from workers internationally who now are operating on the same cognitive level as they are. That is, "knowledge work," cognitive labor, etc. is becoming normalized, measurable (since only then can there be competition!) and put under direct capitalist control. Is that impossible? That is the cry of all skilled workers throughout the history of capitalism: "They can't take my job from me; my contribution is immeasurable; I know too much!" However, skilled worker self-confidence has failed time and again as a defense against restructuring, replacement and displacement. I fear that the optimism of the theory of cognitive capitalism, however, does not prepare us for such a challenge.

c. The Becoming Profit, Rent, and Interest of Surplus Value or the Becoming Rent of Profit? (Marxology)

> We thus have a mathematically exact demonstration of why the capitalists, no matter how little love is lost among them in their mutual competition are nevertheless united by a real freemasonry vis-à-vis the working class as a whole.
> —Karl Marx[69]

An important claim of the cognitive capitalism theorists is that with the rise of cognitive capitalism, there has been a major categorical change in the revenues that Marx analyzed—profit, interest, rent, and wages. The category of profit, especially, is merging into that of rent. Indeed, these theorists claim that Marx had some premonition of such changes, especially in two texts he never finished, *Capital* III and *Grundrisse*. The key evidence they use is the presumably changing role that the capitalists play vis-à-vis the production process. One of their central tenets being that capitalists no longer plan, organize, and directly supervise production in the way that they did in the period of real subsumption. Consequently, if profit is the revenue earned by bosses when they do what bosses should be doing (i.e., finding new ways to exploit workers, intensify work, by-pass workers' refusal of work and, in general, increasing the length, intensity and/or productivity of work), then the importance and integrity of the category of profit is bound to be diminishing.

But even if this were the case—and there is much evidence to question this claim for most the branches of industry, including the knowledge-producing sector—this thesis would not fare well in the light of Marx's theory. Marx himself made a sharp differentiation between "the profit of enterprise" and the

---

[69] Marx, *Capital: Volume III*, 300.

"wages of supervision," and the former was not dependent on the latter.[70] The profit of enterprise is not "locally produced," it is a "field" variable that is the result of a transformation process taking the collectively generated surplus value throughout the system (something of a capitalist common) and redistributing it according to a specific rule of return: if c is the constant capital, v is the variable in a branch of industry and R is the average rate of profit across all industries, then the profit would (c+v)R, with the proviso that there was free movement of capital and labor. Or, in Marx's words, "In a capitalist society, this surplus value or surplus product is divided among the capitalists as dividends in proportion to the quota of social capital that belongs to each."[71]

Consequently, there is no correlation between the cleverness, self-discipline, charisma or brutality of the individual boss and the rate of profit of his/her firm or industry. Some capitalists might be exploiting the hell out of their workers, say in a branch of industry the exploitation rate is 100 percent, but if their firms are in a low organic composition industry (roughly, the ratio between machines and labor-power employed in the production process), they must "share" the surplus value created in their industry with the capitalists in industries at the high organic composition end of the system of production whose actual exploitation rate is 10 percent! The key is the amount of capital (constant and variable) employed in the production process. This is capitalist justice: capital itself must get its due, even if individual capitalists, especially the "hard working" ones operating at the lower end of the system and squeezing the most surplus value out of their workers in the face of the greatest resistance, are rewarded by being allowed to keep only a miniscule amount of surplus labor they extracted.

This surplus value transformation process is the material basis of the existence of a single capitalist class. That is what Marx meant in his reference to capitalists' "freemason society" in the epigraph to this section, i.e., a secret society that creates solidarity among members behind the backs of those who see them as competitors in "the religion of everyday life."[72] Marx expressed this solidarity as: "a capitalist who employed no variable capital at all in his sphere of production, hence not a single worker (in fact an exaggerated assumption), would have just as much interest in the exploitation of the working class by capital and would just as much derive his profit from unpaid surplus labour as would a capitalist who employed only variable capital (again an exaggerated assumption) and therefore laid out is entire capital on wages."[73] Thus, a crucial aspect of the category of profit has nothing directly to do with the behavior of the capitalist with respect to the production process; whether capitalists resembled either absconding gods who pay managers to do the dirty work or crucified ones suffering in the bowels of the firm for their salvation is ultimately irrelevant to the

---

[70] Ibid., 503–4.

[71] Ibid., 959.

[72] Ibid., 969.

[73] Ibid., 299.

functioning of the flow of surplus value into the form of profit. Consequently, cognitive capitalism theorists' argument concerning the withdrawal of capitalists from the production process does not quite reach its conclusion unless the very transformation process by which capitalism becomes itself is jettisoned.

The fact that profit of a firm is not determined simply by what goes on in the firm applies in different ways to the other forms of revenue Marx reviewed in the "Trinity Formula."[74] Marx was anxious to escape from the pathos of a "factors of production" approach to revenues positing a one-to-one relationship between a revenue category (profit, interest, rent, wage) and its separate sources. He refused to allow that each category of revenue is "justified" to receive "its share" of the value of commodities and is scathing in his contempt for this piece of "vulgar economics actually does nothing more than interpret, systematize and turn into apologetics of the agents trapped within bourgeois relations of production."[75] For in reality, no one was justified in receiving their revenues according to the tale they tell about their "contribution" to the value creation.

Marx's perspective on the categories of revenue combines objective metabolic transformation of surplus value and subjective confusion and illusion, i.e., everything happens behind everyone's back; what is private becoming common and vice versa. Thus the "trinity formula," capital—profit/interest, land—rent, labor—wages, systematically fetishizes capital, land and labor as the sources of the revenues interest, rent, and wages, respectively. But how can capital (in the form of money, machines, or raw material) expand itself to earn a profit or pay interest thus making, as Marx derides, 4 equal 5? How can land, which has use-value but no exchange-value produce *ex nihilo* an exchange-value, rent? How can "a social relation, conceived as a thing, [be] placed in a relationship of proportion with nature"?[76] Finally, how can labor, which creates value, have a price? Isn't the term "the price of labor" "as irrational as a yellow logarithm"?[77] In the face of these absurdities, Marx proposes another "source" for these revenues: value creating living labor in a vast common pool that appears in another mode as an equally vast mountain of commodities, bodies, money, and machines.

The problem with the cognitive capitalist theorists is that they attribute the sources of revenues like profit and rent to the behavior of profit-making capitalists and to rentiers. Their argument seems to be: if capitalists begin to behave as rentiers, their revenue will stop being profit and begin to become rent. But this behavior *qua* profit-making capitalist or *qua* rentier was not the source of the value appearing as profit and rent, consequently these changes (whatever their empirical status) are logically disconnected with the behavior of the revenues. Cognitive

---

[74] Ibid., 953–70.

[75] Ibid., 956.

[76] Ibid.

[77] Ibid., 957.

capitalism theorists like Vercellone and Boutang do not take into account the relationship between the lowest and highest organic composition poles of the system and the transfer of surplus value from lower to higher branches for the latter to be able to achieve at least an average rate of profit.

This appears to be a "mathematical" constraint, but, on the contrary, it is based on the vagaries of class relations: the only way to resist the falling rate of profit throughout the system is to continue to introduce industries with low organic composition to offset the growing organic composition of the industries that are usually associated with knowledge sector. But where are these industries to come from? They arise in areas where there is relative overpopulation that makes labor-power cheap, since there is an "a quantity of available or dismissed wage-labourers."[78] In these regions, low organic composition industries can start up and make it possible to transfer created there to the high organic composition industries and also produce a countertendency to the falling rate of profit. This is exactly the story of the industrialization of China in the context of the increasing organic composition of production associated with IPIIs in the United States and Western Europe. The increasing power of Chinese factory workers will have epochal consequences for the profits of capitalists around the planet, independent of whether they have invested in Chinese firms or not.

Conclusion: Searching for a Synoptic View of Global Struggles

> Let us imagine, with your permission, a little worm, living in the blood, able to distinguish by sight the particles of blood, lymph, &c., and to reflect on the manner in which each particle, on meeting with another particle, either is repulsed, or communicates a portion of its own motion. . . . He would be unable to determine, how all the parts are modified by the general nature of blood, and are compelled by it to adapt themselves, so as to stand in a fixed relation to one another.
> —Spinoza to Oldenburg (1665–66)[79]

The cognitive capitalism theorists' work has brought a welcome excitement to the study of contemporary capitalism. Their approach is certainly unconventional and filled with categorical topsy-turvies where apparent victory becomes real defeat and apparent weakness becomes real strength. For example, what conventional Marxist wisdom racks up as a defeat—deindustrialization and globalization—has, in cognitive capitalism theorists' eyes, been a victory for the proletariat in Europe and United States (since their struggles have, in effect, driven capitalists out of the production process). Moreover, capitalism in its

---

[78] Ibid., 343.

[79] Benedict de Spinoza, *On the Improvement of the Understanding, the Ethics, Correspondence* (New York: Dover, 1955), 291.

cognitive stage is extremely vulnerable, since workers now are using their powers of cooperation and self-determination in the very process of applying their living knowledge on the job, while—shades of Hegel's master/slave dialectic—capitalists are reduced to the role of "middlemen," no longer in touch with the production process. By arguing that capital suffers from a deep weakness, and that the cognitariat possesses an even deeper strength, the cognitive capitalist theorists aim to revive the revolutionary élan of the age.

Far be it from me to hinder a path to revolutionary enthusiasm and joy, for no great transformation can take place without them. But I agree with Spinoza in the importance of adequate ideas whose presence or absence differentiates between joy from pride. The characteristic measure of such a conceptual adequacy is the synoptic breadth of the analysis, so that we are not stuck with the "worm in the blood's" limited vision of the human (or social) body (as in this section's epigraph). It is in its lack of a synoptic comprehension that I find the theory of cognitive capitalism most deficient.

The cognitive capitalism theorists' focused scrutiny of the struggles in the knowledge-based sector inevitably makes it possible for them to neglect the class struggle taking place in the huge area of agriculture (especially in the struggles against land displacement) and in factory production worldwide. Just because factory and agricultural production now account for only a quarter of employment in the U.S. does not discount the fact that factory and agricultural production constitute nearly two thirds of global employment, and that is based on ILO statistics that emphasize waged employment. Therefore, the most vital questions concerning the contradictory political impulses arising from the complex composition of the contemporary proletariat of our time are not addressed. This is especially problematic because there seems to be an assumption that workers that are at the highest spheres of capitalist productivity are the most revolutionary.

Silvia Federici and I have previously noted that this assumption is false.[80] In the period of industrial work, it was not the industrial workers who made the revolutions: "Ironically, under the regime of industrial capitalism and factory work, it was the peasant movements of Mexico, China, Vietnam, and to a great extent Russia who made the revolutions of the 20th century. In the 1960s as well, the impetus for change at the global level came from the anti-colonial struggle, including the struggle against apartheid and for Black Power in the U.S."[81] Similar ironies seem to be playing out in this period of cognitive capitalism when "it is the indigenous people, the *campesinos*, the unemployed of Mexico (Chiapas, Oaxaca), Bolivia, Ecuador, Brazil, Venezuela, the farmers of India, the *maquila* workers of the U.S. border, the immigrant workers of the United States, etc. who are conducting the most "advanced" struggles

---

[80] Silvia Federici and George Caffentzis, "Notes on the Edu-factory and Cognitive Capitalism," in *Toward a Global Autonomous University*, ed. Edu-factory Collective (Brooklyn: Autonomedia, 2009).

[81] Ibid., 128–29.

against the global extension of capitalist relation."[82] Indeed, it appears that we are facing a twenty-first-century version of the question, will "the hammer" (in the form of the silicon chip and fiber optic cable) and its bearers once again dominate "the sickle"?[83]

A synoptic theory that can bring together the poles of organic composition and class composition and escape the worm in the blood's dilemma will become the source of the adequate ideas for revolutionary transition from capitalism in the twenty-first century. The theorists of cognitive capitalism have only accomplished part of the job of constructing this theory, and for that we must thank them. The whole, however, remains undone.

---

[82] Ibid., 129.
[83] Midnight Notes Collective, "The Hammer and . . ."

II
MACHINES

ON AFRICA AND SELF-REPRODUCING AUTOMATA

In the same way we may say that the imperialist states would make a great mistake and commit an unspeakable injustice if they contented themselves with withdrawing from our soil the military cohorts, and the administrative and managerial whose services function it was to discover the wealth of our country, to extract it and to send it off to the mother countries. We are not blinded by the moral reparation of national independence; nor are we fed by it. The wealth of the imperial countries is our wealth too.
—Frantz Fanon, *The Wretched of the Earth*[1]

The basic principle of dealing with malfunctions in nature is to make their effect as unimportant as possible and to apply correctives, if they are necessary at all, at leisure. In dealing with artificial automata on the other hand, we require immediate diagnosis. . . . The rationale of this difference is not far to seek. Natural organisms are sufficiently well conceived to be able to operate even when malfunctions have set in. . . . Any malfunction, however, represents a considerable risk that some generally degenerating process has already set in within the machine. It is, therefore, necessary to intervene immediately, because a machine which has begun to malfunction has only rarely a tendency to restore itself, and will probably go from bad to worse.
—John von Neumann, "The General and Logical Theory of Automata"[2]

The following notes begins with a precise, but apparently theoretic or ideal, consideration: the proper Marxist characterization of self-reproducing automata (i.e., machines that reproduce themselves without labor input) before they actually have come into existence. This consideration, however, has politico-economic consequences which are immediately relevant to class struggle in general and to Africa in particular.

The factory system was capital's response to the stranglehold workers' skill as well as their control and appropriation of constant capital ("customary usages") had on Manufacture and Domestic Industry. But the factory system (the concrete

---

[1] Frantz Fanon, *Wretched of the Earth* (New York: Grove Press, 1963), 102.

[2] John von Neumann, "The General and Logical Theory of Automata" in *The World of Mathematics*, ed. James Newman (New York: Simon and Schuster, 1956), 2086.

essence of Modern Industry) itself was in turn held up by the power of the manufacturing workers who built the basic machines (steam engines, self-acting mules, etc.) of that system. Only when machines constructed machines, i.e., when the elements of the factory were themselves the products of factories, could the whole system self-reflexively achieve the relative autonomy from workers' antagonism it was designed for.

Automata are complex machines (heat-engines linked to an integrated array of "simple" machines) whose logical and computational operations are themselves mechanized. Thus an automata system (or subsystem) is a factory system (or subsystem) without the "supervisory attendance" of human workers. In response to factory system operatives' struggles in the post–World War II period, capital introduced automata systems and subsystems in assembly line and continuous-process plants. This strategy has been generalized and automata systems have been widely integrated in the circulatory and social accounting circuits of capital. Spot-welding robots, computerized billing, and genetically engineered cells excreting valuable chemicals are all widely recognized elements of automata systems or subsystems.

But automata are largely designed and built by skilled mental and manufacturing workers, as well as factory operatives who constitute a new antagonistic stranglehold and technical limit on production of and with automata systems. From the desperate strikes of Filipino women in computer-chip factories to computer programmers designing and releasing computational viruses "for the fun of it," the shadow of the "strife between workmen and machine" still disturbs capital's dream of workerless and struggle-less production. The logical escape from these strangleholds and limits is through self-reflexivity. Only when automata create automata, i.e., when the elements of automata systems become products of automata systems, can "post-modem industry" find its fitting foundation. The ideal type of such automata-creating automata is the self-reproducing automaton (SRA).

Machines have been traditionally defined as "aids to labor," and as a consequence, the product of a worker-machine unit is of necessity less complex than the producing unit itself. For a worker-machine unit could, at best, produce another machine but not another worker. Given the contradictory volatility of workers, capitalist thinkers have always been intrigued by the possibility of creating machines that did not require direct human intervention in their operations, i.e., automata.

But the early machines were not complete automata because an enormous amount of skilled labor went into their production, while their repair and "regeneration" required further labor. Was it possible to create a total automaton, i.e., one that would—after the first unit—produce itself out of pure "raw materials," as well as repair and regenerate itself, all without human labor inputs? Let us call such total automata "self-reproducing automata" (SRA).

This new ideal of a machine had von Neumann as one of its primitive conceptualizers in the early post–World War II era. No immediate, widely known model of such automata was available to him, such as the cuckoo clocks and other mechanical "toys" that were the inspiration of so much early capitalist thought. However, as he was working on the mathematical and engineering problems attendant to the production of nuclear weapons, he materially coaxed and theorized the construction of some of the first operational electronic computers. The computers appeared to him as prototypes of SRA for two reasons. First, it was possible to envisage and mathematically describe a computer (called "a universal Turing machine") that literally could "re-create" the operation of any arbitrary computer (including itself). Second, it was even then possible to design computers that would be self-correcting, i.e., capable of diagnosing their own errors and malfunctions and repairing them (within limits).

Von Neumann argued that SRA required four components: (1) raw material, which he called "cells"; (2) a program of instructions; (3) a "factory" that arranges the "cells" according to the program with the proviso that the program is copied in the product itself; (4) a "supervisor" that might receive new "instructions" from the "outside," copy them and transmit them to the "factory." Although at the time of their conceptualization these SRA appeared as "science fiction," the last generation has seen a tendency in capital to approach this ideal in a number of different production environments. Increasingly, computers are used to produce computers, diagnose their errors and repair themselves in assembly lines, satellites, and missiles, as well as in "artificially intelligent" robots. Thus the automatization of automation has taken an enormous leap forward. Further, when we consider the petroleum-internal combustion energy cycle (e.g., the increasing automatization of the drilling, transporting, and refining of petroleum) as well as the uranium electricity cycle (e.g., in the recycling of plutonium) we see the increasing automatization extending its tendrils into the "raw materials" stage.

Von Neumann described the process of self-reproduction in the following words: "There is no great difficulty in giving a complete axiomatic account of how to describe any conceivable automaton in a binary code. Any such description can then be represented by a chain of rigid elements [a program]. . . .Given any automaton X, let f(X) designate the chain which represents X. Once you have done this, you can design a universal machine tool A which, when furnished with such a chain f(X), will take it and gradually consume it at the same time building up the automaton X from the parts floating around freely in the surrounding milieu. All this design is laborious, but it is not difficult in principle, for it is a succession of steps in formal logic. It is not qualitatively different from the type of argumentation with which Turing constructed his universal automaton." Once one has machine tool A, self-reproduction is an easy next step. For A must have its description, f(A), and f(A) can be fed into A and another A will be produced . . . without paradox, contradiction, or circularity.

Perhaps the most profound exemplar of von Neumann's SRA model is in "genetic engineering." Here, all the elements of the SRA are immediately available. Indeed, the merging of automata studies with biogenetic research points to the possible practical total realization of SRA. For the very mechanism of the genetic process (that according to von Neumann, produces "natural" automata) can itself be mechanized to create specially designed products that replicate themselves.

Thus the SRA is slowly making its way from the "heaven" of the capitalist imagination to the "hell" of the production process. For they seem to fulfill capital's dream of a perpetual motion machine: production sans workers and therefore profits without the class struggle. But whose nightmare is this dream?

Dreams and nightmares, apocalypses and utopias, they are the poles of a spectrum of social possibility . . . but whose possibility? Capital, by identifying wealth with value, restricts the logical field of social intercourse to work and its management. From psalm singing in its heaven to furnace stoking in its hell . . . labor is all it can imagine. Indeed, imagination is labor for it. Are SRA the long awaited evolutionary leap to a labor-less Cockagne or the seventh seal of a millennium of work for work's sake?

At first sight, the SRA is a worker's nightmare, for its immediate impact is the excision of the power of refusal in the production process, given that SRA continue to be capitalistically controlled means of production. How can you strike against a "factory" that you never stepped foot in and against an employer that employs no one? Thus an SRA industry would appear to have managed a perfect "lock-out."

Approximations of the SRA "superlockout" are to be found in many of the recent confrontations of the industrial proletariat with a capital that takes on a dream-like quality, ever receding either spatially to low wage sectors or temporally to higher organically composed forms of production. The historic collapse of strike activity in the United States during the last decade is only one among many omens portending the SRA's slouching to capital's Bethlehem to be born. Against such monsters of technical ingenuity, the usual tactics of workers' struggle seem impotent.

But appearances, by definition, deceive. Upon analyzing these SRA in the light of traditional Marxist theory, we see that they have a number of paradoxical qualities. For example, the value of a product and the organic composition of the system producing it are elementary concepts of analysis. Eschewing refinements, the value of a product is the socially necessary labor-time required for its production as a commodity, while the organic composition of a production system is the ratio of constant to variable capital, i.e., the ratio of the value of the "machinery" to the value of the labor-power employed. In brief, the organic composition of an SRA industry would be infinite while the value of its products tends to zero.

The organic composition of the SRA industry is infinite because by definition SRA produce themselves and thus do not require any labor-power in their production, i.e., the variable capital of SRA is zero, and any number divided by zero is infinite (or, perhaps, undefined). The value of SRA tends to zero since the "original capital" of the "parent" SRA gets slowly distributed over the potentially infinite series of its "off spring." Further, the surplus value generated by a commodity (again broadly speaking) is the difference between the value added to the commodity in the production process and the value of the labor-power expended in the production process (added to the product). But again a strange result follows: the surplus value of SRA is zero simply because no labor-power is absorbed in the production of the SRA. Already the dream of capital-production and profit without a struggle begins to invert itself, for such SRA production does not, apparently, produce the surplus value that is essential to capital. This curious combination of infinity and zero opens a threatening anomaly in the system of capitalist production that must be probed.

However, we should not be led astray by the blatant "extremism" of SRA. They are, after all, only machines. And the reasons for their introduction are quite explicable in capitalism. As the succinct writer of "Prologue to the Use of Machines" puts it: "a worker is replaced by a machine when the cost per unit product of the work is greater than for the machine." Let us take a classical case: moving weights over distances. If it costs $1 to move a 100 lb. weight one mile by machine (on average) then any wage higher than $1 will make the worker "replaceable." Hence the use of the machine as a capitalist weapon in the wage struggle, since it appears to put an absolute and objective limit on wage demands. Two corollaries to this principle in the SRA case are obvious, though they might sound strange: (1) SRA will be produced as commodities by other SRA if and only if the cost of the SRA's self-reproduction is less than the wages that must be paid for workers to produce SRA; (2) SRA will be used to produce commodity X if and only if the cost of X's SRA production is less than its cost when wage labor is employed.

But there is another principle of machine introduction in capitalism that does seem to be violated by SRA, viz., the desire to increase relative surplus value. Historically, a great impetus to the introduction of machinery has been working-class struggle that achieved reductions in the workday and improvements in working conditions. The immediate impact of such reduction and improvement was a reduction in absolute surplus value, for the boss literally was able to expropriate less labor time when an effective legislative limit was put on, say, the working day. Such reductions in the working day stimulated capitalists to introduce machinery into production that would make labor more productive or intensive or both. The result of such machinery on the system as a whole, especially in producing the means of subsistence, thereby lowering the value the worker consumes, was a reduction of the "necessary" part of the working day (i.e., the labor time involved in creating the value necessary for the reproduction of the worker or, in short, the real wage). If this introduction of machinery succeeds, then the ratio between surplus labor-time and necessary labor-time can increase quite dramatically, even with a reduction in the length of the working day.

The introduction of SRA would appear to violate this principle since their surplus value production is zero and hence their relative surplus value is zero as well. Thus they would appear useless in the accumulation process unless they contribute to the total expanded reproduction of aggregate capital values.

Even if the cost of their self-reproduction is less than human production and they do actually increase the general rate of profit, SRA remain paradoxical objects in a capitalistic space. They are like "black holes" or "space-time singularities" in the manifold of work processes, for they appear to absorb value but produce none in return. So an SRA industry would be the exact opposite of appearances—instead of being infinitely efficient or productive, it would turn out to be totally "unproductive."

A bit of logic is necessary here. There is a world of difference between "nothing" and "zero." A "nothing" is not a member of a continuum, series, or aggregate, but zero definitely is, i.e., it is the precise starting point of the said continuum, series or aggregate. Thus, while Marx's "yellow logarithm" is not a number at all, zero certainly is. We cannot conclude that processes producing zero value are unproductive. One might be tempted to put SRA into that miscellaneous closet of "luxury" commodities or "incidental expenses of production," the golden bathtubs and cruise missiles of our age. But SRA would not be "incidental" to social production, they might even prove to be "basic commodities" that enter the production cycle of every commodity. Yet, unlike luxury goods that embody surplus value, they would not add one iota of new value.

The logical differentiation of zero from nothing might seem abstract and "semantic," but it goes to the heart of traditional Marxist debates concerning "productive" versus "unproductive" labor. Labor-power that has, or tends to have, zero value (i.e., it is wageless) can be enormously productive of surplus value through the total cycle of value production, while labor-power that might appear to have high value might very well prove entirely "unproductive"—contribute nothing to surplus value production. You can no more determine productive labor by paychecks than you can determine value by stopwatches.

There is a further connection of SRA and Marxist theory. In some of his most crucial revolutionary passages, Marx was preoccupied with the stage of production that would usher in SRA. Consider those passages in the *Grundrisse* and *Capital* where Marx envisages the limit of the relative surplus value generation process driven by working-class struggle and implementing the sciences directly in production. At this limit, Marx sees not a nightmare for the workers but a catastrophe for capital itself. In this Marxist analysis, von Neumann's SRA embody the exact limits of the accumulation process where the whole system of value production "explodes." Now we come to a dichotomy: are first impressions right and will SRA be a worker's nightmare, or is Marx right in claiming that the nightmare will be one for the nightmare owner?

Let us say a particular object or condition is useful to someone, or even more strongly, let us say it is essential to human species existence. Surely that object or condition is an aspect of human wealth but this fact does not confer value on it. An SRA industry could be extremely useful to some and it might begin an epochal process of interspecies evolution . . . BUT for individual capitalists *qua* embodiments of capital the matter of usefulness or species existence is beside the point. For them the SRA riddle is simply put: can SRA "make money" for the SRA owners?

To answer this question we must first adjust von Neumann's vision, for it contains a hidden presupposition: SRA are (or would be) commodities. But that presupposition is debatable. Surely if SRA are commodities, then the SRA industry becomes part of the total commodity production "tree," i.e., the SRA "branch." If, however, these SRA remain outside the logic of commodities and become something like a new "biomechanical" species that can be used by anyone without exchange, then why should capitalists own or produce them at all? Clearly if SRA are not commodities then the riddle would solve itself, so let us assume that SRA become commodities at some stage in the process of capitalist development.

If SRA are commodities then they must have a price, i.e., they must be bought and sold for some exchange-value. But how can they have a definitive price when in the long run they have virtually zero value? Again, we confront an apparent paradox, but one that is easily resolved. Capitalism is exactly the system where price generally does not equal value in the first place; in fact, it is only in very rare circumstances that price is identical to value. In most situations values must be "transformed" into prices in order for the total capitalist system of production to reproduce itself, either simply or on an expanded scale. Many commentators on Marxist theory take the "transformation of values into prices of production" as a "problem" because Marx was not able to elegantly carry out the mathematics of the transformation in the simple models that he presented in the third volume of *Capital*. They seem to forget that the concept of "transformation" Marx uses is a special case of a general and profound feature of life in capitalism, where nothing is left literally "as is." One of the great fascinations (and terrors) of the system is its need for a continual interchange, flow, appearance, and disappearance of its components. The transformation of values into prices is one vital aspect of capital's appearance-disappearance process. It is this transformation that can help us explain how a capitalist can make a profit from a commodity that embodies no surplus value.

In the process of the transformation of values into prices, commodities produced in high organic composition industries have prices greater than their values while commodities produced in low organic composition industries have prices less than their values. This trick is accomplished by the transposition (in the market or by "administered" prices) of surplus value "generated" in the "low" industries into the "high" industries. The capitalists of the SRA industry (the topmost branch of the tree of production) would get their profit sustenance from the tree's gnarled earth-pressed roots. Thus profits can and must be expropriated without exploiting any workers directly if the SRA industry is to exist.

Let us put the point concerning the profitability of an SRA industry in a more precise form. The value of a commodity is the sum of its constant capital (c), variable capital (v) and its surplus value (s), but the price of production is determined by c, v, and r, the average rate of profit that acts as a cybernetic stabilizer for the total capitalistic system in its reproduction. The value, L, of a commodity is therefore:

$$L = c + v + s,$$

while the price of production, P, of a commodity is

$$P = c + v + r(c + v).$$

The "extremism" of SRA lie in that for them $v = s = 0$, $L = c$, and $P = c + rc$. Clearly P cannot equal L, indeed $P - L = rc$, but where does this "rc" come from? Since machines cannot produce value per se the profit in an SRA industry must ultimately come from the famous "sweat and toil" in the "lower" branches and "roots" of the production tree. Hence it is a "pure" profit that derives from the perverse logic of capitalist "justice" requiring that all investment in capital get a "fair" return. This justice simply becomes almost divine in the case of SRA.

What a situation! We have here a branch of capitalist industry that produces no surplus value but absorbs a potentially huge profit. This is only paradoxical to those who think that profits accrue to those who directly exploit. But this is no truer than the presumption that workers who produce the most surplus value get the highest wages. If anything, the exact opposite holds.

Perhaps one might classify SRA capitalists as pure "rentiers," but no, for their industry "produces" something and their return is not based upon some naturally given scarcity. They are no more rentiers than capitalists who control a hypothetical industry producing and selling dirt. Indeed, by its "self-reproducing" status the industry's products are continually growing in mass.

How big is their profit? It is proportional (more or less) to the ongoing average profit rate and the size of c, the part of the constant capital in the SRA industry that is used in the construction of an SRA unit, which might not be trifling. On the contrary, the investment required to actually reach this "ideal" machine industry is enormous, perhaps astronomical. Any reasonable attempt to imagine such an enterprise in actuality must result in a titanic expenditure. Therefore the industry's existence presupposes an enormous absorption of surplus value at whatever the ongoing profit rate. Indeed, if the capitalist system is compelled into creating such an industry, it would be like a gambler staking all his/her "chips" on a rather risky bet.

The move into atomic power plants in the post–World War II can give a hint of such "risks." In response to the struggles of the coal miners of the United States and the nationalist movements in the oil-producing countries the capitalist system viewed the production of extremely high organic composition forms of energy production requiring enormous investment as an acceptable "risk." The result has been the devaluation of hundreds of billions of dollars of investment when the gamble proved unprofitable.

The introduction of an SRA industry will require a immense restructuring of the international form of commodity production requiring an ever greater "economic" distance between the "bottom" and "top" branches of the world's value production tree. This restructuring will not happen "naturally." Rather, a fatal violence whose proportions are hard now to reckon is on the capitalist agenda. Whenever fatality on these dimensions is proposed, the riskiness of the bet is evident.

But this "bet" is not made in an instant. There is an approximate approach, both in terms of investment and conditions of return, in the tendential growth of organic composition in the branches of production tending to the SRA limit. The way this approximate approach first forces itself into recognition is in a radical change in the price structure of commodities. For any large-scale leap in the organic composition of an industry or the system as a whole, especially one that tends to infinity, must "drain" more from the lower branches and roots of the tree (where by "roots" I mean those branches of production where c and v tend to zero). The mechanism of this "draining" and "sapping" is the transformation of prices into values.

This transformation of relative prices must be such that the low or zero organic composition branches and roots will discover low and lower relative prices, while the SRA-tending branches will experience high and higher relative prices.

Other things being equal, if the organic composition of one industry increases while the organic composition of the other remains the same, the price of the first will increase with respect to the price of the second. This is just a mathematical constraint on a system whose aim is the accumulation of value.

This widespread disturbance of relative prices and an ever more excruciating sapping of the surplus value extracted at the "bottom" of the tree of production is, I believe, what Marx was referring to in his "explosion" remarks in the *Grundrisse*. He worked out many of the details in *Capital* to the point that the mechanism is simplicity itself. As the "cost" of labor-power in "real wages" is increased and the working day reduced through working-class struggle, the dominant capitalist response is a dramatic "restructuring" of production. But where is the capital for this investment in higher organic composition industries to come from? Clearly in the transformation of relative prices and the ever-widening and deepening absorption of surplus value throughout the world. For workers at the bottom, or kicked to the bottom, this means in most cases increased exploitation in an absolute sense (e.g., increased workday) and decreased wages, since the "profits" of the "low" capitalist might have to come from the necessary labor-time of the worker.

There is a temporal aspect to this relative price transformation as well, which is seen most starkly in our SRA industry. As was pointed out previously the value of SRA units tends to zero. This is just the mathematical conclusion from the following premises: the series of SRA is potentially infinite while the "initial" capital, C, is finite (though C can be quite large). But

$$C/n \to 0$$
$$\text{as}$$
$$n \to \infty,$$

where n is the number of SRA produced.

The capitalist, however, does not live in mathematical eternity. S/he will not be content to have human, even capitalist, posterity accrue "his" return. S/he will want a return on his investment, with "fair profit" of course, within a reasonable period of time. But the turnover time of his constant capital is literally infinite. There must therefore by a temporal dilation in the period of return, for instead of getting back his C+rC in an infinite time he will need to get it back in a finite, indeed, a relatively short time, or he will not make the investment. Let us say that given the conditions of turnover throughout the system investment will not be made in an SRA industry unless the return takes place in a century. Let us say, however, that only ten SRA are allowed to be produced "profitably" every year. Then the price of the SRA must average C+rC/1000, which will be quite large compared to the real value in them. This "guaranteeing" of profits within a fixed period of time will further intensify the pressure of expropriation on the "bottom."

This situation, presaging and stepping into the period of the SRA, is an "extreme" version of the average response of capitalism to a threat to its current average rate of profit. However, the radicality of the present period lies in the "extremism" of capital's approach and in the breadth and depth of the wage reduction it requires, on the one side, while on the other, the working class possesses an enormous actual and potential knowledge of struggle which can accelerate the circulation of struggle to an unprecedented extent.

This leap of capital's organic composition is therefore exceptionally crucial for Africa (because it generally is at the bottom of the accumulation hierarchy) and is reminiscent of the situation a century before: the Berlin conference of 1885, which organized the rules of the game of the exploitation of Africa, was an essential step in the formation of Tayloristic production. Since Africa is at the bottom of the wage scale and at the top of the absolute exploitation index, it becomes central to capital's adventures in this period. If capital cannot intensify its wage reduction and absolute exploitation here, it cannot escape a level of catastrophic confrontation in the "higher branches" of production (with all due qualifications).

The "debt crisis," the U.S. budget deficit, the ever "worsening" terms of trade for Third World commodities beginning in the 1970s and intensifying in the 1980s, all reveal symptoms of the strains and imperatives of transformation. The infamous IMF conditionalities and austerity programs simply spell out the role Africa is to play in the transformation.

Thus, for Africa, "the consensus" is that wages are too high, that the urbanization of the African proletariat has led to a concentration of class power that was and is too dangerous for a system that is not "productive enough." Knowing the conditions of Lagos, one might be amazed at the perversity of those who would argue that the Lagosian's average wage is "high." Yet "high" is a relative term, relative to a standard, and the standard is relative to a perceived sense of proportion. For the IMF, Keynes's world-historical contribution to the sphere of capitalist institutions, the "highness" of African wages is obvious. Thus the "back to the land" programs, the threats and realities of starvation, the high food and "commodity prices, the appeals to a "self-reliant" poverty, and a return to the notion of an "appropriate technology" of the neolithic period (at best).

Capital must repropose, therefore, a ferocious period of original accumulation for Africa, with the final expropriation of the remaining communal lands from Ethiopia across to Nigeria and down to Zimbabwe.

The preceding chain of notes—from self-reproducing automata to Africa, from the ideal limiting top of contemporary capitalist production to its real sustaining bottom—poses a deep riddle of strategy for the African proletariat. A riddle intensified by the peculiar "convergence" of Left and Right in this period. Both are agreed that the expectations of African youth are too high, that the level of "indiscipline," "petit-bourgeois behavior," "laziness," "backwardness," "antisociality" of the average African urban worker and peasant is too contradictory with "historical and economic reality." Of course one speaks of "lack of class consciousness" while the other of "lack of achievement motivation" and when one speaks of "autarky" the other recommends "domestic inputs." However, both conclude that Africa must wait out this century and a good deal of the next until it is ready either for "true capitalism" or "true socialism." Understanding this agreement of perspective makes it clear that much of what might appear as a "sell-out" by a left- (right-) winger to say, the IMF (Soviet Union), can make much sense from the logic of Left's (Right's) position per se. As a consequence, much political analysis of Africa remains on the level of "moralism," for if one cannot change values, then the natural course is to idealize them.

Yet to accept such assumptions and strategies, even from a "well-meaning" perspective that wishes to do "right by the people," is to collaborate in the condemnation of the African proletariat to the deprivation of the possibilities that objectively exist for a level of production and social intercourse that is unprecedented in human history. For these assumptions and strategies of the Left and Right functionalize and ration these possibilities only to the most select social sectors of "comrades" or "good old boys." One can only presume that the "instability" of governments of both the Left and Right in Africa, and the often inchoate political violence (frequently dismissed as "tribal," "ethnic," or "religious") that characterizes the continent at present, has a clear and rational base in the mass perception that these objective possibilities of production and intercourse are being repressed across the ideological spectrum.

It should be obvious that the logic of these notes point to a totally different direction. It should also not be surprising that this direction is parallel not with the scientific socialist realists' strategies but with the arguments of Fanon. In Fanon, one finds simultaneously a total rejection of capitalist values (which in the mystified form are aggregated into "Western Civilization") with an equally uncompromising strategy of reappropriation. Fanon's argument is simply a forceful application of a Marxist truism, viz., the accumulated wealth, both cultural and physical, of the "advanced capitalist world" is simply the transformation of the labor of Africans which must be returned, as Malcolm X used to say, by any means necessary. As Silvia Federici explains in her essay "Journey to the Native Land," for Fanon, much of the "true history" of Africa is in Europe and the Americas (as, indeed, most of the "true history" of Europe and America) is scarred in Africa.[3] It is only by the reappropriation of that wealth and "true history" that Africans can escape the toil, misery, and wretchedness that is now programmed for them.

This is neither the place nor the hour to discuss the mechanisms of reappropriation but only its logic and consequences. Thus, we argue that without an enormous return of social technique and wealth into the African continent and on Africans' terms: all efforts at "self-help," "self-reliance," "autarky," "living within our means," "substituting domestic inputs," etc. will lead to a further isolation of the African proletariat from the rest of the planet in a period when the very need for world accumulation based upon the most "primitive" forms of exploitation is reaching a peak. A "self-reliance" strategy plus SRA creates a disastrous conjuncture, to say the least, and not only for the African.

---

[3] Silvia Federici, "Journey to the Native Land: Violence and the Concept of the Self in Fanon and Gandhi," *Quest: An International African Journal of Philosophy* 8, no. 2 (December 1994).

The ability to decrease African wages and increase absolute exploitation in Africa is a necessary condition for the success of capital's project of renewal in this period. This project, provoked by the international wage "explosion" and profits "crisis" of the late 1960s and early 1970s, and put into motion in 1973, has been extraordinarily successful (except for a few set-backs in 1979–80). At the moment, resistance to this project at the "higher branches" of production seems muted at best. Attention turns to the "roots" of the tree, for, as any logician will tell you, the failure of a necessary condition of a project is a sufficient condition of the failure of the project.

WHY MACHINES CANNOT CREATE VALUE:

MARX'S THEORY OF MACHINES

The presupposition of the master-servant relation is the appropriation of an alien will. Whatever has no will, e.g., the animal, may well provide a service, but does not thereby make its owner into a master, This much can be seen here, however, that the master-servant relation likewise belong in this formula of the appropriation of the instruments of production; and it forms a necessary ferment for the development and decline and fall of all original relations of property and production, just as it also expresses their limited nature. Still it is reproduced—in mediated form—in capital, and thus likewise forms a ferment of its dissolution and is an emblem of its limitation.
—Karl Marx, *Grundrisse*[1]

There will be machines that make work easier, but first you must work hard to have one.
—Marcel Biefer and Beat Zgraggen, *Prophecies*[2]

Thirty years ago, my generation was told by economists, sociologists, and futurologists to expect a society in which machines had taken over most repetitive and stressful tasks and the working day would be so reduced by mechanization that our existential problem would not be how to suffer through the working day but rather how to fill our leisure time. The coming "affluent society" would, we were assured, make the ancient problems of hunger, disease, and insecurity dim historical memories. The long-term trends showing a reduction in the working day, the rise in real wages and the relative reduction of the waged working population (with, for example, the curbs on child labor and an earlier retirement age) in the early 1960s seemed to confirm such "great expectations."

Not all was future perfect, however. Prophets of the Right and Left projected different dystopias on the basis of these socioeconomic trends. Those on the Right warned of a postindustrial, mass society filled with anomic, "superfluous people"

---

[1] Marx, *Grundrisse*, 501.

[2] Marcel Biefer and Beat Zgraggen, *Prophecies*, ed. Hans-Ulrich Obrist (Zürich and Venice: Sammlung Hauser & Wirth and Aperto 93/Biennale of Venice, 1993).

living on guaranteed incomes, lacking individual initiative, being electronically manipulated by a totalitarian welfare state. Leftist prophets saw in this mechanization a dramatic reduction in the proletariat's ability to struggle against capital, since its labor would be less needed while structural unemployment would increasingly exacerbate race-based divisions between a small sector of highly paid skilled workers and a huge "underclass" of unemployables.[3]

These futurological assumptions and political dystopias turned out to be radically wrong in their common assumptions. The most glaring mistake can be seen in what happened to the length of the working year and the size of the wage labor market. For, just as the increase in capitalist accumulation in the 1840s and 1850s (after the ten-hour-day legislation went into effect in Britain) put into crisis Nassau Senior's claim that the capitalists would lose most of their profits if the ten-hour-day legislation was passed, so too the stubborn refusal of capitalist states since the 1960s to substantially reduce the working day and the labor market participation rate seems to put in question the assumption that capitalism is no more in need of the proletariat's capacity to create value because machines now are the prime value producers.

Since the energy crisis of 1973–74, the work-year in the United States has increased by about 10 percent, while the number of waged workers has also dramatically increased with the introduction of millions of new immigrants and women workers into the wage labor market. More people are working for longer hours (and for lower real wages) than ever before in U.S. history.[4] According to U.S. Department of Commerce 1994 estimates, the total amount of waged work per week in the U.S. has increased by 57 percent between 1970 and 1993, while the number of nonagricultural waged workers has increased from 69,461,000 in 1970 to 107,011,000 in 1993 and their average weekly work increased from 38.3 to 39.3 hours. This trend can be observed throughout the advanced capitalist world (defined as the OECD countries) where, though the average unemployment rate (for waged workers) increased in this period, the total percentage of waged workers in the population increased from 42.8 percent to 46.8 percent.[5] These facts contradicted the sophisticated prophesies concerning "the obsolescence of the proletariat," especially when we take into account the increasing importance of "informal economic activity" ranging from unpaid housework, "off the books" work, and criminal activity in OECD and Third World countries.[6] In addition, the desperate attempts by neoliberal postcolonial and post-Communist governments (with the complicity of

---

[3] See, for example, Mario Savio's "An End to History" in *The New Left: A Documentary History*, ed. Massimo Teodori (Indianapolis: Bobbs-Merrill, 1969), 159–61.

[4] Juliet Schor, *The Overworked American: The Unexpected Decline of Leisure* (New York: Basic Books, 1991).

[5] Organization for Economic Cooperation and Development, *The OECD Jobs Study: Evidence and Explanations* (Paris: OECD, 1994).

[6] J.J. Thomas, *Informal Economic Activity* (Ann Arbor: University of Michigan Press, 1992); Mariarosa Dalla Costa and Giovanna Franca Dalla Costa, *Paying the Price: Women and International Economic Strategy*. London: Zed Books. 1995.

international agencies like the IMF and World Bank) to throw billions of new workers into competition against each other on the international labor market through structural adjustment programs and forced emigration is a further contradiction of the projected trend to less work.

The existence of higher average unemployment rates in the former Eastern bloc countries and in many parts of Africa and the Americas (as well as in Western Europe) does not falsify this account. Increasing unemployment rates do not signal a reduced need by capitalists for work and workers, but rather the creation of unemployment is a standard capitalist strategy for increasing the mass of available labor-power while reducing its value. Irrespective of unemployment trends, the increase in both the duration and mass of work in the United States and internationally in the last generation has occurred in the face of an unprecedented increase in technological transformation (from robotization of industrial work, to computerization of commercial work, to introduction of biotechnical methods in agricultural work). In other words, mechanization has led to an increase, not a decrease, of work.

Why did the most sophisticated analysts of the last generation go wrong and why is there a still continual stream of texts to this day like Rifkin's *The End of Work*, which see in technological innovations the promise of a new era of workerless production? One way to understand this failure is to see that these analysts and texts assumed that technology had a qualitatively new role to play in contemporary capitalism and that machines can create value, hence surplus value and profits. One can locate such a view not only among neoclassical economists who claim that capital (in the form of machines) used in the production of a commodity is partially responsible for the commodity's value, but implicitly or explicitly among many others—ranging from Hannah Arendt and Jürgen Habermas to Antonio Negri and Jean Baudrillard—who took a Marxist analysis of capitalism seriously, but then claimed, often using passages from Marx's as support, that there was a qualitative change in the nature of capitalist accumulation in the twentieth century due to technological change.[7] If machines did create value, one could certainly see the justice of the scenarios implying a qualitative change in capitalism (as postmodernists claim), and of those theorists who have bid a "farewell to the proletariat" and given primacy to a "social movement" and "identity politics" analysis of resistance to capitalism.[8]

Contrary to such claims, what follows is a reanalysis and defense of Marx's original claim that machines cannot produce value. It falls into two parts. The first examines Marx's original claim in the context of the mid-nineteenth-century

---

[7] Hannah Arendt, *The Human Condition* (Chicago: University of Chicago Press, 1958); Hannah Arendt, *The Origins of Totalitarianism* (New York: Harcourt Brace Jovanovich, 1973); Jürgen Habermas, *Legitimation Crisis* (Boston: Beacon Press, 1975); Julius Sensat Jr., *Habermas and Marxism: An Appraisal* (Beverly Hills: Sage, 1979); Jean Baudrillard, *The Mirror of Production* (St. Louis: Telos Press, 1975); Jean Baudrillard, *Simulations* (New York: Semiotext(e)/Autonomedia, 1983); and Negri, *Marx Beyond Marx*.

[8] Andre Gorz, *Farewell to the Proletariat* (Boston: South End Press, 1983); Andre Gorz, *Paths to Paradise: On the Liberation from Work* (Boston: South End Press, 1985); and Caffentzis, "The Work-Energy Crisis and the Apocalypse," 11–57 in this volume.

discussion of machines, energy, and work in political economy, physics, and engineering. The second part deals with Marx's claim from the perspective of the late twentieth century. It is important to do so not simply because almost a century and a half separates us from *Capital*, but also because major theoretical developments in the study of technology have taken place during this period. Marx and the classical Marxist analysts recognized only two theories of machines: the theory of simple machines (developed by Hero of Alexandria and perfected by Galileo and the eighteenth-century mechanists); and the theory of heat engines (developed by Carnot and perfected by Clausius and Thompson in the mid-nineteenth century). These set the framework for their own theory of machines. But a new theory of machines was developed in the 1930s (associated with Turing, von Neumann, Wiener, and Shannon) that could not have been known to Marx and the classical Marxists. The analysis of value-production in the context of communicating Turing machines theoretically capable of feedback and self-reproduction needs to be sketched out in order to understand how Marx's original claim fares in our time.[9]

Marx's Theory and Mid-Nineteenth-Century Thermodynamics

> The energy in A is increased and that in B is diminished; that is, the hot system
> has got hotter and the cold colder and yet no work has been done, only the
> intelligence of a very observant and neat-fingered being has been employed.
> —A letter from Maxwell to Tait in 1867

Machines have been the center of an elaborate scientific and philosophical discourse throughout the capitalist period. A most prominent feature of this discourse has been their use as a trope for organizing thought about Nature. Thus "the mechanization of the world picture" so lamented by nineteenth-century romanticism and Heidegger-inspired ecologists has its roots in early bourgeois thought and its attempt to determine how much work could be expected from natural processes. The romantic lamentation over the "demystification of the world," however, was premature. The last four centuries have seen a "remystification" of nature whereby, instead of taking on the charming or terrifying personifications of Homeric warlords and ladies, nature has become capitalized in the form of a gigantic machine.

The use of this trope was no accident, since the development of machinery and a heightening of the need for a theory of machines is an essential aspect of the development of class antagonism. Once the working class—through its strikes, revolts, and sabotage—makes the path of accumulation via the extension of the working day or the cutting of wages below subsistence risky, the main path of accumulation that lies open is that of increasing relative surplus value. By the introduction of machinery that increases the productivity and intensity of labor, the necessary part of the workday can be reduced (with appropriate qualifications) and surplus value can be increased even if the length of the workday is fixed or the level of subsistence

---

[9] See "On Africa and Self-Reproducing Automata," 127 in this volume.

wages defended. True, in most cases, the capitalist class in general and many individual capitalists are brought kicking and screaming to the showroom of each passing "industrial revolution." And they resist with justice, for the new machines do cost money and "create a lot of problems" especially in the initial phases; but invariably the working-class entropy these recalcitrant capitalists face will force them to buy the new machines or to find a completely new sector of the working class to exploit . . . or, of course, to die *qua* capital.

Marx was rightly critical of the "theory of machines" as he found it in the middle of the nineteenth century. It had barely changed from Hero's day in form (returning to the same old lever, inclined plane, screw, and so on) though its mathematical content had gone through an enormous transformation in the seventeenth and eighteenth centuries. In particular, Marx was critical of its confused categories and its lack of historicity, and so he took to task the machine science of his day: "The weak points in the abstract materialism of natural science, a materialism that excludes history and its process, are at once evident from the abstract and ideological conceptions of its spokesmen, whenever they venture beyond the bounds of their own specialty."[10] He tries to make a beginning on the "history of the productive organs of man" in Part IV of the first volume of *Capital*. Consider a definition of machine that is characteristically Marx's own:

> All fully developed machinery consists of three essentially different parts, the motor mechanism, the transmitting mechanism, and finally the tool or working machine. The motor mechanism is that which puts the whole in motion. . . . The transmitting mechanism . . . regulates the motion, changes its form where necessary as for instance, from linear to circular, and divides and distributes it among the working machines. . . . The tool or working machine is that part of the machinery with which the industrial revolution of the eighteenth century started.[11]

Marx inverts the polar hierarchy that plots the standard narrative of the industrial revolution—in the difference of motive power and tool, analyses of motive power are given prominence. But, Marx argues, it is only with the separation of work and tool in the original labor process accomplished by manufacturing that steam engines became necessary. What held up the application of steam power was not so much the efficiency of steam engines in the eighteenth century, but rather the lack of preconditions for their use.[12]

For if the labor process has "three elementary factors"—the personal activity of man [*sic*], that is, work itself; the subject of that work; its instruments, then, ironically enough, the development of capitalism (whose historical condition is the exploitation of labor) spells a step-by-step disintegration of the labor process. First, primitive accumulation detaches the laborer from the subject of the labor, and then

---

[10] Marx, *Capital: Volume I*, 494.

[11] Ibid., 494.

[12] Ibid., 496–97.

manufacture, through its obsessive attention to the details of the "naturally developed differentiation of the trades" separates the work of the laborer from the instruments of that work to a point where Modern Industry appears to virtually do away with the activity of the laborer all together.

In describing the labor process, Marx gives it the form of an Aristotelian process, complete with starting and finishing points, means and ends, entelechies and dynamae, that is, the labor process is an activity in Aristotelian time. But in its perpetual efforts to rid itself of dependence on the "self-willed and intractable workman" (Ure), capitalist development has certainly destroyed the apparent metaphysical structure of the labor process, though by no means has it destroyed workers and their labor—quite the contrary.[13] For human workers enter into the production process after the introduction of Modern Industry in one of two major ways: (a) as "mere living appendages" of the system of machines, or (b) as "wretches" whose wages are so low "machinery would increase the cost of production to the capitalist."[14]

For The Appendage, the workday is linearized, since the basic form of work is the feeding and tending of machines whose cycles are independent of the laborer's work tempo. The process character of labor (as laid out by Marx originally) is eliminated: "In Manufacture, the organization of the social labor-process is purely subjective; it is a combination of detail workers; in its machinery system, Modern Industry has a productive organism that is purely objective, in which the laborer becomes a mere appendage to an already existing material condition of production."[15] In Modern Industry the laborer undergoes something of a Copernican revolution, finding him/herself transformed from the center of the productive system to its planetary margins . . . and then pumped dry, under the threat of unemployment, the workday is either prolonged or intensified.

Similarly, the introduction of machinery creates The Wretch who, in effect, finds him/herself on the other side of the cost horizon, in the netherworld of production. If the Wretches force their wages above the horizon determined by a possible technological application they annihilate themselves *qua* Wretches, but if they remain below this horizon they know that they will "squander" themselves and their labor-power.

Thermodynamics and Value

The laws that determine the creation and conditions of both Appendages and Wretches constitute Marx's theory of the capitalist use of machines. But while he was working out this theory of machines, another theory of machines—a thermodynamics of heat engines to be precise—was being developed by Joule, Mayer, Clausius, Maxwell, Tait, and Thomson in England and Germany. Indeed, the tension between Marx's theory and thermodynamics and the differing notions of equivalence and limit they espouse, pose one of the most serious questions in the divide

---

[13] Ibid., 490.

[14] Ibid., 517.

[15] Ibid., 508.

between capital and nature: what differentiates human labor-power from other natural powers and human labor from other forms of work? Marx's theory postulates a deep difference between machines and humans—that machines produce no value, while human labor can. By contrast, thermodynamics argues that machines like humans can produce "work." In Marx's theory, the asymmetry between machines and humans is pivotal, while in thermodynamics this difference is not recognized, even though both are theories of work.

Marx was clearly cognizant of this new thermodynamical theory of machines and was concerned about its relationship to his own theory, which presumes the asymmetry of machines and labor. He refers to the work of Grove and Liebig—two of many aspirants to the laurels of discoverer of the conservation of energy—directly in the first volume of *Capital*, in regard to labor and labor-power. These references show that Marx clearly saw labor-power to be integrated (or correlated) with the wide range of forces that were being studied by the energeticists of the mid-nineteenth century. These researches ranged *horizontally*, from heat to light to electricity to magnetism to chemical affinity; and *vertically*, from the inorganic realm (as in the crystallization of atoms into solids) to the vegetable realm (where the minerals of the soil, the carbon and oxygen of the atmosphere and the light and heat of the sun are joined to make plant cells), to the realm of herbivorous animals (which release the energy of plants internally to make their animal motion possible), to the realm of carnivorous animals (which release the energy of plants at a meta-level). Labor-power is situated rather precariously at the pinnacle of this vertical hierarchy, correlating or converting living substances into human motion. Thus it is an object of physics, physiology, and political economy, but not in the way, however, that Foucault saw Labor in the discourse of economics as being homologous to Language in Linguistics and Life in Biology.[16] Rather, labor-power is the *physical precondition* of social production and *the point of intersection* of the law of the conservation of *energy* and the law of the conservation of *value*.

However, Marx was eager to differentiate labor as it appeared in political economy and labor (or work) from its appearance in thermodynamics. He did this in a number of oblique ways. For example, at the end of Chapter 15 of the first volume of *Capital*, Marx criticizes one of Liebig's excursions into political economy— Liebig's praise of John Stuart Mill's expression of the "law of diminishing returns of labor" in agricultural production—by pointing out that Liebig used "an incorrect interpretation of the word 'labor,' a word he used in quite a different sense from that adopted by political economy," implying that even a most sophisticated chemist might blunder in traversing the divide between nature and society, or chemistry and political economy. In the beginning of the first volume of *Capital*, he more directly differentiates (conjunctively) between the physiological and the social aspects of labor: "all labour is an expenditure of human labour-power, in the physiological sense, and it is in this quality of being equal, or abstract labour that it forms the value of

---

[16] Michel Foucault, *The Order of Things: An Archeology of the Human Sciences* (New York: Random House, 1970).

commodities."[17] "This quality" is a social product that is averaged over all the differential physiological loci at one particular temporal instant to create that productive Leviathan, "the total social labour-power of society." Consequently, labor and labor-power in Marx's analysis is related to the work and work-power of the thermodynamically sensitive physiologists in the same way as the total work done by a steam engine is related to the work done by the individual atoms in the steam cloud. There is clearly a relation between the two levels, but the higher one is dependent upon the macroscopic arrangement of the engine's (or a society's productive) parts, while the lower one is theoretically determinable independent of this arrangement.

But this fundamental differentiation of political economy from thermodynamics, between labor and work, does not mean that Marx's theory of machines was not correlated with the then current theory of machines and heat engines of the engineers (Carnot, Joule), physicians (Mayer, Helmholtz, Carpenter), lawyers (Grove), and chemists (Faraday, Liebig) that was so functional to the development of capitalist production and reproduction during this period. For example, central to both Marx and capitalism's technical intelligentsia was the question of the existence of a perpetual motion machine, that is, could there be a machine M such that it has as its only input and output the same "stuff" Q and in every cycle of its operation Q(input) is less than Q(output)? If such a machine M existed, then M would be able to produce any desired quantity of Q, Q(d), for there must exist some n such that $n(Q(\text{output}) - Q(\text{input}))$ would be greater than Q(d), given M's proper operation over n cycles. There can be many kinds of perpetual motion machines depending on the purported quantity Q, and, of course, the more valuable Q is, the more M would be the object of fantasy and desire. The history of the search for such Ms has been the source of many arcane and humorous volumes, and indeed the year 1775, when the Paris Academy of Sciences refused to consider any design that purported to be of a perpetual motion machine, is often considered the terminal year of magical technology.

But in the period between 1775 and the 1840s, when the first formulations of the conservation of energy were published, there was a new temptation to try to find in the nonmechanistic forces of electricity, magnetism, heat, chemical attraction, and physiological vitality some source for a perpetual motion machine. Thermodynamics was based on the denial of this temptation, for it began with postulating the impossibility of a perpetual motion machine (of the first and second kinds). Thus, Liebig begins his essay "The Connection and Equivalence of Forces" with this claim: "It is well known that our machines create no power, but only return what they have received."[18] Indeed, he argues that the conservation of power is simply the obverse of the view that power cannot be annihilated. Liebig goes on, of course, to dismiss the possibility of a perpetual motion machine as did all the other founders of thermodynamics. Many, indeed, inserted an "economic" twist. For

---

[17] Marx, *Capital: Volume I*, 137.

[18] Edward L. Youmans, *The Correlation and Conservation of Forces: A Series of Expositions* (New York: Appleton & Co., 1872), 387

example, Helmholtz in his popular essay on the conservation of energy, "Interaction of Natural Forces," argues that the fascination of the seventeenth and eighteenth centuries with automata and the "real quintessence of organic life" lead many to try to discuss the new philosopher's stone—perpetual motion for profit. He turned to "fable-rich America" for a recent example of an American inventor who argued that the gases produced by electrolytic decomposition could be combusted to turn a steam engine that would drive a magneto-electric machine that would decompose water that would in turn provide the fuel for the steam engine. Such schemes were doomed, of course, but Helmholtz ironically described the hopes they generated, not only in fabulous America:

> Another hope also seemed to take up incidentally the second place [after the attempt to artificially create men], which, in our wiser age, would certainly have claimed the first rank in the thoughts of men. The perpetual motion was to produce work inexhaustibly without corresponding consumption, that is to say, out of nothing. Work, however, is money. Here, therefore, the practical problem which the cunning heads of all centuries have followed in the most diverse ways, namely, to fabricate money out of nothing, invited solution. The similarity with the philosopher's stone sought by the ancient chemists was complete. That also was thought to contain the quintessence of organic life, and to be capable of producing gold.[19]

The conservation of energy (or "force," up until the 1860s and 1870s) as well as Carnot's principle (as phrased by Helmholtz: "only when heat passes from a warmer to a colder body, and even then only partially, can it be converted into mechanical work") put a definitive end to these economic dreams.

Marx entered into this discussion not only by inserting labor-power into the network of forces being correlated by the energeticist program. He also argued quite paradoxically against the economic analysis of perpetual motion machines that provided so much of the ideological stage setting of the early energeticist movement. For the thermodynamicists saw in their laws of the conservation and dissipation of energy a new kind of Puritanism to scourge any neo-alchemical, pseudoscientific "American" offering a "free lunch" contraption. But Marx in his theory of machines did energetic Puritanism one better by claiming that far from perpetual motion machines "fabricating money out of nothing" they would directly produce zero value. To understand this Marxist paradox one must examine Helmholtz's claims like "Perpetual motion [machines] produce work" and "work is money" more carefully from Marx's perspective.

Machines enter into the value-production process, according to Marx's theory of machines, as constant instead of variable capital. Their value is preserved and transferred during the production process to the resultant commodity by the labor expended in the process. This labor has a twofold character, however, for it is (a)

---

[19] Ibid., 213.

useful, concrete labor as well as (b) abstract, value-creating labor. This twofold nature of labor is crucial to understanding what happens in the production process, for the concrete labor "preserves" the value of the machinery which it transfers to the product, while the abstract labor creates new value. Hence in his discussion of the production of yarn, Marx argues:

> On the one hand, then, it is by virtue of its general character, as being expenditure of human labour-power in the abstract, that spinning adds new value to the values of the cotton and the spindle; and on the other hand, it is by virtue of its special character, as being a concrete, useful process, that the same labour of spinning both transfers the values of the means of production to the product, and preserves them in the product.[20]

This division of result arises from the root differential of the commodity itself—the distinction between use-value and exchange-value—and the twofold nature of capital in the production process, for the capitalist purchases raw materials, auxiliary materials and machinery and labor-power to initiate the process. These purchases appear totally symmetric to the capitalist but they have very different consequences: the capital represented by the first remains constant through the destruction of the original utilities into the product, while the capital represented by the labor-power creates new value and thus is variable.

Thus we see that in Marx's theory of value production a machine cannot add value to the product, however efficient and cost-free it might be. Marx does to the perpetual motion enthusiasts of the nineteenth century what the early quantity theorists of money like Locke did to those with lingering alchemical dreams in the seventeenth. The quantity theorists revealed not the physical impossibility of turning, say, iron, into gold, but rather they exposed alchemy's self-defeating character. Increasing the supply of gold would, by that very fact, decrease the relative price of gold while increasing the general price level. Far from realizing their visions of infinite wealth, the alchemists would destroy the very ideal they premised their vision on.

Similarly, Marx argues that a perpetual motion machine would create *no* value directly at all as a machine, nor would it have part of its value transferred to the product since it would be costless by definition. It would be the goose that laid the golden egg, but the egg would embody less value than the regular henhouse variety. Marx wrote of perpetual motion machines in his 1858 *Notebooks* and claimed that they were ideal machines: "If machinery lasted for ever, if it did not consist of transitory material which must be reproduced (quite apart from the invention of more perfect machines which would rob it of the character of being a machine), if it were a perpetual motion machine, then it would most completely correspond to its concept."[21] Such ideal machines would join with all the other "powers of society" that cost capital nothing, like the division and cooperation of labor, scientific power and population growth, but are

---

[20] Marx, *Capital: Volume I*, 308.

[21] Marx, *Grundrisse*, 766.

in themselves incapable of creating or positing value. Marx recognized that it was easy to confuse the ability to create use-values with the ability to create value:

> It is easy to form the notion that machinery as such posits value, because it acts as a productive power of labour. But if machinery required no labour, then it would be able to increase the use value; but the exchange value which it would create would never be greater than its own costs of production, its own value, the value objectified in it. It creates value not because it replaces labour; rather, only in so far as it is a means to increase surplus labour, and only the latter itself is both the measure and the substance of the surplus value posited with the aid of the machine; hence of labour in general.[22]

The perpetual motion machine as the embodiment of the ideal Marxist machine would not make money, as Helmholtz claimed, by doing work. Rather, it would make money through reducing the value of the commodities it was involved in producing by (a) reducing the transfer of value from it to the product relative to less efficient and more costly mechanical rivals and (b) reducing the socially necessary labor-time required in the production of the said commodities. A perpetual motion machine could only make money for capitalists by reducing the value of the commodities it produced. The paradox is thus both resolved and further intensified in the pages of the *Grundrisse* when Marx notes that the capitalist desire for a perpetual motion machine has within it, in its most extreme form, the very drive that will destroy itself:

> On the one side, then, [capital] calls to life all the powers of science and of nature, as of social combination and of social intercourse, in order to make the creation of wealth independent (relatively) of the labour time employed on it. On the other side, it wants to use labour time as the measuring rod for the giant social forces thereby created, and to confine them within the limits required to maintain the already created value as value. Forces of production and social relations—two different sides of the development of the social individual—appear to capital as mere means, and are merely means for it to produce on its limited foundation. In fact, however, they are the material conditions to blow this foundation sky-high.[23]

Just as the dream of the alchemists has within it the destruction of a gold-based economy, so too the moneymaking schemes of the perpetuum mobilists implicitly speak of the end of a moneymaking economy. For they call up all "the powers of science and nature" (indeed, call beyond these powers) merely to make . . . values.

Marx proves his own version of the impossibility of a perpetual motion machine by invoking a law of conservation in the realm of value: No machine can create new value nor transfer more value to its product than it loses. This law parallels the laws of conservation of force and energy found in the classical theory of machines

---

[22] Ibid., 767–68.
[23] Ibid., 706.

and in the theory of heat engines. Machines are not seen as producers of force or energy in either tradition; they merely transform, more or less efficiently, input forces or energies. Indeed, this is one of many laws of value conservation to be found in Marx's critique of political economy. For example, there is the law of the exchange of equivalents and its converse: "Circulation, or exchange of commodities, creates no value" in the first volume of *Capital*.[24] Then there are the laws of the conservation of total value and total surplus value that he postulates in the discussion of the transformation of values into prices in the third volume of *Capital*.[25]

The Zerowork Paradox

But in the fashioning of these conservation theorems, Marx had to deal with a number of phenomena that involved an amplification/dissipation of value in the production process. The most blatant one was the extraordinary existence of profits in successful industries that employ relatively little direct labor (and thus even less surplus labor). Since the total value produced in a developed capitalism comes largely from the work of Wretches and Appendages, then it would appear that the fewer the direct workers involved in a particular sphere of production, the less the surplus value created there. But this is clearly not the case. As Marx recognizes: "How therefore can living labour be the exclusive source of profit, since a deduction in the quantity of labour needed for production not only seems not to affect the profit, but rather to be the immediate source of increasing profit, in certain circumstance, at least for the individual capitalist?"[26] Indeed, Marx even mentions the possibility (though an "exaggerated" one) of a capitalist employing no laborers and still generating an average profit rate on his machinery and other elements of constant capital alone.[27] Here, it would seem, is proof positive that machines do produce value!

Marx's solution to this "zerowork" paradox lies in his claim that commodities are not exchanged (in most cases) at their value and that the profits of capitalists in different spheres of production are not identical to the surplus value created there. On the contrary, "the process of capitalist production as a whole," which synthesizes individual spheres of production and local conditions of circulation with global constraints, cannot operate on the basis of such identities. Each of the spheres of production has its own "organic composition" (a chemical term originally), which crystallize or congeal value in its commodity products. In exchange and circulation, however, the ratios of value are only accidentally one-to-one. On the contrary, commodities produced in spheres of high-organic-composition production generally exchange above their value, while commodities produced in spheres of low organic composition generally exchange below their value. This

---

[24] Marx, *Capital: Volume I*, 266.

[25] Marx, *Capital: Volume III*, 266; Marco Lippi, *Value and Naturalism in Marx* (London: New Left Books, 1979), 50–51.

[26] Marx, *Capital: Volume III*, 270.

[27] Ibid., 299.

breakdown of "equal exchange" is necessary to preserve the existence of an average rate of profit and make possible the existence of high-organic-composition spheres of production.

This process takes place in a world of fluctuations, "removed from direct observation," and is something of a "mystery" which takes place "behind the backs" of individual capitalists and workers. Capitalists have a glimmering of it when they recognize that "their profits are not derived solely from the labor employed in their own individual sphere" and that they are involved in the collective exploitation of the total working class. Indeed, it explains the very existence of the capitalist class as a class. "Here, then, we have the mathematically exact demonstration, how it is that the capitalists form a veritable freemason society arrayed against the whole working class, however much they may treat each other as false brothers in the competition among themselves."[28] Thus in the "transformation process" we have a truly organicist vision of capitalist production and reproduction, with the vegetative roots of the system sucking up the labor nutrients and transferring them vertically to the herbivores, which in turn are devoured by the carnivores, who finally transfer the original labor to the nervous pinnacles.

The transformation of values into prices solves the "zerowork" paradox by simply pointing out that the "zerowork" capitalist, who invests only in constant capital (machinery, buildings and raw materials) and nothing in variable capital (labor-power), receives an average rate of profit due to the transformation of value from spheres of production that operate with much variable capital. Thus, this capitalist's machines do not produce or create new value at all; rather, they at most preserve and conserve the value of the constant capital consumed in the production process. These totally automatic machines simulate the role of a worker's concrete useful labor, but they cannot create value as the worker can by actualizing his/her labor-power into abstract labor. Indeed, the very existence of spheres of production with such high (tending toward infinite) organic compositions necessitate the existence of a much greater mass of labor-power exploited in spheres of production with extremely low organic composition. Otherwise the average rate of profit would fall dramatically.

But all this behind-the-scenes circulation of value from lower to higher spheres is not arbitrary. It is determined by the chemical-like composition of capital in its exchange reactions and the various conservation laws like "the sum of the profits for all the different spheres of production must accordingly be equal to the sum of surplus values, and the sum of the prices of production for the total social product must be equal to the sum of its values."[29]

The Strategy of Marx's Theory of Machines

The context of Marx's theory of machines is not only to be found in the development of the science of energetics or even of Darwinian evolution or indeed of any particular discipline. Still less is its center to be found in his philosophical and

---

[28] Ibid., 270.
[29] Ibid., 273.

methodological debates with the Hegelian tradition. Marx's theory of machines was deployed in a political struggle; it was not the result of some suprahistorical, *a prioristic* ratiocination. Theoretically, Marx could have taken different paths in the understanding of machines and still remained anticapitalist. For example, he *could* have argued that machines create value but that this value was the product of a general social and scientific labor that *ought not* be appropriated by the capitalist class. Such an approach was indeed taken up by Veblen and others in the early twentieth century, although it of course has its roots in Saint Simon and Comte.

Marx's choice of theoretical weapons against the value-creativity of machines was rooted in the complex political situation he and his faction of the working-class movement of Western Europe faced during the U.S. Civil War and the formation of the International Working Men's Association (IWMA). On the one side, capitalist ideologists were increasingly putting the working-class initiative on the defensive through their claim that machines could break the resistance of the movement and that the future belonged to those who could conceive of and own the "crystal palaces" of Modern Industry. On the other, there was an "anti-economistic" faction of the IWMA (which included first Lassalleans and later Bakuninites) who combined this capitalist ideology and the wages fund theory to conclude that the capitalist class was increasingly becoming independent of the working class and that therefore the wages fund was diminishing. The "anti-economists" drew political implications from these conclusions that were definitely at odds with the Marxist line, arguing that trade union activity was ultimately useless.

On top of these ideological and political struggles were historical realities that Marx was responding to: the revolutionary end of the Civil War in the United States and the wave of strikes that followed the end of that war in Europe. Within that moment, inevitably, there were echoes of Luddism and the "antagonism of workers and machinery." The leaders of an organization that named itself "the International" faced a mass call for a strategy of action. Marx was thus certainly feeling the heat in the mid-1860s. His writings and speeches leading up to and including the publication of the first volume of *Capital* were his effort at a response. And one of the most important questions he had to deal with was the complex "question of machinery."[30]

The first element of the question was the intensive propaganda campaign that industrial capitalists in Britain launched against the Ten-Hour Day Law in the 1830s and 1840s and later against the legalization of unions in the 1850s and 1860s. In both campaigns, their secret tool was the ability to make those who were most exploited—and hence those most essential to the existence of capitalism—appear to be the most superfluous of beings. In both campaigns, the "question of machinery" was central.

One of the most important intellectual agents of capital in the first period was Andrew Ure—though, ironically, he was a man whom Marx did more to memorialize than anyone else. Ure's *Philosophy of Manufactures* was a paean to the capitalist use of machines to thwart, subvert and eventually crush working-class resistance to their

---

[30] See G.D.H. Cole, *Socialist Thought: Marxism and Anarchism 1850–1890* (London: Macmillan, 1969) and Julius Braunthal, *The History of the International, Volume 1: 1864–1914* (New York: Praeger, 1967).

masters' rule. Indeed, Ure seems to positively rejoice in the capitalist's recruitment of science to tame and, if need be, eliminate workers. His book is full of tales showing how cooperation between capitalists and engineers can inevitably create devices that will make redundant factory operatives who try to become "Egyptian taskmasters" over their bosses. Ure epigrammatically eulogizes, "when capital enlists science in her service, the refractory hand of labour will always be taught docility."[31] He is especially proud of the story of the inventive engineer, Mr. Roberts, who took on the project of constructing "a spinning automaton" at the behest of strike-plagued spinning mill owners of Lancashire and Lanarkshire. In the course of a few months, he succeeded in creating "the *Iron Man*, as the operatives fitly call it, [which] sprung out of the hands of our modern Prometheus at the bidding of Minerva—a creation destined to restore order among the industrious classes, and to confirm to Great Britain the empire of art. The news of this Herculean prodigy spread dismay through the Union, and even long before it left its cradle, so to speak, it strangled the Hydra of misrule."[32] Ure thus consigned class struggle on the shop floor to the rank of an unscientific superstition. In fact, so confident was Ure of the insuperable power produced by the union of science and capital that he saw the major obstacle to capitalist development to be the factory masters themselves. For if the masters were dissolute and irreligious, their hands would follow their example, and only this form of self-destruction could be the path of perdition for capital. "It is, therefore, excessively the interest of every mill-owner, to organize his moral machinery on equally sound principles with his mechanical, for otherwise he will never command the steady hands, watchful eyes, and prompt co-operation, essential to excellence of product."[33] Industrial Reformation, he concludes, is the key to success now that the working class has been tamed by the Iron Man.

This Urean image was a dominant feature of nineteenth-century capitalist ideology. For example, the grand industrial exhibitions of 1851 and 1862 were not simply places for intercapitalist information exchange about the latest technological breakthroughs. They were housed in the Crystal Palace in London at great expense in order to show the machines to the working-class public as well. These exhibits had the quality of armed parades whose intent is to forestall attack by awing the enemy with the public display of the power of one's weapons. Its success was such that the machine and its power had become the literary expression of capital in general. This, at any rate, was the message the Crystal Palace transmitted from London throughout Europe even to the streets of Petersburg. By 1864, in the heat of Marx's work in preparing the Inaugural Address for the IMWA, Dostoevsky was writing in *Notes from the Underground*: "we have only to discover these laws of nature, and man will not longer be responsible for his actions and life will become exceedingly easy for him. . . . Then . . . new economic relations will be established, all ready made and computed with mathematical exactitude, so that every possible question will vanish in a twinkling, simply because every possible answer to it will be provided. Then the crystal palace will

---

[31] Andrew Ure, *The Philosophy of Manufactures* (New York: Augustus M. Kelly, 1967), 368.
[32] Ibid., 367.
[33] Ibid., 417.

be built."[34] The Crystal Palace meant to the petty bureaucrat speaking in the *Notes from the Underground* a final loss of his humanity, the crushing of "human" resistance to capital by scientific means.

The theme of machines becoming the arbiters of social existence in general had captured the European imaginary by the 1860s. And not only in Europe. In 1863, Samuel Butler wrote and published "Darwin among the Machines" in New Zealand. He argued, ironically playing upon and then validating the machine=capital metaphor, that machines were best conceived as the next evolutionary step beyond the human species. The problem this evolutionary tendency posed was: What would be the proper human stance, resistance or cooperation? The working out of the resistance-option could be seen later in *Erewhon* (1872), which describes a society that destroyed all its machines in a horrendous civil war after the publication of a prophetic text, *The Book of Machines*. That book's argument was that machines were quickly becoming the masters of the human race and that unless they were destroyed (at the cost of infinite suffering) the human race would eventually be annihilated or totally dominated.

Not surprisingly, *Erewhon* was written in large part during the Franco-Prussian War and the massacre of the Paris communards. Indeed, at the end of that utopian novel, Butler has the Italian captain who saves the hero from drowning simply assume that he had come from the siege of Paris.[35] Butler's semi-satiric intent indicates the ambivalence of the discourse on machines that was current in the mid-nineteenth-century bourgeoisie. On one side, the metaphorical identification of science with capital originated as a salubrious "moderating" influence on the demands of workers but, on the other, it gradually lost a clear class referent and even began to be identified with an alien force that was threatening to the marginal bourgeoisie itself. Such are the vicissitudes of class weapons!

It is in this context of capitalist imaginary that Marx's theory of machines operated to great effect. Marx argues that the forces that lead to the metaphor are not simply tactical moves in the class struggle. Working-class struggle leads to the era of relative surplus value production and a tremendous unleashing of the productive powers of labor that, necessarily, in the capitalist system appear as powers of capital itself. His texts are replete with this point:

> the forms of socially developed labor—co-operation, manufacture (as a form of the division of labor), the factory (as a form of social labor organized on machinery as its material basis)—all these appear as forms of the development of capital, and therefore the productive powers of labor built upon the forms of social labor—consequently also science and the forces of nature—appear as productive powers of capital . . . with the development of machinery the conditions of labor seem to dominate labor also technologically while at the same time they replace labor, oppress it, and make it superfluous in its independent forms.[36]

---

[34] Feodor Dostoevsky, "Notes from the Underground," in *Existentialism*, ed. Robert C. Solomon (New York: Modern Library, 1974), 37.

[35] Samuel Butler, *Erewhon* (New York: Lancer Books, 1968), 337.

[36] Karl Marx, *Theories of Surplus Value, Part I* (Moscow: Progress Publishers, 1963), 390–91.

In the face of the ideological attack arising from the depths of the system, Marx needed a direct reply. It was, of course, to point out that surplus value was the thin reed that the whole capitalist system was based upon. For all the thunder of its steam hammers, for all the intimidating silence of its chemical plants, capital could not dispense with labor. Labor is not the only source of wealth, but it is the only source of value. Thus capital was mortally tied to the working class, whatever the forces that it had unleashed that were driving to a form of labor-less production. This was the political card that Marx played in the political game against the ideological suffocation of the machine = capital metaphor. It was an ironic card, but it has proved to be a useful one not only in the struggles of the 1860s.

The other side of the functionality of Marx's theory of machines was in his internal battles with members of the IWMA, which revolved around the possibility of working-class action to increase wages. The IMWA originated in the strike waves throughout Europe during the latter part of the U.S. Civil War, and it was effectively terminated with the bloody defeat of the Paris Commune. This period of eight years saw the beginning of a rise in real wages in Western Europe and the United States as well as the formation of major trade union organizations. Marx saw in the wage struggle and trade unions a positive direction for the working-class movement, and he rejected both the state-collaborationist and insurrectionist wings of the International. Marx argued on behalf of the trade unionists of the IWMA that the working class can autonomously raise wages while in the process precipitate a profits crisis for capital and empower itself for the overthrow of capitalism. He thus positioned himself between the IWMA's Lassallean and Bakuninite tendencies. Lassalle argued that the industrial proletariat cannot change the "iron law of wages" and so required state-collaboration to deviate from the law, while Bakunin argued that the power to overthrow the capitalist system can only come from the margins, that is, from the rural peasants or the lumpenproletariat at the margin of cities who were not rendered impotent by the powers of industrial capital.

At the root of both positions was a doctrine that quite rightly gave political economy the epithet "dismal." This doctrine was a synthesis of the "wage fund" theory and an analysis of the labor/wage displacing aspects of machinery that has its roots in Ricardo's *Principles* and was refined by J.S. Mill. The "wage fund" theory has had many variations, but in essence it claims that in each period of production the quantity of wage goods destined for working-class consumption is fixed. If that quantity is W and the average wage is w and the number of wage workers is n then $w = W/n$. Clearly, given the fixity of W, the only way for w to rise is through a fall of n; when individual workers or subgroups of workers struggle for higher wages, they simply redistribute W not w, that is, the wage struggle is a zero-sum game played against other workers.

The other "dismal" part of the doctrine arises from an analysis of the construction and introduction of machinery into a capitalist economy. Given a distribution of workers in the industrial and agricultural sector that produces a wage fund W, imagine now that a capitalist decides to construct a new machine. This would either directly or indirectly draw off labor from the agricultural sector and would then reduce the wage fund in the next period, W. This would then lead to a reduction of the average wage, w. At the end of the process of construction are we sure that W will equal or be greater than W? This does not necessarily follow, for it would depend upon the uses of the machine, its eventual impact on agricultural productivity, and so on.[37]

Synthesizing these two aspects of the dismal doctrine we gaze on the specter of a fixed (or even falling) wage fund being shared by an ever-increasing number of industrial wage workers. This would lead to periodic Malthusian crises that would equilibrate average wages at the point of physical subsistence. Thus mechanization threatened to intensify the effects of a system that was destined to Malthusianism anyway. The bourgeois economists thus advised the workers to forget their riots and strikes and stop up their sexual lusts. The Lassalleans called on the State to intervene in the operation of the laws of civil society and offer large sectors of workers alternatives to employment in capitalist industry. Finally, the Bakuninites could only see salvation in an apocalyptic end to the wages system precipitated outside it by the lumpen in city and country.

Marx, of course, rejected these ways out because he saw in the great strike wave stretching from the cotton plantations of Georgia to the wheat fields of Poland through the great factories and mines of Western Europe another possibility. But it required organizational cohesion and a theoretical understanding among those in the center of the wave. Thus he needed to dispel the specter of the "dismal doctrine." The first aspect of the doctrine was easy enough: there was no fixed wage fund since national production continuously changes and the ratio between the wage and profit parts of that production also shifts. His speech before the General Council of the IWMA in June 1865, later titled "Value, Price and Profit," dealt the wage fund theory a decisive blow.[38] But what of the labor/wage-displacing character of machinery? Couldn't the capitalists direct their investments so that the construction of machinery would increase their profits while reducing the wage rate? Certainly, if machines were creators of value, then this would be the golden (for capital) but dismal (for workers) path of accumulation. But if machines do not create value, another consequence looms. Every time capitalists introduce machinery in response to working-class efforts to increase wages and/or reduce the working day, they threaten the average rate of profit. That is, the wage struggle intensifies mechanization, which in turn causes the relative diminution of the variable (and value creating) part of capital. Thus, the immediate impact of strikes and other forms of shop floor action might not invariably be to increase wages but to strengthen the tendency of capital to reduce the average rate of profit while simultaneously reducing the necessary part of the average working day. And the main way the capitalist class can find out of this

---

[37] See Mark Blaug, *Economic Theory in Retrospect* (Homewood, IL: Richard D. Irwin, 1962) and Samuel Hollander, *The Economics of John Stuart Mill, Vol. 1: Theory of Method* (Toronto: University of Toronto Press, 1985).

[38] Karl Marx, *Value, Price and Profit* (New York: International Publishers, 1935).

trap is to further expand the net of capitalist labor market.[39] It is this consequence that Marx saw as central to the argument of the IWMA. For it makes it possible to follow an Ariadne's thread from apparently reformist trade union struggles to the international revolutions implicit in the strategy of the First International. A key element to it was the inability of capital to solve its crisis internally through the self-creation of value via machines.

Marx and the Turing Machine

> I would prefer not to.
> —Melville, *Bartleby the Scrivener*

Marx's theory of machines was deeply implicated in the theory of heat engines that developed in the mid-nineteenth century under the rubric of thermodynamics. The strategic motivation for Marx's restriction of value creativity to human labor was given "scientific" support through an obvious analogy with the restrictions that thermodynamics places on perpetual motion machines of the first and second kind, that is, on machines that violate the first (conservation of energy) law and the second (entropy) law of thermodynamics. But a new theory of machines was developed in the 1930s (and its ideological impact began to be increasingly felt in the years after the revolts of the 1960s) that Marx did not deal with. This section turns to this twentieth-century theory, the theory of Turing machines—often called "universal computers" or "logic machines"—and poses the question of value creativity in their case.

A good place to begin this discussion is the *annus mirabilus* for the class struggle in the United States, 1936. On the one side, that year saw the River Rouge live-ins and the peak of the CIO's mass worker organization drive, and on the other it saw the publication of Turing's (and Post's [1936]) work on universal computers. The former phenomenon spelled the limits of Taylorization in practice, while the latter was a theoretical starting point for a new science of machines and, consequently, of the labor process. Turing originally presented his the notion of the Turing machine in a paper titled "On Computable Numbers, an Application to the Entscheidungsproblem." This is not the place to enter into the details of Turing's classic paper, but it is worth pointing out that its fetishistic charm is the utter simplicity and plausibility of its starting point. The basic elements of the Turing machine are the following:

> The machine is supplied with a "tape" (the analog of paper) running through it, and divided into sections (called "squares") each capable of bearing a "symbol" ["blank" or "1"]. At any moment there is just one square . . . which is "in the machine." We may call this the "scanned square." The symbol on the scanned square may be called the "scanned symbol." The "scanned symbol" is the only one of which the machine is, so to speak, "directly aware."[40]

---

[39] Marx, *Capital: Volume I*, 772–81.

[40] Alan Turing, "On Computable Numbers," in *The Undecidable*, ed. Martin Davis

There are a finite set of "conditions" or states the machine may be in when it scans a square and the specification of the state the machine is in and the symbol that the machine is scanning is called the machine's configuration. The configuration determines which among the following four operations the machine can do:

> In some of the configurations in which the scanned square is blank . . . the machine writes down a new symbol ["1"] on the scanned square: in other configurations it erases the scanned symbol. The machine may also change the square which is being scanned, but only by shifting it one place to right or left. In addition to any of these operations the [state] may be changed.[41]

A Turing machine is thus machine with (1) a suitably inscribed tape, (2) a finite set of internal states, (3) a capacity to execute the four operations, and (4) a set of instructions that completely determines the next step of the machine for any possible configuration, with the proviso that one possible next step is halting the operation of the machine. In fact, every kind of Turing machine can be described completely by its set of instructions, which after all is simply a set of symbols that can be written on a tape as well. This description is what Turing called "the standard description" of the Turing machine that is controlled by the given instructions.

The first mathematical tour de force of "On Computable Numbers" is the demonstration that a Turing machine is capable of computing any function a human or any other computer can compute. (Or, à la Jacquard, a Turing machine, starting off with a blank tape, can produce any numerical pattern that a human or any other pattern-maker can produce.)

Yet the second major result of his work was even more remarkable. For he showed that "it is possible to invent a single machine which can be used to compute any computable [function]." The key to this result is the recognition that the standard description of a given Turing machine's table of instructions can be represented as a number printed on the tape of a special machine, the universal Turing machine (UTM). On the basis of such a number plus other information inscribed on its tape, the UTM determines what the given Turing machine can compute and proceeds to compute the function the Turing machine was designed to compute. In other words, the UTM is the universal simulator.

The UTM's capacity for universal simulation mimics the classical self-reflexivity of thought, for the UTM can take the number representing the standard description of its own instructions as an input on its own tape. Indeed, using this reflexivity technique, one can try to construct all sorts of specialized machines to examine themselves and other machines and test whether they can do certain specified tasks. For example, we might wish to construct a machine that, given the standard descriptions of any two Turing machines, can determine whether they compute the

(Hewlett, NY: Raven Press, 1965), 117.
[41] Ibid.

same function. Or, perhaps, we might wish to construct a machine that would allow us to determine whether it halts, that is, it reaches a state for which there do not exist any instructions for further action. For example, we might ask if there is a machine that, given the standard description of any arbitrary machine M, can determine whether M will halt or not?

The third major achievement of Turing's "On Computable Numbers" is his proof that there are certain important questions about Turing machines (and hence about computable functions and computers, human or otherwise) that cannot be answered by Turing machines. The first such example of a demonstrably mechanically undecidable question is exactly the previous query, sometimes called "the halting problem." Turing proved that no Turing machine could determine in general whether a given Turing machine will halt or not. Therefore, *mutatis mutandis*, a human computer cannot start out computing a function given some set of precise instructions and always know beforehand that the job will be done in some finite time. Indeed, it is in this aspect of his work that Turing charts the limits of mechanization of computation, and hence the limits of computation itself. The undecidability of the halting problem is for the new science of computation what the Second Law of thermodynamics was for heat engines: a limit on the constructability of machines.

There had been many previous attempts to characterize the computation process before Turing's, of course, but Turing devised an intuitively appealing and mathematically precise way to capture the notion of "following a rule" in general. It is important to see that human beings can be "Turing machines" that follow rules as well. Indeed, in Emil Post's version of the theory a worker carrying out a specified set of (repeatable and objectifiable) actions is the equivalent of a Turing machine. Consequently, Turing machine theory deals with productive processes irrespective of the physical construction of the subject of the process.

Moreover, Turing showed convincingly that the Turing machine can compute any function or can manipulate any string of function symbols that any rival system or scheme of computation known at the time could. This fact gave great support to an observation made by Alonzo Church made in the mid-1930s, later termed Church's Thesis. This thesis necessarily has many formulations. One sober one would be:

> The notion of a function computable by a Turing machine is a realization of
> the notion of a finite decision procedure, that is, a set of rules and instructions
> that unambiguously determine a step-by-step operation, and, moreover, any
> past or future formulations of the latter notion will be equivalent to Turing's.

Church's Thesis is not strictly a mathematical or logical theorem, rather it is a claim about the capacities of any computer, whether human or not, similar to the formulation of the First Law of thermodynamics that prohibits the existence of perpetual motion machines of the first kind. If a system produces results that are the product of computation, then its behavior should be simulatable by a Turing machine. Moreover, if anyone claims to come up with a new decision procedure, the Thesis claims that it ought to be equivalent to Turing's.

Church's Thesis still holds to this day even though an impressive number of new formulations of the notion have been developed since 1936—for example, Kolmogorov's and Markov's notion of algorithm, McCulloch and Pitts's notion of the neural net, Post's notion of a formal system, a wide variety of new computer programming "languages"—and the intuitive power of Turing's formulation of such decision procedures was decisive in persuading most mathematicians that Church's Thesis marks off the limits and content of computation.

More important still, however, has been the ability of Turing's work to show that mathematics was no longer the dividing line between mental activity and manual labor. For Turing machines can replicate the behavior of any human worker who is following (consciously or not) any fixed, finite decision procedure whether it involves manipulating numbers, discrete physical objects or well-defined, publicly identifiable environmental conditions. A data entry technician at Los Alamos, a hole-puncher in an auto assembly line, a quality-control tester, a typesetter or anyone else working in conditions typical of the industrial "Modern Times" capitalism of the 1930s and 1940s are Turing machines whose behavior can be simulated by the universal Turing machine. In a word, Turing's machine theory reveals the mathematics of work.

Although the technological implications of Turing's work were almost immediately recognized, its political economy still remains problematic. If, as some versions of technological determinism have it, the steam engine set the conditions for a classical period of economic reflection, does the Turing machine create the conditions for a postclassical form of economic reflection? Or, does the Turing machine create the conditions for a new type of conflict between worker and machine *qua* capital? And finally, though most crucial for our work, even if we grant Marx his claim that simple machines and heat engines do not create value, do Turing machines create value?

The short answer to these questions is that the value-creating aspect of human labor seems to be essentially unaffected by the Turing machine approach. Indeed, it seems to give more concrete support for Marx's claim that the use-value of labor, that is, that labor has different levels of skill and kinds of results, is not crucial for analyzing the value-creation aspect of human labor. Rather, simple average labor as the expenditure of human labor-power is the crucial object for study. Just as thermodynamics gives us the measure to compare all sorts of human energy expenditure so, too, a Turing machine analysis allows us to see the quantitative basis of skill. It makes precise the "various proportions in which different kinds of labor are reduced to simple labor as their unit of measurement are established by a social process that goes on behind the backs of the producers; these proportions therefore appear to the producers to have been handed down by tradition."[42] Thus, a computational analysis of tailoring and

---

[42] Marx, *Capital: Volume I*, 135.

weaving make clear that "though qualitatively different productive activities, are each a productive expenditure of human brains, nerves and muscles, and in this sense are human labour." The mystique of skill (especially mental skill) is deflated by a Turing machine analysis, and a fundamental continuity between labor—mental and manual—is verified.

The Self-Negativity of Labor

> I am forced to the conclusion that this was a deliberate act. In a man of
> his type, one never knows what his mental processes are going to do next.
> —A British coroner commenting on Alan Turing's suicide (1954)

The theory of the Turing machine and Church's Thesis have a fundamental contribution to make to Marxist value theory by extremizing the possibilities of mechanization. For if the notion of computation is properly generalized into any activity that is rule-governed, then one of its implications is that all labor (whether mental or physical) that is repeatable and standardized (and hence open to value analysis at all) can be mechanized. Thus, if value is created by labor per se and all its positive features can be accomplished by machine (via Church's Thesis), then machines can create value. But this is a *reductio ad absurdum* for Marxist theory: consequently one must look to other features of the transformation of labor-power into labor that cannot be subsumed under Church's Thesis.

This transformation nexus between labor-power and labor is, of course, central to value theory. It is here, after all, that the creation of surplus value is to be found, that is, the difference between the value of labor-power and the value created by labor. On the labor-power side of this nexus is the weight of physiology and history, while on the labor side is an activity that is totally simulatable by machine, but it is in its gap that value creativity is to be found. For if machines cannot create value, then why can labor? The answer cannot lie in some positive feature of labor per se, since it is arguable that any particular well-defined piece of labor can be modeled or simulated by a complex machine (in theory at least). That is, let us grant that a universal simple machine powered by a universal heat engine guided by a universal Turing machine can imitate or instantiate any rule-governed act of labor. If there was, therefore, a positive aspect of labor that created value, either individually or collectively, then one can conclude that machines also, at least theoretically, can produce value.

Consequently, if labor is to create value while (simple, heat or Turing) machines do not, then labor's value-creating capacities must lie in its negative capability, that is, its capacity to refuse to be labor. This self-reflexive negativity is an element of the actuality of labor that very few models of Marx's theory can capture. Thus in linear algebraic Marxism, this negative capacity of labor is not revealed. On the contrary, the formal equational symmetries seem to bedevil the interpretation making "iron," "corn," "machines," or any other basic commodity as capable as labor to produce value (and to be exploited!).[43] Certainly, these linear algebraic systems do not convincingly interpret Marx's theory because they seem to take Sraffa's method as basic: that capitalism is a positive, self-reflexive system of commodities produced by commodities per se. But Marx insists that labor has no value and is not a commodity, though it is the creative source of value, that is, capitalism is a system of commodities produced by a noncommodity.

Thus, labor is something like a singularity in the apparently total and homogeneous field of value or a kinetic energy trajectory in a potential field. It is not commensurable in kind with the objects of the discipline—the "immense [mountain cavern] of commodities" that begins Volume I of *Capital*—though its volatility creates the value of these very objects. Labor is outside of political economy in a way opposite to the exoteric character of use-values, for the discovery of the externality of labor to the field of value makes it possible for there to be a "critique of political economy" at all, whereas use-values simply direct us to consumer catalogues and the semiotics of fashion.

In a nutshell, we can thus formulate the Marxian reason why machines cannot create value: because they are values already.

A good, if enigmatic place to look for this gap between the being and the becoming of value is in the suicide of Alan Turing himself. Turing's suicide deprived the British government and industry a highly skilled mathematician, cryptanalyst, and computer theorist. On June 7, 1954, he ate an apple dipped in cyanide, leaving behind neither note nor explanation.[44] The circumstances behind the suicide are not clear, but it did follow his arrest under the "Gross Indecency contrary to Section 11 of the Criminal Law Amendment Act 1885" and his being forced by the court to undergo "chemotherapy" to "cure" his homosexual "tendencies." Was his suicide a protest against his treatment at the hands of the authorities (whom he had served with such effectiveness in the Second World War and in the initial period of the computer "revolution")?

This we do not know. We do know, however, that he was a state employee in the midst of an antihomosexual purge. Its very lack of explanation gave his suicide a sort of "Bartleby-effect" (after the mysterious Scrivener in Melville's 1851 story who would "prefer not"): an act that evinces the ability of labor-power to refuse to be realized as labor whether within or without a contractual bond and for reasons that are not necessarily dictated by the immediate conditions of the labor. Turing's suicide (when an employee of the state) or Bartleby's refusal to move (when an employee of a private firm) demonstrates that *the crucial ability giving human work its value is not its nonmechanizability, but rather its self-negating capacity.* As long as it can be refused, as long as the transformation of labor-power into labor is self-reflexively nondeterministic, then it can create value in its actualization. This self-reflexive negativity is no simple matter, as Hegel pointed out

---

[43] Spencer J. Pack, *Reconstructing Marxian Economics: Marx Based upon a Sraffian Commodity Theory of Value* (New York: Praeger, 1986).

[44] Andrew Hodges, *Alan Turing: The Enigma* (New York: Simon and Schuster, 1983), 487–96.

in his master-slave dialectic long before and as Fanon demonstrated shortly after Turing's suicide. For this negativity brings into play a history not so much of life and death, but of killing or being killed.

This analysis of value-creation allows us to see that class struggle is basic to the capitalist mode of production in the region of "mental" labor just as it is to be found in the realm of physical production. It is basic not because it is a sign of the special quality of mental labor, but because it is simply labor. Though complex, this capacity for labor-power to refuse its actualization into labor is not some mysterious aspect of humanity, it is a presupposition of the existence of contractual society in the first place.

MARX, TURING MACHINES, AND THE LABOR OF THOUGHT

Introduction

In 1936, in the depths of the Great Depression and amid the great strikes on the assembly lines in the industrial cities of the United States and Europe, a young British mathematician published a technical paper entitled "On Computable Numbers, with an Application to the Entscheidungsproblem" in an academic journal. The point of the paper was to solve an important, but theoretical problem in the foundations of mathematics. Although it would not have been of much immediate interest to the workers and bosses struggling in the factories of the day, Turing's paper was to radically transform the conception and practice of industrial production. For in order to arrive at the solution to a complex mathematical theorem, Turing abstractly defined a new kind of machine—later to be dubbed a "Turing machine"—which was to become the basis of the "computer revolution."

The Turing machine quite simply is a machine that is capable of computing any mathematical function a human or any other machine can compute. Let us consider a simple example of a computable function, e.g., the square function. The square function is a *function* because for any whole number, say ten, it assigns one definite whole number, in this case, one hundred. The square function is *computable* because there is a set of rules and instructions that unambiguously determine a step-by-step operation ending in a definite result, in this case, multiplying the given number by itself. Because the square function is computable, one can instruct a worker to carry out a multiplication procedure (even if the worker does not understand the concept of multiplication) as one can design many different kinds of machines that would also multiply numbers by themselves. The Turing machine allows for a unified way to describe the set of rules and instructions (in contemporary parlance, the "program") that allows anyone or anything to compute a mathematical function or carry out any other patterned activity that can be described mathematically, e.g., knitting, weaving, detecting DNA strands. In other words, every actual computer is just a different realization of an abstract Turing machine.[1]

During the Second World War, the technological implications of Turing's work were recognized in fields as varied as cryptography and nuclear weapons design.[2] After the end of the war, the Turing machine gradually replaced the heat engine as the paradigm machine metaphor of the twentieth century.

But even as we enter the twenty-first century, the fundamental "economics" of the Turing machines still remains problematic. If, as some versions of technological determinism have it, the steam engine set the conditions for a classical period of economic reflection, does the Turing machine create the conditions for a postclassical form of economic reflection? Or, as a Marxist would put it, does the Turing machine create the conditions for a new type of conflict between worker and machine? *And finally*, even if we grant Marx his claim that simple machines like the lever, gear and pulley, and heat engines do not create value, *do Turing machines create value?*

A Short History of the Manual/Mental Distinction

The first step in answering these questions is to determine what is "new" about Turing machines in comparison to the other types of machines—the simple machine and the heat engine—familiar to technological thought. It is exactly that, thought. Although simple machines and heat engines were obvious models for manual labor, the Turing machine's operations appeared to be a model for thought *qua* mental labor. This model marks a decisive turning point in the bourgeois relation to thought. For on one side, bourgeois philosophy in the seventeenth century began with transforming thought from activity to labor, and on the other side, it proposed a new set of divisions between manual and mental labor. This twofold transformation is a complex one that is often confused by theorists and critics of bourgeois ideology like Sohn-Rethel.[3] It is useful to have an understanding of this complexity, at least in outline, in order to adequately assess the meaning of Turing machines for the question of value-creativity.

---

[1] This statement is referred to as "Church's Thesis" after the mathematical logician, Alonzo Church, who in the 1930s hypothesized that any past or future formulation of a finite decision procedure can be simulated by a Turing Machine.

[2] Hodges, *Alan Turing*.

[3] Sohn-Rethel, *Intellectual and Manual Labour*.

First consider the difference between mental labor and mental activity. Sohn-Rethel, Thomson, and Farrington see a continuity between the division of mental and manual labor in capitalism and a similar distinction in ancient Greece.[4] But there is an important difference as well. In capitalism, the products of mentality are commodifiable and are conceived as a species of labor. This is not so in ancient philosophy. Thus in Platonic and Aristotelian philosophy thought is not considered labor nor can it be commodified. In Plato, the distinction between thought and money is sharply drawn and not merely for rhetorical purposes: thought is a contemplation of and participation in the activity of ideal forms that cannot be owned. Therefore, the results of thought cannot be private property, they cannot be alienated and thought's masters, the philosopher kings and queens of *The Republic*, must be absolute communists. Similarly in Aristotle, thought is an end in itself, it is an activity that is radically distinguished from labor that has a process structure (beginning-middle-terminus) and has a detachable result or *telos*. The act of knowing is, on the contrary, one of identification with its object, an intuition of an inexhaustible common of forms, literally outside of time. Thus, for Aristotle, the knower could no more own knowledge of the sun than s/he can own the sun.

The distinction between the mental and the manual for Plato and Aristotle is not of two different species of labor, but rather the "servile" labor of the slave mode of production is seen not to have a genus in common with the mental activity of the masters. There is simply no exchange between the master and slave classes in ancient Athenian philosophy. But in the transition to capitalism, thought *does* become laborious. And although capital in its early stages had many different philosophical strategists, they were agreed that *ideas* (the general word used in seventeenth- and early eighteenth-century discourse on thought and knowledge) were not "givens," they had to be worked on, struggled with, refined, or computed to be worth something.

Consider the rather divisive set of early bourgeois strategists or philosophers consisting of Locke, Hobbes, Bacon, and Descartes. They hardly agreed on anything, but they did on this: *knowing thought is not, should not, and cannot be a natural, spontaneous activity.* Thus:

- The venom behind Locke's critique of "innate ideas" is his concern that no one get the impression that knowledge can be gotten "for free," in a magical manner, and without much effort.
- Bacon's critique of Aristotle lies in The Philosopher's claim that knowledge is natural and that the process of induction is ultimately a spontaneous thing instead of being a product of an elaborate (and laborious) masculine penetration and manipulation of a feminine Nature.
- Descartes's method is the epitome of manufacturing model of knowledge production whose first step is the rejection of all "givens," whether social, historical, or sensory.

---

[4] Ibid.; George Thomson, *The First Philosophers* (London: Lawrence and Wishart, 1955); Benjamin Farrington, *Science in Antiquity* (Oxford: Oxford University Press, 1969).

• Hobbes's transformation of mental activity into mental labor required the transformation of thought into an explicit mechanizable process and here, as a mediator, the mental labor of computation proved a likely candidate. Hobbes, the archetypical mechanist, put this point clearly in the *Leviathan*:

> When a man reasoneth, he does nothing else but conceive a sum total, from additions of parcels; or conceive a remainder, from subtraction of one sum from another; which, if it be done by words, is conceiving of the consequence of the names of all the parts, to the name of the whole and one part, the name of the other part. . . . These operations are not incident to numbers only, but to all manner of things that can be added together, and taken one out of the other. . . . In sum, in what matter soever there is place for addition and subtraction, there is place for reason; and where these have no place, there reason has nothing at all to do.[5]

Thus, though Hobbes, Locke, and Bacon were ontologically, genetically, and methodologically (respectively) at opposite poles from Descartes, they shared the "constructivist," laborious approach to thought that was to become the hallmark of bourgeois philosophy down to the present.

It is true, of course, that modern philosophers distinguished mental from manual as did the ancient Greek philosophers; but the point of the differentiation had changed. For once manual labor is juridically freed from its servile status and mental activity is transformed into mental labor, the conditions of a unification are set, since both thought and physical motion become comparable units to be included in the division of labor. True, a division between mental and manual labor still remains, but it develops historically in the capitalist era. We might take Sohn-Rethel's breakdown as suggestive.[6] Following Marx and supplementing him, he argues that there are three stages of production, corresponding to regimes of accumulation and technical starting points:

Manufacture	mercantile	labor-power
Machinofacture	laissez-faire	machinery
Continuous flow	monopoly	labor

Each stage represents a different division between mental and manual labor, with mathematics, science, and management techniques separating themselves off from the workers who experience them as apparently alien powers of capital, although they too are essential parts of social labor.

Yet, Sohn-Rethel ends his analysis of the relation between manual and mental labor with Taylorism and the time-and-motion techniques applied to

---

[5] Thomas Hobbes, *Leviathan* (Indianapolis, IN: Hackett Publishing Co., 1994), 22.

[6] Sohn-Rethel, *Intellectual and Manual Labour*, 140–74.

continuous-flow production methods. The 1930s and 1940s constituted both the triumph and crisis of such a method of analysis with organizations of mass workers learning how to effectively struggle against the dictatorship of speed-up. A new initiative for the integration of mental and manual labor via Turing machine theory was launched at the very moment of this triumph and crisis. For what this new analysis considered crucial was not the spatio-temporal form of the labor process, but its computational structure throughout all levels of production. Consequently, not only the manual parts of the labor process are analyzed and made comparable to each other, but the mental aspects of labor could be made commensurable to them as well.

Marx and Mental Labor

The analysis of thought as the labor of a Turing machine should have been congenial to the Marxist project. Turing, both in his formal and philosophical analyses, rejected the metaphysical exceptionality of the mental and, although never a Marxist, he was from his childhood a proponent of a materialist ontology. His ironic comments on the "theological argument" (i.e., "Thinking is a function of man's immortal soul; God has given an immortal soul to every man and woman, but not to any other animal or to machines; hence no animal of machine can think") indicate this quite clearly:

> We like to believe that Man is in some subtle way superior to the rest of creation. It is best if he can be shown to be necessarily superior, for then there is no danger of him losing his commanding position. The popularity of the theological argument is clearly connected with this feeling. It is likely to be quite strong in intellectual people, since they value the power of thinking more highly than others, and are more inclined to base their belief in the superiority of Man on this power. I do not think that this argument is sufficiently substantial to require refutation. Consolation would be more appropriate: perhaps this should be sought in the transmigration of souls.[7]

Certainly Marx shared with Turing a materialistic rejection of the ontological autonomy of thought. Moreover, the inventor of an early version of the Turing machine in the nineteenth century, Charles Babbage, had a major influence on Marx's own theory of machines. Yet, Marx has no explicit reference to Babbage's chapter "On the Division of Mental Labour" in *Economy of Machinery and Manufactures*, even though Marx quoted extensively from the book in *Capital*. Indeed, the mechanization of mental labor, Babbage's *idée fixe*, seemed to play no role in the development of Marx's critique of thought.

On the contrary, mental labor enters into Marx's in a variety of other ways throughout his work:

---

[7] Alan Turing, "Computing Machinery and Intelligence," *Mind* 59, no. 236 (May 1950): 444, 15 (italics added).

(a) *as an essential aspect.* We presuppose labour in a form in which it is an exclusively human characteristic. A spider conducts operations which resemble those of the weaver, and a bee would put many an architect to shame in the construction of its honeycomb cells. But what distinguishes the worst architect from the best of bees is that the architect builds the cell in his mind before he constructs it in wax."[8]

(b) *as a cost of circulation in the form of "bookkeeping,"* e.g., "Book-keeping, however, as the supervision and ideal recapitulation of the process, becomes ever more necessary the more the process takes place on a social scale and loses its purely individual character."[9]

(c) *as the work of "unproductive" ideologists,* like priests and vulgar political economists, whose work and its "immaterial products" are not directly purchases by capitalists in order to create surplus value; Marx tends to treat this aspect of thought with large heaps of irony, e.g., "With given conditions of production, it is known how many labourers are needed to make a table, how great the quantity of a particular kind of labour must be in order to make a particular product. With many 'immaterial products' this is not the case. The quantity of labour required to achieve the result is as conjectural as the result itself. Twenty priests together perhaps bring about the conversion that one fails to make; six physicians consulting together perhaps discover the remedy that one alone cannot find. In a bench of judges perhaps more justice is produced than by a single judge who has not control but himself."[10]

(d) *as a form of labor per se that is part of the process of production, namely the labor of superintendence and management,* which "necessarily arises where the direct production takes the form of a socially combined process, and does not appear simply as the isolated labor of separate."[11]

(e) *as scientific and technological labor that in the period of modern industry,* when "all the sciences have been pressed into the service of capital," becomes a distinct part of the division of labor, e.g., "invention then becomes a business, and the application of science to direct production itself becomes a prospect which determines and solicits it."[12]

Marx's notion of mental labor was evidently ambivalent, ambiguous, and incomplete (for he does not place his own type of mental labor in the production system). As a consequence, along with his suspicion of the reductionist materialism of the Enlightenment, there is very little temptation in his work to deal with mental labor as a separate category of class analysis. (For example, Marx provides

---

[8] Marx, *Capital: Volume I,* 283–84.

[9] Marx, *Capital: Volume II,* 212.

[10] Marx, *Theories of Surplus Value, Part I,* 268.

[11] Marx, *Capital: Volume III,* 507.

[12] Marx, *Grundrisse,* 704.

no analysis of intellectual property law, i.e., the rise of patents and copyright, as it existed in the mid-nineteenth century.) Indeed, Sohn-Rethel notes this lacuna as essential to his project:

> There is furthermore a lack of a theory of intellectual and manual labour, of their historical division and the conditions of their possible reunification. In the "Critique of the Gotha Programme" Marx makes reference to this antithesis that a "higher phase of communist society" become possible only "after the enslaving subordination of individuals under division of labour, and therewith also the antithesis between mental and physical labour, has vanished." But before understanding how this antithesis can be removed it is necessary to understand why it arose in the first place.[13]

True, the classical Marxist tradition is replete with discussions of ideological production and, via Western Marxism, the capitalist manipulation of the infinite Maya of commodity fetishism in advertising and propaganda. But only with the work of Braverman, Gorz, Nobel, and Sohn-Rethel himself in the last generation has the actual "work of the mind" become a vital concern in a Marxist political economy (simultaneously with the neoclassical interest in the "economics of knowledge and information"). This new interest should not be surprising, according to Marxian theory, since the new stage of incorporating mental labor in social production through its mechanization has been realized in the last generation with the advent of the computerization of the spheres of production and circulation.

Computation and the Labor Process

How does Turing machine theory affect Marx's theory of machines? We can definitely say that Turing's analysis of a finite decision procedure or computation process does reveal in an *unprecedented* way the extent and importance of calculation and computation in social production. True, this aspect of production was known to pre-Marxist theorists of machinery like Babbage and Ure.[14] Thus, the Jacquard loom was, after all, the mechanization of the computational knowledge of the silk weavers of Lyons. In general, it was well known that most developments in machine technology, especially in the period of manufacture, required a thorough appropriation of the computational knowledge of the workers themselves.

Though Marx was certainly sensitive to the computational knowledge of workers, he analyzed it under the rubrics of skilled and unskilled labor. As his account of Manufacture concludes:

> Hence, in every craft it seizes, Manufacture creates a class of so-called unskilled labourers, a class strictly excluded by the nature of handicraft industry.

---

[13] Sohn-Rethel, *Intellectual and Manual Labour*, 3–4.

[14] Charles Babbage, *On the Economy of Machinery and Manufactures* (London: Charles Knight, 1832); Ure, *Philosophy*.

If it develops a one-sided specialty to perfection, at the expense of the whole of a man's working capacity, it also begins to make a specialty of the absence of all development. Alongside the gradations of the hierarchy there appears the simple separation of the workers into skilled and unskilled.[15]

But what distinguished skilled and unskilled labor? Until Turing, there was no uniform method for representing and homogenizing the computational aspect of the labor process. Although the time-and-motion studies of Taylorism presented an ultimately analog, mimetic and inadequate representation of worker behavior (whether skilled or unskilled), Taylorism could not give an objective, uniform measure of the computational complexity of a task.

A Turing machine approach to the labor process is clearly superior, since it allows one to estimate the costs, the complexity and the productivity of a computational procedure that is included in and yet obscured by the notion of "skill." Thus, a Turing machine analysis of the skill of physicians, air-traffic controllers, machinists, paper makers, phone-sex workers could be given a uniform representation and be mechanized via "expert systems," "robots," "digital control devices," "virtual reality machines," etc. Much public attention has been focused on the often spectacular programming and mechanization of these skills, but what is even more important for both technological development and the prosecution of class struggle has been the conceptual precondition of mechanization: a Turing machine analysis of the labor process which is the condition of its mechanization. *Just as a thermodynamical analysis of the transformation of mechanical, electrical, chemical and biological energy made a uniform approach to industrial and agricultural processes possible in the nineteenth century, so too a Turing machine analysis of the computational procedures implicit in all parts of the division of social labor provides a similar conceptual unification in the late twentieth century.* Consequently, the addition of a Turing machine analysis to heat engine and simple machine theory creates the basis of a more thorough Marxist analysis account of the labor process.

Does this addition, however, change the fundamental principle of Marxist analysis of machines: Only the transformation of human labor-power into labor creates value, machines cannot create value? No. The value-creating aspect of human labor seems to be essentially unaffected by the Turing machine approach. Indeed, this twentieth-century analysis of labor seems to verify Marx's nineteenth-century claim that the use-value of labor is not crucial for analyzing the value-creation aspect of human labor.

Marx refused to grant a qualitative hierarchy to different performances of labor. He claimed that simple average labor as the expenditure of human labor-power is the crucial object for study of capitalist production. *Just as thermodynamics gives us the measure to compare all sorts of human energy expenditure so, too, a Turing machine analysis allows us to see the quantitative basis of skill.* It makes precise the "different proportions in which different sorts or labour are reduced to unskilled labor as their

---

[15] Marx, *Capital: Volume I*, 470.

standard, are established by a social process that goes on behind the backs of the producers, and, consequently, appear to be fixed by custom."[16] Thus, a computational analysis of tailoring and weaving make clear that "although they are qualitatively different productive activities, are both a productive expenditure of human brains, muscles, nerves, hands etc., and in this sense both human labour."[17] The mystique of skill is penetrated by a Turing machine analysis, and a fundamental continuity between labor—mental and manual—is verified.

The Self-Defense of Mental Skill

This result, of course, has a particularly ominous aspect for those who are identified with mental labor and who believe that their work would be immune from the type of mechanization that manual and industrial laborers have faced since the dawn of capitalism. This anxiety has been the basis of much of the debate around the possibility of defining what is essentially "human labor" as the labor that cannot be mechanized, i.e., labor that is "creative," intelligent, irreducible to finite routines, "infinite." The limit theorems of Turing machine theory—the insolvability of the halting problem and the incompleteness of arithmetic (Gödel's Theorem)—just as the entropy law of thermodynamics, have been the horizon that these debates have played about. Thus, if there are noncomputable numbers and functions and if there are nonprovable truths of arithmetic, then it would appear that here is the space for deploying that unmechanizable but essential otherness of human mental labor. Hence, the intellectual worker could be forever safe from mechanization, if such a noncomputable space exists.

Just as many in the nineteenth-century thought that a vital essence would account for the existence of evolving life forms in apparent violation of the entropy law so, too, twentieth-century philosophers and scientists like Penrose, Lucas, Dreyfus, and Searle have created arguments using the limit theorems and other apparently noncomputable aspects of thought and experience to define a distinctively human, if meritocratically achieved, labor. Indeed, most of debate around "artificial intelligence" and "the philosophy of mind" in the last half-century has revolved around the attempt of many in the intelligentsia to defend their place in the hierarchy of social labor in the face of their own threatened obsolescence. For, as Turing pointed out, the strength of what often might appear to be archaic arguments based on the mysterious exceptionality of thought "is likely to be quite strong in intellectual people, since they *value* the power of thinking more highly than others, and are more inclined to base their belief in the superiority of Man on this power."[18]

The soundness of such arguments is important in determining whether capitalism has a future and what future might that be. If there is a noncomputable, nonmechanizable mental space where value (*and surplus value*) can be created, then that would define an objective division between mental and other forms of labor *and*

---

[16] Ibid., 134.

[17] Ibid.

[18] Turing "Computing Machinery and Intelligence," 444.

a permanent division between workers and within the working class itself. In former U.S. Secretary of Labor Robert Reich's terms, the "symbolic analysts" operating in this mental space would then be free of the dilemma all other workers face: if one struggles to better wages and working conditions, s/he faces being replaced by machines, but if one does not struggle, one inevitably receives wages below subsistence and wretched working conditions. The "symbolic analysts," confident in the non-mechanizability of their skills, can demand better wages and working conditions, even though their "nonsymbolic" sisters and brothers both in the United States and around the planet sink into a slave-like status. Hence, though the arguments in this debate are at times arcane, they implicate the destiny of a unified struggle to end capitalist relations of production.

Turing's philosophical work is as central to this debate as was his mathematical performance in the 1930s. In the early 1950s, he argued against the existence of an unmechanizable space of mental labor for such a space was increasingly being claimed by those intellectuals whose anxiety about being displaced by a machine was leading them to justify a sharp machine/human dichotomy in the realm of mental labor. He decided that the question of whether machines could think required some behavioral criterion for an answer, i.e., a "test" of what constitutes thinking. Turing argued that if a machine can play a question-and-answer game that (with a "level playing field," e.g., the human interlocutor could not see the machine) would consistently give an interlocutor the impression that it is human, then the machine would have passed the test, and any fair-minded person would be forced to admit that the machine can think. Turing was convinced in 1950 that it would be possible to build such machines by the end of the twentieth century and "the use of words and general educated opinion will have altered so much that one will be able to speak of machines thinking without expecting to be contradicted."[19] Here, indeed, his social acumen failed, for it is exactly those "mental laborers" that form "educated opinion" who would be most recalcitrant in attributing thought to machines.

Turing's test has been the target of those who have wanted to claim for human thought a nonmechanizable essence. These opponents can be divided into two groups: (a) those like J.R. Lucas who argue that a machine could never pass the Turing test and (b) those like John Searle who argue that even if a machine could pass the test, one should still not attribute thought to it. Group (a) arguments abound from ones that claim that machines can never write sonnets to ones that deny machines the ability to love.

However, J.R. Lucas in his 1961 "Minds, Machines and Gödel" devised an argument using Gödel's Theorem to purportedly prove that a human can always know a machine is a machine. Lucas argued that since a Turing machine can be taken to be equivalent to a formal system, and, as Kurt Gödel proved, any formal system with the power of proving the theorems of arithmetic is incomplete, i.e., it has true formulae that cannot be proven in the system, then the human who can formulate and recognize these truths is in some way superior to the machine. "In a sense, just

---

[19] Ibid., 442.

because the mind has the last word, it can always pick a hole in any formal system presented to it as a model of its own workings. The mechanical model must be, in some sense, finite and definite: and then the mind can always go one better."[20] In the context of the Turing test, all the interlocutor need do is to pull out a true but unprovable Gödelian sentence tailored for the Turing machine being interrogated and the machine would be stumped in an incriminating manner. Thus, according to Lucas, the machine is finite while the (or, more precisely, some) human mind(s) is (are) inexhaustible for "any system which was not floored by the Gödel question was *eo ipso* not a Turing machine, i.e., not a machine within the meaning of the act."[21]

Group (b) arguments tend to impute to mental labor an essential aspect that would not be detectable by the Turing test. Again many varieties of such claims abound, but the now classic version is Searle's "Chinese Room" example. In 1980, John Searle wrote "Minds, Brains and Programs," taking us inside a Turing machine during a Turing test the machine has passed to argue that the machine that is being interrogated can ultimately only deal with language (and hence its responses to an interlocutor) syntactically and neither semantically nor performatively. That is, the machine does not really understand the responses it is making to the questions. To make his point, he described a situation where the human interlocutor was Chinese and wrote out her questions in Chinese, while inside the machine was the reader who did not understand Chinese but was given a rather elaborate rule book that, if properly followed, would produce plausibly correct answers in Chinese as the output from the room. Hence, though the Chinese room would pass the Turing test, the operator within the room would not understand even one ideogram of Chinese!

The debate around the Turing test opened by Lucas's and Searle's efforts has been elaborate, intense, but remain unsolved to this day. Consequently, the truth of Turing's prediction—that by the year 2000 "educated opinion" would accept the thought capacity of machines as common sense—is looking less and less likely. With every claim of success the defenders of Turing machines and "artificial intelligence" make, a counter claim has been produced of either the Lucas or Searle variety to show that machine will not or cannot replace human mental labor. This should not be surprising from a Marxist perspective, for it is always those whose labor is threatened with competition who are apt to find in it a special, irreplaceable "something." On an ideological level, this debate is reminiscent of all those skilled workers who have claimed throughout history that the specialty steel they produce, the exquisitely weaved flannel they market, or the especially fragrant perfumes they distill, cannot be produced by a machine, and if a machine produces something like their product then . . . it's ersatz!

Therefore, the pharisees and special pleaders for the mind present their case before a skeptical audience—whether it be made of capitalists or unskilled laborers—for they have heard it all before. The intellectuals, the academics, and mental

---

[20] J.R. Lucas, "Minds, Machines and Gödel," *Philosophy* 36, no. 137 (April–July 1961): 117.

[21] Ibid., 126.

workers should not expect a special hearing, since the capitalist no more identifies him/herself with mental labor than the proletarian identifies him/herself with manual labor. Indeed, Marxist analysis would reject the claim of the irreplaceability and unmechanizability of certain types of hyperskilled labor as presented by Searle and Lucas, by the following reasoning: if any rule-governed activity is computable, then all repeatable and standardized labor (whether mental or physical) producing commodities is mechanizable. If, *pace* Lucas, the detection of Gödelian sentences (i.e., true sentences that are not provable with respect to a particular formal system) becomes a "job," then a Turing machine can be built on the basis of a more powerful program that could carry out this detection as well. There are no absolutely Gödelian sentences. Similarly, *pace* Searle, the condition of alienation from work described in his "Chinese room" parable is the generalized condition of work in capitalism, where one works in a system that is designed not to be "understood." But this alienation has never been a hindrance to the creation of value. On the contrary, it is an essential component in the process of exploitation.

Where, then, can value-creativity be found, if not in some special human feature of labor that is unsimulatable by machines? One should look to the general condition of labor in capitalism as the source of value-creativity, i.e., in the conflict between the laborer (whether mental or manual) and the exploiter of his/her labor-power. Labor creates value because of the human potential to refuse the transformation of their labor-power into labor. It does not lay in labor's inherent unmechanizablity. The Detroit factory occupations of 1936 that we began with are classic examples of this potential.

CRYSTALS AND ANALYTIC ENGINES:
HISTORICAL AND CONCEPTUAL PRELIMINARIES TO A NEW THEORY OF MACHINES

> [I]n this there is very great utility, not because those wheels or other machines accomplish the transportation of the same weight with less force or greater speed, or through a larger interval, than could be done without such instruments by an equal but judicious and well organized force, but rather because the fall of a river costs little or nothing, while the maintenance of a horse or similar animal whose power exceeds that of eight or more men is far less expensive than it would be to sustain and maintain so many men.
> —Galileo[1]

In this chapter, I claim that immaterial labor, as defined by its advocates like Hardt and Negri, does not exist. In order to defend this claim, I examine how labor has been understood in the history of capitalism through the study of machines, and argue that the most successful theory of machines in capitalism is Marx's. I rely on this theory to defend my skepticism concerning immaterial labor.

However, Marx's theory itself must be defended. One of Marx's most sophisticated critics, Philip Mirowski, has charged him with being "envious" of two contradictory physics theories at once: the substance-theory of energy of the 1840s and the field-theory of energy of the 1860s. Mirowski argues that Marx could not decide which to take as his model for labor—machines and value—so he used both and ended up with a contradictory theory of value and machines.

In part one, I defend Marx's theory by demonstrating that the very binary Mirowski deploys to criticize Marx's theory (the categories of substance versus field) is not a binary at all and that Marx's theory is consistent.

In part two, I show that Marx's theory of machines is incomplete. Though it included the theory of simple machines and of heat engines, it did not comprehend Turing machines, even though Charles Babbage had developed the first version of a

---

[1] Galileo Galilei, *On Motion and On Mechanics*, trans. I.D. Drabkin and Stillman Drake (Madison: University of Wisconsin Press, 1960), 150.

Turing machine thirty years before the publication of *Capital*. This incompleteness encourages thinkers like Hardt and Negri to argue that services, cultural products, and especially knowledge, and communication require immaterial labor for their production.

A New Theory of Machines that was complete would show how services, cultural products, knowledge, and communication are material goods, thus would support my initial claim.

Introduction

Karl Marx often sardonically noted that the capitalist ethos evoked a magical, "something for nothing" imaginary concerning the profit-making potentialities of science and machinery. This attitude was precisely captured in the seventeenth century by Ben Jonson in his play, *The Alchemist*, and in the nineteenth century by the get-rich-quick cranks like Charles Redheffer and John W. Keely, who had perpetual motion machines and schemes eternally buzzing in their brains.[2] For Marx, capitalists, far from being the sober and rational agents depicted by Max Weber's ideal type, promote an irrational understanding of the uses of machinery, just as capitalism famously inculcates a fetishism with respect to commodities that is more thorough going than the reverence West Africans were supposed to express toward their wooden idols. Far from defining humanity's inevitable future, capitalism is inherently unable to understand the very machines that serve as the distinctive tools and symbols of this supposed future.

In what follows, I analyze Marx's theory of machines in capitalism. I do this in order to contribute to the ongoing debate concerning immaterial labor. I take an extreme position in this debate: immaterial labor as defined, for example, by Hardt and Negri in *Empire*—"labor that produces an immaterial good, such as a service, a cultural product, knowledge, or communication"—does not exist.[3] I argue that services, cultural products, knowledge and communication are "material goods" and the labor that produces them is material as well (though it might not always be tangible). The products of services, from stylish hair cuts to massages, are embodied material goods; cultural products like paintings, films, and books are quite material; communication requires perfectly material channels (even though the material might be "invisible' electrons); and finally, knowledge as presently understood is, like goals in soccer games, a specific material transformation of social reality.

However, in order to make my case, it is not enough to present some counter-examples as I have just done. I need to present a model of work in response to the "immaterialists" and like all such models, they need a *machine substitute*, for the model of understanding human labor in capitalism is the machine that can replace it in the course of capitalist production. The identification of human labor with the action of machines is special case of a general situation. Marx doggedly points out, again and again, from the *1844 Manuscripts* to the third volume of *Capital*, that capital in the form of machines falsely presents itself as productive of value and the creator of surplus

---

[2] Arthur W.J.G. Ord-Hume, *Perpetual Motion: The History of an Obsession* (New York: St. Martin's Press, 1977).

[3] Hardt and Negri, *Empire*, 190.

value. Living labor repeatedly appears as dead labor, even in the case of our own living labor. This transformation is not an ideological choice, it is a *reflex* of this mode of life. (This reflex is something like the "Moon Illusion," i.e., why the moon looks bigger on the horizon than when higher up, transposed from the realm of sight to social understanding.) Marx writes about it in the following passage, "with the development of machinery there is a sense in which the conditions of labor come to dominate labor even technologically and, at the same time, they replace it, suppress it, and render it superfluous in its independent form."[4] This is one of hundreds of possible citations in Marx's work that makes the same point, illustrating how obsessive he became in trying to expose this false transformation. Indeed, Marx's theory of machines microscopically analyzes this reflex that makes capital "a highly mysterious thing" and he specifies the conditions of the demystification of machines.

In this chapter, I defend Marx's theory of machines from charges of inconsistency, but I also find it incomplete. I argue that it needs to be extended to include another category of machine: the Turing machine (i.e., the common mathematical structure of all computers, formally isolated by Alan Turing in the 1930s).[5] A complete theory of machines that included Turing machines as well as simple machines and heat engines would demonstrate, on the one side, the materiality of all labor and, on the other, the lineaments of a strategy to liberate labor from its bondage to capital.

Although Marx was far from being an anti-industrial "back to the land" activist, he was a prime debunker of the economic claims capitalists make for machines which function as a form of conceptual terrorism against workers' struggle.[6] He argued that active human labor is the only source of value, that however cleverly designed or gigantic in size, machines produce no value at all and that, at best, they can only transfer their own value to the product.

Marx's attitude was similar to that early modern critic of machine magic: Galileo.[7] In the same paragraph from which the epigraph of this piece was culled, Galileo ridicules "designers of machines" who believe that "with their machines they could cheat nature."[8] He claims that machines do not in themselves create force or motion, they simply make it possible to substitute less "intelligent" and less costly sources of force and motion for the more "intelligent" and more costly ones. The problem for the mechanic is to design machines so that "with the mere application of [the mover's, say, a horse's] strength it can carry out the desired effect."[9] The mechanic introduces intelligent design into the world, but s/he cannot add even a cubit of force or motion to it.

---

[4] Marx, *Capital: Volume I*, 1055.

[5] Alan Turing, "On Computable Numbers with an Application to the Entscheidungsproblem" in *The Essential Turing: Seminal Writings in Computing, Logic, Philosophy, Artificial Intelligence, and Artificial Life, Plus: The Secrets of Enigma*, ed. Jack Copeland (Oxford: Clarendon Press, 2004 [1936]).

[6] See "Why Machines Cannot Create Value: Marx's Theory of Machines," 139 in this volume.

[7] Galileo, *On Motion and On Mechanics*; and Stillman Drake, *Galileo at Work: His Scientific Biography* (Chicago: University of Chicago Press, 1978).

[8] Ibid., 150.

[9] Ibid.

This might not appear to be so, if one looks at the books of mechanics from Hero of Alexandria's to Galileo's own, which are filled with the diagrams of the mediating machines; but its true realm is in the world of costs and wages. In other words, simple machines—the inclined plane, lever, pulley, screw, wheel, and axle (capstan)—"judiciously organize force," they do not create it.[10]

Many physicists after Galileo, especially nineteenth-century architects of thermodynamics like Sadi Carnot and Hermann von Helmholtz, were anxious to make this anti-magical lesson evident in the context of heat engines as well (e.g., by proclaiming the principles: no perpetual motion machine is possible, energy cannot be created or destroyed).

Marx, undoubtedly influenced by the two "laws of thermodynamics" being developed in his time, agreed with Galileo and, if one substitutes "value" for "force" or "energy," one can see his effort to establish conservation laws for value that block any attempt to "cheat society" with machines. Machines do not create value, they merely "judiciously organize" it and, most important, they make it possible to substitute less costly for more expensive (and/or resistant) labor-power. As Andrew Ure, the nineteenth-century "philosopher of machines," wrote:

> The effect of improvements in machinery, [lies] not merely in superseding the necessity for the employment of the same quantity of adult labour as before, in order to produce a given result, but in substituting one description of human labour for another, the less skilled for the more skilled, juvenile for adult, female for male.[11]

That is why they can become such powerful weapons against the working class, so that "the instrument of labor strikes down the worker."[12]

Though they appear often to be behemoths of power (as in the steam engines of the nineteenth century) or angels of intelligence (as in computers of the twenty-first century), machines' weakness—the fact that they cannot create value—has enormous consequences for the whole capitalist system. Industries that employ a large amount of machinery and a relatively small amount of labor cannot create within their production process the surplus value necessary to constitute an average rate of profit for the investment in constant capital (machinery, for the most part) and variable capital (wages). However, if capitalists do not receive at least an average rate of profit, they inevitably leave their branch of industry over time and new investors shun them. Soon, these branches of industry would stop functioning, due to bankruptcies and low investment. But what if these branches of industry (e.g., oil extraction) were required for the reproduction of the system? How would the profits of such branches be provided for, if the workers in these branches could not generate them? This question is especially important to answer since increasing the use of machinery

---

[10] Ibid.

[11] Quoted in Marx, *Capital: Volume I*, 559–60.

[12] Marx, *Capital: Volume I*, 559.

to respond to workers' struggles is a crucial strategy in the eternally rolling, though often low-intensity, class war.

Marx's response to this conundrum is that there is a transformation of surplus value created in some branches of industry with relatively low ratios of investment in machinery to wages into the profits of branches that have relative high ratios. This process takes place "behind the backs" of capitalists in the competitive process, and forms the foundation of the remarkable unity of capital, given the apparent competitive character of the system.[13] Investment in machines is promoted by the system in general, even though it does not lead to an increase in surplus value in particular (although, of course, surplus value can be created by workers in the production of these machines just as in the production of any other commodity).

In Part I of this chapter, I defend an important tenet of Marx's theory of machines from claims that it is rooted in a fundamental inconsistency of the theory. This tenet is the notion of a transformation of surplus value generated by some branches of production into the profits of other branches of production.

Part I. A Conceptual Preliminary: Is Marx's Theory of Machines Consistent?

> I could be a rich man if I could have taken along only what I merely needed to pick up and break loose. In some places I found myself in a veritable garden of magic. What I beheld was formed most artistically out of the most precious metals. In the elegant braids and branches of silver there hung sparkling, ruby-red, transparent fruits and the heavy trees were standing on a crystal base inimitably wrought. One hardly trusted one's senses in those marvelous places and never tired of roaming through those charming wildernesses and delighting in their treasures, on my present journey too I have seen many remarkable things, and certainly the earth is equally productive and lavish in other countries.
> —Novalis[14]

Marx's theory of machines postulates the existence of a fundamental transformation principle of capitalist life: profits tend to be equalized across all branches of industry, even though the ratio between the investments in machinery and the payment of wages varies tremendously between them. If this transformation is not operative, then there would be no incentive to invest in machinery in order to escape working-class struggle or even to ensure the system's own material reproduction. For if surplus value is created by labor, but very little labor is employed in essential industries like oil extraction, then there would be little or no profit for such an industry that requires large investments in fixed capital.

But does such a transformation of surplus value into profit take place literally "behind the backs" of the participants of the system? The debate on the mathematical and methodological validity of Marx's "transformation" has been the staple of the academic polemics between Marxists and anti-Marxists since Böhm-Bawerk's *Karl*

---

[13] Marx, *Capital: Volume III*, 273 forward.

[14] Novalis, *Henry von Ofterdingen* (New York: Frederick Ungar Books, 1964), 88.

Marx and the Close of His System first published in the late nineteenth century.[15] Indeed, in the last century, every time there was an intensification of the class struggle and a penetration of Marxist intellectuals into the academy, capital's schoolmasters took out that old chestnut from the closet to be roasted again. The sophistication of the technical ripostes on each side, however, has definitely been increasing. Thus in response to the campus rebellions of the 1960s, Paul Samuelson (1971) leveled his analytic arsenal on the old Moor only to find that a whole literature modeling Marx's theory in linear algebraic terms sprouting in its defense. This literature, with its Sraffaian, "analytic" and "recursive" solutions, has shown us that the technical problems of the "transformation" can be resolved *if* one accepts rather stilted mathematical models of Marx's fluid, chemically active description of the capitalist system of production *and* rejects one or more of Marx's conservation principles or mathematical procedures.[16] The status of this debate, therefore, has entered into a more interesting stage. For what is at stake is the very reason for having a labor theory of value in the first place.

A sign of this change appeared with the publication of Philip Mirowski's *More Heat than Light* where Marx is no longer charged with making elementary mathematical errors or being ignorant of analytic techniques that were invented a generation or two after the publication of *Capital*.[17] Rather, Mirowski tries to show that the transformation problem is a problem because it reflects a major tension not only in Marx's theory, but in all scientific endeavors during the mid-nineteenth century. Natural philosophy was transforming itself into physics in this period, Mirowski points out, and the ontology of science was turning from "substance" to "field" entities (or from "substance" to "function" in Cassirer's [1953] formulation).

Mirowski claims that Marx found himself on the "cusp" of this transition and his value theory reflected it, "in fact there ended being not one but *two* Marxian labor theories of value, the first rooted in the older substance tradition, the other sporting resemblances to nascent field theories in physics."[18] The first type Mirowski calls "the crystallized-labor or substance approach," while the second type is called "the real-cost or virtual approach."[19] They have very different, even contradictory methodological implications. For the first is like the caloric theory of heat which identified heat as a substance that "flowed" from hotter to cooler bodies in the way that water flowed from higher to lower elevations, while the second identifies heat as one aspect of a generalized energy field that can be transformed into many different states, phases, and forms. Indeed, the intellectual struggle in the development of thermodynamics from the publication of Sadi Carnot's *Memoire* in 1824 to the publication of Clausius's

---

[15] Eugen von Böhm-Bawerk, *Karl Marx and the Close of His System* (London: Porcupine Press, 2006 [1896]).

[16] Ian Steedman, et al., *The Value Controversy* (London: Verso, 1981); and Anwar Shaikh, "Marx's Theory of Value and the 'Transformation Problem,'" in *The Subtle Anatomy of Capitalism*, ed. Jesse Schwartz (Santa Monica, CA: Goodyear Pub. Co., 1977).

[17] Philip Mirowski, *More Heat than Light: Economics as Social Physics, Physics as Nature's Economics* (Cambridge: Cambridge University Press, 1989).

[18] Ibid., 177.

[19] Ibid., 180.

entropy-defining paper of 1865 could be read as marking the transition from substance to field theories in physics.[20] Marx's theory then would be like many theories developed in the 1840s by those who accepted both Carnot's caloric explanation of the work performed by the steam engine and early versions of the conservation of energy.

In particular, the crystallized-labor theory makes it clear that exploitation can only have its origin within the process of production. Since value is a substance, it is conserved both *locally* (when, for example, it is used in productive consumption as in the case of food for a worker or gasoline for a tractor) and *globally* (when the total sum of value is conserved in the complex transformation from one branch of production to another). These flows of value seem to have all the charm of "the hallowed tradition of natural-substance theories, which were intended to imitate the structure of explanation in the Cartesian natural sciences."[21] The metaphors emanating from such a view of value, of course, have a powerful political appeal as well, for the sense of theft during the capitalist process of production can be directly referred to. After all, the worker produces a certain amount of value-stuff and s/he only gets part of this value-stuff back in the form of wages, the difference being the only source of revenue for capitalists, bankers, priests, and landlords.

The problem, Mirowski points out, with such a simple but powerful crystallized-labor theory is that it was *passé* at the moment of its most sophisticated employment in the Marxian critique of political economy. Caloric had been replaced with a much more subtle, field-theoretic entity, energy, whose continuity of motion, metamorphoses, conservation and dissipation was not to be modeled in the fluid dynamics of Cartesian vortexes. This subtlety is illustrated in what Cassirer writes of Mayer's energetic equation of potential with kinetic energy:

> If the mere elevation above a certain level (thus a mere state) is here assumed to be identical with the fall over a certain distance (with a temporal process), then it is clearly evident that no immediate substantial standard is applied to both, and that they are not compared with each other according to any similarity of factual property, but merely as abstract measuring values. The two are the "same" not because they share any objective property, but because they can occur as members of the same causal equation, and thus be substituted for each other from the standpoint of pure magnitude. Energy is able to institute an order among the totality of phenomena, because it itself is on the same plane with no one of them; because, lacking all concrete existence, energy only expresses a pure relation of mutual dependency.[22]

The "cost-price" approach was Marx's incipient awareness of this new energetic-field-of-relations approach in his own work. In this approach, a commodity can possess

---

[20] Sadi Carnot, *Reflections on the Motive Power of Fire*, ed. and trans. Robert Fox (Manchester: Manchester University Press, 1986 [1824]); Rudolf Julius Emanuel Clausius, "Entropy," in *A Source Book in Physics*, ed. William F. Magie (Cambridge, MA: Harvard University Press, 1965 [1865]).

[21] Mirowski, *More Heat*, 184.

[22] Ernst Cassirer, *Substance and Function* (New York: Dover, 1953), 199–200.

a value only relative "to the contemporary configuration of production."[23] Thus its value can be changed by, for example, technological alterations anywhere in the economy (e.g., the development of new programming techniques) or even market phenomena (e.g., good harvests) that had no direct connection with the production of the commodity in question.[24] However, the creation of value can no longer be identified with labor, profit with the exploitation of labor in the production process, nor the flows and transformations of value with continuous (though unobserved) processes. Indeed, in the cost-price world, machines could also produce (or deduct) value. Mirowski suggests that this approach would have solved many of the major analytic problems of Marx's program, though at the impossible cost of "throwing history out the window," where by "history" Mirowski simply means that present conditions are partly determined by past events and processes.[25]

Let us chart the consequences of contrasting approaches:

Substance Theory	Field Theory
crystallized labor *approach;*	*real-cost* or virtual *approach;*
labor "buried" in the commodity is *source of value*	*source of value* in the field;
the *quantity of value* is determined by labor-time;	the socially necessary direct replacement costs determine the *quantity of value;*
the *history of production* is important to the determination of the value of commodities;	The *history of production* is irrelevant to the determination of the value of commodities;
profit can only be generated in production;	*profit* can be generated in exchange and market transactions;
labor *value* is conserved;	"windfalls" are ubiquitous and throughout the system *values* can be created or destroyed instantaneously.

But in trying to juggle between these two inconsistent ontologies Marx was bound to crash, according to Mirowski, who locates this catastrophe in "the transformation problem" where the conservation of crystallized value and surplus value can not be reconciled with the equalization of rates of profit while the cost-price

---

[23] Mirowski, *More Heat*, 181.

[24] Ibid.

[25] Ibid., 184.

values can easily enforce equalized rates of profit but must falsify the claim that "surplus is only generated in production and is passed around among industries in the pricing process."[26] The transformation of values to prices does not pose a mathematical problem per se, Mirowski argues, but rather it is a symptom of a deeper logical and methodological incoherence.

This is a serious critique. However, what is charming about Mirowski is that he seems to be relatively innocent of the blatant Cold War motivations that have driven similar efforts in the last couple of generations of scholarly debate on these matters. Indeed, Mirowski's effort is one of the first in the new post–Cold War turn of a rather hoary genre. A sign that Mirowski is operating in a new critical space is expressed by the fact that he applies to the work of neoclassical theorists like J.B. Clark and, yes, Paul Samuelson the same hermeneutical device he uses to detect tensions and contradictions in Marxism (i.e., the substance versus field approaches). He also finds a shared, root failure in both the Marxist and the neoclassical research programs: *an ill-understood "physics envy" which ironically is often ignorant of the complexity of the object of its envy or is fixated on one historical embodiment of physical theory.* In a word, the contemporary neoclassical research program has become "helplessly locked into the physics of circa 1860" while Marxism is locked in the physics of the 1840s.[27] Mirowski speaks for a new theoretical initiative that would, on the one hand, open economics up to models of physics that superseded the proto-energetics of the nineteenth century and, on the other, look for models outside of physics altogether. But is this type of critique useful in general or accurate as a way of interpreting Marx's writings?

The main problem with Mirowski's hermeneutics in general is that the central distinction between substance and field theories he relies on is far from clear in itself and, furthermore, it is not easily inserted in a historical narrative. First consider theories like Newtonian mechanics, the kinetic theory of heat, the relativity theories and quantum mechanics: are these "substance" or "field" theories? Well, they are a bit of both. Thus Newton's gravity acts as a field force, but his notion of mass is substantial; the microscopic billiard balls of the kinetic theory are ideal type substances, but the macroscopic states they create (like temperature, pressure and volume) are field-like entities; Einstein's general theory of relativity seems to posit a substantial character for space-time while his special theory seems to give it a field-like aspect; as for the notorious quantum mechanics, one can easily add a "substance"–"field" duality to top off and sum up the Tower of Babel dualities it poses to the interpreter. Thus, most theories in physics at least have substance as well as field elements in them and it is in the intersection of these elements that their complex potentialities for paradox emerge: in Newtonian mechanics, the mass point and the gravitational field; in the kinetic theory of gases, the molecule and temperature; in Einstein relativities, the mass point and the manifold of space-time; in quantum mechanics, the wave and the particle. *One might perversely argue that the uniqueness of these theories is to be found in the paradoxical heart of this intersection.*

---

[26] Ibid., 185.
[27] Ibid., 394.

Thus we see that Mirowski's concepts of "substance" and "field" are not found unmixed in any historically given theory in physics. But even as ideal types, these concepts are far from mutually exclusive polarities. One can argue that an ideal field is simply a highly complex substance defined by an infinite set of internal relations while an ideal substance is simply a pure field defined by a small to null set of internal relations. In other words, *the "substance"–"field" distinction is not one of absolute kind but of dialectical degree.* And in the history of science one can often find nodes of transition from substance to field and then back again. Think of the complex dialectical, crisscrossing dance in the history of quantum mechanics from wave (field) to particle (substance) and back again.

Therefore, it is very difficult to use these ontological notions in a historical narrative. From the Newtonian-Cartesian debates of the seventeenth century to the wave/particle dualities of the twentieth, it is clear that "substance" and "field" are dialectical polarities in the theory-construction toolbox first of natural philosophy and then of physics. Mirowski credits Meyerson, an early twentieth-century French philosopher and historian of science, with explaining why the process of reification was so central to science of the post-Aristotelian period. Meyerson showed how "substance" ontologies underlie conservation laws and these laws make it possible to apply mathematical methods to the "external [but noncelestial] world."[28] But substance ontologies have been replaced by field ontologies for equally powerful mathematical reasons, and the reasons for this replacement can hardly be said to be determined by the internal logic of the dialectical spirit.

If Mirowski's "substance"–"field" dichotomy is not a general tool of theoretical hermeneutics, the question remains whether his critique of Marx and the Marxist theory of value is cogent. Does Marx have two divergent theories of value? Does Marx fetishize labor and in so doing reify it into the very substance-thing that bourgeois economists so superstitiously worship? Mirowski's criticisms certainly reflect the contemporary Zeitgeist, for poststructuralist critics like Baudrillard reject Marxist analyses because of their purported "objectivism" and "representationalism."[29] But are these criticisms accurate? In order to answer this question let us go directly to the center of Mirowski's criticism: *the crystal.* After all, he dubs Marx's substance theory of value "the crystallized-labor approach" because for Marx, "labor time extracted in the process of production is reincarnated (or perhaps "buried" is a better term, since Marx calls it "dead labor") in the commodity, to subsist thereafter independent of any market activity."[30] But is a crystal a substance?

At the beginning of the nineteenth century, the crystal became the focus of research programs in mineralogy and in chemistry. Mineralogists saw that most solid inorganic bodies were composed of microcrystals while chemists, following Hauy, argued that every chemical substance had a unique crystalline structure. Hauy's hypothesis initiated an immense theoretical and empirical activity that eventually

---

[28] Ibid., 6.

[29] Baudrillard, *Mirror of Production.*

[30] Mirowski, *More Heat than Light*, 180.

ended in its rejection. But these research programs and their fate would undoubtedly have interested Marx (and Engels) not only because they appealed to their general mathematical interests but also because of the role which that most precious of minerals, gold, played in political economy.

By the 1860s a new energetic turn in the crystalline story was taken. It was understood that a mineral's crystalline form was not a given of nature. A crystal was merely "a state of energetic equilibrium reflecting the most stable level of energy under given external conditions."[31] Grove, in a work cited by Marx in the first volume of *Capital*,[32] clearly makes this point:

> There is scarcely any doubt that the force which is concerned in aggregation is the same which gives to matter its crystalline form; indeed, a vast number of inorganic bodies, if not all, which appear amorphous are, when closely examined, found to be crystalline in their structure: we thus get a reciprocity of action between the force which unites the molecules of matter and the magnetic force, and through the medium of the latter the correlation of the attraction of aggregation with the other modes of force may be established.[33]

Thus the crystalline aggregation, which had been studied throughout the early nineteenth century as a way of differentiating chemicals, was seen as part of the great round of the correlation of forces. Grove points out that via the correlation of aggregation force and magnetic force a new theory of the crystal is made possible. For the crystal simply is a store of energy that in the various mineralogical processes is released and then reabsorbed. Increasingly the internal structure of inorganic bodies were seen by physicists, chemists, and mineralogists as a more or less complex pool of "tensional" or "potential" energy.

The whole of the theory of energetics was interested in the relation between this "potential energy" and the "actual energy" that is exhibited to the observer. Rankine put the problematic of energetics in his 1853 paper "On the General Law of the Transformation of Energy," in which he introduces the notion of "potential energy" for the first time:

> ACTUAL, OR SENSIBLE ENERGY, is a measurable, transmissible, and transformable condition, whose presence causes a substance to tend to change its state in one or more respects. By the occurrence of such changes, actual energy disappears, and is replaced by
>
> POTENTIAL, OR LATENT ENERGY; which is measured by the product of a change of state into the resistance against which that change is made.

---

[31] Rene Taton, ed., *Science in the Nineteenth Century* (New York: Basic Books, 1965), 302.

[32] Marx, *Capital: Volume I*, 664.

[33] Quoted in Youmans, *Correlation and Conservation of Forces*, 172.

Vis-à-vis of matter in motion, thermometric heat, radiant heat, light, chemical action, and electric currents, are forms of actual energy; amongst those of potential energy are the mechanical powers of gravity, elasticity, chemical affinity, static electricity, and magnetism.

The law of the Conservation of Energy is already known, viz.: that the sum of all energies of the universe, actual and potential, is unchangeable.[34]

Potential energy is, of course, a typical field variable, since it can change due to variations in the field (whether these changes are gravitational, electrical, magnetic, or chemical) while it can remain static over long periods of time. Actual energy is quite different. It is by its very nature realizing and annihilating itself at its locale of action.

Not surprisingly then, the process of potential turning into actual then back into potential energy was to serve Marx as a model for the shift from living into dead labor that is then transferred in the production process. For example, he refers to commodities "As crystals of this social substance [i.e., human labor], which is common to them all, they are values—commodity values."[35] The crystal is the ideal model for a potential energy store whose structure is formed by the actual energies employed in the crystal-generating process but whose total potential energy is determined by the whole potential field. Value is therefore analogous not to actual, but to potential energy, for labor is valueless while being a creative, transforming, preserving, determining action, but once stored, dead, objectified, determined, congealed labor is value. This dead labor (like its analogous potential energy) is measured by the socially necessary labor-time, not by the living labor that has vanished into time, and is only *represented* in the value of the commodity.

Thus, commodities have locked within them value due to the labor (both useful and value creating) that has gone into them. They form the crystalline "storehouse" cave of capital in the same way that Helmholtz describes the objects in "the general store-house of Nature" that lock force within them:[36]

The brook and the wind, which drive our mills, the forest and the coal bed, which supply our steam engines and warm our rooms, are to use the bearers of a small portion of the great natural supply which we draw upon for our purposes, and the actions of which we can apply as we see fit. The possessor of a mill claims the gravity of the descending rivulet, or the living force of the wind, as his possession. These portions of the store of Nature are what give his property its chief value.[37]

---

[34] Quoted in C.A. Truesdell, *The Tragicomical History of Thermodynamics, 1822–1854* (New York: Springer-Verlag, 1980), 259.

[35] Marx, *Capital: Volume I*, 128.

[36] Quoted in Youmans, *The Correlation and Conservation*, 227.

[37] Ibid., 227.

Just as the potential energy of a rivulet can be changed by shifts in the potential field (e.g. by the reduction of the height of the water's fall by an earthquake) so too can the value of constant capital engaged in a particular process of production be changed by events outside of that very process. But the possibility of changes in the potential energy does not turn potential into kinetic energy, for these changes occur, so to speak, "outside" of the locus of the potential energy. Similarly, changes in the stored value of circulating and fixed capital can occur "outside" of the process of its production. For example, cotton bought in a previous year and sitting in the storehouse of a spinning mill will increase in value if there is a bad cotton harvest this year, or the value of an already operating spinning machine can decrease if a new less expensive technique for building such machines is put into play. But in both cases, these changes take place "outside" the immediate production process. Within the actual production process of spinning cotton, however, the machine and the cotton "cannot transfer more value than [they possess] independently of the process."[38] Keeping with the analogy, once the potential energy of a body is determined, then the kinetic energy it releases can not be greater than itself.

This excursus into the bowels of Marx's theory of value production and machines is not meant to show that Marx's theory was devised with a strict analogy to energetics in mind. On the contrary, there were many different analogies, metaphors, metonymies, tropes, etc. that Marx had in mind in the composition of *Capital*. Darwinian biology, infinitesimal calculus, debates in geology, developments in organic chemistry and more were often directly and, even more often, indirectly cited in the text. Marx, Engels, and indeed much of the workers' movement of the day were not suffering from "physics envy," rather they were deeply enamored with the tremendous theoretical and practical productivity of the sciences of the day. But certainly pride of place was given to energetics (or the discipline of thermodynamics) during the mid-nineteenth century, and it would be surprising if Marx did not explore the relation between labor and energy in his theory. Marx was clearly knowledgeable about energetics and its primary theoretical distinctions (like kinetic versus potential energy). Therefore, Mirowski's critique of Marx—that he was on the "cusp" between substance and field theories—is not convincing.

However, we might turn this reply to Mirowski's Marx-critique around into an even more pointed Marx-critique (that is similar to Mirowski's critique of neoclassical economics). Namely, if Marx was perfectly conscious of the anti-substantial developments in mid-nineteenth-century energetics and patterned much of his value theory on them, why should twenty-first-century critics of capitalism take *his* theory seriously? After all, physics has moved into major new conceptual and methodological territory since the grey beards of thermodynamics finally cracked the contradiction between Carnot's caloric theory and the conservation of energy. Do relativity theory, quantum mechanics, chaos theory not offer better and more interesting insights than labor- and wretch-obsessed Marxism in order to understand the contemporary postmodern situation? Mirowski calls on his colleagues in neoclassical

---

[38] Marx, *Capital: Volume I*, 318.

economics to let go of their dependence on outdated (and ill-understood) physical theory and try something new. A similar point has been made by post-Marxists and other "antisystemic" thinkers who were previously sympathetic to Marxism.

Well, why not? The answer is simple: *choose whatever model you wish, but what is to be modeled—our social reality—is still rooted in the past.* We cannot avoid or "go beyond" the categories of labor, value, money, surplus value, exploitation, capital, crisis, revolution, and communism because capitalism is still very much in existence. True, much else is in existence now that was not in the mid-nineteenth century, but has it made a crucial difference in understanding capital? Answers to a question like this are, of course, complex, but who could really say in 2007 that money, work, wages, profit, interest, and rent do not *really* matter? Of course they do, and any application of contemporary scientific theory to contemporary social and economic life that ignores them would not *really* matter.

However, there have been genuine changes in the world of machines since the mid-nineteenth century, especially the development and industrialization of the Turing machines. This is an area that definitely calls for an extension of Marx's theory of machines, as I will argue in Part II.

Part II. Historical Preliminary: Ure versus Babbage

> The Turing machine is an idealization of the human computer. [Turing explained,] "We may compare a man in the process of computing a real number to a machine which is only capable of a finite number of conditions . . . called 'm-configurations.' The machine is supplied with a 'tape' . . ." Wittgenstein put the point in a striking way: "Turing's 'Machines': These machines are *humans* who calculate."[39]

Marx's theory of machines was deeply implicated in the theory of heat engines that was developed in the mid-nineteenth century under the rubric of "thermodynamics" in the same way that Galileo's theory of machines was implicated in the theory of simple machines initially developed especially by thinkers in Hellenistic Egypt like Hero of Alexandria and later by Arabic and medieval European mechanicians.[40] Indeed, much of the motivation for Marx's restriction of value-creativity to human labor arose on analogy with the restrictions thermodynamics places on perpetual motion machines of the first and second kind, i.e., on machines that violate the first—conservation of energy—law and the second—entropy—law of thermodynamics. In this part of the essay I will turn my attention to the kind of machines studied by the theory of Turing machines—often called "universal computers" or "logic machines."

---

[39] Jack Copeland, ed., *The Essential Turing: Seminal Writings in Computing, Logic, Philosophy, Artificial Intelligence, and Artificial Life, Plus: The Secrets of Enigma* (Oxford: Clarendon Press, 2004), 41.

[40] Marshall Clagett, *The Science of Mechanics in the Middle Ages* (Madison: University of Wisconsin Press, 1959), 3–68.

Marx *might* be forgiven for having neglected Turing machines, for the mid-1930s are often celebrated as the origin-time of their theory while World War II is frequently seen as the "hot-house" that forced the transformation of Turing machine theory into actual, functioning hardware. I qualify what I say because the origin of the theory and practice of universal computers or logic machines *can* be antedated by at least a century. True, the uncertain origin of a scientific or technological concept like that of the universal computer is by no means unusual and in this "postist" period suspicion of origins is *de rigueur*. But this particular antedating is important for my argument since it will highlight an early tension in Marx's theory that can explain why the later Marxist tradition (in both its Stalinist *and* libertarian tendencies) has traditionally confused the labor process (which they glorified) with the value-creativity of labor.

This case of anteceding origins takes us to a figure quite familiar to Marx and the readers of the pages on machinery in the first volume of *Capital*: Charles Babbage. Marx quoted Babbage's *On the Economy of Machines and Manufacturing* (1832) at least five times in Part IV, "The Production of Absolute and Relative Surplus Value," but he seemed to have a rather ambivalent stance toward him.[41] On the one side, Marx credits Babbage with the definition of machine he uses, but on the other, he relegated him to the role of an antiquary, someone interested not in *au courant* Modern Industry (the automatic factory) but rather in *passé* Manufacture (the workshop). In an interesting footnote, he compared Babbage to a contemporary of the 1830s, Andrew Ure, whose *Philosophy of Manufactures* (1835) Marx referred to sixteen times in the first volume of *Capital*:

> Dr. Ure, in his apotheosis of Modern Mechanical Industry, brings out the peculiar character of manufacture more sharply than previous economists, who did not have his polemical interests in the matter, and more sharply even than his contemporaries—Babbage, e.g., who, though much his superior in mathematics and mechanics, treated large-scale industry from the standpoint of manufacture alone.[42]

That is, Babbage was still mired in marveling at the remaining aspects of the detail laborer, at the workshop and handicraftsman work, while Ure was interested in the use of machinery to escape the stranglehold skilled laborers in manufacturing had on capital.[43]

This assessment is surprisingly off the mark. From the perspective of the twenty-first century, Babbage was clearly involved in a project whose consequences would be more momentous than simply the polemical "reduction" of skilled into unskilled labor discussed by Ure. For Babbage's work would eventually lead to an

---

[41] Marx, *Capital: Volume I*, 643–74.

[42] Ibid., 470.

[43] Ibid., 563–64.

understanding of what skill was in the first place.[44] However, Marx could be excused his rather conventional assessment of Babbage, since Babbage's very project required an interest in a kind of labor that was not yet within the ken of "Modern Mechanical Industry" and still required all the resources "Manufacture" could provide in this period. Babbage wished to build at least *one* universal computing machine out of metal and wire, which required the assemblage of some of the most skilled artisans of Britain to build a machine whose requirements of precision tested the limits of mechanical knowledge. The process of putting together this machine was the basis of his research that went into *On the Economy of Machinery and Manufactures* (1832). As one of his biographers writes:

> Babbage's study of machinery and manufacturing processes originally started in a manner so extraordinary that it has passed almost without comment, as if no one could believe what he was really doing: he settled down to study all the manufacturing techniques and processes, more particularly all the mechanical devices and inventions he could find, searching for ideas and techniques which could be of use in the Difference Engine. The manner in which this research led to the elegant devices embodied in the Calculating Engines is itself a fascinating study.[45]

This "one step back to go two steps forward" motion was Babbage's fate and Marx was by no means the only one who treated him as a brilliant Victorian quasi-crank. There was evidence enough for his crankiness. For example, when Marx was involved in the process of forming the International Working Men's Association and preparing its London inauguration in September 1864, Babbage was in the heat of his widely publicized campaign against barrel-organists and other street musicians which eventually lead on July 25, 1864, to propose "An Act for the better regulation of Street Music within the Metropolitan Police District" or, "Babbage's Bill." In support of his campaign, Babbage devoted a whole chapter of his 1864 autobiography *Passages from the Life of a Philosopher* to "Street Nuisances." What follows is Babbage's description of the chapter:

> Street Nuisances
> Various classes injured—Instruments of Torture—Encourages; Servants, Beer-Shops, Children, Ladies of elastic virtue—Effects on the Musical Profession—Retaliation—Police themselves disturbed—Invalids distracted—Horses run away—Children run over—A Cab-stand placed in the Author's street attracts Organs—Mobs shouting out his Name—Threats to burn his House—Disturbed in the middle of the night when very ill—An average number of Persons are always ill—Hence always disturbed—Abusive Placards—Great Difficulty of getting Convictions—Got a

---

[44] See "Why Machines Cannot Create Value: Marx's Theory of Machines," 139 in this volume.

[45] Anthony Hyman, *Charles Babbage: Pioneer of the Computer* (Oxford: Oxford University Press, 1982), 105.

Case for the Queen's Bench—Found it useless—A Dead Sell—Another
Illustration—Musicians give False Name and Address—Get Warrant for
Apprehension—They keep out of the way—Offenders not yet found and
arrested by the Police—Legitimate Use of Highways—An Old Lawyer's
Letter to *The Times*—Proposed Remedies; Forbid entirely—Authorize
Police to seize the Instrument and take it to the Station—An Association
for Prevention of Street Music proposed.[46]

One can see how this cantankerous seventy-three year old philosopher of
machines in 1864 could look a bit "off," and not just in the eyes of a communist
revolutionary in the process of writing the text that refuted the value-creativity of
machines and organizing the First International!

But, like it or not, Babbage was working on his Calculating Engines before
Sadi Carnot published his *Reflexions on the Motive Power of Fire* (1824)—the beginning of classical thermodynamics—and certainly by 1834, Babbage had theorized
the universal computer or, anachronistically, the Turing machine. Consequently,
one cannot say that the theory of heat engines antedates the theory of universal
computers. That is, in the period when Carnot was studying, *in general*, the motive
power of fire and finding it in "differences in temperature,"[47] Babbage was studying
"the whole of the conditions which enable a *finite* machine to make calculations
of *unlimited* extent."[48] The product of that research, Babbage's Analytic Engine,
had the major five components of the modern computer, as Dubbey pointed out:

(a) the *store* containing the data, instructions and intermediate calculations;
(b) the *mill* in which the basic arithmetical operations are performed ["con-
    trol of operations in the Mill is by a microprogram represented by studs on
    the surface of a barrel (after the manner of a music box or barrel organ)"];[49]
(c) the *control* of the whole operation, in Babbage's case by means of a
    Jacquard loom system;
(d) the *input* by means of punched cards;
(e) the *output* which automatically prints results.[50]

Moreover, the Analytic Engine could repeat instructions, make conditional
decisions and store programs in a library. However, the full generality of what a
universal computer that recursively operates on its own program could simulate
was not fully comprehended at the time by either Babbage or his associates like

---

[46] Charles Babbage, *Passages from the Life of a Philosopher* (New York: A.M. Kelley, 1969
[1864]), 389–90.

[47] Carnot, *Reflections on the Motive Power of Fire*, 67.

[48] Hyman, *Charles Babbage*, 170.

[49] Ibid., xiii.

[50] J.M. Dubbey, "The Mathematical World of Charles Babbage," in *The Universal Turing Machine: A Half-Century Survey*, ed. Rolf Herken (New York: Oxford University
Press, 1995), 217.

General Menabra and Lady Lovelace. Whereas Carnot presumed the intellectual background of a "cosmology of heat" that identified the determining form of nature and life as an effect of heat, the most that Babbage claimed was that "the whole of the developments and operations of analysis are now capable of being executed by machinery."[51] Even Lady Lovelace, when it came time for her to employ her most Byronic of hyperboles, could only refer to the mathematical world:

> The bounds of arithmetic were however out stepped the moment the idea of applying the [Jacquard] cards had occurred; and the Analytic Engine does not occupy common ground with mere "calculating machines." It holds a position wholly its own; and the considerations it suggests are most interesting in their nature. In enabling mechanism to combine together general symbols in successions of unlimited variety and extent, a uniting link is established between the operations of matter and the abstract processes for the most abstract branch of mathematical science. A new, a vast, and a powerful language is developed for the future use of analysis, in which to wield its truths so that these may become of more speedy and accurate practical applications for the purposes of mankind than the means hitherto in our possession have rendered possible. Thus not only the mental and material, but the theoretical and the practical in the mathematical world, are brought into more intimate and effective connexion with each other.[52]

That is, Babbage's engines appeared to be *mathematical* computers and computers were apparently *mathematical* things. True, these mathematical results can have "practical applications," but they are not in themselves "practical." The fact that Babbage's Analytic Engine was a *universal* computer could not yet connect with a "cosmology of computation" which was, alas for Babbage, to be the creation of the mid-twentieth century. Was this failure inevitable? The cyberpunk novelists William Gibson and Bruce Sterling in *The Difference Engine* (1990) did not think so, since they imagined a Victorian world where the connection between the computer and the steam engine was made and materialized in a complete mode of capitalist production.[53] If their novel shows us that this gap was not inevitable, since the connection was imaginable, then why was it not made?

Here are parts of the answer as to why Marx, along with the British Government and "venture capitalists" after 1834 and almost everyone else, ignored Babbage's engines in the nineteenth century: (a) they were conceived, even in the most florid of settings like the one above, as mathematical instruments; (b) the crisis of clerical labor had

[51] Donald Stephen Lowel Cardwell, *Turning Points in Western Technology: A Study of Technology, Science and History* (New York: Science History Publications, 1972), 89–120; Babbage, *Passages from the Life of a Philosopher*, 68.

[52] Quoted in Charles Babbage, *Charles Babbage and his Calculating Engines: Selected Writings by Charles Babbage and Others*, eds. Philip Morrison and Emily Morrison (New York: Dover, 1961), 252.

[53] William Gibson and Bruce Sterling, *The Difference Engine* (London: Victor Gollancz Ltd., 1990).

not yet materialized; (c) the computational aspect of all labor processes had not yet been understood. For in the mid-nineteenth century the heat engine and not the computer stood at the center of Modern Industry's factories, as Ure lyricized, "In these spacious halls the benignant power of steam summons around him his myriads of willing menials [and assigns to each the regulated task, substituting for painful muscular effort on their part, the energies of his own gigantic arm, and demanding in return only attention and dexterity to correct such little aberrations as casually occur in his workmanship]."[54]

Clerical, or mathematical labor, also appeared to be a rather minor aspect of Modern Industry closeted away somewhere in a dusty office above the behemoth of steam on the factory floor. Indeed, such labor gets barely a mention in Babbage's own *On Economy of Machinery and Manufactures*.[55] Consequently, Babbage's engines could be relegated to the status of an item on a scientist's or mathematician's "wish list" as late as 1878 when a prestigious committee of the British Association for the Advancement of Science advised, "not without reluctance," the Association not to invest any funds in building one of them.[56] Whereas the colossi of steam were on the minds of nineteenth-century industrialists, military strategists and revolutionaries, the machines of computation were considered purely supplementary to the serious work of industry.

This estimate was to change in the transition from the paleo-capitalistic period of absolute surplus value to the contemporary period of transferred surplus value.[57] A mark of such a change can be found in the changing position of clerical groups within the composition of the waged working class between the mid-nineteenth and mid-twentieth centuries. As Braverman pointed out:

> The census of 1870 in the United States classified only 82,000—or six-tenths of 1 percent of all "gainful workers"—in clerical occupations. In Great Britain, the census of 1851 counted some 70,000 to 80,000 clerks, or eight-tenths of 1 percent of the gainfully occupied. By the turn of the century the proportion of clerks in the working population had risen to 4 percent in Great Britain and 3 percent in the United States; in the intervening decades, the clerical working class had begun to be born. By the census of 1961, there were in Britain about 3 million clerks, almost 13 percent of the occupied population; and in the United States in 1970, the clerical classification had risen to more than 14 million workers, almost 18 percent of the gainfully occupied, making this equal in size, among the gross classifications of the occupational scale, to that of operatives of all sorts.[58]

This change in the size of the clerical workforce from the mid-nineteenth to the mid-twentieth century, however, took place with a concomitant change in its

---

[54] The unbracketed part is quoted by Marx, *Capital: Volume I*, 545.

[55] Babbage, *On the Economy*, 176–77.

[56] Hyman, *Charles Babbage*, 254.

[57] See "The Work/Energy Crisis and the Apocalypse," 11 in this volume.

[58] Harry Braverman, *Labor and Monopoly Capital: The Degradation of Work in the Twentieth Century* (New York: Monthly Review Press, 1974), 295.

predominant gender (from male to female) and its relative wage (from about twice the average wage for factory operatives to below the operatives' wage).[59] This transformation could not have happened without a substantial change in the machinery of the office, most especially in the use of computers. And it was imperative that this change take place for all of capital since, for example, a sudden doubling of the wage of almost 20 percent of the workforce *ceteris paribus* would have meant a 20 percent increase in the total wage bill itself and potentially a substantial drop in profit. This gradual wage crisis of clerical labor, therefore, put a premium on the development of computing machines that would subvert the wage demands of a highly skilled part of the working class. But this crisis was not yet even on the horizon in the 1830s nor, indeed, even by 1867. Babbage's Analytical Engines could not attract the sustained attention of the "central committee" of the capitalist class until the dimensions of the crisis of clerical labor began to appear, which was not to happen for more than half a century after publication of the first volume of *Capital*.

A more important reason for the neglect of Babbage's Engines was that neither Babbage, nor Marx, nor anyone else at the time saw the essential connection between computation and *all* forms of the labor process, even though the key was staring Babbage and Marx in the face all along. That key was Jacquard's loom. It proved essential, as mentioned above by Lady Lovelace, for the creation of the Analytical Engine or the universal computer. The problem was that Babbage took this transposition as that of an industrial device being used for mathematical purposes while Marx (following Ure) saw it as one more chapter in the continuous saga of the struggle between workers and machinery.[60] This is not to say that either was wrong per se, i.e., Jacquard's device was implicitly a mathematical device *and* explicitly a weapon in the industrial class struggle, but rather that Babbage's *transposition* of the two itself marked a moment in the self-reflection of the labor process that was not understood until the 1930s.

Let us consider more extensively each part of the matter:

First, Babbage described the role of the Jacquard loom in the development of his Analytic Engine in the following passage.

> It is known as a fact that the Jacquard loom is capable of weaving any design which the imagination of man may conceive. It is also the constant practice for skilled artists to be employed by manufacturers in designing patterns. These patterns are then sent to a peculiar artist, who, by means of a certain machine, punches holes in a set of pasteboard cards in such a manner that when those cards are placed in a Jacquard loom, it will then weave upon its produce the exact pattern designed by the artist. Now the manufacturer may use, for the warp and weft of his work, threads which are all of the same color; let us suppose them to be unbleached or white threads. In this case the cloth will be woven all of one colour; but there will be a damask pattern upon it such as the artist designed. But the manufacturer might use the same

---

[59] Braverman, *Labor and Monopoly Capital*, 296–98.

[60] Marx *Capital: Volume I*, 553–64.

cards, and put in the warp threads of any other colour. Every thread might even be of a different colour, or of a different shade of colour; but in all these cases the *form* of the pattern will be the same—the colours only will differ. The analogy of the Analytic Engine with this well-known process is nearly perfect. . . . The Analytic Engine is therefore a machine of the most general nature. Whatever formula it is required to develop, the law of its development must be communicated to it by two sets of cards. When these have been placed, the engine is special for that formula. The numerical value of its constants must then be put on the columns of wheels below them, and on setting the Engine in motion it will calculate and print the numerical results of that formula.[61]

Or, as Lady Lovelace put it, "the Analytic Engine *weaves algebraical patterns* just as the Jacquard-loom weaves flowers and leaves."[62] Thus, Babbage and Lovelace saw in the Jacquard loom principle—that of using *seriatim* a set of partial instructions to weave a total textile—a *form* that could be transposed into a mathematical space of operations on numbers in order to mechanize them. But for Babbage and his supporters the connection between the Jacquard loom and the Analytic Engine was exactly that, a *transposition* from an industrial setting to a mathematical one, instead of an indication of a third, mathematical-industrial space that characterized the labor process in general. This insight was lacking, of course, not only in Babbage and Marx but also in most of those who studied the labor process until the 1930s. For example, Taylor's "scientific management" efforts of the turn of the century were still engaged with the time-and-motion studies that linearly fractionalized the work process in order to reduce its temporal components in order to speed up the whole. But Taylorization left the deep computational structure of the labor process unexamined.

Second, Marx, following Ure, saw in Jacquard's loom another "invention . . . providing capital with weapons against working-class revolt."[63] Jacquard's loom was surely that, for it was aimed against one of the most militant parts of the European working class, the Lyons silk workers. As a commentator on "the artisan republic" of Lyons pointed out:

> In the eighteenth century, the silk industry, or the *fabrique*, had become a capitalistic putting-out system with a few hundred merchants commissioning a few thousand master weavers to produce the silk. Masters' dependence on merchants' hiring and piece-rate (or wage) practices forged a bond of solidarity between masters and their "employees" or journeymen. One consequence was a tradition of economic militance. As early as 1709, silk weavers boycotted merchants to get higher piece-rates; in 1786 and again in 1789 and 1790, they struck for a general piece-rate agreement. . . . [After the

---

[61] Babbage, *Charles Babbage and His Calculating Engines*, 55.

[62] Quoted in Douglas R. Hofstadter, *Gödel, Escher, Bach: The Eternal Golden Braid* (New York: Random House, 1980), 25.

[63] Marx, *Capital I*, 563.

Revolution] silk workers and local authorities returned to the *ancien regime* concept of collective contracts guaranteed by the government in 1807, 1811, 1817–19 and 1822. Moreover, silk workers formed authorized voluntary versions of their old corporations and used these mutual aid . . . societies as covers to organize strikes.[64]

According to Ure, in the face of such a historically intransigent sector of workers, Bonaparte and Lazare Carnot (Sadi's father), set Jacquard to work to develop a loom that would circumvent the skill of the silk weavers:

[Jacquard] was afterwards called upon to examine a loom on which from 20,000 to 30,000 francs had been expended for making fabrics for Bonaparte's use. He undertook to do, by a simple mechanism, what had been attempted in vain by a complicated one; and taking as his pattern a model-machine of Vaucanson, he produced the famous Jacquard-loom. He returned to his native town [Lyons], rewarded with a pension of 1000 crowns; but experienced the utmost difficulty to introduce his machine among the silk-weavers, and was three times exposed to imminent danger of assassination. The *Conseil des Prud'hommes*, who are the *official* conservators of the trade of Lyons, broke up his loom in the public place, sold the iron and wood for old materials, and denounced him as an object of universal hatred and ignominy.[65]

All this pre-Luddite rage in 1807 was not misconceived. The Jacquard punch-card device "halved the time needed to mount the looms, eliminated the weaver's helper, and quadrupled productivity," hence reducing piece-rates, and by 1846 about one-third of the silk looms in Lyons had Jacquard devices.[66] Ure, of course, took the resistance of the silk weavers of Lyons to the Jacquard loom as a typical short-sighted response of the workers to the inevitable and beneficial consequences of mechanization, although Ure also notes later: "it appears that there has been a constant depreciation of the wages of silk weaving in France, from the year 1810 down to the present time [1835]."[67] But Ure was sure that this action and reaction of the classes around the Jacquard loom was just another moment in a more general struggle that would be won by an alliance of capital with a properly chastened working class.

Ure and Marx, who inversely followed him, saw in the transition from Manufacture to Modern Industry *a general process*: "to substitute mechanical science for hand skill, and the partition of a process into its essential constituents, for the division or graduation of labour among artisans."[68] But this description is rather vague and infinitely variable in its realization. The questions, "*How* does one substitute mechanics for hand skill?" and "*What* are the essential constituents of a labor

---

[64] Mark Lynn Stewart-McDougall, *The Artisan Republic: Revolution, Reaction, and Resistance in Lyon, 1848–1851* (Kingston: McGill-Queens University Press, 1984), xiv–xv.

[65] Ure, *Philosophy*, 256–57.

[66] Stewart-McDougall, *The Artisan Republic*, 12.

[67] Ure, *Philosophy*, 264.

[68] Ibid.

process?" are open ended. Neither Ure nor Marx saw that this substitution could have a specifically identifiable character that would at the same time be universalizable, aside from it being reducible to abstract labor through the labor market in the case of Marx. Therefore, the realization that Babbage's induction of the Jacquard principle into the mechanization of mathematics had within it a general description of the labor process remained stillborn.

This insight was to be the result of the theory of Turing machines and the concomitant "cosmology of computation" generated in the 1930s and 1940s. By then, a number of new factors had come into play: (a) mathematics itself had been remarkably generalized; (b) the wage crisis of the clerical working class had matured; (c) the limits of a time-and-motion form of analysis of the labor process had been reached in the formation of the Congress of Industrial Organizations (CIO) and other forms of "mass worker" class organization. Thus, the stage had been set for a new theory of computing machines and the labor process, or, more precisely, the self-conscious application of Babbage's forgotten, never fully cognized theory of universal computation.

Conclusion: A New Theory of Machines or an Old Theory of Capitalism—or Both?

The result of these conceptual and historical preliminaries is apparently a contradiction. On one side, Marx's hoary theory of the role of machines in capitalism is vindicated as internally consistent against the claims of critics like Mirowski; on the other, Marx's theory of machines is clearly found to be incomplete, since it does not explain how the introduction of Turing machines (the descendants of Babbage's Analytic Engine) affects the work process, the generation of surplus value and modalities of class struggle.

Philip Mirowski argues that both Marxist and bourgeois economists should question their allegiance to theories patterned on old theories of physics that have been left behind in the twentieth century. This argument, as I showed in Part I, is invalid. But Mirowski does have something right. There *is* a tension between the old and new in our historical condition with respect to science and machines that needs to be isolated and resolved. It is simply that the enormous productivity (and violence) brought about by introducing a new order of machines into the work process is putting even more stress on the categories of capitalist (and anticapitalist) self-understanding. It is important at this juncture not to appeal mindlessly to that old Marxist chestnut, "the contradiction between the forces and relations of production," and leave it at that. For this contradiction, as Mario Tronti pointed out long ago, does not necessarily lead to another post- and anticapitalist system of production, as Marx envisioned.[69] Indeed, in most cases, it merely stimulates the development of capitalism itself.

Therefore, Marx's consistent but incomplete theory of machines in capitalism needs to be extended to the realm of Turing machines. One immediate consequence of this extension would be a new conception of the powers of the labor process itself and the manner by which surplus value is created. This process and its powers are

---

[69] Mario Tronti, "Workers and Capital," *Telos* 14 (1972): 25–62.

inherently neither immeasurable nor subversive, nor is it a tale of "immaterial labor," as some have recently argued.[70]

How would the new theory of machines that I described help support my claim that there is no immaterial labor? It would show that contemporary technology is haunted neither by "magical" forces nor mysterious "ideational" novelties. What appear to be "immaterial" products of labor are the result of pattern production that can be accomplished by machines (whether they be composed of wood, iron, and paper cards, and powered by heat engines or of plastic, silicon, and copper and powered by electric currents). These machines are fully "physical," in the usual sense of the word, as are the patterns they produce and, most importantly, reproduce. For at the core of capitalist commodity production is the reproduction of a pattern, whether it be "composed" of pure silk or pure electrons. A new theory of machines would help explain the capitalist consequences of the ability to produce these patterns mechanically.

The Lyons artisans who smashed the Jacquard looms recognized a truth important for the class struggle that should be inscribed in such a theory. Machines can reproduce the patterns that they—intelligent and creative humans—weaved. Millions of artisans, craftspeople, engineers, clerks, and computer programmers have learned the same lesson since. No reproducible commodity production is essentially unmechanizable.

As a corollary, the new theory of machines would definitely provide a critique of "immaterial labor" as defined by Hardt and Negri. To see this, let us review the three types of labor they unite under the rubric of "immaterial labor": (1) "the production and manipulation of affects and requires (virtual or actual) human contact, labor in the bodily mode"; (2) "an industrial production that has been informationalized"; (3) "the immaterial labor of analytical and symbolic tasks, which itself breaks down into creative and intelligent manipulation on the one hand and routine symbolic tasks on the other."[71]

Of course, Hardt and Negri are free to coin any term they wish to express their insights. They seem to have chosen "immaterial"—an adjective fraught with metaphysical and political baggage—as a way of differentiating their view of capitalism from the "materialist" Marxist tradition. In making this choice, however, also they enter into a field with a history of its own that needs to be considered. For example, after the women's movement's long struggle to have "housework," "reproductive" work and the body be recognized as central to the analysis of capitalism, it is discouraging to have two men come along and describe the very embodied reproductive work done largely by women as "immaterial"! Indeed, we see this tension in their very definition of this kind of immaterial work, "labor in the bodily mode." The dissonance between immateriality and a bodily mode should alert us to a problem in using a term like "immaterial labor."

The new theory of machines would further support a critique of the term "immaterial labor." After all, the very distinction between "intelligent manipulation"

---

[70] Hardt and Negri, *Empire*.

[71] Ibid., 293.

and "routine task" is put into question by Turing machine theory as is the notion that analytic and symbolic tasks are inherently irreducible to perfectly mechanizable operations. If Turing exorcized "the ghost from the machine" more than half a century ago, Hardt and Negri's return to a Cartesian mind/body, material/immaterial rhetoric would re-"spiritualize the machine" at the cost of a great confusion. Moreover, the notion that information is "immaterial" was successfully countered in the development of Information Theory (again more than half a century ago) that saw information as the inverse of entropy. The fact that information, like entropy, is not "tangible" does not mean that it is not "physical" (hence, it is not "immaterial").

Let me return, then, to my initial claim: *immaterial labor does not exist.* By this, I simply mean that the term "immaterial labor" fails to bring out important common features of labor like housework and computer programming, and that the adjective "immaterial" participates in a semantic field that provokes a discourse that has been problematic for centuries. Following Hardt and Negri and the other theorists of "immaterial labor" into that field would not be a wise "exodus" for the anticapitalist movement.

However, Hardt and Negri are right in insisting on the importance of the Turing machine for twenty-first-century struggle. As with all machinery, the Turing machine defines a terrain of struggle with its own landmarks and history that are still in formation. A new theory of machines that brings together simple machines, heat engines, and Turing machines would make it possible to survey this terrain and go beyond simply noting the continued existence of the contradictions and conflict between worker and machine in twenty-first-century capitalist production. I hope these preliminary efforts will invite others to join in the work.

III
MONEY, WAR, AND CRISIS

FREEZING THE MOVEMENT
AND THE MARXIST THEORY OF WAR

I found the following set of "posthumous notes" recently while I was cleaning up a closet. They were written, on the basis of memory and textual evidence, in the spring of 1983, right before I left the United States to live and teach in Nigeria. Some of the material in these notes went into a couple of articles that were published then. One was in the *Posthumous Notes* (1983) issue of *Midnight Notes* and the other was in a piece entitled "The Marxist Theory of War" in the *Radical Science Journal* issue on the anti–nuclear war movement (1983). But they have since been unread and untroubled.

My rediscovery of these notes puts them and me in a tight logical spot. I was supposed to have been dead (and reborn) according to these notes . . . but I clearly am neither. So their circulation now immediately falsifies them. Self-negating or not, I am hoping that these notes from the dead might be of use to the living at a time when nuclear war is again on the agenda.

Anyway, please receive these notes as a gift on the Day of the Dead.

November 2, 2003

> Oh that I had in the wilderness a lodging place of wayfaring men; that I
> might leave my people and go from here! for they be all adulterers, and as-
> sembly of treacherous men.
> —Jeremiah, *Lamentations* 9:2

A Lamentation

"The existence of the bomb paralyzes us. Our only motion a gigantic leap backward in what we take to be the minimal conditions of our existence whereby all desires, demands, struggles vanish; only our biological existence appears a valid cause. Don't kill us, exterminate us, burn us alive, make us witness the most horrid spectacle the mind can imagine [?????], lived thousands of times in our fears watching the 7:00 News, reading the 'scientific medical reports.' Please let us live, that's all we ask, forget what this life will be like, forget about our now seemingly utopian dreams."

But isn't this declaring we're already dead? Isn't this admitting the explosion has already worked, that we've already been blown to pieces hundreds of times when, of all our needs and struggles, only the will to survive remains? Worse yet. Isn't this declaration a most dangerous path? For when only people on their knees confront the powers that be, these powers feel godlike and justified, not restrained by the fear that should they dare so much, whoever of us will be left will make life impossible for them as well.

Why a freeze then? Freezing what? Just our brain it seems, in the false assumption that the *status quo* may hold at this moment any guarantee for us. Freeze is accepting to live with the blackmail of the bomb. Accepting to bring children into a world threatened by a nuclear explosion. Freeze is to allow THEM to periodically toy with the threat of blowing us up. Are we so mad that we can watch on TV a discussion of our future disposal as if the Jews had been allowed to witness the plans for the construction of the gas chambers. Are we going to bargain—ask for 10 instead of 100 or 1,000 crematory ovens—debating on their size, expediency and efficiency? Shall we ask how many people will they put to work or out of work? Or do we harbor the secret hope that they are readied for somebody else—perhaps in Europe, more likely the Middle East.

Reflections on a Summer of Peace

They that were brought up in scarlet embrace dung heaps.
—Jeremiah, *Lamentations* 4:5

One of the pleasures of the posthumous state is that we are free, finally, of compromise, self-deception, all the tricks of exchange. Without myself, what is there to exchange? Let us share the posthumous state for a while to discover the refreshing breeze of the last judgment before we part company. Flip out of our body; hovering over our mythical blast shadow, reflecting on the debris, it is time now for positing reasons for all this.

Certainly we go to haunt the assorted generals, capitalists and consultants cowering in their bunkers, but are they reason enough? It is time now perhaps to remember ourselves.

It was a summer of extraordinary peace. In the midst of the deepest period of unemployment, bankruptcy, and social wage cutbacks since the Great Depression, the only movement in the streets was the "Peace" Movement.

The summer began on June 12, 1982, with the largest demonstration in memory gathered in NYC before the disarmament sessions at the UN. The demonstration took many months to plan in Washington and NY and many others throughout the country obviously made it the focus of their political and creative efforts. Almost one million people from all over the United States (with other marches in the west) converged on the city. Writes one observant marcher:

> The spectacular aspects of the march were the most powerful and even now, a month later, they are still vivid in my mind's eye. I suppose you have seen some of the floats: a blue whale a hundred feet long with a slogan on its side: SAVE THE HUMANS. A white dove actually fabricated from huge bolts of white cotton that was elevated by poles and which the afternoon breeze animated into a floating life high above the people along Fifth Avenue. The puppets I think were seen by millions—earthy, peasant and fantasy-life figures of women and children that glided fifteen and twenty feet into the air. Banners of all kinds. Absence of uniformity of slogan, poster or placard—a big difference with the Solidarity Day March in Washington.

Indeed, the contrast to the other events of the summer of 1982 was remarkable. From the traditional unionized working class came a profound peace, perhaps the silence of the grave, with only a few desperate exceptions like the Iowa Beef strike. It was long and bitter and led to the calling of the National Guard with guns drawn, assisting scabs to the plant. The strike was bitter because it was held in the midst of the lowest strike activity since World War II and also, characteristically, because it was over not how much the wage increases were at stake, but how much the "give backs" would be! Only the professional baseball players could strike and win that summer.

With the "unwaged" part of the working class, there was the same peace. It was the beginning of the "riot summer" in the U.S. ghettos, and not a riot was to be found in the face of the most direct attacks on the social wages of Blacks and Hispanics. The silence was so noticeable that the *New York Times*, at the end of the summer, could editorialize with a sigh about it and the *Wall Street Journal* sent an investigative report team in to find out about the nonexistent. Even the most "activist" Black groups went on vacation that summer!

Thus in 1982, the most direct "observable" protest movement in the Reagan period was neither to be found in the factories nor in the ghettos, but in Central Park, Fifth Avenue, and UN Plaza. The two old centers of insubordination and revolt were apparently paralyzed.

Composition, Organization, and Divisions in the Peace Movement

> For the sins of her prophets, and the iniquities of her priests, that have shed the blood of the just in the midst of her. They have wandered as blind men in the streets, they have polluted themselves with blood, so that men could not touch their garments.
> —Jeremiah, *Lamentations*, 4:13,14.

Who were those who brought their multitudes into the streets of the city that summer? They have a past, indeed, immediate predecessors in the angels of the anti–nuclear energy movement. The Peace movement is a generalization of the anti–nuclear energy movement that began to homogenize the "new working class" in the period between the spring of 1977 through the spring of 1980, the first boom of the Crisis, with so much effect. In fact, the previous mass demonstration in NYC in September 1979 was an anti–nuclear energy demonstration and concern that drew more than a quarter of a million people and was the biggest such demo of the movement in that period. The intervening three years have lead to a "broadening" of the numbers of people involved; on the other side, it has lead to a "shallower" movement. If anything, we have now reached the limit that the anti–nuclear energy movement was hunting for, beyond it lies the uncharted social seas.

But in going to the limit, there is a stark and qualitative change that makes one almost nostalgic for the "good old days" of 1979! This can be seen on three counts: the "grass roots" organization, the tactics, and the leadership groupings.

For all the possible critiques that one might have had about the anti–nuclear energy movement, one thing must be singled out as important; its creation of new social configurations on the microscopic social level that brought together people from radically different layers of the division of labor, inhabited by the nonindustrialized worker (although excluding the Black or Hispanic ghetto dweller). The "affinity group" filled the need for a new mix-master that the party and union increasing could not fill in the late '70s. Thus he had the Hard Rains, the Shads, the Tomatoes, the Clams, the Abalones, etc. On the contrary, we find the peace movement organized along occupation, party or church lines. Consider the following list:

Lawyers Alliance for Nuclear Disarmament

Artists for Nuclear Disarmament

Writers for Nuclear Disarmament

Communicators for Nuclear Disarmament

Computer Programmers for Nuclear Disarmament

Educators for Social Responsibility

Psychologists for Social Responsibility

Architects for Social Responsibility

Nurses for Social Responsibility

United Campuses to Present Nuclear War

etc.

Oh, let us not forget Business Alert to Nuclear War! As well as the church groupings from the Quakers to the Catholics and the Democratic Party fronts— and the CP fronts too. In going to the limit, the "new working class" is attempting to define itself on a work basis or in a representational form (through political or theological representation), but as a consequence the movement becomes congealed before it can find some possible new social level, or "strange loop" with which to connect disparate sectors of the class.

Second, the leadership structure is quite different. The anti-nuke movement had a mythology of "no leaders" which was quite delusive; however, its leadership cadres were relatively diffuse. This is not so for the Peace Movement, whose evident center is in Washington, DC, in the "neoliberal" [an anachronistic "*sic*" here!] think tanks and the halls of Congress. Though the Left attempts to not do just their dirty work, the real initiatives have come directly from the liberal Democrats.

Third, the median tactic (i.e., the action form that typifies a movement, from which it can escalate or descend) of the anti–nuclear energy movement was "civil disobedience," which we previously analyzed as an attempt to use human capital against high-organic composition capital to "shame" the latter with the degradation of the former.[1] The Peace Movement's median tactic is the vote and the "tribute" relation with its adherents. For example, the Freeze Movement defines itself in a purely representational way: *qua* referenda, the winning of congressional seats, and legislation immediately. Further, it relates the movement's masses in the same representational form. It asks (like CISPES, from which it has learned much) a sort of movement "tax" or "tribute" from the base in order to do the movement's work. There is a presumption that the "average person" is too busy for direct political participation and that therefore s/he should pay a tax to have this work done for them. This tax is levied as bodies in a weekend demo or in funds for organizers.

But getting to the limit is not all, because the limit of the type of worker currently involved in the Peace Movement is still not wide enough. And so it becomes crucial to deal with other class elements. The first elements were the Blacks who formed a part of the movement in the demos throughout the country in a way that was not true of the anti–nuke energy movement's demos (which shows that the previous movement still had some time to go before it reached its barriers). The tangled story of the "difficult relations" between Blacks and the anti-nuke war movement can be seen in the preparation of the June 12 demo, which started in the fall of 1981. The first Black groups, however, were approached only in January 1982, at least in NYC. One of the participants writes that the points agreed to on January 29, 1983, in the National Coordination Committee were the following: "all campaign literature would include paragraphs linking the arms race with U.S. interventionism in the Third World and with racism at home; that at least one third of the members of each leadership body of the Campaign would be Third World, and that a caucus of Third World Organization would choose who would represent them on the leadership bodies."

But by March 8, 1982, the "main stream" groups moved to form a "corporation to produce the June 12th event." A number of "main stream" groups (including the Riverside Church Disarmament Program, American Friends Service Committee,

---

[1] Midnight Notes, "Strange Victories: The Anti-nuclear Movement in the U.S. & Europe," *Midnight Notes* 1, no. 1 (1979).

the National Nuclear Weapons Freeze Campaign and SANE) sent a letter to the "centrists" (including Mobilization for Survival, War Resisters League, U.S. Peace Council, Women's International League for Peace and Freedom, and the NY Public Interest Research Group) arguing for the new approach which would make the agreements with the Black and Third World groups null-and-void. The object of the exclusionary effort was the Black United Front and a variety of white left-wing party groupings. So as the Spring progressed the splits between the mainstream groups, the mediating while Left groups and the Black Left parties grew and festered, until finally the threat of having a separate demonstration forced the mainstream groups to opt for some sort of "harmony" and they allowed the "Third World Leadership" in the June 12th Rally Committee. The tension, however, was so intense that there were rumors of fist-fights behind the stage, while Bruce Springsteen played for the gathered million, between Black speakers and the organizers who were arguing for more minutes with "the Boss."

Such are the soap operas of a movement that is trying to overcome its class limits, so goeth the adulteries, the marriages and murders. Indeed, the road of reconciliation with the Black movement was so rough that it quite possibly was the reason for the peculiar silence after June 12. For there was no set of "local" initiatives that spread a kind of "anti-nuke" small pox across the land. After June 12 there was peace too from the peace movement. And this was inevitable, for it learned that to be able to keep its class composition in order, it can allow for very little movement. By going to the limit, it must Freeze itself.

Paradoxically, the very working-class vacuum of 1982 gave this movement an enormous relative momentum: it couldn't stand still. It could even consider itself and its cadres, drawn from the social and electronic technologists thrown up by the Crisis, as prophets of a New New Deal. For all their hesitancy, their timidity and haste for compromise, they saw in the emptiness the ability to bargain the fate of the class relation. But to do this, the Freeze captains had to go out in search of the Moby Dick of the proletariat, the Great White Worker. In order to find him let us chart the seas.

The Peace Movement and the U.S. Class War in the 1970s

> All thine enemies have opened their mouth against them: they hiss and
> gnash the teeth: they say, We have swallowed her up; certainly this is the day
> that we looked for; we have found, we have seen it. The Lord hath done that
> which he devised.
> —Jeremiah, *Lamentations* 2:16, 17

And in an instant I remembered everything. I saw the profits of Capital decline from 1965 through 1973 heading to the node of euthanasia, under the continual assault of riot, strike, sit-in, mutiny, refusal to work, to fuck, to not fuck, etc. And before me came the image of the Great Beast of Reaction: the Energy and Money Crisis.

This Crisis changed the very organic physiognomy of capital itself. The mass assembly lines, the steel and rubber plants slowed and, at times, halted altogether. While the lay-offs continued, there was an enormous expansion of the poles of the economy: on one side, the capital-intensive "high-tech" information and energy industries and, on the other, by the labor-intensive "reproductive" and "service" sectors of the economy. Whole new industries (like software programming and biogenetic engineering) found billions of dollars of investment available on the basis of a "good idea" while dinosauric meat-packing plants and archaic steel mills were palmed off on their workers, prone to cardiac arrest, for suicidal wages and self-managed drudgery.

I saw the very body of the working class transformed. No more muscles and beer bellies. The waged workers have become both feminized and "alien," through a rapid increase in legal and illegal immigrants at the bottom of the labor market, while on the top we find the white-male-technocrats of the social or computational machines. The tendency for the homogenization of wages, which reached its peak in 1968, was definitely broken in the 1970s and the wage gaps between different branches of industry and sectors of the working class are reaching historical peaks.

And the very land did change. Cities that were the traditional centers of working-class power were systematically depopulated and the Blacks' tactical hold on the centers was broken. It was a period of exile, wandering in the desert, transport and, for the recalcitrant, internment.

The wage struggle was demobilized and profits rose with a sigh in the post-1973 period. The Black movement was not only destabilized geographically but also, through the impact of immigration, new divisions have been introduced into the lowest waged and unwaged part of the class; the women's movement found itself immediately in struggle against the traditional white unionized workers and the Blacks in an ever tightening labor market. These division and tensions intensified by the depressions of 1974–1976 and the 1980–1983 exhausted much of the initiative of these movements so that real wages fell for over a decade for the first time since the 1920s.

The Crisis did what it was devised to do, but at the cost of enormous instability; so now the time had come to decide more coherently for a model of accumulation of capital that could last into the next century, past the second millennium. To envision the possibilities think of the production of values and the reproduction of labor-powers.

In the realm of value production: the first is a revival of the old post–World War II "Keynesian" form of production pivoted on assembly line production, though this time undoubtedly under a new form of "social contract" in which a chastened working class would accept lower wages in return for job security in an "export" oriented economy. The second model would be an intensification of the physiognomy of capital in the crisis: wiping out the last vestiges of "old capital," investing in the informational-computational-anti-entropic industries and creating special reservation of low-capital/high labor, verities with a new humbleness or a more risky and more polarized economy: "reindustrialization" or "postindustrialization."

But to produce value you must reproduce its producer, labor-power. And again two models or Ideas dominated. On one side, the "patriarchal traditionalist" family model which would attempt to return the male to the center of the reproduction problematic; it would be pro-natalist hence anti-gay, anti-abortion, anti-feminist. It signals a yearning for a return to the most Protestant mortification in defense of bourgeois family units. The second model is the "freedom of choice" model that insists on an equally hoary bourgeois demand: autonomy of the individual as the route of reproductive efficiency. It is Filmer versus Locke all over again, but now Locke has become a gay, sex-changed single demanding an abortion!

When these dichotomies cross, a matrix is formed that locates the four pure types of capitalist politics of the future. It is upon these types that deals with the class can be made as well as compromises within capital can be coordinated. Let us review each for the moment

	Postindustrialization	Reindustrialization
Freedom of choice	A11	A12
Patriarchal	A21	A22

A11: This is the utopia of computer freaks and scientistic production embedded in an environment of alternative "lifestyles", from clean living to S&M prowlers.

A12: This is the utopia of the Left, a good day's work at the plant producing "useful" materials, and a free, "socialized" form of housework.

A21: This is the image of the '50s, if there were no '60s and '70s, crew-cut tech daddy returns to the happy family, no incest and no dildoes.

A22: Here the factory worker returns home, the wife and kids shut up, while the Jews and Blacks weep.

Am I being facetious? Perhaps. Let the dead have their fun, I think you get my point, anyway. But the Freeze Movement arises exactly during the moment when historic choices must be made among the ideal types, more precisely it arises as part of the process of choice. It constitutes the military policy of the social struggle that is pushing for a form of production to be found in the upper right portion of the matrix. If it is to win, the Great White Leviathan must be lured or snared near A12. But why is the military policy necessary? In order to see this we have to take a trip down a dark tunnel where we can hear the voices of past friends.

The Pure Theory of War

> He hath bent his bow, and set me as a mark for the arrow. He hath caused the
> arrows of his quiver to enter into my reigns. I was a derision to all my people,
> and their song all the day. He hath filled me with bitterness, he hath mad me
> drunken with wormwood. He hath also broken my teeth with gravel stones,
> he hath covered me with ashes.
> And thou hast removed my world far from peace; I forgot prosperity.
> —Jeremiah, *Lamentations* 3:12–17

> War is a matter of vital importance to the State; the province of life or death;
> the road to survival or ruin, it is mandatory that it be thoroughly studied.
> —Sun Tzu, *The Art of War*

There are three stages down the tunnel of war before we come to the light. First
we hear the classic accents of Marx and Engels, then in imperialist voice, the dialectics
of Rosa Luxemburg, Lenin and Hilferding, and finally the living voices of Sweezy,
O'Connor, and Vietnam vets talking Keynesian Marxism. They give us the three moments of the Marxist theory of War: the relation between violence and production.

Marx and Engels developed their theory of War in the middle of a century
of capitalist peace *in Europe* between 1814 and 1914. (I'd wager that more people
were killed on the barricades of Paris and in the massacres of workers in mining and
industrial towns than in the *official* wars fought *on the European soil* of that century.)
The classical bourgeois political mercantilist policy of military intervention and
power is an essential element of the process of accumulation. After the Napoleonic
Wars, these theorists dominated the strategy of the system of European national
capital arguing for a homeostatic market mechanism to dominate interstate affairs
while emphasizing internal class management: a shift from army to police, from war
to class struggle. Hence there developed an ongoing bourgeois critique of military
spending and "waste" through the nineteenth century.

This context, of course, shaped Marx's and Engel's theory of war not only
because of their appreciation of capitalist strategy but also due to internal debates
within the workers' movement. Proudhonists, socialist quacks like Dühring and an-
archists continually argued that capitalist production was fundamentally illegitimate
since property is "theft," a system built on violence and armed expropriation. One
consequence of the debate was a life-long dispute over the tactics of working-class
insurrection, especially of the efficiency of wage struggle and legal reform. For surely,
many argued, if Capital lives by the sword, it must die by the sword. But Marx
argued that violence and conquest form only an efficient cause for the eventual development of a mode of production, they did not determine it. This is true even in
the most extreme instances:

> The Mongols, with their devastations in Russia, e.g., were acting in accor-
> dance with their production, cattle-raising, which vast uninhabited space are
> a chief precondition. . . . It is received opinion that in certain periods people

lived from pillage alone. But, for pillage to be possible, there must be something to be pillaged, hence production. And the mode of pillage is itself in turn determined by the mode of production. A stock-jobbing nation, for example, cannot be pillaged in the same manner as a nation of cow-herds.[2]

This piece was written in the context of a critique of Proudhonist economists to be found in the *Grundrisse* and the *Critique of Political Economy* in 1857. Twenty years later, in an attempt to correct a pacifist line in the German Social Democratic Party being proposed by Dühring, Engels went on the attack. He pointed out that Dühring's phrase, "property founded on force," is wrong, since property "already existed, though limited to certain objects; in the ancient primitive communes of all civilized peoples." He concluded:

> The role played in history by force as contrasted with economic development is therefore clear. Firstly, all political power is originally based on an economic and social function, and increases in proportion as the members of society through the dissolution of the primitive community, become transformed into private producers, and thus become more and more alienated from the administrators of the common functions of society. Secondly, after the political force has made itself independent in relation to society and has transformed itself from its servant into its master, it can work in two different directions. Either it works in the sense and in the direction of the natural economic development, in which case no conflict arises between them, the economic development being accelerated. Or it works against economic development, in which case, as a rule, with but few exceptions, force succumbs to it.[3]

This complex dialectic of emphasizing and then de-emphasizing the importance of force has its tactical dimension since Comrades Marx and Engels were continually attempting to steer the worker's movement between Blanquist insurrectionism and social pacifism. Ultimately they tell the movement that it is pointless to employ force unless economic development is already taking society to the brink of breakdown. In actual practice, the message is ambiguous, as Marx's flip-flops on the Paris Commune showed.

But Marx's economic analysis of military expenditures was much more consistent with, in fact, the bourgeois consensus of that period. That is, he agreed with Smith, Ricardo, and Mill that "the whole army and navy are unproductive labourers" paid out of the revenue and not in any way productive of capital. Certainly Marx never committed any ideological stupidity on this matter, as his beautiful critique of the "grasshopper and ant" theory of primitive accumulation demonstrates:

> But as soon as the question of property is at stake, it becomes a sacred duty to proclaim the standpoint of the nursery tale as the one thing fit for all

---

[2] Marx, *Grundrisse*, 98.

[3] Frederick Engels, *Anti-Dühring* (Peking: Foreign Language Press, 1976), 234.

age-groups and all stages of development. In actual history it is a notorious fact that conquest, enslavement, robbery, murder, in short, force, play the great part. In the tender annals of Political Economy, the idyllic reigns from time immemorial. Right and "labour" were from all time the sole means of enrichment, "this year" of course always excepted. As a matter of fact, the methods of primitive accumulation are anything but idyllic.[4]

Capital "comes dripping from head to foot, from every pore, with blood and dirt" but the producers of this blood, the soldiers and sailors, and the instruments of this production, the Krupp guns and Mauser rifles, are "incidental expenses of production." Marx's discussion of military expenditures arises in the debate with the "vulgar economists" who argue, contra Smith and Ricardo, that often cannot distinguish between productive/unproductive labor since servants, senators, sergeants, saxophonists and sex workers do produce services (spiritual or material) that can be as essential as steel mills. True, Marx retorts, but what constitutes productive labor from capital's point of view is not whether it produces pleasures but whether the expenditures for that labor produce profits (surplus value).

Although Marx's discussion is rather sloppy, fragmentary and, at times, genuinely confused and inconclusive, it does come out quite clear on the question of war and military expenditures. Marx does this in this discussion of Nassau ("Last Hour") Senior's claim that a soldier who, because of the unsettled state of the country, must stand guard over the fields is as productive as the farmers that sow and reap. The soldier is as crucial as the stoop laborer, his gun is as essential as the hoe, Senior claims as the Sam Huntington of his day. Now it might be true that you can't dig coal with bayonets, but what if it were the case that you cannot dig coal without them, wouldn't bayonets and their wielders be as productive as shovels and coal miners? Senior wrote:

> There are countries where it is quite impossible for people to work the land unless there are soldiers to protect them. Well, according to Smith's classification, the harvest is not produced by the joint labour of the man who guides the plough and of the man at his side with arms in hand; according to him, the ploughman alone is a productive worker, and the soldier's activity is unproductive.[5]

Marx's retort to this critique of Smith displays one of his great failures of categorization which was characteristic of much of his work in the field of productive and unproductive labor: "The soldier belongs to the incidental expenses of production, in the same way as a large part of the unproductive labourers who produce nothing themselves, either spiritual or material, but who are useful and necessary only because of faulty social relations—they owe their existence to social evils."[6] If

---

[4] Marx, *Capital: Volume I*, 874.

[5] Marx, *Theories of Surplus Value, Part I*, 288.

[6] Ibid., 289.

the "faulty social relations and evils" disappeared "the material conditions of production, the conditions of agriculture as such, remain unchanged." We could remain for much time here within the tunnel, wrangling over these passages. For example, is it because military presence is not part of the "normal conditions of production" and so it does not effect the "labor-time social necessary" which determines the value of the commodities produced under the shadow of the gun, that military expenditures (e.g., the wages of the soldier and the cost of his M-16) are incidental? But before we do, it is worth noting that Marx's categorization of military expenditures as unproductive, hence on par with the wages of parsons and tax clerks, led to a critique of colonialism that was quite in line with the classical nineteenth-century liberalism of J.S. Mill. In his articles during the 1850s for the *New York Daily Tribune*, Marx continuously drummed on the "waste" and "inefficiency" of the British rule in India on purely cost-accounting grounds. He concludes one of his articles with the following:

> It is thus evident that individuals again largely by the English connection with India, and of course their gain goes to increase the sum of the national wealth. But against all this a very large offset is to be made. The military and naval expenses paid of out of the pockets of England or Indian account have been constantly increasing with the extent of the Indian dominion. To this must be added the expense of Burmese, Afghan, Chinese and Persian wars. . . . Add to this career of endless conquest and perpetual aggression in which the English are involved by the possession of India, and it may well be doubted whether, on the whole, this dominion does not threaten to cost quite as much as it can ever be expected to come to.[7]

That is, the incidental expenses of producing poppies in the fields of Bengal, processing them into opium and transporting it from Calcutta (which constituted more than a half of all Indian exports in dollar terms) far outweighed the income generated. But since the income was private while the expenses were public, Marx suggested, the lack of "surplus" was tolerated by the British state, and indeed it was a way of taxing the English working class for the benefit of capital.

The final position of Marx and Engels on war is not at all straight-forward but perhaps in summing together the social and economic analysis we can get this picture: war is absolutely essential in the period of "primitive accumulation" in order to create the conditions of accumulation (especially the expropriation of laborers from the land) but with the establishment of a capitalist mode of production war-related expenditures become increasing antithetical to the accumulation process.

The Marxist theory of war underwent a profound change with the rise of capitalist "Imperialism" in the midst of the Great Depression (1873–1896). Instead of expanding the "free trade" ideology of nineteenth-century liberalism there followed the "scramble for Africa," the redivision of China, the Rough Riders, etc. War,

---

[7] Karl Marx, "British Incomes in India," in *Karl Marx on Colonialism and Modernization: His Dispatches and Other Writings on China, India, Mexico, the Middle East and North Africa*, ed. Shlomo Avineri (New York: Doubleday and Company, 1968), 225.

invasion, and massacre become the order to the day along with a dramatic increase in military investments, e.g., in Britain consider the growth of military expenditures both absolutely and relatively:

	Total expenditure of government	Military	Military/Total
1820	50	12.5	.25
1850	50	10	.20
1880	80	30	.37
1900	120	60	.50

*(Amounts in millions of £)

The theorists of the Second International attempted to explain the rise of Mars over Mammon (apparently) by postulating aspects of capital that Marx did not recognize or did not foresee adequately. We shall only stop to speak of Luxemburg, Hilferding, and Lenin but in them we see the growing shift in the evaluation of military expenses: increasingly they appear to enter into the accumulation process as essential components rather than incidental expenses.

For Red Rosa, Marx erred because he did not see that capitalism could not both be accumulating and reproducing on an extended scale *and* be a closed system of capitalists and workers. If it were closed, then who would there be to sell the surplus commodities that are the product of expanded reproduction? Her answer: the realization of surplus value must require noncapitalist consumers outside the system of direct capitalist relations, i.e., those in the world who still live on the level of simple commodity production. They are the fresh blood the system absolutely needs for continued accumulation, hence the imperialist scramble to divide up the remaining and dwindling noncapitalist parts of the planet. In this battle of the vampires, a form of reverse Malthusianism, war and the instrumentalities of violence are essential conditions for the realization of surplus. Military policy becomes fundamentally aggressive, but not as a matter of "choice" or "opportunity." It is now war or death that, according to her model, mathematically intensifies as the remaining noncapitalist areas diminish until, no doubt, the holocaust ignites over the last noncapitalist peasant in Borneo!

Though Hilferding's explanation of Imperialism was quite different from Luxemburg's, he also agrees that the character of war and war preparation dramatically shifted between the middle and the end of the nineteenth century. In his analysis, the cause is the rise of Finance Capital, i.e., the enormous concentration of capital brought about the stock-corporation which made it possible for the banking system to coordinate large parts of industrial capital in the form of cartels and trusts, but the formation of national monopolies forces the monopolist to seek outside investment outlets as the only source of expansion in markets not dominated by domestic monopolies; this simultaneous search in the context of a finite world immediately leads to national conflict and annexation. It is a zero-sum game, with more players joining every year (in the form of newly industrialized capitalist societies like Japan, Germany, Italy, etc.) and the pot fixed by the geographical limits of the planet. Hence the inevitability of, and necessity for, war. Hilferding writes:

> Finance capital, finally, needs a state which is strong enough to carry out a policy of expansion and to gather new colonies. Where liberalism was an opponent of state power politics and wished to insure its own dominance against the older power of aristocracy and bureaucracy, to which end it confined the state's instruments of power within the smallest possible compass, there finance capital demands power politics without limit; and it would do so even if the outlays for army and navy did not directly assure to the most powerful capitalist groups an important market with enormous monopolistic profits.[8]

Hilferding dismisses the usual liberal critique of military expenditures as the product of conspiracy and corruption between military contractors and government official. Military power is necessary for accumulation, it enters into the very conditions of the capitalist mode of production. Outlays for the army and navy are no more discretionary and incidental, they are part of doing business in the reign of Finance Capital.

Lenin develops Hilferding's theory of Finance Capital with special emphasis on the question of War, i.e., the burden of Lenin's argument in his 1916 pamphlet on Imperialism is to show that the development of monopoly capital (whose details he ultra-derives from Hilferding) inevitably leads to war. It is a polemic against Kautsky and others who argued that international cartels prefigure a period of "imperialism" when the different national monopoly capitals will join together in a peaceful "joint exploitation of the world." In the middle of the First World War, you can excuse Lenin's bile! His argument is quite straight-forward: the only conceivable basis for this "ultra-imperialism" is a mathematical equality of different national capitals with respect to their "strength" and that all changes in these strengths will be even. This is impossible, Lenin points out. Indeed, this is where he introduces his theory of war; military power is the *form* of the economic *content* of monopoly capitalism, and this form expresses itself during the period of instability: "Finance capital and the trusts do not diminish but increase the differences in the rate of growth of the various parts of the world economy. Once the relation of forces is changed, what other solution of the contradictions can be found under capitalism than that of force?"[9] Content, Form, and Force are Hegelian categories that undoubtedly arise from his reading both of Hegel's *Science of Logic* and the Hegelian military theorist, Clausewitz. Lenin takes as his theme, "War is a continuation of policy by other means," and he applies it to the era of imperialism, an era of "bad infinities" of war and "peace":

---

[8] Quoted in Paul Sweezy, *The Theory of Capitalist Development* (New York: Monthly Review Press, 1942), Appendix B, 375.

[9] V.I. Lenin, *Imperialism: The Highest Stage of Capitalism* (New York: International Publishers, 1967), 752.

"Inter-imperialist" or "ultra-imperialist" alliances . . . no matter what form they may assume, whether of one imperialist coalition against another, or of a general alliance embracing *all* of the imperialist powers, are *inevitably* nothing more than a "truce" in periods between wars. Peaceful alliances prepare the ground for wars, and in their turn grow out of wars; the one is the condition of the other, giving rise to alternating forms of peace and non-peaceful struggle out of *one and the same basis* of imperialist connection and the relations between world economics and world politics.[10]

War and military expenditure become essential and necessary for the capitalist mode of production, and so, in contradistinction to Marx's notion of "incidental expense of production," Lenin commits himself to a radically different relation of value to "force." Marx is quite right when he points out that the corn grown under the shadow of a gun tastes the same and has the same value (i.e., incorporates socially necessary labor time) as the corn grown in unguarded fields; the wages of the soldier and the cost of his/her gun are extras that might be made up because, say, of the extraordinary "fertility" of the field. But what if *all* fields must be guarded? This appears to be the case with the scramble to divide and redivide the world by the imperialist powers. Does military expense become part of the "normal conditions of production"? Apparently so; hence these expenditures in part determine the value of commodities. Here, as in much else in *Imperialism*, we find Lenin to be quite the revisionist renegade! With that, he vanishes in disgust as we are drawn further down the tunnel.

Paul Baran appears to speak for himself and the living Sweezy and O'Connor. Hiroshima and the entrance of the Red Army into Berlin ended the nauseating alternating circuit of imperialist war; however, another nausea developed. The United States emerged as the dominant capitalist power, "interimperialist" war ended, but the U.S. entered into innumerable anti-insurrectionist wars either directly or through client regimes in the "Third World," as well as carried on "virtual" nuclear war with the Soviet Union. Immense sums went into military expenditures. Given the extraterrestrial powers of nuclear weapons, no satisfactory explanation based on the notion of "national defense" is possible. Then why war? A new explanation arose that quite different from the Imperialist-analysts of the early twentieth century. Baran and Sweezy defined this approach on the basis of a new "law" of capitalist development to be found with the establishment of monopoly capitalist: the law of rising surplus, i.e., the growing gap between "what a society produces and the costs of producing it." This was to express the increasing contradiction between the productive capacities of industrial technique and the social limits of capitalist accumulation; a conflict ultimately between use-value and exchange-value. In a few words, the Baran and Sweezy argument is that the normal operation of capitalist enterprise produces much more than is necessary for the reproduction, on a profitable basis, of

---

[10] Ibid., 770.

constant and variable capital and so some way must be devised for this surplus to be "absorbed" without violating the basic principles of capitalist social relation.

A corollary of this argument is a new theory of war: war expenditures, aside from their lingering imperialist uses, are the best way to absorb the surplus. They write: "Here at last monopoly capitalism had seemingly found the answer to the 'on what' question: on what could the government spend enough to keep the system from sinking into the more stagnation? On arms, more arms, and ever more arms."[11] This argument, reminiscent of J.S. Mill's critique of government spending in the 1860s, appears to reinvoke Marx's distinction between productive/unproductive labor, but it does it with a twist. The "unproductive" worker *qua* lathe operator in a missile plant is essential for the existence of capitalist production: s/he is only unproductive for a "rational society's" point of view. There is a real charm in this picture of war, for in a period of the production of the most devastating weapons imaginable, Baran and Sweezy tell us they are ultimately capital's toys, the "conspicuous consumption" of monopoly capital! and further, that the working class in the United States are passive accomplices to this fundamental fraud who "rationalize" their submission to the needs of monopoly capital with anticommunist ideology.

Baran and Sweezy's work reflected the "war" Keynesianism of the immediate post–World War II years, in which the class struggle appeared to be channeled into collective bargaining rituals of the mass industries. But between 1965 through 1973, the "union-management" formulation of struggle broke down both in the factory proper (through the "wildcat") and especially in the "social factory" (the ghettos, universities, army and "home"). The immediate response by the state was to both increase military expenditures as well as "welfare" funding ("Vietnam" plus "the Great Society"). James O'Connor attempted to extend Baran and Sweezy's theory of war to account for these developments. He argued that the capitalist state "must try to fulfill two basic and often contradictory functions—accumulation and legitimation. Expenditures that fulfill accumulation functions are "social capital" while those that fulfill legitimation functions are "social expenses," the first are productive (expanding surplus value) while the second are not. Military spending as well as "welfare" expenditures fall into the category of legitimating social expenses.

> The function of welfare is not only to control the surplus population politically but also to expand demand and domestic markets. And the warfare system not only keeps foreign rivals at bay and inhibits the development of world revolution . . . but also helps stave off domestic economic stagnation. Thus we describe the national government as the *warfare-welfare state*.[12]

The basic function of military spending, therefore, is to increase the capitalist state's "legitimacy," i.e., the "loyalty and support" for capitalism within the working

---

[11] Paul Baran and Paul Sweezy, *Monopoly Capital: An Essay on the American Economic and Social Order* (New York: Monthly Review Press, 1966), 213.

[12] James O'Connor, *The Fiscal Crisis of the State* (New York: St. Martin's Press, 1973), 150–51.

class. While "welfare" is seen as something like bread to the "surplus" population, the military apparatus appears to be the circuses of the modern proletariat. Indeed, O'Connor's conception of a "surplus population" is not far from the riotous proletariat on the banks of the Tiber whose only function is the production of "prolis" (children) for the state. They too must be kept back from the revolutionary turmoil by the modern version of the *lex frumentaria*, e.g., AFDC and "food stamps," they too have their votes bought with "poverty programs" and the gladiatorial games and combats that provided the pleasures of violence, temporary omnipotence, the delights of distant terror all for free (as well as being an ongoing source of employment), produced by the military. As Seneca described it: "The spectators demand that the slayer shall face the man who is to slay him in his turn; and they always reserve the latest conqueror for another butchering. The outcome of every fight is death, and the means are fire and sword."[13] So, too, the military, aside from its obvious imperialist purpose, provides the spectacle necessary for the legitimation process which, according to Habermas (a key influence on O'Connor), an "advanced capitalist state" needs:

> The state apparatus no longer, as in liberal capitalism, merely secures the general conditions of production (in the sense of the prerequisites for the continued existence of the reproduction process) but is now actively engaged in it. It must, therefore—like the pre-capitalist state—be legitimated, although it can no longer rely on residues of tradition that have been undermined and worn out during the development of capitalism.[14]

But how does the state "elicit generalized motives—that is, diffuse mass loyalty" without eliciting "participation"? Surely the H-bombs, the laser-beamed "Star Wars" satellites, the apocalyptic rumors and missiles have a "game" element (a huge, expensive technology *built not to be used*, supposedly!) They make you feel the power, the violence, and terror of the state, or at least they did . . . it is the nearest earthly thing to God, after all.

So O'Connor's theory of war goes somewhat further than Baran and Sweezy's, for besides recognizing the surplus absorbing character of military expenditures (they "stave off domestic economic stagnation") he adds the "legitimizing" element: a monstrous investment in a machine that produces mass feelings.

Baran smiled as we were drawn further down the tunnel and slowly there emerged a light that began to grow in intensity until it became a pure crystal, clear illumination, bright and radiant, but it didn't hurt my eyes. I emitted queries and questions in a gentle ironic voice:

> Why is the working class so irrational that it puts up with all capital does?
> Is capital so self-limiting?

---

[13] Lucius Annaeus Seneca, *Moral Epistles*, trans. Richard M. Gummere (Cambridge, MA: Harvard University Press, 1917), Letter VII.

[14] Habermas, *Legitimation Crisis*, 36.

Why is the bulk of exchanges of "unproductive" commodities?

Where do the bodies for autopsies come from?

Was Hitler's extermination of "deviant" gays, the "mad," gypsies and Jews a product of bureaucratic irrationality or capitalist reproductive policy?

More and more questions flowed and heat began to build in me. And then I saw in a flash the huge amount of WORK that is required to produce the essence of all capital: labor-power. And I saw how so much capital and the Left have kept it *invisible, wageless, made of it a natural identity first of all for women*, and maligned those who demanded wages for this work. Like an island rising out of the sea, reproductive work came into sight filled with unnamed animals, insects, and plants wet with submarine obscurity breathing in the light!

Just as capitalist production only *incidentally* (though necessarily) creates use-values in order to produce value, so also in capitalist reproduction is labor-power the object, while the human animals that embody it are only created *by the way*. From capital's viewpoint these animals are only human if they embody labor-powers and a set of such animals form a population only if they can become variable capital. But the transition from animal to human, from animal to capital, is by no means "natural." It requires work, and therefore is a, perhaps *the*, ground of struggle. The birth of an animal is by no means the birth of labor-power and the death of an animal is by no means the death of labor-power: the class struggle is not a struggle over birth and death, but more fundamentally a struggle over what is being born or being killed. Here we can know the reproductive function of war. Nassau Senior's example of the soldier guarding the field from bandits so that they don't take the produce is superficial, but then again so were Marx's comments on it: what if the soldier's presence was necessary for the laborer to be there, what if it was an essential part of the labor-power expended?

The theme of war, genocide and work is, of course, basic to the classical political economy through Malthus's "principle of population" that explains war as one of the great "checks to population" when the number of animals produced by the sexual vitality of the working class confronts inadequate space and food supplies leading to "those two fatal political disorders, internal tyranny and internal tumult, which mutually produce each other." Marx's relentless critique of Parson Malthus's "Principle" just shifts the causation of war from Nature to Capital:

The law of capitalist accumulation, mystified by the economists into a supposed law of Nature, in fact expresses the situation that the very nature of accumulation excludes every diminution in the degree of exploitation of labor and every rise in the price of labor which could seriously imperil the continual reproduction, on an ever larger scale, of the capitalist relation. It cannot be otherwise in a mode of production in which the worker exists to satisfy the need of the existing values for valorisation; as opposed to the inverse situation in which objective wealth is there to satisfy the worker's own need of development.[15]

---

[15] Marx, *Capital: Volume I*, 771–72.

A prime material vehicle in the eternal attempt to "exclude" any tendency to "seriously imperil" capitalist accumulation is clearly to be found in the "human slaughter industry" and its products: Corpses and Terror. Surely Hitler was not the first to note the importance of war in "demographic" policy; his originality lay simply in the objects of that policy (Europeans) and the era (the twentieth century).

Therefore, the distinction between "warfare" and "welfare" expenditures made by many on the Left was superficial and tactical at best. Both are essential elements in the "reproduction, on an ever-enlargening scale, of the capitalist relation." As a former self preached to the deaf:

> "War" and "defense" are an essential, though unrecognized part of the reproduction of labor-power, which can dictate the death of millions of workers. Auschwitz, Dachau, Belsen were extermination factories whose product—the suffocation and death of tons of bodies—was an essential moment in capital's labor policy. . . . Moreover, "social welfare" spending by the state can be defense spending.[16]

These two types of state expenditures were essential to the maintenance of a "proper" quantitative ratio between the laboring population and the social capital that set into motion. War and control of natality being mechanisms required to produce the "law of population peculiar to the capitalist mode of production." Thus, the class struggles around the state's war-making powers and its control of the uterus were the most basic and subversive. For if capitalism lost control of the ratio between the quantities of surplus labor (capital) and total labor, the system would be unable to reproduce itself. Capital was not a struggle of Death against Life, of Thanatos against Eros per se: as any demographer could see, it had unleashed enormous sexual powers as well as cosmic immortal forces. No, it is a Law that correlated Eros and Thanatos, loving and killing, to produce accumulated values. The class struggle was then a struggle against capital's Law and Purpose, and not *for Life* (whatever that meant!).

But war was crucial not only for the determination of quantitative ratios, it was also part of the determination of the quality of labor-power; war and its threat, i.e., Terror, could be used to control the general wage level as well as a given hierarchy of wages. The most obvious example of this was the direct control of wages and the composition of labor during the course of an officially declared war. But this is only the most superficial instance, for the microapplication of army, police and paramilitary organization at points of "interface" between capital and working class during wage struggles is too common an experience to even document. Indeed, capital's theorists during peaks of wage struggle (e.g., Hobbes) simply identify the state as the social institution that must resort to violence in defense of property and the conditions of property production (work), i.e., the state as the famous "body of armed men." There was also, however, a global impact of war and Terror on the

---

[16] Caffentzis, "The Work/Energy Crisis and the Apocalypse," 11 in this volume.

wage, the availability for work, and the maintenance of wage hierarchies, for the wage measures the value of labor-power, i.e., the amount of labor-time necessary to reproduce a unit of labor-power, and Terror (fear of death) can dramatically reduce this value [*sic*]. True, there are limits to this Terror, as we dead know, but it is effective whatever the routes the worker believes the instruments will take to strike her/him down. For example, it is irrelevant for this effect whether the workers believed their wage struggle would "weaken" Capital in their own state and so it would retaliate, or that another state will "take advantage" of this weakness and strike.

Further, the "human slaughter industry" was indispensable during any period or "primitive or original accumulation" of the working class. Surely all those here remember the violence that was necessary for capital to unleash in order to expropriate European from their fields, Africans from their continent and the Indians from their tribes in order to create an international proletariat "free" for exploitation. The need for this quantity of violence did not end with the seventeenth century, however, for two reasons. First, large pockets of potential labor-power were left out of capital's initial inventory of the world's labor and further some sectors were able to "drop out" of the account book (e.g., Haiti for a part of the nineteenth century). Second, and even more important, during any epoch of capitalist development part of the working class manages to acquire means of subsistence that, though they may be compatible with an older mode of capitalism, must be destroyed in order to create a new mode of accumulation. There is a moment in every major change in capitalist development that can be described as the eternal return of primitive accumulation. The older ways must be destroyed, the proletariat must be "freed" from its past and the only way for this to occur is through the blood and fire of war and its violence. The Napoleonic wars that lead to the creation of European factory proletariat and the First and Second World Wars that led to the formation of the post-1945 "boom" are clear examples of the "echo" of original accumulation.

War was not only requisite for the creation, quantity and quality of the working class, it had been the laboratory, testing ground and factory for new forms of work organization. We need not chew on the old chestnut ("the model of industrial production was the army and the prison") nor need we re-image the correlation between the mass armies of the World Wars and the assembly lines of the United States, Europe, and Japan in the 1950s to get the point: military experience is the basic paradigm of capitalist cooperation. But here's a new chestnut: the use of women in the U.S. Army during the post-Vietnam era was clearly a test of a new form of work that involved women's reproductive powers directly in the production process instead of indirectly, as in the previous period. The difficulties of this integrated sexuality could be studied and manipulated with enormous ease in the bowels of the state. This was just the latest applications of the general "function" of War and Army as an area for the development of work productivity and new patterns of cooperation.

Finally, the military and police extirpate unproductive and anti-productive workers as well as increasing the efficiency of work relation. Indeed, these were not unrelated tasks. The most benighted knew that even, or especially, very productive employments of labor-power created highly entropic human "wastes" that must be extracted from the production flow, killed and then dumped. The smoothest machine creates its share of "used up," "burnt out," "degraded" energies that must be expelled at the completing of every cycle or the next cycle will become extremely inefficient. This is true for variable capital as well as constant, and so even the most sophisticated form of capitalism confronts its share of "criminals," "bandits," "guerrillas," "terrorists," "revolutionaries," "perverts," and "witches," who cannot be recycled. The trick is to find them, hence the need for detectors—spies, agents, and dossiers—and then to destroy them. The long history of executions, assassinations, death squads, "antiterrorist" campaigns, and "counterinsurgency" warfare is a story not of "incidental expenses" arising from anomalous "faulty social relations." These things were as essential to capitalist production as a condenser is to a heat engine.

And so I saw before me the Pure Theory of War: the snakes of Annihilation, Terror, Expropriation, Discipline and Extirpation wet with blood and feces twisting and squeezing. The voice that called up this obscene crystal of War had vanished. I was left alone.

Alone with a sickness and a knowledge of the system I had escaped where war was essence. Alone with memories of the last days when those who claimed to bring peace hid new Machines of War in their cloaks and Armies in their minds.

"Light, Cheap, Many"/" Export or Die": The New Military Thought and Reindustrialization

> When a country is impoverished by military operations it is due to distant transportation; carriage of supplies for great distances renders the people destitute. Where the army is, prices are high; when prices rise the wealth of the people is exhausted. When wealth is exhausted the peasantry will be afflicted with urgent exaction.
> —Sun Tzu

The fourfold pathway of capitalist development for the rest of the century that they thought they had, necessarily involved the ability to create a military policy that would "accelerate" the proposed model and would create an appropriate reproduction of the working class.

As a consequence, each of the models had to develop a military "strategy" and "sell" it to both capital and significant sectors of the working class to make a deal. This was especially true if significant changes were to be made in the direction the accumulation process had taken since 1973. Military policy and procurement plays such an enormous part in the development of different kinds of capitalist development not only because of the function of military expenditures on the reproduction of the working class, i.e., the production of workers *qua* workers. It is also crucial in the shaping of the domestic production process on "home" industries. In the United States, military procurement is the fundamental form of direct government investment and subsidy for constant capital. It might be a small part of the GNP, which is much too "gross" to measure anyway, but it is qualitative different from other types of investment both in form and effect. In comparison with other forms of direct investment in constant capital, military expenditures can be dynamic, in the sense that enormous amounts of capital can be transformed literally "out of the skies"; it is not dependent upon the immediate profitability, the eternal complain of liberalism against the military; there is state power behind the expenditures and so all local restriction, labor regulations, etc., can be neglected; by being willful and discretionary, it is accelerating in effect.

Reagan's defense policy that emphasized immense new investment in extremely capital-intensive and even "science-intensive" weaponry, from MXs to particle-beams, clearly had a particular model of constant capital for the new millennium. Not accidentally, Teller, the protégé of von Neumann and philo-H-bomber, was a primary technical advisor. A new military doctrine was necessary if another, anti-Reagan development model, was to be proposed. So it is not surprising that the "Peace" movement over night turned into the "Freeze" movement.

Indeed, behind the Freeze was a whole new military-industrial complex, and that is why the road to the Freeze was so smooth. Anyone going to a typical Freeze or Ground Zero gathering remembers being impressed by the "centrist" names in attendance, the jackets and ties, the professional women and the "official" backing whether it be political (as in the Democratic Party) or institutional. Even William Colby, former CIA head, supported it. It surely was enough to get one paranoid! *Reader's Digest* and Reagan took to red-baiting the whole thing, saying the masses (always well intentioned!) are being manipulated by the KGB (of all things). But here, Reagan and friends were left high and dry because the "manipulators" were more likely to be found in the Congressional delegations, corporate headquarters of the auto industry, and the "neoliberal" Washington think tanks than in Moscow. And the manipulated? We, the "masses" were not so well-intentioned and some parties were looking around for a better deal, apparently from the Muscovite stooges! That is why, for example, in the spring of 1982 the major newspapers of the Northeast (especially the *New York Times* and *Boston Globe*) consistently overestimated attendance at pre–June 12 Freeze events where the scruffy anti–nuclear energy movement literally had to fight for coverage.

The reason for the impressive backing of the anti–nuclear war movement was simple: a good part of capital was skeptical of the stability of the Reaganite model of a polarized realm and, moreover, some parts that were destined to die if the mixture works were refusing to march off the historical stage peacefully. These elements seen in the Freeze movement, and in the military-industrial complex associated with it, promised survival for themselves and a more stable system in the future. And, perhaps more deeply, they realized that nuclear weapons are obsolete militarily, i.e., the threat to capitalist control did not reside in mass territorial war but in molecular, capillary and diffuse infections needing precise yet extensive application. Could a Nike really "solve" the "problem of El Salvador"?

The publicist for the "new strategic thinking" had been unquestionably James Fallows (and his book, *National Defense*, published in the first Reagan year), who not only laid out the main arguments of the approach but nicely captured the tone of a former Vietnam war resister who had come back to the fold, but who demands reasonability and "humanity" from the system as the price. The essence of his approach is to build cheap and many: "small is beautiful" in military weapons as long as it is bountiful. Thus, consider the procurement list recommended by the *Washington Monthly*, Fallows's and the "liberals'" house organ:

Weapons the Military Could Use

1. A light, maneuverable long-range bomber to replace the B-52.
2. Increased procurement of A-7 attack plane now used only by the National Guard.
3. Increase procurement of A-10 close support plane.
4. Renewed procurement of F-4 and F-5 fighters.
5. Small, diesel-powered submarines, both for attack and missile-launching capability.
6. Cheap, small "fast boats" that avoid radar.
7. 106mm recoilless (cannon) rifle for use as an antitank weapon.
8. GAU-8 30mm cannon for use as an antitank weapon.
9. Increased procurement of Sidewinder missiles.
10. Battalions of motorcycles to improve maneuver warfare capability.
11. Increased procurement of Remote Piloted vehicles (unmanned target locators and distractions for enemy antiaircraft).
12. Small, light tank for Marines.

The key words, of course, are "light," "small," "cheap," and "maneuverable." Fallows and friends took aim at the "culture of procurement" and the continual attempt to find high-tech "magical" solutions to the problems of "defense." To get a sense of Fallows's rhetorical tactics consider his comment on the Pentagon's perversion of "the business of spending money":

This is corruption, but not in the sense most often assumed. The bribes, the trips to the Caribbean in corporate aircraft do occur, but they distort the essence, as Abscam distorts the essence of Congressional irresponsibility, and payoff in the General Services Administration distort the pathology of the civil service. The real damage is not spectacular but routine: it is the loss of purpose in the daily operation of the military machine, the substitution of procurement for defense. This is the true corruption, and it affects all the relevant groups: soldiers, who are converted to sales agents, rewarded for skills that count in real estate; contractors, whose productive core is corroded by contact with the nonperformance culture, and finally the rationality and civility of public discussion about defense, what are sabotaged by the hidden purpose of continuing to spend money.[17]

Here we have a voice of "reason," not a sniping, cynical, lesbo-Marxist snarl, but someone who has seen both sides of the defense picture and can bring a proper balance, who only is asking that the "job" get done "right." Compare Fallows's earnest prose with the nervous complement of *Business Week*'s "Reindustrialization" team:

> Too often chief executives send mixed signals to their staffs. On the one hand they demand creativity and on the other they regard numbers . . . the easiest way for executives to feel comfortable with alien technological or marketing concepts is to devise a technique for measuring them. Not only had internal rate of return and discounted cash flow replaced educated instincts for deciding on new projects, but quantitative approaches—or at best, formularized ones—have even pervaded human resource management. The old days of motivating employees by example and by general day-to-day closeness to the field have given way to consultants' techniques such a behavior modification climate and attitude control and the like. It is little wonder that top management has become isolated from its employees.[18]

Though speaking with different rhythms, the pathos is the same: "the method has been put before the result," say these mechanics as they looked at the engine of the stalled system.

The relation between Fallows's thinking and that of the "reindustrializers" was by no means rhetorical, for in Fallows's books, and in the thinking of the defense strategists who eventually developed as one part of the Freeze movement, the Freeze is an essential element of the "reindustrializers'" policy. It was essential in two ways: (a) it allowed for a perfectly acceptable compromise way to allow the state to intervene in the domestic economy through a new procurement policy in order to reintroduce mass industry and revive older branches of the economy; and (b) it attempted to develop a force for intervention internationally that would suitable for the new role of the United States in the international division of labor.

The success of the Freeze movement per se would have put defense procurement in the hands of a part of the defense establishment that was trying to develop a "new look" that goes beyond Reagan's bipolarism. The whole defense establishment was split on whether all capital's eggs should be put in the Cold War nuclear basket. A clear indication of this debate was in the remarks of Admiral "Bobby" Inman, the real head of the CIA for some time, in explaining his resignation from the CIA in April 1982. He said, "I reject out of hand the likelihood that we could

---

[17] James Fallows, *National Defense* (New York: Random House, 1981), 62–63.

[18] "The Reindustrialization of America," *Business Week* (special edition), June 30, 1980, 81.

be surprised with a Pearl Harbor kind of attack. And the same pretty well holds true for the eastern front, central part of Europe."[19] The problem arises "in following political and economic trends abroad" in "dealing with instability in many areas of the world, trying to cope with the fervor of religious movements." In other words, the problem of intelligence is not a bipolar one. The question is: will the United States "steward" the planet through missiles-bombers-aircraft carriers or through machine guns-knockout gas-lasers, i.e., through weapons directed at the Soviet Union or directly at insurgencies in the local or foreign proletariat. The payoff for the reindustrializers is, of course, that the rejection of the Reagan Cold War would reorder the Defense Department's priorities. From the "high-tech" liberals to Kennedy, from Rohatyn to the *Business Week* publicists, this shift would be the opening wedge to the type of "partnership" between "government, the unions and business" that they desire. What a short cut to the partnership this type of military development would be.

The Freeze would have been the type of military policy "reindustrializers" needed in foreign affairs. For the Freeze, if it merely became a limit (like the limit imposed on the size of factories of the length of the working), would simply have allowed or, even better, forced capital to develop more intensively in new directions. The direction that would be more propitious in one that totally directs itself to the revolutionary disruptions of international capitalist trade. Indeed, the "reindustrializers" were using, on one side, the world market as a club to whip the American proletariat. On the other side, it is necessary to get a return from the U.S. proletariat that has been stopped outside of the United States by the increasingly successful resistance of the European and "Third World" proletariat.

Wage struggle in the post–World War II period within the United States was the decisive impetus that sent U.S. capital on its multinational path of production, first into Europe and then throughout the Third World. In Europe, wage rates began to accelerate past U.S. rates and in the Third World, revolution and insurrection intensified even in the face of violent reaction and tortuous defeats. As a consequence, there is a renewed interest in the U.S. proletariat and a desire to come back "home" again. Such a return, however, would have brought capital to a situation that was more reminiscent of the Imperialist period of the late nineteenth century. Therefore, the type of military policy that was not bipolar would become essential.

Indeed, the *Business Week* team sees a new place for the U.S. as the mix of the "First World" and the "Third World":

> The United States, unlike its major competitors, has a rapidly growing labor force, much of it unskilled and U.S. wages will be declining relative to those abroad. The economy will therefore have the resources to staff mass-production industries, such as autos and textiles, that the other advanced countries will begin to de-emphasize because of incipient labor shortages and rising wages. But the United States will have to make these industries much more

---

[19] *New York Times*, April 28, 1982, A16.

efficient, since it will be coming into increasing competition with the newly industrializing countries of Asia and Latin America, where labor costs will be much lower.[20]

What is the function of military policy in this "export-based" political economy? In their only reference to it, the Team says, in reference to the "handicapping to U.S. exporters" by the government, " the United States must find more suitable and cost-effective means, ranging from foreign aid to military intervention in specific situations abroad." Though standing alone, this mention is quite telling, for it speaks to a form of export imperialism of the last century quite baldly. As the Team says, in the title of this section: "Export or Die."

The Draft: Variable Capital and Moby Dick

Is there anywhere where our theory that the organization of labor is determined by the means of production is more brilliantly confirmed than in the human slaughter industry?
—Marx to Engels (1866)[21]

Once I had seen the essential relation of the Freeze campaign to the political economy of reindustrialization, the question arose: where were the soldiers to come from, who were they to be? Was there to be a "volunteer army" or a draft?

Inevitably the military reindustrializers (through their whole spectrum) had a radically different view than the Reagan Administration concerning the draft. After all, the "army of labor" and the mass armies of this century have been essential parts of the mass organization of work embodied in the assembly line. The Reagan Administration was abandoning the mass worker and so it viewed the post-Vietnam "volunteer" army as a perfect image of its preferred working-class composition: on the bottom the army is a pure "free enterprise zone" of labor conscripted by wages, given the starkness of the labor market; on the top, well paid "professionals" and even "consultants" of the high-tech war machine. When the "liberals" cried (what the "conservatives" used to cry about)—"You can't run an army on money alone"—Reagan answered (with Friedman behind him): "Why not? We run the rest of the damn system on it!" In those days capital's left wing took out the old patriotic snot rag to sob in: Money is not enough! Fallows wailed for the military "spirit" thusly: "Before anything else, we must recognize that a functioning military requires bonds of trust, sacrifice, and respect within its ranks, and similar bonds of support and respect between the Army and the nation it represents. . . . I believe that will not happen unless we reinstitute the draft."[22] Of course, of course . . . How could the reindustrializers hope to fight

---

[20] "The Reindustrialization of America," 120.

[21] Karl Marx and Friedrich Engels, Selected Correspondences, 1846–1895 (London: Lawrence & Wishart, 1936), 209.

[22] Fallows, National Defense, 173.

their trade wars in Africa and South America when their troops were all Black and Hispanic? How were they to get the Great White Youth back into uniform? Clearly, if the reindustrializers did reintroduce a full employment" economy, the why should white youths join a "volunteer" army, unless the military wage were prohibitively high. Where are the "bonds of sacrifice" to pull the pale Leviathan in, if not from the whirl-pool of wages, then spur of prison. As the editors of the *Washington Monthly* wrote:

> Pentagon planners like to point out that last year they met their recruiting goals with enlistees of improved quality. What they don't like to mention is the major reason for these gains: the worst economic recession since the 1930s. If the economy ever revives, the recruiting problems will return, particularly since the national recruiting pool of 15-to-21-year-olds will decline by 15 percent by 1990.[23]

They were right, of course, in their haughtiness, but wrong in their expectations. If Reagan did get the political economy of his model there would not be a revival of "full employment" to undermine the "military spirit." In this matter the Reaganites proved to be more serious than their opponents, who were reaching for the base pedal when talking so disgustingly of the "Ol' Army." Reagan had more respect for the evident resistance the 15–21-year-olds have to the "Officer and Gentleman" routine (as the cautious, temporizing way with handling the resisters to registration showed).

This stance to the draft made clear that the thinkers of the "new military" need-ed the reindustrializers as much as the reindustrializers needed the new militarists: no one expected to sell the draft to white kids, much less to their parents, unless it was part of a "package deal." Only when one could reasonably argue that the future was real, that it held some guarantees of employment and high wages could the State demand a present "sacrifice" and hope to get away with it. For example, aside from mass jailings, the only credible weapons against draft evasion could be employment discrimination, but if the typical white riot punk did not have much possibility to find a job in the part of the labor market that demanded a high level of certification, then why register for the draft in the first place? A clear case of this dialectic between the present and the future can be seen in the case of the Blacks' relation to the draft and registration. The huge expansion of the "underground economy" envisioned by the Reaganauts which could absorb the many millions of "illegal aliens," cons, drifters with a minimum of documentation, would make a "fair, equitable" registration rate of 85 percent an impossible dream. It is clear that without the reindustrializers' success the notion of a mass army is hot air, even, militaristic heart-throb and soft core S&M.

Somehow, the Great White Whale had to be lured into the vicinity of the liberal's *Pequod*. On the one side, they offered their old jobs back with a lower wage, but with a promise of lower levels of exploitation ("labor participation in manage-ment decisions"), on the other side, they claimed to be able to cut a deal with the

---

[23] George Ott, "Three Modest Proposals," *The Washington Monthly* 14, no. 2 (April 1982): 35.

Russians that would safeguard them and their real estate from the only conceivable threat to their total existence: nuclear war. They promised a saner, more reasonable, polyvalent world. No more titanic struggles between the forces of Good against the "focus of evil" fought with MXs and lasers, just a few trade wars and border disputes, a limited dose of social democracy in selected areas of the Third World and some charity for the basket cases. Illusions were rife then . . .

Nuclear Strategies: Who's Kidding Whom?

> The atom bomb is a paper tiger which the U.S. reactionaries use to scare people. It looks terrible, but in fact it isn't. Of course, the atom bomb is a weapon of mass slaughter, but the outcome of a war is decided by the people, not by one or two new types of weapons.
> —Mao (1946)[24]

The political economy behind the Freeze was a revival of the Keynesian state based on a mass assembly line industry impelled by a revived mass army. But for all their rhetoric about "saving humanity" the Freezers were in as an untenable position as Reagan. For they reproposed a model of class relations that the working class had taken to be unacceptable in the first place. They were going back to square one of the crisis, hoping against hope that the Whale had been tamed after the latest bout with Depression. But as the 1982 Chrysler strike showed, even through all the lining up to take a few shit jobs at $4.00 an hour, the "inflationary pressures" were far from dead. Chrysler workers simply refused to accept a contract that coordinated their wages with the position of Chrysler in the capitalists' pecking order. At least they expected their wages to be coordinated with the workers in the rest of the U.S. auto industry, i.e., they insisted on the *converse* of the old saw, "A fair day's work for a fair day's pay."

It is this skepticism that gave reality to Reagan's policy even though it was obviously unstable and contradictory. Reagan's, in some weird way, points in the direction of working-class energies, in an "inverted" form of course. At the very least, there was little enthusiasm for "going back home"! *Reagan, for all of his 1950s mugging and his wattles, faced the class future, the Left (in its liberal, social democratic or marxist-leninist forms) the past.* That was his power and not the accumulated violence at his disposal. This was by no means an original point, it was made again and again by the "opinion polls": like it or not, we were stuck with him unless . . . And indeed, unless there was a leap of their energies, we might very well have rotted in the pot of history a lot longer than the "holocausters" gave credit for.

The Freezers offered a "sensible deal," it seemed, especially given the alternative: Reagan' nuclear build-up and the increased danger of nuclear war. Their argument was simply: the nuclear build-up was so dangerous for human survival

---

24 Mao Tse-Tung, *Selected Works of Mao Tse-Tung Vol. IV* (Peking: Foreign Languages Press, 1969), 100.

that any effort made to stop it independently of the rest of the class dynamics is imperative and possible. The basis of this argument was laid down most eloquently by E.P. Thompson, working-class historian and leader of the British anti-nuke movement. He was not a Freezer, but his "Exterminism" article had a great impact on the Nuclear Freeze Campaign. In this article, he coined a word and built an argument for the "relative autonomy" of nuclear-weapons systems from the entire economic, scientific, political and ideological support system to that weapons-system—the social system which researches it, "chooses" it, produces it, policies it, justifies it and maintains it in being." True, Thompson admits, there is capitalism, imperialism, and all that; indeed, they might have brought exterminism into existence but once in existence it developed a "life" of its own, so to speak.

> Class struggle continues, in many forms, across the globe. But exterminism itself is not a "class issue": it is a human issue. Certain kinds of "revolutionary" posturing and rhetoric, which inflame exterminist ideology and which carry divisions into the necessary alliances of human resistance are luxuries which we can do without.[25]

Thus, in the blaze of x-rays from the mushroom cloud, the human race *qua* human race is born as a political entity. In the moment of the most extreme weakness against the Bomb, Thompson sees a United Front of Humanity whose main demand addressed to the Demons of Exterminism is: let us live! The bipolar collision of the United States and the USSR is taken up by Thompson with the same reverence that Reagan speaks of it. But this assumption of isomorphism that is the root of his exterminism argument is unsound, first and foremost because he "forgot" that there was no "U.S." and "USSR," rather, there was a class system within both: Soviet and American capital and working class. At the very least, one must speak of a "trapezoid of forces"; it is only in the class mechanics of this trapezoid could we begin to understand the logic of "nuclear war." These mechanics had twelve directions instead of two: i.e., not:

USSR*   *USA

but:

USSR Cap*   * USA Cap
USSR WC*   *USA WC

E.P. Thompson, the historian of working-class self-activity, abandoned class analysis when confronting late twentieth-century weapons technology. But the

---

[25] E.P. Thompson, "Notes on Exterminism: The Last Stage of Civilization," in *Peace Studies: Critical Concepts in Political Science*, ed. Mathew Evangelista (New York: Routledge, 2005), 211.

very extraterrestrial energies of these weapons, ironically, made Absolute War in Clausewitz's sense impossible, i.e., War with the aim of "overthrowing the enemy," of compelling "the enemy to fulfill our will" ended. Only Real or "Partial" nuclear War could be played out—"a half-and-half production, a thing without a perfect inner cohesion." Napoleonic grandeur vanishes and an elaborate game of nuclear thrust-and-parry remained. (Hence the "hot line" between Washington and Moscow and Sen. Jackson's nuclear war utopia where Russian and American analysts debate the cities to be destroyed in an atomic exchange somewhere in the Indian Ocean!) For, after all, who is nuclear war against?

The danger of Real nuclear war arises only when it is in the interests of both U.S. and Soviet capital. This is especially true on the U.S. part, given the undoubted ability of its military to destroy Soviet fixed and variable capital under any circumstances (for all of Casper's howling). Even in the "worst-case scenario," our trusty nuclear planners envision a U.S. President with his land-based missiles wiped out, along with 15 million souls, hesitating to launch an attack on selected Soviet cities from Polaris and Trident submarines; the cities being completely un-protected and the Soviet citizens in them hostages. But then under what circum-stances would nuclear war, a real one, have made sense for both? Undoubtedly it could have been under very delicate conditions, i.e., only when the class forces have reached a mass point concentrated enough to be used as hostages in a swap—Detroit for Kiev! The "problem" for the poor, idle nuclear planners was that these conditions required both a deep, deep crisis in the internal class relations and a belief on capital's part that a physical elimination of a targeted sector of the work-ing class would not lead to a level of insurrection and revulsion that would end in a collapse of the system. If neither of these conditions held, then the risks would not be worth it for either side.

Certainly in 1983, such a crisis was not in the offing for U.S. capital, al-though it did arise within a few years. In between, the irony was that the intrac-tableness of the Soviet proletariat saved everyone from a kind of "Nuclear Chess" that military gamers dreamed. Soviet planners were not so sure that any major disruption would be controlled. The shame was that the U.S. working class's "cri-sis behavior" did not stir similar fears in U.S. capital. If anything, the Reaganite rigidity might very well have been a warning to the "Russians" to end their dilly-dallying with the Soviet proletariat and "peasantry."

If "the danger of nuclear war" was really the problem of the "Peace" move-ment, then there would be only one possible strategy. Certainly the Freeze could not be a reasonable response, for it merely reproposed the problem on another (lower) level of armaments. Rather, the only logical strategy would have been to develop the ability to threaten any attempt at Real nuclear war with revolution. That is, to have made clear to Soviet and U.S. capital that any attempt to dramatically and "instan-taneously" devalue the working class would only lead to a complete loss of control, dropping one Bomb would destroy the whole game. Those who argued that all nuclear war must be Absolute were full of it, "partial" or "controlled" nuclear war was certainly *technically* possible; it is only an insurrectional proletariat that could make sure than any "partial" war would be "absolutely" catastrophic for capital. Indeed, in any revolutionary juncture in the U.S., nuclear weapons complicate matters, for it would be necessary to pass that delicate point between endemic crisis and breakdown extremely quickly or at a different point from the Soviet proletariat. Certainly, the "Peace" movement never took this strategy up, only a few desperadoes took this as their motto: *Nuclear War will be Absolute or Nothing, no more Apocalyptic Pathos.*

Though the "Peace" movement never planned for the response for nuclear war, capital was knowledgeable about the possibilities of revolutionary consequences of nuclear war and was quite worried about them, as could be seen in the Congressional study prepared for the Joint Committee on Defense Production, published in 1979 (at the beginning of the build-up). The study ends with a chapter on "The Social and Political Implications of Nuclear Attacks" in which we find the following telling words concerning the post–nuclear war environment:

> A significant risk of total loss of political legitimacy may develop, accompanied perhaps by real efforts on the part of survivors to change the leadership or the system forcibly or, at a local level, to take matters into their own hands. While a sense of national emergency and solidarity may operate to sustain the support of survivor for some time in the post-attack period, the failure of the government at any level to achieve rapid and meaningful recovery process, to explain satisfactorily the causes of the attack, or to demonstrate a genuine concern for social needs and pre-attack values could lead to widespread dissatisfaction and perhaps result in serious challenges to the authority of government itself.[26]

This fear was our greatest defense against nuclear war. The Freeze attacks the unpredictability of the working-class response, the certainty of unpredictability, by committing itself to the very process and institutions that would bring on war in the first place (as the German Social Democrats "reluctantly" voting for war-credits did at the start of the World War I) since it guaranteed civil peace in the midst of nuclear war. Thus, for example, in *Nuclear War: What's in It for You?*, the official book of the Ground Zero group, the description of a postnuclear "scenario" has no mention of insurrectional consequences or possibilities. Rather we are given a picture of a gripping, depressed population whose most dangerous occupations are an occasional food riot and some dabbling in the black market. This is no accident; such an image is the product of how the Freezers want us to be in the prenuclear state: upset, but not so upset as to do anything rash.

The desperadoes' strategy did not demand "negotiations" with anyone, for it ultimately did not depend upon what they did or not: they were not upset about whether they built MXs or not per se. They organized themselves so that they could make a middle ground of "partial nuclear war" a mathematical catastrophe.

---

[26] Joint Committee on Defense Production, *Economic and Social Consequences of Nuclear Attacks on the United States* (Washington, DC: US Government Printing Office, 1979), 148.

They believed that if capital was not convinced that it must risk all to continue the threat of War, then it would risk all. Now I know they did not see the cusp, the discontinuity.

True, I remember that the Freeze was something more than an elaborate scheme of capitalist reorganization. It did have its own class "objective possibilities." First, by being a direct communication between the U.S. proletariat and Soviet capital and working class, it was extremely destabilizing to Reagan's Administration. Indeed, if it were not destabilizing, then it could not have been used by the reindustrializes for their own lever to change the course and model of U.S. capitalist development. The Freeze leaders, of course, did not want these objective possibilities to get out of their control, and as long as it filtered through the representative form, it did not. However, even the electoral blitz of 1981 and 1982 (where the Freeze resolution was passed in many states and localities) was dangerous for the Freeze leaders because it "rushed things along too quickly," i.e., before other elements of the "game plan" could mature. So they had to slow the movement down to control it and pick its proper fruits, but this risked a contradiction in the temporal horizons of its supporters. After all, if "we are on the verge of total annihilation," then "we must proceed with all haste" (is the slogan they use to stimulate the movement), but at the same time the leaders had to slow down the rush by cautioning, "Well, the Apocalypse has been postponed 'til the elections of 1984." The Apocalypse was a rather heavy horse to handle tactically, but they managed largely because the riders were indecisive and even a child could lead them.

For the U.S. proletariat appeared to be willing to make a deal for its skin. For example, in Massachusetts the "Freeze" resolution in 1982 passed (approximately) 75 percent to 25 percent while at the same time a referendum on capital punishment which called for the reintroduction of executions into the state passed 60 percent to 40 percent. Under the most "favorable" interpretation (vis., all who voted against the Freeze voted for capital punishment) at least 35 percent of those who voted for the Freeze voted for the right to "fry" those condemned to death. They were willing to make peace with the Soviet Union (which had the power to attack them) in exchange for the right to declare war against those on death row. The White Whale was ready for the harpoon.

When I remembered this and the numerous treacheries of the class, its racism, its rapes, its meanness, I wanted to remain here in the tranquility, this vanishing of all worries. All around me a living, pale golden glow streamed and flowed. But I felt a barrier, I wanted to go into the glow . . . but I couldn't, something stopped me . . .

Coda: Theory and Practice

All had to drink a measure of this water, but those who were not preserved by wisdom drank more and as each drank they forgot everything. After they had slept and it was the middle of the night, there was a clap of thunder and an earthquake and suddenly they were carried upward to birth in different

directions, rushing like stars. Er himself was forbidden to drink of the water.
He did not know how and in what way he arrived back in his body, but look-
ing up suddenly he saw himself lying on the pyre at dawn.
—Plato, *The Republic*

Somewhere in the *Social Contract*, Rousseau argues that humans would never
have left the delicious, anonymous state of savagery unless they were under the
threat of an overwhelming natural catastrophe requiring a "summing of forces" to be
overcome. The Contract created a network of constraints that combined the given
forces of each individual canceling out the total threat to human existence. Why
enter into the chained labyrinth of bourgeois rights and obligations without the
impulse of a collective natural necessity?

A new necessity has appeared, the Contract is broken now. Amid the lingering fires and the swirling dust I see the others are coming now as we agreed. It is
time for new things.

THE POWER OF MONEY:
DEBT AND ENCLOSURE

T his is an "interview" I conducted with myself in 1995. I wanted to ask myself the "simple" questions that others in the mid-1990s were not asking me or themselves. The following are my answers.

> What originally appeared as a means to promote production [i.e., money] becomes a relation alien to the producers. As the producers become more dependent on exchange, exchange appears to become more independent of them, and the gap between the product as product and the product as exchange value appears to widen. Money does not create these antitheses and contradictions; it is, rather, the development of these contradictions and antitheses which creates the seemingly transcendent power of money.
> —Karl Marx, *Notebook 1* (1857)

Why do the IMF and WB, which are, after all, just glorified banks that lend money, charge interest, and engage in foreign exchange manipulations, have such "transcendental" powers, as you claim?

Here is my argument: The WB and the IMF are the coordinators of flows of money, the payments of debt and the determination of interest rates among the states of the world. And money, debt, and interest are essential for the survival or extinction of governments today. *Therefore*, the WB and IMF have enormous power.

Why is money so important? In one sense it is obvious—just try to do without it—but *why* it is obvious is *not* obvious. For most of human history, money either did not exist (before roughly the seventh century BC) or it was of marginal importance for most people on the planet (until roughly the nineteenth century AD). Why is it so important now?

Many economists now tell a sweet tale, brimming with reason, about money in order to explain why money is indispensible to rational social life. Come, listen:

Money becomes vital only in societies where buying and selling (commodity exchange) affects every aspect of life. Simple commodity exchange (or barter) has a notorious flaw: some one might want to exchange A for B, but no one in the vicinity who owns B might want to exchange it for A. This lack of coincidence of desire (which has within it the presupposition that people who produce A are not in communication with or are hostile to the desires of those who produce B) is often taken to be the motive force for the development of money. Barter also has very high "transaction costs" (since it takes much time, energy and risk for sellers to find suitable buyers); the institution of money (which cuts down on time, energy and risk) in a network of commodity exchangers "saves" *everyone* an enormous "cost." Since everyone is better off, then it is reasonable to accept money once it is introduced. This is the way the origin of money is discussed in "economics."[1]

But this economist's fairy tale poses more questions than answers. For example, Is the cost of money clearly less than barter? Why has "everyone" become buyers and sellers? And finally, why have the hypothetical people in the tale become so distant or hostile to each other?

Let us take them in order.

Is the social cost of the money system less than that of a barter system?

Money too has its "transaction costs," as that most voluminous yet most penurious writer on the topic of money, Karl Marx, wrote: "Money can overcome the difficulties inherent in barter only by generalizing them, making them universal."[2] As people who live in a monetary society, we can well attest to the fact that the lack of coincidence of desires often occurs with a vengeance where money predominates, for those with money are often not interested in spending it on any particular commodity (they hoard it or try to get more money with it) and those without money often have nothing to sell to get it. These mutually antagonistic "failures of coincidence" have enormous costs: from depressions, famines, and slavery to police, prisons, and execution chambers to banks, stock markets, and all sorts of expensive "financial services."[3] How much *they* cost and *who* suffers the cost is not often

---

[1] The "transaction cost" approach to telling the tale of money is one of the most sophisticated; for a now classic exposition of this approach see R.W. Clower, "A Reconsideration of the Microfoundations of Monetary Theory," *Western Economic Journal* 6, December 1967, 1–8.

[2] Marx, *Grundrisse*, 149–50.

[3] Suzanne de Brunhoff, *Marx on Money* (New York: Urizen Books, 1976).

quantified by the tellers of the tale of the rationality of money, but certainly this cost is enormous, and the billions who suffer the cost are rarely those who tell the tale.

The money system's priests always present it as an abstract but purely rational reality, as not only the ideal language of commodities but as the truly universal mode of human coordination transcending the vast and endless multiplying varieties of human intercourse on the planet. They say: "only the irrational can refuse it." But it is perfectly rational to survey the *total cost* of the money system and conclude that it is much greater than the alternatives.

Why is it then that "everyone" is involved with the money system, if it is not based on an utterly transcendental reasonability, i.e., if its costs can be greater than its benefits?

Most people can find in their genealogy or in their own lives some point when their ancestors or they themselves were forced from lands and social relations that provided subsistence without having to sell either one's products or oneself, i.e., they suffered Enclosure. Without these moments of force, money would have remained a marginal aspect of human history. These moments were mostly of brutal violence, sometimes quick (with bombs, cannon, musket, or whip), sometimes slower (with famine, deepening penury, plague), which led to the terrorized flight from the land, from the burnt-out village, from the street full of starving or plague-ridden bodies, to slave ships, to reservations, to factories, to plantations. This flight ended with "producers becoming more dependent on exchange" since they had no other way to survive but by either selling their products or selling themselves or being sold. Thus did "exchange become more independent of them," its transcendental power arising from the unreversed violence that drove "everyone" into the monetary system.

It often is money itself that serves as the pretext for this expropriating violence, for unpaid debt has frequently been the basis for being taken into slavery, or losing one's land, or giving up "a pound of flesh." For those on the margins of a monetary society, debt can be a way to try to buffer for a while the demands of surviving in a monetary system or to try to enter into the system with some strength. But since these debtors are on the margin, when conditions change and expectations prove faulty, repayment becomes impossible. The power of money then becomes positively Jehovah-like, all escape is blocked, and the debtor is ruined, i.e., everything he/she had to subsist is taken away by banks, the police or the debt collector's goons, and what was to have been a way to "promote production" becomes "alien to the producers."

This scenario happened often in the past to individuals and groups, but recently there have been New Enclosures where unpayable national debt is used by the IMF and WB and complicitous national governments to change laws that restricted the expropriation of land that provided some guarantees of subsistence to workers. The classic example of this New Enclosure was the Salinas government's repeal of Article 27 of the Mexican Constitution in 1992 in accordance to the SAP that had been put into place in the mid-1980s under the guidance of the WB and IMF. Before Article 27's repeal, Mexican farm workers had the right to claim some of the land they were working on and no one could buy the land they owned, now they have no such legal aims and they can be forced to sell their land because of bad loans.

The essence of these structural adjustment programs (SAPs) in Mexico and in the more than eighty other countries, then, is to make it impossible for anyone to retreat from the monetary system and make them totally subject to the "transcendental power of money."

Once one is forced into a monetary system why does it often appear impossible to create other alternatives?

Clearly there is a whole array of powerful (and armed) organizations that immediately threaten such attempts (from police, to death squads, to armies), but there appears to be another more reasonable and even more inexorable force blocking the escape from money, the famous "flaw" of nonmonetary social exchange: the lack of coincidence of desires. The continued existence of money depends on this lack of coincidence of desires while the money system and its agents develop and deepen this lack in their relentless effort to convince everybody that collective discussion and understanding of desires can never lead to coincidence. The cultivation of hostility, suspicion, competition and fear of scarcity (*especially* the scarcity of money) creates the preconditions for everyone to depend on money for exchange (with all *its* flaws). These preconditions are also consequences of the monetary system's production and reproduction so that the only terror worse than money is its lack.

The WB's and IMF's power, therefore, lies not only in their ability to directly threaten governments, political parties, labor unions, indigenous organizations that attempt to escape the circuit of money with a commodity blockade and to subtly suggest a subsequent violent invasion by contras, the UN "humanitarian" army, or former colonial forces. The Bank's and Fund's power depends upon the "transcendental power of money" itself which it is their sworn duty to develop throughout the planet *ad infinitum*. Hence their innate, instinctual hostility to the use of land (or any other potentially "commons," e.g., the field of linguistic exchange, electromagnetic frequencies, the high seas, the atmosphere, the past) for the development of antimonetary forms of social coordination, so that human beings can again gain confidence in creating fatal (for the money system) coincidences of desire.

Consider the WB's new policy toward the "cultural property" of indigenous people in, for example, the Amazon Basin or the rainforest of southern Mexico. Places of religious, traditional, and artistic importance have been loci where people, especially indigenous people, have coordinated together the widest spectrum of their needs and desires (including plotting war against invaders), often without having to pay an admission fee. But now the WB is committing itself to investigate what goes on in these places and to transforming the "good" ones into investment opportunities.

In keeping with this new "respect for indigenous cultures," the WB issued its 1992 Operational Directive on Cultural Property. The following is a WB description of this directive:

"Cultural property" refers to sites, structures, or remains with archaeological, historical, religious, cultural or aesthetic value. It is Bank policy to protect and, where feasible, to enhance a country's cultural property through its policy dialogue, lending operations, and economic and sector work. The operational directive will be grounded in the recognition that maintaining a society's cultural values is important for the sustainability of its development, particularly where those values are reflected in cultural property of national or regional significance.[4]

Thus, the WB is now arrogating into its hands the very places that are often used by people to gather together to plan struggles against SAPs. Under the cover of a newly discovered concern for the indigenous peoples, it is trying to turn these sites of free coordination into places of monetary "value" and "significance" (the dimensions of which its experts will decide, in consultation with the indigenous communities, of course). In this touching display of multicultural awareness, the WB shows itself on par with the Nazis who were also concerned not to lose the invaluable "indigenous knowledge" of the Central European Jews, so that they gathered the best Jewish scholars together and had them construct a "Museum of the Extinct Species" in Prague. After cataloguing, interpreting, and placing the beautiful artifacts of the Prague ghetto in the Museum's archive according to their Nazi masters' specifications, the scholars were taken out and shot.

---

[4] World Bank, *The World Bank and the Environment* (Washington, DC: World Bank, 1992), 108.

NOTES ON THE FINANCIAL CRISIS:
FROM MELTDOWN TO DEEP FREEZE

These notes were inspired by the political-financial crisis (often called the "Wall Street Meltdown") in September 2008, when many U.S. financial corporations were, in effect, nationalized—some temporarily, some to this day—in response to the bankruptcy of several major investment and commercial banks.[1] They were also prompted by the fact that for a year after the "meltdown" there has been remarkably little political activity in the streets, union halls, retirement communities of the United States demanding a resolution of the crisis in favor of the millions who are losing wages, houses, and pensions.

There are many ways of explaining this deep freeze. One factor might be that money and the financial sector of capitalism that deals directly with it have been inherently opaque to working-class political analysis and action for more than a century. (Although workers are often obsessed by money or its lack, the last time there was a self-conscious working-class debate on a national level concerning the money form was the 1896 election when the fate of money hung on "a cross of gold"). Ironically, the time lag between capital's large-scale financial action and the proletarian response is increasing in this era when financial information and transactions circulate at light speed. This lag gives a sense of the sluggishness of contemporary class struggle.

---

[1] I learned a lot from Harry Cleaver's careful analysis of an earlier version of this text when he kindly sent his comments in the fall of 2008. Thanks, Harry. I also want to thank Silvia Federici for her help in the formulation of the remarks on financialization. Of course, neither Harry nor Silvia is responsible for the final product. This essay was written in Portland, Maine, between October 12, 2008, and December 18, 2009.

The purpose of these notes is to present in outline a way of understanding this crisis as developing out of class struggles taking place in the United States and internationally in the last decade. This can be useful, I believe, since if class struggles had the power to create the crisis, then understanding them might guide us to the path that would lead out of the crisis with more class power. This maxim is not mine alone, of course. It has constituted the web of continuity of the political projects my comrades and I have been weaving since the early 1970s, especially in the journal *Zerowork* and later with the Midnight Notes Collective, which began more than thirty years ago.

These notes also constitute a methodological experiment. I want to see how far the interpretation of the Marxian categories of value, surplus value, profit, interest and rent that my comrades and I have developed over the last forty years can be used to understand the present crisis. At the moment, most methodological experiments emerging from anticapitalist mental labs tend to stretch Marx's basic categories beyond their elastic limit, e.g., declaring the end of value, identifying finance and industrial capital, or conflating rent and profit.[2] I am assuming here the continued functioning of Marx's categories and distinctions in contemporary capitalism, including the transformation of surplus value into profit, interest, and rent (although I, too, do some "stretching" of these categories).

As a result, I recognize that these notes might look like dry stuff from the outside, but I have three things to say about their style. First, however dry, the contents of this analysis concern the fate of millions of people, including our own. Secondly, the pace of this analysis has been deliberately made to take one step at a time to slow down the speed of thought concerning this crisis in order to combat the artificial acceleration it has been imbued with. Third, I neither take on an "apocalyptic" tone nor open up a sweeping historical perspective—however tempting these rhetorical options are in crisis situations—because I do not pretend to anticipate the contours of the struggle to come.

Financial crises are difficult to understand from the point of view of average class politics, for the standard Marxist model of class struggle to this day is still the factory, farm and office where the workers' labor-power is bought, through the payment of a wage, by capitalist firms and put to work along with machines and other inputs to produce a product that is sold for a profit. Workers are worked harder, longer, more dangerously and/or more productively in order to make a larger profit. They respond to this work regime by a combination of means, from compliance to a thousand-and-one ways of passive resistance, to strikes, factory takeovers, while capitalists devise strategies to resist this resistance. This struggle can take a myriad of forms, sometimes involving the most refined application of social and psychological sciences and sometimes the most brutal forms of assassination and torture, but the factory-office-farm model is categorically straightforward: waged workers resist exploitation and capitalists resist their resistance; with profits and wages most often

---

[2] Christian Marazzi, *Capital and Language: From the New Economy to the War Economy* (Los Angeles: Semiotext(e), 2008).

moving inversely. It is all apparently simple, but it can become complex because in a struggle there are many deceits and tricks each side plays both on each other, as well as on observers—present and future.

When it comes to money and the financial corporations that operate with it—banks, mortgage loan corporations, hedge funds, and other money market firms—this model of class struggle seems not to operate. Why? There are at least four primary reasons.

First, money is quite a different "product" than either physical things such as cars, services like massages, or paradigms like software programs. Money is a bit mysterious. Words that combine the philosophical and necromantic like "magical," "abstract," "fetishistic," and "universal" are often used to describe money and to immediately give the impression that, compared to other commodities, the usual rules do not apply. For example, money is a unique kind of commodity that exchanges with all other commodities, a role that no other commodity plays. By calling money a "commodity" I do not mean that it is a physical thing as it was during the era of precious metal coinage that stretched from Lydia (in contemporary Turkey) in the seventh century B.C. to the twentieth century A.D. But contemporary money is exchanged by the hundreds of billions of dollars a day, it is bought and sold, it is loaned, and it accumulates.

Second, while industrial firms require the production and sale of a nonmonetary commodity in order to "make money," financial firms make "money from money." They seem to operate in an abstract realm without a spatial location or, if they do locate in a huge metropolis like New York or London, they make the city itself abstract.[3] This adds to the weirdness of the financial firms that during the history of capitalism have always attracted both fascination and hostility from other capitalists and workers. "We work so hard for our money," the workers and industrial capitalists say—with different meanings of work, of course—while they find the money-people literally creating money by some nefarious scheme or other.

Third, the financial capitalists claim a different form of income than other capitalists and workers: Interest. When it comes to making money they make it in the form of interest on loans to capitalists, who pay interest out of "their" profits, and workers, who pay interest out of "their" wages. In other words, the value financial firms "make" through money-lending is created "elsewhere" by those who work for nonfinancial capitalists. The workers of the financial firms themselves may be exploited—e.g., be forced to work long hours and get paid in worthless stock bonuses—but the income that the firms' owners receive does not derive from these employees' efforts in producing a product. Its value comes from the profits and wages of those who received loans who are, in most cases, not their employees.

Where does the "right" to earn interest come from? How is it determined? These kinds of questions haunt our understanding of financial firms, since it appears that in a society where work is the source of value, interest appears to be like "creation out of nothing"!

---

[3] Simmel, *Philosophy of Money*, 503–5.

There are two aspects of capitalism that should be remembered at this juncture. First, it is a system of continual transformations and conversions so that at the end of a cycle there is no direct connection between the creation of surplus value and its appearance. Secondly, surplus value is an unowned creation of the system; it only appears as a value that is owned by individuals or firms when it is transformed into profit, interest, and rent. It is one of the great ironies of history that capitalism—the moral system of greed and mineness—is actually founded on the creation of a common pool of value that is shared by those most protective of private property.[4] This aspect of capitalism is now being recognized in the work on the "embeddedness" of the economy in relations of trust and in the importance of "social capital."[5]

The fourth difficulty in the typical class struggle scenario is that "financialization" adds a new twist to the story. Financialization is a term with multiple meanings that is now used to mark the fact that in this historical period finance capital has played new roles in addition to its traditional one. This change has been widely recognized in the Left—from the *Monthly Review* perspective, who baptize this period as one of "Monopoly-Finance Capital,"—to the autonomist Marxist views of Antonio Negri, Michael Hardt, and Christian Marazzi, although with different emphases.[6] One thing is for sure: financial capital firms are no longer serving just their traditional functions of pooling together money capital and either lending it to corporations or giving investors an alternative short-term road to profit when the average rate of profit begins to decline in the industrial production.

What are these new functions and what are their sources? Some see this novelty as part of an increasing immateriality of contemporary capitalism where the "money of the mind" begins to substitute for both money and the mind. However, I trace this novelty to the need for a new tool of control once either structural adjustment programs (SAPs), operated by state and international agencies like the International Monetary Fund and World Bank, and/or war, reach their limits.

The emergence of financialization indicates that capitalists found a way to get their problems solved through the invention of new roles for money. As with so much else in capitalism, financialization is a process that takes a different form when directed to workers or to capitalists: (a) financialization provides protection to investors through hedge funds and derivatives indicating that the level of uncertainty has increased due to the higher level of resistance; (b) financialization allows for aggressive war against governments by monetary means; (c) financialization undermines workers' struggles. It describes a situation where capital is able to move freely from country to country, hence intimidating governments and even more importantly putting struggles on their knees. This can be seen in South Korea during the "Asian

---

[4] Marx, *Capital: Volume III*, 270.

[5] Francis Fukuyama, *Trust: The Social Virtues and the Creation of Prosperity* (New York: The Free Press, 1995).

[6] John Bellamy Foster and Robert W. McChesney, "Monopoly-Finance Capital and the Paradox of Accumulation," *Monthly Review* 61, no. 5 (October 2009); Michael Hardt and Antonio Negri, *Multitude: War and Democracy in the Age of Empire* (New York: Penguin, 2004); Marazzi, *Capital and Language*.

financial crisis" in the mid-1990s when the South Korean workers' struggle was halted in its tracks by the financial crisis that engulfed them.[7] Financialization is also a process that eases the creation of bubbles, driving up the prices of vital commodities like food and oil, which could also be used to stop people's struggles. What SAPs and War do not accomplish, financialization can, by enhancing some of their most destructive results. And, as billions of people have learned to their chagrin, it is very hard to fight the consequences of monetary flows since they operate outside of state control and the national territory.

On each of these counts then, financial firms do not fit into the factory-office-farm model of class struggle. There is undoubtedly a form of struggle that financial firms in their nature are involved in that has an ancient origin: the struggle of debtor versus creditor. For when a firm lends out money to a person or firm, the debtor makes a promise to repay this loan with interest at some time in the future. The failure to do so in ancient times often led to slavery or mutilation, i.e., the famous "pound of flesh" the creditor was allowed to cut from the body of the defaulting debtor. In contemporary capitalism, besides criminal sanctions in the most egregious cases, default on loans leads to bankruptcy for capitalist firms and liens on the property and future income for workers. This debtor-creditor struggle differs from the wage struggle in many regards—e.g., temporal, workers usually get paid after their work is over, while the debtor gets the loan money before repaying the loan.

There is clearly a struggle going on in the United States today concerning money and finance, but how best to understand it? Workers versus capitalists, debtors versus creditors, or some new way? What are the political demands that are being voiced in this crisis? After all, the struggle is about how the social surplus, which in communal societies was to be shared, is distributed.

To answer these questions, we must get back to the basics and how they apply to contemporary capitalism. Before examining the "bailout" legislation, however, let us look to the elements of capitalism that are involved: F, the financial sector; I, the industrial sector, which includes all the information/computation firms, since they exploit quite material workers in order to produce "immaterial commodities"; W, the working class.

Are the next few years going to be the epoch making ones we have expected would come? That will depend on whether those "in" W, the working class, are ready to struggle against its subordination.

Also, we must remember that the act of assigning a "W" to represent the working class does not magically unify this class. W's referent has a complex class composition that is continually in transformation.[8] It has a *technical composition*, a *sociological composition*, as well as a *political composition*, and they do not neatly fit into each other. For example, the most powerful and technologically advanced sectors of the working class might be at a particular moment politically the least aggressive,

---

[7] Midnight Notes Collective, eds., *One No, Many Yeses* (Brooklyn: Autonomedia, 1998).

[8] Midnight Notes Collective, eds., *Midnight Oil: Work, Energy, War* (Brooklyn: Autonomedia, 1992).

while those workers on the lowest levels of technology might be the most demanding and effective.

Moreover, the working class is profoundly divided by the wage itself. Some workers get higher wages than others, and a large part of the working class is unwaged. These unwaged workers in a money economy are often subordinated to their wage-earning fellows. These divisions and hierarchies appear as racism, sexism, and many of the other sources of class weakness. Most important, we need to recognize that the workers involved in this crisis story are not simply those in the territorial United States.

Given these elements, we will have to look at the relations and struggles between F and I (the finance sector and industrial sector); F and W (the finance sector and the working class); and, of course, W and I (the working class and the industrial sector). Thus there is an intraclass and well as an interclass struggle—i.e., one between wages and profits and wages and interest—but also one between profits and interest. The entrance of wages into the class equation concerning finance is very important because there has been a profound shift in the twentieth century concerning our notion of interest.[9] In the nineteenth century and before, waged workers were never important direct players in the financial world, since they had almost no property that could be used as collateral to take out loans from financial institutions, and they had almost no savings to be used as deposits in banks. As Marx writes, "Interest is a relationship between two capitalists, not between capitalist and worker."[10] In fact, the many mutual aid and credit union organizations that sprang up in the nineteenth century were due to the fact that banks and other financial institutions considered themselves as having solely capitalists (large and small) as their customers, or that workers were too suspicious to hand over their hard-earned savings into the hands of financial capital. This is no longer the case. Consequently, when we speak of financial crisis in the twenty-first century, we must speak of interclass conflict as well as conflict between factions of capital.

What is the source of the financial crisis and the "bailout"? At first, it appears like every other financial crisis in history: the inability of debtors to pay back old loans and the inability of financial firms to make new loans. Instead of money creating money out of nothing, we now have money creating nothing.

But this way of looking at it is almost tautological. For another explanation, we should examine the class relations. There are at least three reasons for this crisis: in the condition of the U.S. working class, in the globalization of financial flows, and in the phenomenon of financialization.

The ignition of the current crisis in the financial sector has much to do with working-class homeowners instead of capitalists not being able to sell their

---

[9] This is one reason why Marx's work in the third volume of *Capital* is only of limited assistance while, at the same time, being tremendously needed in this period. For the third volume of *Capital* is the place where Marx attempts to trace the transfers of value that are continually taking place "behind the backs" of both workers and most capitalists and makes for the hellish sense of capitalism's invisible invulnerability.

[10] Marx, *Capital: Volume III*, 506.

production for a profit large enough to pay the interest on their loans, which was the usual origin of a crisis scenario in the nineteenth century. In this case, worker's wages were not large enough to pay the interest and principal on the loans they took out to purchase their homes. Indeed, there was a bout of real wage stagnation at the very moment when the housing market was booming and housing prices bubbled. So, the inability to sustain a successful wage struggle in the twenty-first century United States is at the heart of the present financial crisis. *Although, if such a struggle were successful, an altogether different kind of crisis would have resulted.*

The second aspect of the crisis is the restriction in the flow of new investment funds into the U.S. financial system. Vast flows of capital into the financial sector, especially from China, led U.S. financial firms to offer mortgages and extend credit to U.S. capitalists and workers. Here the word "flow" is important, for as long as there is new capital coming into the sector, "bad" loans could be "rolled over," and payments delayed without any serious problem. However, when there are significant constraints in these flows the mechanisms of deferral cannot be used, and loans are defaulted on while new loans cannot be transacted

China was the major—though not the only—source of restriction of flows into the United States for two reasons. First, the recent reduction of the growth rate of the Chinese economy indicates that there has been a decline in the average rate of profit in China. Secondly, Chinese workers have recently been able to dramatically increase their wages and better their working conditions. This has lead to increased Chinese investment within China itself, and the cultivation of the domestic market in government planning. These trends have negatively affected the flows of Chinese foreign investment into the financial sector of the United States. Thus, the China's sovereign wealth fund has refused to come to U.S. capitalism's rescue. These factors have been part of the reason why the U.S. government has to make up for the short fall.[11]

Thus we see how the mortgage crisis in the United States is the effect of at least two proletariats. First, the U.S. proletariat's inability to increase wages (there have been almost no strikes of significance in the United States in the last few years), and workers' use of credit and equity to satisfy their subsistence needs—traditionally the attributes of rentiers. Secondly, the Chinese proletariat's success, thorough thousands of strikes and protests, in increasing wages and forcing more investment in its social reproduction.

Given these causes rooted in class struggle, let us examine the "bailout" legislation as a set of "deals" between different elements of contemporary capitalism, coordinated by the state. By a "deal," I mean something like a tacit agreement between two enemies that sometimes appears in, but often underlies, the official legislative formulation of a social contract.[12] We use this language to indicate that the concept of a social contract is too formal and irenic (i.e., peaceful) a structure to capture the

---

[11] Midnight Notes Collective and Friends, *Promissory Notes: From Crisis to Commons* (Brooklyn: Autonomedia, 2009); Niall Ferguson, *The Ascent of Money: A Financial History of the World* (London: Penguin Books, 2008), 338–39.

[12] p.m., *bolo'bolo* (Brooklyn: Autonomedia, 2011 [1984]); Midnight Notes Collective, "Outlaw Notes," *Midnight Notes* 8 (Brooklyn: Midnight Notes, 1985).

often unspoken aspects of these agreements that are dependent on the state of power relations and grow out of a protracted and open-ended struggle. Antagonists can agree on the rules of the struggle until the rules become the object of struggle: this is the first axiom of "agonology," the study of struggles.

Let us take each of these sectors and examine the deal that is being offered by the state to them in outline:

F (the financial sector): This sector must agree to government imposed open-ended restrictions on their freedom of action and government regulation of their money capital movements. It also agrees to at least temporary nationalization of certain branches of the industry. In exchange, it will get a large-scale "socialization" of debt losses across the board (not just in so-called subprime mortgage loans). Implicitly, there is an assumption that this socialization will not be adversarial—i.e., the personnel involved in choosing the debts to be purchased by the government will not be looking out only for the government's interest. The Obama Administration has definitely lived up to this part of the deal with the appointment of and support for Larry Summers and Tim Geithner.

I (the industrial sector): This sector must agree to support the "rescue" of the financial sector in exchange for a government guarantee of a continuous access to credit—the end of the "credit crunch"—and an implicit indication that the principle "too big to crash," used to judge which firms in the financial sector would be "bailed out," would also be applied to this sector.

Of course, the distinction between these two sectors is not clear superficially, for many industrial firms have financial subsidiaries and many financial firms are invested in industrial corporations. Moreover, the accounting category used to describe accumulation in both sectors is the same: profit. According to this semantics, banks make profits as do car companies (or, at least, they hope to), even though they have a different relation to the surplus value produced throughout the system.

W (the working class): Our class must agree to a dramatic wage decrease, either through debt-inspired inflation and exchange rate devaluation, or the theft of the Social Security Fund, or both in exchange for a return to relatively full employment relatively quickly—with the nature of the "relatively" a matter to be determined by struggle.

The configuration of the relations between *F, I, W* in the immediate future is described below:

F-I (the relation between interest and profit and financial and industrial capitalists): This coming period will repose the "eternal conflict" between the financial sector (and its claim to interest) and the industrial sector (and their claim to "the profits of enterprise") after a period of hegemony of the financial sector. Economic rhetoric will be filled with snide remarks about pure money magicians and rocket scientists who land their projectiles in teacups and the need for "real" investments, especially in the energy sector.

F-W (the relation between wages and interest or working class and financial capitalists): The coming period will be, on the one side—in the face of a tremendous downward pressure on wages—replete with moralistic and largely ineffectual

demands for debt cancellation or abatement and, on the other side, draconian sanctions for breaking loan agreements, for falling behind the mortgage schedule, and
for sending money to cover the credit card statement *too late*. This prediction has
already been confirmed by the "bail out the homeowner" laws that were passed in
the last two years, which have assisted a risible number of people facing foreclosure.

*I–W (the relation between wages and profits, and between workers and industrial
capital)*: The Bush Administration's "ownership" society begins to look quaint in
the Obama era. As a consequence, the efforts by workers to regain their previous
levels of income will no longer rely on finding a "financial" exodus—through stock
ownership or house purchasing—and will have to confront capital directly around
wage struggle, broadly conceived. For by "wage struggle," I do not only mean pickets
around the factory gate. I include the struggle to have the power not to have to sell
one's labor-power and to have increasing control of the means of production and
subsistence. For much of the history of the working class, this power to be able to
refuse work has been rooted in the existence of common property resources or commons that people could access independent of their status as wage workers. Thus, in
my view, "wage struggle" includes the power to preserve old commons and to create
new ones.[13]

All classes and sectors, however, agree that much of the ideology and some of
the practice of neoliberalism will be turned into relics. "Government" is now trump-
ing "governance" on all levels of the economy (not, of course, that the state was ever
aiming to wither away, as some postmodern thinkers were led to believe during
the last decade). Just as developments after September 11, such as the invasions of
Afghanistan and Iraq showed, the center-less and "flat" world of globalization was
more an advertising gimmick than a reality. Similarly, the return of the surveillance
state with the "war on terrorism" showed that the internet was no field of open
communication. So, too, events in September and early October 2008 have shown
that the era of the symbolic, future-centered economy operating at light speed has
reached its limits in a meteor shower of falling stock prices, bankrupt investment
houses, foreclosed homes and tent cities.

It is also clear that the bailout deal is only as strong as the results it produces.
There is no guarantee that either buying up hundreds of billion of dollars of "toxic"
loans will be adequate to "restore" confidence in the financial sector, or that the
credit flows will resume to the extent that will make an economic "upturn" possible,
or that there will be a return to historically normal levels of employment after a period of "turbulence." Moreover, some parts of the system might eventually reject the
deal previously accepted when confronted with demands that were merely implicit
in the initial offering. For example, how will workers respond to a demand that
the Social Security fund be invested in stocks after just seeing the latest of a series

---

[13] See for example: Federici, *Caliban and the Witch*; Chris Carlsson, *Nowtopia: How
Pirate Programmers, Outlaw Bicyclists, and Vacant-Lot Gardeners Are Inventing the Future
Today* (Oakland: AK Press, 2008); Peter Linebaugh, *The Magna Carta Manifesto: Liberties and Commons for All* (New York: Penguin, 2007); Massimo De Angelis, *The Beginning of History: Value Struggles and Global Capital* (London: Pluto Press, 2007).

of stock market crashes? Will the financial sector "masters of the universe" balk, if they are regulated too stringently? Will a "collapse" of neoliberalism lead to a more powerful anticapitalist movement in the United States, or something resembling what we would call "fascism"? These are the kind of questions that will be central to understand the class politics of the crisis of neoliberalism.

Critics of neoliberal globalization might take a moment to gloat about the destiny of its antagonist—but only a moment, for the consequences of this "bailout" are momentous and need to be considered carefully from the point of view of the state and from the point of view of the proletariat.

The great debate with China that the U.S. government was engaged in for more than a decade concerning the role of the state in capitalism has been won by the Chinese, at least for this round. This is an important strategic outcome of the "bailout" and is often referred to when the international fall-out of the crisis is discussed. The bailout is an ideological blow of major proportions. How can the U.S. government seriously push financial deregulation at the very moment when it is practicing the exactly opposite policy? It is true that consistency is not to be expected in the world of power. After all, the U.S. government has been preaching the abolition of agricultural subsidies to the governments of Africa at the very moment when it has substantially increased its subsides to its own farmers! But there are limits to political hypocrisy and the Chinese government (and others like it) to which the United States is preaching financial deregulation have the capacity to resist its embrace.

On the contrary, the Chinese model of strong state control of the financial sector and the exchange rate has proven the winner in this period not only over the Russian transition from Communism to Capitalism but now, apparently, in the U.S. transition from a "straight no chaser" doctrinaire Neoliberalism to a form of Neoliberalism Plan B (or Financial Socialism for the Sake of the Market). But this victory also has consequences for the development of a full political economy. What will the reentrance of the state into the micro-organization of the economy mean for the whole system? Neoliberalism has been a political and a cultural paradigm as well as an economic one. It will require much research to anticipate how these areas of life will be affected by its collapse. How would a Chinese-like economic model bleed into the United States politics and culture?

Finally, can the U.S. working class inspire world society out of this crisis of neoliberalism? The electronic assault on the politicians in Washington via the Internet and the telephone system that led to the first defeat of the bailout bill in September 2008 gave many around the world some hope, but it was not followed by a more sustained resistance and was defeated in one week. On the basis of the wavering political response to the Bush administration's "blitz," then, the immediate answer must be "No." Right-wing talk radio patter and left-wing Internet petitions were ultimately weak tokens in this particular struggle. Indeed, by taking "subprime" mortgages as the origin of the crisis, the working-class demands for reliable housing and income security have been branded to be systematically "toxic" to the credit system (to use the reigning metaphor of our day). The blockage of the credit route out of the long-term stagnation of the wage will have major strategic consequences. Since capital will not allow the U.S. working class to be a class of rentiers—living off the ever increasing value of their stocks and of the equity on their homes—workers must return to the hard terrain of the wage struggle in the widest sense in the coming era, however unpropitious it appears.

Are there any indications that the "deep freeze" of struggle that generated these notes is thawing? One sign is to be found in the renaissance of the student movement in California in the fall of 2009. For one of the most important "deals" with the working class in the Neoliberal era has centered on university education. A tremendous wage premium existed for those who were able to graduate university, especially for those enrolled in the relatively cheaper public universities, compared to proletarians who only managed to graduate high school. The huge student loan business thrived exactly on this wage gap.[14] One aspect of this crisis has been its use by government officials and capitalists to attack this deal by dramatically increasing tuition fees in public universities and equally dramatically reducing government financial support.

In response to this "last fair deal going down," as Robert Johnson used to sing—i.e., to this widely recognized end of the "public university" ladder to a higher wage—young proletarians, from the University of California, and the City University of New York, to Chile and the Quebec university systems, are finally organizing mass resistance. The fate of this resistance in the "edu-factories" in the coming months will tell us much about the power relation at the end of crisis moment of this cycle, perhaps more than the coming struggles in the "real" factories, farms and offices. If so, it would constitute an important shift in the physiognomy of class struggle in the United States.

---

[14] Jeffrey Williams, "The Pedagogy of Debt," in *Towards a Global Autonomous University: Cognitive Labor, the Production of Knowledge, and Exodus from the Education Factory*, eds. Edu-factory Collective (Brooklyn: Autonomedia, 2009).

ON THE NOTION OF A CRISIS OF SOCIAL REPRODUCTION:
A THEORETICAL REVIEW

W hat is the role of extramarket relations in the process of social reproduction, when market relations become the paradigm of social exchange? Are "extramarket" relations and activities (e.g. having a friendly conversation, parenting a child) just a shadow of the central, radiating presence of the market, or are they the bulk of social matter? Is paying exclusive attention to market phenomena—the tip of the social iceberg—justified, or is this a prescription for conceptual and practical disaster? These questions have long been essential to the self-definition of sociology, as opposed (until recently) to economics.

To get a concrete idea of the issues involved, imagine the telephone calls made or e-mail messages sent in a day in any city of the United States. We may label them as market exchanges, as most calls and messages are bought from a telephone company, and many are made in the context of market activities. But what about the nonmarketable exchanges made possible by them? What about the calls and messages that people make, not to buy or sell, but in the context of family relations, love affairs, struggles, including those against the telephone company? These calls and messages certainly have a "use-value." Can we say that it is irrelevant to social wealth?

As Marx writes, "The wealth of societies in which the capitalist mode of production prevails, appears as 'an immense accumulation of commodities.'"[1] In the case

---

[1] Marx, *Capital: Volume I*, 125.

of a telephone company, wealth presents itself in the form of the company's revenues. But revenues do not reveal the web of information and social coordination that moves through the wires. What is the relation between this informing, imaginative wealth and the commodity form? We know that a telephone workers' strike, or an increase in the interest rate will affect how many calls are made and their price. But what about the social wealth produced in these exchanges? Can all be measured by market means?

If we extend the example of the telephone calls and e-mail messages to include all material exchanges (e.g., conversations, amorous encounters), we begin to discover the great "Other" of the market. This realm, subsisting outside the circulation of commodities and money, has been, since the late 1960s, a pole of attraction for the social sciences. For there has been a growing realization that nonmarket exchanges can challenge and disrupt the formal economy, and yet are essential to its existence.[2] Thus, measuring their quantity, and assessing their potential have become crucial questions in social theory. This is especially true in the study of societies in many areas of Africa, Asia, and the Americas, where the commodity form is not dominant, and in the study of housework and the other activities involved in the reproduction of labor-power, which are mostly performed outside the space of formal market exchanges in most of the planet.

To describe the sphere of nonmarket relations new terms have been developed by the last generation of political theorists: the "unwaged work" sector,[3] the "social factory,"[4] the "shadow economy,"[5] the "general economy,"[6] the "moral economy,"[7] the "informal economy."[8] With them, a new set of social-economic polarities has emerged: formal/informal, production/reproduction, market/moral, rational/customary, modern/postmodern, and a deconstruction of social forms has begun. For no sooner were apparent dichotomies identified, than their presumed positive and negative poles were displaced, or inverted, to reveal new fields of relations. Once, for instance, reproductive work, including subsistence farming, was made visible, it could no longer be ignored that the quantity of unwaged labor dwarfs the mass of wage labor, which was previously given pride of place in economic analysis, Marxist and non-Marxist alike.

The first question this theoretical revolution poses for us concerns the status of the older concepts in light of these developments. How has the reappraisal of the

---

[2] Richard Swedberg, "Economic Sociology: Past and Present" in *Current Sociology* 35 (1987): 1–221; Richard Swedberg, ed., *Economics and Sociology: Redefining Their Boundaries, Conversations with Economists and Sociologists.* (Princeton: Princeton University Press, 1990); Neil J. Smelser and Richard Swedberg, *The Handbook of Economic Sociology* (Princeton: Princeton University Press, 1994)

[3] Dalla Costa and James, *Power of Women.*

[4] Mario Tronti, "Capitale Sociale," *Telos* 17 (1973): 98–121.

[5] Ivan Illich, *Shadow Work* (London: Marion Boyers, 1981).

[6] Georges Bataille, *The Accursed Share* (New York: Zone Books, 1988).

[7] E.P. Thompson, *Customs in Common* (New York: The New Press, 1991).

[8] Serge Latouche, *In the Wake of the Affluent Society: An Exploration of Post-Development* (London: Zed Books, 1993).

importance of nonmarket relations in social life transformed the concept of social reproduction, previously analyzed by political economy on the basis of the market alone? More specifically, how does the notion of a "crisis of social reproduction," intended as a break in "normal" market exchanges, and associated (by Marx and the classical economics tradition) with depressions, panics, and bubbles, relate to this realm? Can we develop a more general notion of such crises, by analogy to those rooted in commodity exchanges? Can famines, genocides, wars, and other "breaks" in social reproduction be explained through a generalization of the classical notion of crisis?

These questions are the focus of this essay, as they have been for social theory since the 1980s, when it was recognized that famines, and many other catastrophes are by no means natural disasters, but are socially imposed consequences of the negation of entitlements—to food, land, and other factors of subsistence—as the work of Amartya K. Sen and others has demonstrated.[9]

My discussion starts with an analysis of Marx's theory of social reproduction, still the most sophisticated classical economic theory on the matter. I then identify three alternative approaches that acknowledge the importance of nonmarket relations, but differ in the way they account for them. The first approach explains nonmarket exchanges by generalizing the commodity form, the second generalizes the social-exchange relation, the third stresses the value-producing aspects of nonmarket phenomena. Each also provides a different perspective on the concept of a crisis of social reproduction, which, in my view, is a test of their explanatory power. I conclude that the third approach has the greatest potential for explaining crises of social reproduction like famines.

Social Reproduction: Genealogy and Crisis, A Marxian View

"Social reproduction" is an odd term. "Reproduction" evokes naturally reoccurring biological cycles, while "social" connotes a set of intentional and voluntary interactions. Nevertheless, the belief that modern capitalist societies have natural reproductive cycles has been central to the development of economics and sociology. The tension present in the concept is evident in the continuing tension between these disciplines. The reasons for it can be illustrated etymologically. "Sociology" is rooted in the Latin *socius*, that stands for a freely chosen companion with whom there are no blood ties. "Economics" derives, instead, from the ancient Greek word *oikos* ("hearth and home"), that describes the bonds of blood and slavery. One could talk about the reproduction of the *oikos*, because the household was not seen as a terrain of choice and freedom, but as the threshold between nature and convention, *physis* and *nomos*, thus sharing the automaticity and repetitiveness of the physical world. From this viewpoint, economic relations were in the realm of necessity. They occurred between husband and wife, parents and children, masters and slaves, and

---

[9] Amartya K. Sen, *Poverty and Famines: An Essay on Entitlement and Deprivation* (Oxford: Clarendon Press, 1981); Joanna Macrae and Anthony Zwi, eds., *War and Hunger: Rethinking International Responses to Complex Emergencies* (London: Zed Books and Save the Children (UK), 1994); Alexander De Waal, *Famine that Kills: Darfur, Sudan, 1984–1985* (Oxford: Clarendon Press, 1989).

their reproduction was rooted in seemingly "natural" rhythms. Social relations, instead, were in the realm of freedom, being established by mutual agreement among equals, free from "natural" bonds. It was inconceivable that these unique relations, built on desired coincidences, could be reproduced. At best (as in Aristotle's *Ethics*), rules could be set for their preservation.

The Greco-Roman distinction between *socius* and *oikos* eroded, however, with the development of capitalism, as familial, subsistence production was replaced by dependence on monetary exchanges (the foundation of the bourgeois concept of "freedom"). From this development that affected both the proletariat (after the enclosures) and the rentiers (who had been accustomed to consume goods produced on their estates)—originated the very concept of "society," as a term describing human togetherness, and later the concept of "political economy," where the Greek *politikos* was made synonymous with the Latin *socius*. Locke's "social contract" theory formalized the perception, widespread among the seventeenth-century bourgeoisie, that the "natural" relations of the *oikos* (husband-wife, father-children, master-servant) were becoming "social," that is, a matter of individual decision and contract among equals. But a converse recognition was also taking shape, revolving around the idea that society too has a biological metabolism and reproductive cycle. This recognition led to the concept of "social reproduction," the main object of study for political economy in the period of the Enlightenment.

The first theory of social reproduction was presented by Quesnay in the *Tableau économique*, in the mid-eighteenth century. With a new approach, Quesnay asked how a collection of associated individuals, members of specific classes (rentier, capitalist, worker) and connected only by contract, could reproduce itself in such a way that, after a cycle of production and circulation of commodities, the same individuals and classes would reappear. As Marx was to point out, the analytic power of Quesnay's approach derived from the fact that he rooted his analysis in the old locus of the *oikos*: land and agricultural production. Yet, this was also the limit of the *Tableau*, as manufacturing appears in it only as an embarrassing "miscellaneous," though, by the late eighteenth century, industrial production, in Western Europe, was beginning to overshadow agriculture.

In the trajectory from Quesnay to Marx, the most important development in the analysis of social reproduction was Adam Smith's theory that value production must include industrial labor.[10] But it was Marx, the theorist of the capitalist crisis and proletarian revolution, who elaborated the most definitive analysis of the conditions for the reproduction of capitalism.

This subject is treated in Volume II of *Capital*, where Marx shifted from the class struggle (the focus of Volume I) to the analysis of those social phenomena of capitalism that return to themselves: circulation, rotation, turnover, circuit, reproduction. Instead of changes in linear variables (e.g., rises in wages, falls in profit), in Volume II, Marx examined those changes that return a system to its starting point,

---

[10] See Joseph Schumpeter, *Economic Doctrine and Method* (New York: Oxford University Press, 1967) for further discussion of the relation between the Physiocrats and Smith.

showing how the transformations it undergoes in the process are crucial for both the reproduction of the system as well as its subversion.

The model Marx used to analyze the reproduction of capital in the second volume was the mechanical theory of heat, developed by mid-nineteenth-century physics, which explains macroscopic phenomena as the products of millions of microscopic events and entities.[11] In conformity with this method, Marx described the macroscopic aspects of capitalism as the product of millions of microevents, and accounted for the reproduction of social capital on the basis of the circuits of individual capitals, with their microphysical orbits, different velocities and periods. Marx gave a graphic account of the movement from the micro to the macro level in the Introduction to Part III that deals with "The Reproduction and Circulation of Social Capital":

> . . . the circuits of individual capitals are interlinked, they presuppose one another and condition one another, and it is precisely by being interlinked in this way that they constitute the movement of total social capital. Just as, in the case of simple commodity circulation, the overall metamorphosis of a single commodity appeared as but one term in the series of metamorphoses of the commodity world as a whole, now the metamorphoses of the individual capital appears as one term in the metamorphoses of the social capital.[12]

Marx's vision of capitalist economy is that of an immense collection of exchanges, with individually coherent circuits, where value is conserved, increased or decreased, and where commodities and money leap back and forth to other circuits in the course of each exchange, transmitting impulses in every direction.[13] It is an image reminiscent of the play of the atoms in the organic chemistry diagrams so popular in Marx's time. For we can imagine capitalist A (i) selling the produced commodity to another capitalist B who uses it as means of production, (ii) taking part of the money so realized and buying some luxury goods from capitalist C, (iii) buying labor-power from worker D and new means of production from capitalist E who, in turn, energizes new circuits of other individual capitals.

---

[11] Physicists like Maxwell demonstrated that one can mathematically explain why a gas noticeably heats up when its volume is decreased by assuming that the gas is made up of millions of invisible, microscopic molecules in constant motion, colliding with other molecules and the walls of the gas's container.

[12] Karl Marx, *Capital: Volume II: A Critique of Political Economy* (London: Penguin Books, 1978), 429–30.

[13] Marx's study of this network of microcircuits of value led to many important insights concerning capital, e.g., the deduction of the mathematical relation of turnover time and the rate of profit. But at the heart of the model was a retelling of the story of society and its reproduction. Marx rejected Locke's tale of rational individuals tacitly agreeing to exchange their natural rights for a system that is to protect their property. He substituted a more complex but realistic story of millions of daily commodity exchanges between capitalists and workers weaving society together.

However, exchange must be profitable for the system to reproduce itself, on the micro and macro level. Thus, "common to all three circuits is the valorization of value as the determining purpose, the driving motive."[14] But no exchange is necessary or guaranteed; each connection can be broken, or its purpose may not be realized; hence the permanent possibility of microcrisis and even the dissolution of the system as a whole.[15] Marx attributes a tremendous importance to the possible breaking of the exchange symmetry. On the breaking of the microbonds of capital's circuit, rests for him the possibility of the crisis and the end of capitalism, as we can see from the following passages published (respectively) in 1859 and 1867. "The division of exchange into purchase and sale . . . contains the general possibility of commercial crises . . . because the contradiction of commodity and money is the abstract and general form of all contradictions inherent in the bourgeois mode of labor."[16] And again:

> Hence, if the assertion of their external independence proceeds to a certain critical point, their unity violently makes itself felt by producing—a crisis. There is an antithesis, immanent in the commodity, between use-value and value, between private labour which must simultaneously manifest itself as directly social labour, and a particular concrete kind of labour which simultaneously counts as merely abstract universal labour, between the conversion of things into persons and the conversion of persons into things; the antithetical phases of the metamorphosis of the commodity are the developed forms of motion of this immanent contradiction.[17]

For Marx, the crisis brings to the surface the truth of the capitalist system of social reproduction. The metamorphosis of the commodity into money and profits, requires a continuous suppression of needs and glaring contradictions. But once the bond between the commodity and money temporally loosens, a gap grows that can

---

[14] Marx, *Capital: Volume II*, 103.

[15] J.B. Say ruled out the possibility of a crisis of social reproduction of the sort later described by Marx. He expressed what was later called "Say's Law" in his *Treatise on Political Economy or The Production, Distribution and Consumption of Wealth* with the following words: "It is worth while to remark, that a product is no sooner created, than it, from that instant, affords a market for other products to the full extend of its own value. When the producer has put the finishing hand to his product, he is most anxious to sell it immediately, lest its value should diminish in his hands. Nor is he less anxious to dispose of the money he may get for it; for the value of money is also perishable. But the only way of getting rid of money is in the purchase of some product or other. Thus the mere circumstance of the creation of one product immediately opens a vent for other products." Jean-Baptiste Say, *A Treatise on Political Economy or the Production, Distribution and Consumption of Wealth* (New York: Augustus M. Kelly Reprints of Economic Classics, 1964), 134–35.

[16] Karl Marx, *Contribution to a Critique of Political Economy* (New York: International Publishers, 1970), 96.

[17] Marx, *Capital: Volume I*, 209.

explode all the contradictions of capitalist life. As we know, the main contradiction for Marx is in "the bourgeois mode of labor." This may appear irrelevant in the sphere of circulation, since people generally buy goods to satisfy their needs, not because of who made them. But the primary objective of market-exchanges is the expansion of value, and here the labor that goes into the commodity becomes the key factor. Its "contradictions," beginning with workers' struggles, can cut into the capitalists' profits, and put the circulation process into crisis.

As Marx pointed out, the process of social reproduction brings everything back—Money, Commodity, Production—to the starting point. But this return is not guaranteed, since in reproducing itself, capitalism also reproduces its contradictions. "Capitalist production, therefore . . . produces not only commodities, not only surplus value, but it also produces and reproduces the capital-relation; on the one side the capitalist, on the other the wage-labourer."[18] Far from being natural, the reproduction of the contradictory, conflictual capitalist relation, is permanently vulnerable to the possibility of crises and catastrophe.

The Crisis of Marx's Theory of Social Reproduction

Not surprisingly, then, from the publication of the first volume of *Capital* in 1867 to the late 1960s, "crisis theory" has been a key component in the development of Marxist thinking, while the attempt to exorcise the danger of the crisis, in theory and practice, has been the driving force of bourgeois economics. Marxists largely accepted and often revisited Marx's account of social reproduction.[19] But their main concern was establish the possible causes of its crisis, and here Marx's explanation was of little help. Did crises arise from a disproportion in the production of consumer- goods versus producer-goods? Were they caused by a chronic insufficiency of aggregate demand, or were they a response to the falling rate of profit during periods of expansion and investment?[20] Though many times reinterpreted, the text of *Capital* could not resolve the matter.

Still, "crisis theory" generated provocative hypotheses. From Luxemburg's, Hilferding's, Lenin's, and Bukharin's underconsumptionist explanations of imperialism to Kalecki's "political business cycle" theory during World War II to Baran and Sweezy's "realization" hypothesis and Paul Mattick's "rate of profit" retort in the 1960s, the field of crisis theory was contentious.[21]

---

[18] Marx, *Capital: Volume I*, 724.

[19] Christian Palloix, *Les firmes multinationales et le procès d'internationalisation* (Paris: Francois Maspero, 1973); De Brunhoff, *Marx on Money*.

[20] Duncan Foley, *Understanding Capital: Marx's Economic Theory* (Cambridge, MA: Harvard University Press, 1986).

[21] Rosa Luxemburg, *The Accumulation of Capital* (New York: Monthly Review Press, 1968); Nikolai Bukharin. *Imperialism and World Economy* (New York: Howard Fertig, 1966); Michal Kalecki, *Selected Essays on the Dynamics of the Capitalist Economy, 1933–1970* (Cambridge: Cambridge University Press, 1971); Baran and Sweezy, *Monopoly Capital*; Paul Mattick, *Marx and Keynes: The Limits of a Mixed Economy* (Boston: F. Porter Sargent, 1969). A brief description of these crisis theories is in order. Undercon-

Soon after the publication of Volume I of *Capital*, bourgeois political economy itself underwent a major change. Under the newly adopted name of "economics," it ceased all attempts to explain the totality of social exchanges, and turned its attention to the way in which fields of desire and modes of rational calculation lead to the maximization of utility in individual subjects (whether consumers or firms) at any particular time. Older questions of social reproduction were either refracted in the categories of the new discourse, or became meaningless for economists. For late nineteenth-century economists such as Walras, Pareto, Jevons, and Menger, there could not be such a thing as a crisis. The market was supposed to tend toward an equilibrium, assuring the full employment of all factors of production, and maximizing every one's desires (although under budget constraints). Thus, any movement away from equilibrium had to take the form of a "shock," i.e., it had to be a phenomenon exogenous to the sphere of economic relations, as, e.g., a change of customs and tastes, an earthquake, or a government decree. The result, for the most part, was that a century of oblivion enwrapped the Marxian problematic of reproduction and crisis in economics. This state of affairs came to an end, however, in the 1960s, when the growth of new social movements worldwide threatened the foundations of capitalism and forced a reappraisal of both the Marxist analysis of the reproduction/crisis nexus, and its evasion in bourgeois economics.

The problem with Marxist theory was that it could only explain the reproduction of the capitalist-waged-worker relation. But the revolutionary subjects of the '60s were mostly unwaged. They were subsistence farmers in the Third World, housewives, students, and all the "minorities" that make up the bulk of the world's population. Marx's theory was practically silent about these figures, leading many Marxists to underestimate the political potential of the anticolonial movement, the welfare mothers' and Black power movements, the student movement, the women's movement, and, today, the indigenous peoples' movements.

A similar problem confronted bourgeois economics, as the "unemployed," the "underemployed," the "nonproductive" of the neoclassical economic synthesis

---

sumptionist explanations identified the cause of capitalist crisis in the inability of the working class to purchase consumption goods, and the overproduction of the means of production. Rosa Luxemburg's version of this theory is the most resonant for the late twentieth century. She argued that capitalism needs a noncapitalist world to absorb its surplus production (and realize the surplus value embodied in it). In her view, the control of the noncapitalist regions of Africa, Asia, and Oceania was crucial for the survival of various national capitals. Thus, interimperialist war was an inevitable outcome of a capitalism that had largely subsumed the land and labor of Europe and the Americas. For Luxemburg, capital enters in a final crisis when the last noncapitalist world regions are absorbed into the capitalist mode of production. "Just as soon as reality begins to correspond to Marx's diagram of enlarged reproduction, the end of accumulation is in sight, it has reached its limits, and capitalist production is *in extremis*. For capital, the standstill of accumulation means that the development of the productive forces is arrested, and the collapse of capitalism follows inevitably, as an objective historical necessity" (*Accumulation of Capital*, 417). Luxemburg's theory will be decisively tested in the next decade of "globalization." By contrast, Kalecki's business cycle theory sees crisis as a political choice of the state aimed to control wage demands.

were making history; and were becoming the subjects of government policies and corporate investment. New paradigms were needed; governments and corporations demanded new reports; and obligingly, the economists came to the rescue with new theories reappraising the economic significance of nonmarket spheres, from family, to sexuality, racial discrimination, education, health. In both the Marxist and bourgeois research programs, the analysis of what had been left to the rest of the social sciences, especially sociology, now became a priority. The core of this new activity was the reexamination of the concept of social reproduction.

Three new research programs directed at social reproduction emerged in this period, in response to the shortcoming of bourgeois and Marxist political economy. Each can be understood as a generalization of one, or another, moment of the commodity-money-production circuit, as presented in Marx. As we know, this process begins with the commodity, C, that is exchanged for money, M, with which the means for producing the commodity are bought and put into action in the production process, P, leading to a new commodity, C', that incorporates more value than the money invested in the production process. Each moment of this process, that moves from the commodity (C), through a series of exchanges (M and P), to the commodity C', as increased by the surplus value, allows for a generalization of the economic into the social. The new theories of reproduction and crisis differ from each other with regard to what part of the social reproduction circuit they generalize.

The Totalization of the Commodity Form: The Market Is All

The first approach explains social reproduction through a generalization of the commodity form. Classical political economy defines a commodity as something that is owned and can legally be exchanged. But even in "advanced" money economies, where the commodity form seems to dominate all aspects of life, there is much that escapes its grip. Much housework is unpaid, and so are many instances of sexual intercourse, most babies are not produced in exchange for money, most votes are not directly bought. Moreover, a large part of the U.S. population is not made up of wage earners nor of private capitalists, and most of the average person's day is not directly involved in wage or profit-earning activities. The vast terrain of love, friendship, sleep and dreams, sickness and death, as well as much religious, scientific, or artistic activity are crucial aspects of social reproduction, though they escape the hold of the commodity form. Or so it seems. For there are economists, like Becker, who are ready to dispute that we can ever exit from the world of commodities.

As Blaise Pascal showed in the seventeenth century, a market logic can be applied even to the question of the salvation of the soul, as he argued that a reasonable person should believe in God and wager his/her energies in living a Christian life, even if there is only an infinitesimally small probability that Christian beliefs may be true. For the infinite pain of going to Hell multiplied by the small probability that Christian beliefs may be true is still much greater than the discomfort of leading a moral life multiplied by the large probability that Christian beliefs may be false.

Pascal's famous wager provides a model for what some have called "the economic approach to human behavior," or the "rational choice theory," "neoliberalism" and still others have described as a form of "economic imperialism."[22] If the soul can be treated as if it were a commodity to be invested in, then our leisure time, our children, sexual desires, even our taste for revolution are open to the same treatment under the dominance of capitalism. This, at least, has been the contention of Nobel Prize winner Gary S. Becker, who claims that his economic approach stems from: "The combined assumptions of maximizing behavior, market equilibrium, and stable preferences, used relentlessly and unflinchingly, form the heart of the economic approach as I see it."[23]

The ideal object of Becker's analysis is the "behavior" of a set of "agents" (e.g., a married couple who behaves like an ideal firm), who treat every decision they make (whether or not to have a child, sleep or stay up, brush their teeth) as if they were rational consumers choosing to buy a car. Becker's model, in effect, applies the logic of commodities to things and activities that are legally or morally inalienable, e.g., children, votes, life, sexuality, or are not given an explicit economic value (rarely, e.g., anyone is paid to dream). Becker and other "rational choice" theorists explain how people make choices about their personal lives by taking the market as the model. A "rational agent" would treat all the alternatives "as if" they were commodities with a price attached, calculated by how much time and money it would take (for instance) to bring up a child, or spend an evening with one's lover, where the value of one's time is measured by the amount of money one could earn in the formal labor market in same time period. The "rational agent" would likely have a budget constraint that would be calculated as a quantity of time, valued at its market value; and s/he would then have to choose the combination of "as if" commodities that would maximize his/her utility. Becker does not claim that actual human beings behave according to these "economic assumptions," but he believes that every actual "behavior" can be compared to what an ideally rational being, embodying the "economic" assumptions of the market, would do and that the distance between the actual and ideal results can be computed.

Not only has the "rational choice" approach allowed economists to apply their analyses to regions of social life that economics had largely ignored (because it considered them economically irrelevant or because of legal restrictions on their commodification). The growing hegemony of a neoliberal perspective in the 1980s that makes of the market the arbiter of all social decision-making has given this theory a new use. Surrogate mothering, the adoption market, the legal traffic in organs—all have drawn upon it, in their attempt to acquire a legal status.[24] Neoliberals want

---

[22] Richard McKenzie and Gordon Tullock, *The New World of Economics: Explorations into the Human Experience* (Homewood, IL: Richard D. Irwin Inc., 1978); Gordon Tullock, "Economic Imperialism," in *The Theory of Public Choice*, ed. James M. Buchanan and Robert D. Tollison (Ann Arbor: University of Michigan Press, 1972); Kenneth Boulding, "Economics as a Moral Science," *American Economic Review* 59, no. 1 (1969): 1–12.

[23] Gary Becker, *The Economic Approach to Human Behavior* (Chicago: University of Chicago Press, 1976), 5.

[24] For a discussion of a neoliberal approach to the "organ shortage" see Paul Menzel,

these new "trades" to be fully legalized, they want polices devised so that bottlenecks in these areas (e.g. the resistance of a surrogate mothers to relinquishing "her" commissioned child) are eliminated, and the social utility of these exchanges maximized. They also want to erase the stigma still attached to the commercialization of these sphere of life, and this is where "rational choice theory" becomes important. The logical conclusion and aspiration of neoliberal politics is to apply Becker's "economic approach" to every aspect of social and individual life, so that commodity logic can prevail even in fields where moral or psychological prejudices have so far barred its application.[25]

Once "rational choice" theory is applied to such fields as demography, then it can claim to provide a general theory of social reproduction, taking into account nonformal as well as formal exchanges. Thus, it is no coincidence that this generalization of commodity logic has led to a "new institutional economics" that tries to provide a "rational explanation" (and justification) for the very existence of commodities, money, firms and capitalism itself (in this way, it gives capitalism the same boost that medieval philosophy gave to the Church, when it devised "proofs" for the existence of God).

One of the key question for "institutional economics" is how to account for the existence and reproduction of superindividual structures, given the dramatic changes in the preferences of the individuals who create them.[26] If every aspect of social life is determined by a commodity logic, based on atomized human desires, and if human preferences are continually changing, why (it is asked) do some institutions, for example, the monetary system, survive over long historical periods? The answer given rests on the concept of "transaction costs," these being the additional costs involved in the carrying out of exchanges, production and consumption. A classic example of "transaction costs" are transport costs, but there are other costs as well, e.g., the cost of acquiring information about market prices. A now classic account argues that the "transaction costs" of monetary exchange are lower than those of the alternative, the barter system, because the transportation and information costs of finding someone who has what we want, and wants what we have, in a barter system are very high.[27] A monetary system, enabling us to exchange commodities for money, short-circuits these costs, and this (we are told) is what makes the institution of a money system reasonable for all market participants. According to this "institutionalist" approach, once a monetary system comes into being its positive features become evident to all, and this is why it survives and is reproduced through time.

Strong Medicine: The Ethical Rationing of Health Care (New York: Oxford University Press, 1990), 182–86; and Arthur Caplan, "Beg, Borrow, or Steal: The Ethics of Solid Organ Procurement," in *Organ Substitution Technology: Ethical, Legal, and Public Policy Issues*, ed. Deborah Mathieu (Boulder: Westview Press, 1988).

[25] Richard Posner, *Sex and Reason* (Cambridge, MA: Harvard University Press 1992), 3–4.

[26] Oliver Williamson, "Transaction Cost Economics and Organization Theory" in *The Handbook of Economic Sociology*, ed. Neil Smelser and Richard Swedberg (Princeton: Princeton University Press, 1994).

[27] Clower, "A Reconsideration."

It is easy to see why this "economic approach" is a perfect expression of neo-liberal ideology. By explaining superindividual structures as the result of rational choices among individuals, it generalizes the commodity form to all aspects of life, and presents the basic components of capitalism as the embodiment of Reason in the social world. However, this approach ignores the beliefs and desires of the very subjects whose behavior it supposedly explains. Many women, for example, have demanded Wages for Housework, but not to become little entrepreneurs, but to refuse more work and economic dependence.[28] Similarly, subsistence farmers have struggled, throughout this century, under the slogan "Tierra and Libertad." But this did not mean "Real Estate and Cash Crops." The demand for land, as in the Mexican revolution of 1910–1917 and the Zapatista movement of 1994, expressed the desire to decommodify the earth, and disentangle it from real estate and the grip of agribusiness.[29]

A further problem with "rational choice" theory is that it cannot conceptualize the crises of social reproduction except as shocks exogenous to the commodity system. The shocks must come from "outside," because every process "inside" the system is driven by the decision of rational agents facing budget constraints, and by a predetermined commodity distribution that is supposed to lead to an equilibrium. This explanation is similar to the way in which standard crises are explained in neoclassical economics. According to the latter, changes in tastes and in the natural or social environment (from a craze for chocolates to the discovery of new oil fields) transmit, through the price mechanism, information concerning new desires, new commodity stocks, or new restrictions. As the explanation goes, rational economic agents interpret the new price structures with their budgets in mind, and then shift their pattern of exchanges. As it filters through the market, this shift, at first, can cause catastrophic results, e.g., sudden pockets of unemployment or large stocks of unsold commodities. But, in time, the equilibrium is presumably restored: the unemployed move to areas of high employment, or accept a lower wage at their present jobs; and the unsold commodities are reduced in price or destroyed, if storage costs are greater than any likely future return on their sale. A new equilibrium is reached, with all the market participants (or, at least, those who managed to survive) maximally satisfied at the end of the adjustment, as they were prior to it.

However, once this neoclassical model is generalized to encompass *all* areas of social life previously excluded from the study of formal market relations, a logical problem appears. Once the commodity logic is generalized, e.g. to the realms of psychology and politics, then changes in these realms cannot be treated as exogenous, nor can they function as the source of shocks to account for the origin of crises. If a new set of desires or a new governmental policy is the product of rational choice, then it cannot be an extrasystemic source of crisis. It becomes part of the formal market. Consequently, one has to either invent a new extrasystemic sphere, or accept

---

[28] See Federici, "Wages against Housework," in *Revolution at Point Zero* (Oakland: PM Press, 2012), 15–22.

[29] George Collier and Elizabeth Lowery Quaratiello, *Basta! Land and the Zapatista Rebellion in Chiapas* (Oakland: Food First, 1994).

the possibility that the system of rational choice is not equilibrium tending, but creates within itself perturbational forces. In other words, *the generalization of commodity logic to the realm of social reproduction puts the logical framework of neoclassical theory itself into crisis.*

Exchange Generalized

The second approach to social reproduction sees commodity exchange as a special case of a more general social exchange relation. The main spokesmen for this theory that I will comment on are Granovetter and Foucault, who argue that market relations are "embedded" in a wider network of social relations. Granovetter, echoing the work of Karl Polanyi, emphasizes the importance of trust and obligations as essential conditions for the existence of market relations and the formation of markets. He argues that without some protection against generalized malfeasance and opportunism, and some guarantees of mutual confidence, even the simplest market transactions would not be possible. How could we go to a market—the argument runs—if we could not obtain any trust-worthy information, or ever turn our eyes from our possessions without fear of losing them?

The claim is that protection and guarantees are provided by the "embeddedness" of market relations in "networks" of concrete personal relations.[30] In other words, social reproduction rests on relations of reciprocity and redistribution, as well as market exchanges.[31] According to Granovetter, we can only understand the "altruistic" behavior required for the operation of a commodity market driven by egoistic buyers and sellers in the context of nonutilitarian personal relations of loyalty and mutual recognition. Paradoxically, the existence of an economic agent capable of "standing true" to a contract depends on noneconomic forms of social behaviors that can be learned only in an environment preexisting outside the market. In effect, Granovetter "humanizes the market" by claiming that trust, community solidarity, and reciprocity are preconditions, not consequences, of a market society. This position, however, faces a major contradiction: inherent to the advance of market relations is the tendency to destroy the very relations of trust, solidarity, and reciprocity the market presumably depends upon.

For both Granovetter and Polanyi it is this tendency that is responsible for crises of social reproduction Polanyi, for example, has described how the rise of capitalism in the sixteenth through eighteenth centuries—the "Great Transformation" of Land, Labor, and Money into commodities—destroyed the sociality that was at the root of market relations in medieval Europe.[32] But how could the "Great Transformation" occur, and why, would the market destroy what is vital to its

---

[30] Mark Granovetter, "Economic Action and Social Structure: The Problem of Embeddedness," in *The Sociology of Economic Life*, ed. Mark Granovetter and Richard Swedberg (Boulder: Westview Press, 1992), 60.

[31] Karl Polanyi, "The Economy as Instituted Process," in ibid.

[32] Karl Polanyi, *The Great Transformation: The Political and Economic Origins of Our Times*. (Boston: Beacon Press, 1957 [1944]).

survival? If we accept Granovetter's and Polanyi's assumptions, such phenomena are bound to remain incomprehensible.

This impasse is evident in the politics of "communitarianism," the movement in which the theories of Granovetter and Polanyi have found their political expression. With its revaluation of volunteerism, its praise of "nongovernmental organizations," and its foregrounding of the "nonprofit sector," communitarianism makes a stand in favor of a market economy but with a "human face."[33] Like Granovetter, the communitarians believe that a triumph of commodity logic—as in the aspirations of the neoliberals—undermines the very market society it wants to consolidate. Thus, nongovernmental organizations inspired by this approach have rushed into the various catastrophes caused by neoliberal structural adjustment policies around the planet (from Detroit to Somalia) to save "humanity." But, in this process, they have also helped save "the market" and, by the same token, the very policies that allowed for the development of such catastrophes.

These contradictions may in part explain why, in the intellectual tides of the post-1968 period, Granovetter's (and Polanyi's) analyses have been overshadowed by the work of Michel Foucault. Like other theorists of the "sociology of economic life," Foucault agrees that noncommodifiable relations condition the possibility of capitalist exchange. But, while Granovetter highlights the moral virtues necessary to the life of *homo economicus*, Foucault questions the very concept of "rationality" and the "rational economic agent." In a series of historical works, written between the early 1960s to the early 1980s, he argues that not only is rationality a social construct, but it is shaped in a field of power relations, forming a "general economy" that does not function according to the calculations of a preexistent rational ego (as believed by the theorists of commodity logic), because it is precisely these power relations that define what "rationality" and the "ego" must be in any particular epoch.[34]

Power relations are as essential to Foucault's account of social reproduction as they are to Marx's. In place of the optimistic picture presented by Granovetter and Polanyi, of a network of reciprocity relations surrounding any economic agent, his work confronts us with a somber scenario, where economic rationality is genetically the offspring of regimes organized to produce pain, confinement, control, and of technologies by which power is exercised over its Others (the mad, the ill, the criminal, the sexually deviant).

Foucault rejects, however, the traditional view of power. First, he criticizes the "juridical/monarchical" model of power that poses a central stabilizing axis (the Rule of Law, or the Divinely Sanctified King) at the peak of the social hierarchy

---

[33] Amitai Etzioni, *The Moral Dimension: Towards a New Economics* (New York: Free Press, 1988). Amitai Etzioni, ed., *New Communitarian Thinking: Persons, Virtues, Institutions and Communities* (Charlottesville: University Press of Virginia, 1995); Rifkin, *End of Work*.

[34] Michel Foucault, *Madness and Civilization: A History of Insanity in the Age of Reason* (New York: New American Library, 1971); Foucault, *Order of Things*; Foucault, *The Birth of the Clinic: An Archeology of Medical Perception* (New York: Pantheon Books, 1973); Foucault, *Discipline and Punish* (London: Allen Lane, 1977); Barry Smart, *Foucault, Marxism and Critique* (London: Routledge and Kegan Paul, 1983), 123–37.

legislating, and repressing any deviations from the norm. Echoing Nietzsche's slogan "God is dead," he asserted that there is no Ruling Class, Judge, or King imposing the law on all social agents and punishing its transgressions with death. Nor is there an opposing class struggle against its rule and prohibitions. In the place of the "binary and all-encompassing opposition between rulers and ruled" serving as a "general matrix" for all power relations, he identified a manifold of omnipresent "relationships of force" that "come into play in the machinery of production, in families, groups, institutions, and are the basis for wide-ranging effects of cleavage running through the social body."[35]

Foucault also rejected the assumption that "power" operates only, or primarily, through a structure of prohibitions, and emphasized instead its productive character. Power relations do not only forbid or restrict social or individual possibilities, but produce new strategies, techniques of control (as exemplified by the development of "Reason" and "economic rationality") and, correspondingly, new capacities in the social individual.

As is well-known, much of Foucault work is concerned with the description of the emergence of new regimes of Power. Particularly influential, in this context, has been his analysis of the development of "biopower," which he identifies as the distinguishing feature of European societies in the "modern era," beginning with the eighteenth century. Through this term Foucault describes the forces upon which the social reproduction of capitalist relations has historically depended, and capitalism has in turn developed. Thus, "biopower" is largely reminiscent of the Marxian "labor-power" and, indeed, Foucault admitted that capitalism would not have been possible without the controlled insertion of bodies into the machinery of production and the adjustment of the phenomena of population to economic processes.[36] But he adds that "this was not all it required, it also needed the growth of both these factors, their reinforcement as well as their availability and docility; it had to have methods of power capable of optimizing forces, aptitudes, and life in general without at the same time making them more difficult to govern."[37]

Thus, while Marx concentrated on power relations in the factory, Foucault looked at the development of the sciences of sexuality (from demographics to psychoanalysis) that arose in the nineteenth century to control and develop that main component of biopower: sexuality. In this way his theory anticipated some of the insights of the feminist and gay movements that equally have stressed sexuality and the family as terrains of power relations. This is, undoubtedly, one of the reasons for the popularity his theory has enjoyed among post-1968 radicals. However, his concern with disentangling power relations from any specific political and economic structure, his insistence on the omnipresence of power relations, and above all his suspicion toward any liberationist project have prevented him from playing a role for the post-1968 generation that Marcuse played for the activists of the 1960s.

---

[35] Michel Foucault, *The History of Sexuality, Volume One* (Harmondsworth: Penguin Books, 1981), 94.

[36] Ibid., 140–41.

[37] Ibid.

Further, in his effort to stress the productive (rather than repressive) character of power relations, Foucault has often seemed oblivious to the fact that (a) the "production of life" in the "modern era" has had a purely instrumental character, being finalized to the development of the capacity of work; (b) the production of death has been a permanent component of the capitalist political economy, in all of its stages, as essential to its goals as the "production of life," as proven by the history of colonial conquest, the mechanized slaughters of the First and Second World War, the continuing threat of atomic annihilation, and the economic and ecological catastrophes today plaguing, with increasing frequency, people all over the planet.

By contrast, he firmly assumes that, starting in the eighteenth century, the goal of the state became the "production of life" and his description of the emergence of bio-power on the historical scene almost recalls a myth of origin, if not the textbook tales, still so often rehearsed to establish the progressive character of capitalism:

> The pressure exerted by the biological on the historical had remained very strong for thousands of years; epidemics and famine were the two great dramatic forms of this relationship that was always dominated by the menace of death. But through a circular process, the economic—and primarily agricultural—development of the eighteenth century, and an increase in productivity and resources even more rapid than the demographic growth it encouraged, allowed a measure of relief from these profound threats: despite some renewed outbreaks, the period of great ravages from starvation and plague had come to a close before the French Revolution; death was ceasing to torment life so directly.[38]

There is no trace here of the famines, massacres, executions that have been the stigmata of capitalism from its beginning to the present. Nothing is said of the slave trade, of imperial conquest in the ancient and new world, which transferred to Europe tremendous amounts of vital resources; instead, productivity has the lion share in the alleged displacement of death from history. Again no mention is made of the Irish famine of 1846. Concern with population growth and the techniques to stimulate it under the Ancien Regime, as the mercantilists well realized, also goes unacknowledged.[39]

Foucault's theory also fails to explain crises of social reproduction, because for him crisis and discontinuity are permanent condition of social reproduction. As mentioned, Foucault rules out both the neoclassic assumption that social reproduction is governed by a centripetal, equilibrium-tending market and the Marxian view of crisis as a product of class conflict. Rather, he pictures it as the result of "unbalanced, heterogeneous, unstable, and tense force relations." This means that crisis is literally everywhere; it is another name for Power itself, it is the norm in a society where, à la Hobbes, war is omnipresent, so that war itself needs no special explanation.

However, this nominalist view leads to logical difficulties. How are the great breaks, "the radical ruptures, [and] massive binary cleavages" possible? How, for

---

[38] Ibid., 142.

[39] Eli Heckscher, *Mercantilism. Volume Two* (London: George Allen & Unwin Ltd., 1955).

example, did the great transformation of the eighteenth century from "the Right of Death to the Power over Life" take place? How did the regime of biopower begin to reproduce itself?

Foucault does not say. Instead, he resorts to Heideggerian statements that project the whole problematic in the realm of metaphysics. Such are the claims that the emergence of biopower represents "The entry of life into history"[40] and that "modern man is an animal whose politics places his existence as a living being in question."[41] We are here reminded of the Heracliteans of old, who forced to explain the large-scale features of the universe, reverted to "harmonies in tension" and the Logos.

The Production Process Generalized

The third approach, that I describe as resulting from a generalization of the Marxian idea of production, is the one developed by the feminist theorists and activists politically associated, in the 1970s, with the "Wages for Housework" campaign and the "housework debate."[42]

Fundamental to this approach is the argument that value is created not only by the work needed for the production of commodities, but also by the work needed to produce and reproduce labor-power.[43] This contrasts with Marx's view that value is only created in the process of commodity production.

For Marx, the value of labor-power was measured by the value of the commodities consumed in its production, i.e., by a bundle of "wage goods." Marx refused to give an ontological determination to the value of labor and rejected any supply-and-demand theory of wages. The value of labor-power is for him the product of a "historical and moral" struggle, like that over the length of the working day. Marx, however, did not recognize the unwaged labor that is consumed in the production of labor-power and did not include it in the realm of "productive labor." Aside from a few exceptional passages, he barely took note of the labor involved in child birth, child rearing, housework, the care of the sick and elderly. This aversion to recognizing the productivity of housework has persisted for almost a century in the Marxist tradition, although the "Woman's Question" was crucial in the development of socialist and communist ideology and state planning.

---

[40] Foucault, *History of Sexuality*, 141–42.

[41] Ibid., 143.

[42] Ellen Malos, ed., *The Politics of Housework* (London: Allison and Busby, 1982). In the 1960s and early 1970s a number of French Marxist anthropologists applied a "mode of production" analysis to African societies in ways parallel to the work of Dalla Costa and James. Chief among them was Claude Meillassoux who saw two systems of production coexisting in colonial Africa. One was a system of domestic production whose result was the production and reproduction of labor-power exploited by the colonial regime and the other was a mode of commodity production, see Claude Meillassoux, *Maidens, Meal and Money: Capitalism and the Domestic Community* (Cambridge: Cambridge University Press, 1981).

[43] Dalla Costa and James, *The Power of Women*.

While not the first to challenge this Marxist omission, feminists in the early 1970s like Dalla Costa and James forcefully argued that housework is a value producing activity, and that labor-power is not a natural given, but something that has to be produced and reproduced as an essential condition for social reproduction. The early work of *The Power of Women and the Subversion of the Community* was subsequently developed by James, Dalla Costa and others within the same political and theoretical framework.[44] This perspective was hotly debated within feminist circles throughout the 1970s, and many of its insights have become the starting point for feminist economics and social theory. But though this approach was developed at the same time as Becker's and Foucault's theories of social reproduction, there was very little direct confrontation between them.[45]

Dalla Costa and James argued that the primary subjects of the reproduction process—commonly referred to as "housework"—are women, who do not receive any direct payment for their work, although this work is directly productive of value. These facts explain the invisibility of housework, the dependent status of women in capitalism, the persistent concern by both employers and the state with the stability of "the family." Since housework has largely been unwaged and the value of workers' activities is measured by their wage, then, women, of necessity, have been seen as marginal to the process of social production.

The invisibility of housework hides the secret of all capitalist life: the source of social surplus—unwaged labor—must be degraded, naturalized, made into a marginal aspect of the system, so that its producers can be more easily controlled and exploited. Marx recognized this phenomenon in the case of the nineteenth-century European wage-earning proletariat. But the post-1968 generation of feminists, who identified the work of reproducing labor-power as an unpaid source of value, generalized his analysis to encompass the work of housewives. In time students, subsistence farmers, child laborers, the increasing number of workers, especially sex workers, in near slave conditions were included in the same category.[46] All the unwaged repro-

[44] Mariarosa Dalla Costa, "Riproduzione e emigrazione" in *L'operaio multinazionale in Europa*, ed. Alessandro Serafini (Milan: Feltrinelli, 1974); Mariarosa Dalla Costa, *Famiglia, Welfare e Stato tra Progressismo e New Deal* (Milan: FrancoAngeli, 1983); Leopoldina Fortunati, *The Arcane of Reproduction. Housework, Prostitution, Labor and Capital* (Brooklyn: Autonomedia, 1995); Silvia Federici and Leopoldina Fortunati, *Il Grande Calibano* (Milan: FrancoAngeli, 1984); Mariarosa Dalla Costa and Giovanna Franca Dalla Costa, "Development and Economic Crisis: Women's Labor and Social Policies in Venezuela in the Context of International Indebtedness" in *Paying the Price: Women and the Politics of International Economic Strategy*. eds. Dalla Costa and Dalla Costa (London: Zed Books, 1995).

[45] With the exception of Federici and Fortunati, *Il Grande Calibano*.

[46] Selma James, "Wageless of the World," in *Sex, Race, and Class—The Perspective of Winning: A Selection of Writings 1952–2011* (Oakland: PM Press/Common Notions, 2011); Maria Mies, *Patriarch and Accumulation on a World Scale* (London: Zed Books, 1986); Caffentzis, "The Work/Energy Crisis and the Apocalypse," 11 in this volume; Silvia Federici, "The Debt Crisis: Africa and the New Enclosures," in *Midnight Oil: Work, Energy, War, 1973–1992*, ed. Midnight Notes Collective (Brooklyn: Autonomedia, 1992); Mariarosa Dalla Costa, "Capitalism and Reproduction," in *Emancipating Marx, Open*

ductive activities that orthodox economic theory had either ignored, included in the "wage bundle," or put in the realm of "indirect costs," were introduced by feminist theorists as hidden variables essential to explaining the process social reproduction.

This is not to say that social reproduction is reducible to the reproduction of labor-power. The reproduction of commodities, C, of money, M, and of the production processes themselves, P, require labor-power, but are not defined by it. The complex circuits of exchanges that Marx described in the second volume of *Capital* remain crucial for an explanation of social reproduction. However, adding the production and reproduction of labor-power to Marx's theory of social reproduction, changes the whole Marxist paradigm on a practical and theoretical level. Practically, it changes the concept of "workers' struggles." In Marx, the site of class conflict is the factory, the exemplary place of value production. But if the unwaged also produce value, then their struggles are a key aspect of the class struggle, and can threaten the production of value. Consequently, "social movements"—whose negotiations/ antagonism with capital (public and private) have comprised much of the overt social struggle of the last twenty years (from welfare women's, to gay rights, indigenous people's, environmental, and antinuclear movements)—become *class movements*.

Theoretically, the "addition" of housework and the circuit of labor-power reproduction changes our perspective on social reproduction. It is well-known that money (M), commodities (C) and the commodity production process (P) can have dichotomous meanings for waged workers and capitalists.[47] For the capitalist, money is a means for investment, while money for the waged worker is the primary access to the means of subsistence. But the inclusion of housework circuit, L, brings a new "perspective" on M, C, and P: the perspective of the unwaged, mostly female worker. This perspective reveals the power relations and divisions within the working class. For example, money is a means of control of her behavior by waged workers who do not recognize the housework as an object of exchange. The "household money" the house worker spends does not give her the autonomy that wages—the result of a socially recognized exchange between capitalist and worker—do. A network of "informal" but determining, often violent power relations among workers themselves is inscribed in this money with "strings attached."

The exploration of the power relations operating in the generalized process of social reproduction (C, P, M) from the perspective of the unwaged worker transforms Marxist class analysis and makes it possible to analyze racism and sexism (in all their material embodiments) as class phenomena. It also provides a more subtle foundation to the explanation of crises of social reproduction. A classical Marxist can easily explain how a series of successful strikes in the large plants of a capitalist country can lead to an "economic crisis." But the labor-power production approach allows one to see how "the subversion of the community," through, for example, women's mass refusal to conceive children or to train their children to accept certain kinds of work and wages, can also lead to a crisis of social reproduction. For a break

---

Marxism 3, eds. Werner Bonefeld et al. (London: Pluto Press, 1995).

[47] Harry Cleaver Jr., *Reading Capital Politically* (Oakland: AK Press, 2000 [1979]).

in the L circuit brought about by a large-scale (though often silent) struggle of the unwaged house workers can have more serious effects on capitalism than a thousand strikes. The great factory struggles of the late 1960s and 1970s in Italy undoubtedly affected capital, but the decision of Italian women since the late 1960s to struggle for a family size below replacement levels has had probably a much greater impact.[48]

The problem of this approach to crises of social reproduction is that the methodology needed to apply it is subtler and the data it requires are not found in the standard volumes of national economics statistics gathered by governments or international bodies. The UN Development Program is only beginning to record the amount of unwaged housework done in many countries as part of its "human development index." There has been little study of the relationship between variables, like the length of the "labor-power reproduction work day," and other more well-known measures of economic and social crisis. But these practical problems are outweighed by the contribution of this approach to an understanding of crises of social reproduction. First, it does not need to find an exogenous source of crisis. Crisis is endogenous to the capitalist system not only because of the asymmetry between buying and selling (as noted by Marx), crisis is also caused by the inability of individual capitalists to satisfactorily complete the metamorphoses of their capital at a proper rate of profit, i.e., due to a contradiction between expectations in the orbit of circulation and the realities of conflict in the terrain of production.

The labor-power approach also brings out another conflict within capitalism, one that Marx ignored: the conflict between the needs of capitalist production and the demands of those whose work is centered in the arena of the social reproduction of labor-power. This conflict can lead to major crises of reproduction appearing as dramatically falling (or rising) birth rates, urban riots, or agrarian revolts. These crises are often seen from the point of view of the market as exogenous, but once the activities of social reproduction are introduced into the cycle of capitalism they become as relevant as the strikes of unionized workers. The reproduction of labor-power is not a variable that can be determined by Keynesian "manpower planning" or neoclassical theories of the labor market: just as the regular commodity market has the struggle of their producers inscribed within it, so too the labor market has the struggle of those who produce labor-power inscribed within it. And that struggle is not dictated by the commodity status of its results or by the demands of its purchasers. Certainly, there is no preestablished harmony leading to the best of all possible worlds when buyer and seller meet, even if it is over the kitchen table.

The labor-power production approach, then, shares Foucault's recognition of the permanent possibility of crisis, but rejects his claim for the permanent actuality of crisis. Capitalism has laws, material preconditions, and class divisions that are standard to the system, and therefore it has a historical form, reproducible over centuries and continents. Indeed, much of the social standardization that is such a marked aspect of contemporary reality (and is mistakenly called "westernization") is simply the repetition of this form throughout the planet on many different scales.

---

[48] Dalla Costa, "Riproduzione e emigrazione."

Specific forms of capitalism are so reproducible that international agencies like the World Bank and the IMF are applying a prepackaged template of neoliberal capitalism for its realization in locales as widely divergent as Equatorial Guinea and Tajikistan. The apparent reality of infinite microvariations of the power model that Foucault employs is vacuous, for there is a drive to totalization within the capitalist mode of production that makes these variations extinct even before they can take on a virtual existence. One of capital's laws, of course, is to make the reproduction of labor-power completely dependent upon the wage form and hence to keep the reproducers of labor-power both invisible to and controlled by the system. That is the reason for the relentless attack on any guarantees of subsistence, especially to those who reproduce labor-power that has been recently termed the New Enclosures.[49] Foucault's theory of polyvalent, decentered and fragmented force relations cannot account for the crises caused by ability of workers to successfully struggle against their expropriation from the commons of subsistence.

Thus, the labor-power production approach escapes the metaphysical flaws of both Becker's Parmenideanism and Foucault's Heracliteanism and can give endogenous accounts of crisis because it posits the antagonism between circulation/production and accumulation/reproduction as essential to the existence of capitalism.

---

[49] Midnight Notes Collective, *Midnight Oil*, 317–33.

BIBLIOGRAPHY

Anderson, Nels. *The Hobo: The Sociology of the Homeless Man*. Chicago: University of Chicago Press, 1923.

Aronowitz, Stanley. *False Promises: The Shaping of American Working Class Consciousness*. New York: McGraw-Hill, 1973.

Aronowitz, Stanley, and William Di Fazio. *The Jobless Future: Sci-Tech and the Dogma of Work*. Minneapolis: University of Minnesota Press, 1994.

Arendt, Hannah. *The Human Condition*. Chicago: University of Chicago Press, 1958.

_____. *The Origins of Totalitarianism*. New York: Harcourt Brace Jovanovich, 1973.

Babbage, Charles. *Charles Babbage and His Calculating Engines: Selected Writings by Charles Babbage and Others*. Edited by Philip Morrison and Emily Morrison. New York: Dover, 1961.

_____. *On the Economy of Machinery and Manufactures*. London: Charles Knight, 1832.

_____. *Passages from the Life of a Philosopher*. New York: A.M. Kelley, 1969.

Baran, Paul, and Paul Sweezy. *Monopoly Capital: An Essay on the American Economy and Social Order*. New York: Monthly Review Press, 1966.

Bataille, Georges. *The Accursed Share*. New York. Zone Books, 1988.

Baudrillard, Jean. *The Mirror of Production*. St. Louis: Telos Press, 1975.

_____. *Simulations*. New York: Semiotext(e)/Autonomedia, 1983.

Becker, Gary. *The Economic Approach to Human Behavior*. Chicago: University of Chicago Press, 1976.

Biefer, Marcel, and Beat Zgraggen. *Prophecies*. Edited by Hans-Ulrich Obrist. Zürich and Venice: Sammlung Hauser & Wirth and Aperto 93/Biennale of Venice, 1993.

Blaug, Mark. *Economic Theory in Retrospect*. Homewood, IL: Richard D. Irwin, 1962.

Bonefeld, Werner, et al. *Emancipating Marx, Open Marxism 3*. London: Pluto Press, 1995.

Boulding, Kenneth. "Economics as a Moral Science." *American Economic Review* 59, no. 1 (1969): 1–12.

Boutang, Yan Moulier. "Cognitive Capitalism and Entrepreneurship: Decline in Industrial Entrepreneurship and the Rising of Collective Intelligence." Paper presented at the Conference on Capitalism and Entrepreneurship at Cornell University, September 28–29, 2007.

Braudel, Fernand. *The Wheels of Commerce*. New York: Harper & Row, 1982.

Braunthal, Julius. *The History of the International, Volume 1: 1864–1914*. New York: Praeger, 1967.

Braverman, Harry. *Labor and Monopoly Capital: The Degradation of Work in the Twentieth Century*. New York: Monthly Review Press, 1974.

Butler, Samuel. *Erewhon*. New York: Lancer Books, 1968.

Bukharin, Nikolai. *The Economic Theory of the Leisure Class*. New York: AMS Press, 1970.

_____. *Imperialism and World Economy*. New York: Howard Fertig, 1966.

Business Week. "The Reindustrialization of America." Special issue, *Business Week*, June 30, 1980.

Caffentzis, George. "Immeasurable Value? An Essay on Marx's Legacy." In *Reading Negri*, edited by Pierre Lamarche, Max Rosenkrantz, and David Sherman, 101–24. Chicago: Open Court, 2011.

_____. "On the Fundamental implications of the Debt Crisis for Social Reproduction in Africa." In *Paying the Price: Women and the Politics of International Economic Strategy*, edited by Mariarosa Dalla Costa and Giovanna Franca Dalla Costa. London: Zed Books, 1995.

_____. "A Review Article on Antonio Negri's *Marx Beyond Marx: Lessons on the Grundrisse*." *New German Critique* 41 (Spring–Summer 1987): 186–92.

Caplan, Arthur L. "Beg, Borrow, or Steal: The Ethics of Solid Organ Procurement." In *Organ Substitution Technology: Ethical, Legal, and Public Policy Issues*, edited by Deborah Mathieu. Boulder: Westview Press, 1988.

Cardwell, Donald Stephen Lowel. *Turning Points in Western Technology: A Study of Technology, Science and History*. New York: Science History Publications, 1972.

Carlsson, Chris. *Nowtopia: How Pirate Programmers, Outlaw Bicyclists, and Vacant-Lot Gardeners Are Inventing the Future Today*. Oakland: AK Press, 2008.

Carnot, Sadi. *Reflexions on the Motive Power of Fire*. Translated and edited by Robert Fox. Manchester: Manchester University Press, 1986 [1824].

Cassirer, Ernst. *Substance and Function*. New York: Dover, 1953.

Clagett, Marshall. *The Science of Mechanics in the Middle Ages*. Madison: University of Wisconsin Press, 1959.

Clausius, Rudolf Julius Emanuel. "Entropy." In *A Source Book in Physics*, edited by William Francis Magie. Cambridge, MA: Harvard University Press, 1965 [1865].

Cleaver, Harry, Jr. *Reading Capital Politically*. Oakland: AK Press, 2000 [1979].

Clower, Robert W. "A Reconsideration of the Microfoundations of Monetary Theory." *Western Economic Journal* 6 (December 1967): 1–8.

Cole, G.D.H. *Socialist Thought: Marxism and Anarchism 1850–1890*. London: Macmillan, 1969.

Collier, George, and Elizabeth Lowery Quaratiello. *Basta! Land and the Zapatista Rebellion in Chiapas*. Oakland: Food First, 1994.

Copeland, Jack, ed. *The Essential Turing: Seminal Writings in Computing, Logic, Philosophy, Artificial Intelligence, and Artificial Life, Plus: The Secrets of Enigma*. Oxford: Clarendon Press, 2004.

Dalla Costa, Giovanna Franca. "Development and Economic Crisis: Women's Labor and Social Policies in Venezuela in the Context of International Indebtedness." In *Paying the Price: Women and the Politics of International Economic Strategy*, edited by Mariarosa Dalla Costa and Giovanna Franca Dalla Costa. London: Zed Books, 1995.

Dalla Costa, Mariarosa. "Capitalism and Reproduction." In *Emancipating Marx: Open Marxism 3*. Edited by Werner Bonefeld et al. London: Pluto Press, 1995.

_____. *Famiglia, Welfare e Stato tra Progressismo e New Deal*. Milan: FrancoAngeli, 1992.

_____. "Riproduzione e emigrazione." In Alessandro Serafini (ed.) *L'operaio multinazionale in Europa*. Milan: Feltrinelli, 1974.

Dalla Costa, Mariarosa, and Giovanna Franca Dalla Costa, eds. *Paying the Price: Women and International Economic Strategy*. London: Zed Books, 1995.

Dalla Costa, Mariarosa, and Selma James. *The Power of Women and the Subversion of the Community*. Bristol: Falling Wall Press, 1972.

De Angelis, Massimo. *The Beginning of History: Value Struggles and Global Capital*. London:

Pluto Press, 2007.

De Angelis, Massimo, and David Harvie. "Cognitive Capitalism and the Rat Race: How Capital Measures Immaterial Labour in British Universities." *Historical Materialism* 17, no. 3 (2009): 3–30.

De Brunhoff, Suzanne. *Marx on Money*. New York: Urizen Books, 1976.

De Waal, Alexander. *Famine that Kills: Darfur, Sudan, 1984–1985*. Oxford: Clarendon Press, 1989.

Depastino, Todd. *Citizen Hobo: How a Century of Homelessness Shaped America*. Chicago: University of Chicago Press, 2003.

Devereux, Stephen. *Theories of Famine*. New York: Harvester/Wheatsheaf, 1993.

Dostoevsky, Feodor. *Notes from the Underground*. In *Existentialism*, edited by Robert C. Solomon. New York: Modern Library, 1974.

Drake, Stillman. *Galileo at Work: His Scientific Biography*. Chicago: University of Chicago Press, 1978.

Dubbey, J.M. "The Mathematical World of Charles Babbage." In *The Universal Turing Machine: A Half-Century Survey*, edited by Rolf Herken (New York: Oxford University Press, 1995), 217.

Edmond, Wendy, and Suzie Fleming, eds. *All Work and No Pay*. Bristol: Falling Wall Press, 1975.

Edu-factory Collective. *Towards a Global Autonomous University: Cognitive Labor, the Production of Knowledge, and Exodus from the Education Factory*. Brooklyn: Autonomedia, 2009.

Engels, Frederick. *Anti-Dühring*. Peking: Foreign Language Press, 1976.

Etzioni, Amitai. *The Moral Dimension: Towards a New Economics*. New York: Free Press, 1988.

————, ed. *New Communitarian Thinking: Persons, Virtues, Institutions, and Communities*. Charlottesville: University Press of Virginia, 1995.

Fallows, James. *National Defense*. New York: Random House, 1981.

Fanon, Frantz. *The Wretched of the Earth*. New York: Grove Press, 1963.

Farrington, Benjamin. *Science in Antiquity*. Oxford: Oxford University Press, 1969.

Federici, Silvia. *Caliban and the Witch: Women, the Body and Primitive Accumulation*. Brooklyn: Autonomedia, 2004.

————. "The Debt Crisis: Africa and the New Enclosures." In *Midnight Oil: Work, Energy, War, 1973–1992*, edited by Midnight Notes Collective. Brooklyn: Autonomedia, 1992.

————, ed. *Enduring Western Civilization*. Westport, CT: Praeger, 1995.

————. "The God that Never Failed: The Origins and Crises of Western Civilization." In *Enduring Western Civilization: The Construction of the Concept of Western Civilization and Its "Others,"* edited by Silvia Federici. Westport, CT: Praeger, 1995.

————. "The Great Witch Hunt of the Sixteenth and Seventeenth Century." *Maine Scholar* 1 (1988): 31–52.

————. "Journey to the Native Land: Violence and the Concept of the Self in Fanon and Gandhi." *Quest: An International African Journal of Philosophy* 8, no 2 (December 1994): 47–69.

————. "Wages against Housework." In *Revolution at Point Zero: Housework, Reproduction, and Feminist Struggle*, edited by Silvia Federici. Oakland: PM Press/Common Notions, 2012. Originally in *The Politics of Housework*, edited by Ellen Malos. London: Allison and Busby, 1982.

_____. "War, Globalization, and Reproduction," *Peace and Change* 25, no. 2 (April 2000): 153–65.

Federici, Silvia, George Caffentzis, and Ousseina Alidou, eds. *A Thousand Flowers: Social Struggles against Structural Adjustment in African Universities.* Trenton, NJ : Africa World Press, 2000.

Federici, Silvia, and George Caffentzis, "Notes on the Edu-factory and Cognitive Capitalism." In *Toward a Global Autonomous University*, edited by Edu-factory Collective. Brooklyn: Autonomedia, 2009.

Federici, Silvia, and Leopoldina Fortunati. *Il Grande Calibano.* Milan: FrancoAngeli, 1984.

Ferguson, Niall. *The Ascent of Money: A Financial History of the World.* London: Penguin, 2008.

Foley, Duncan. *Understanding Capital: Marx's Economic Theory.* Cambridge, MA: Harvard University Press, 1986.

Fortunati, Leopoldina. *The Arcane of Reproduction. Housework, Prostitution, Labor and Capital.* Brooklyn: Autonomedia, 1995.

Foster, John Bellamy, and Robert W. McChesney. "Monopoly-Finance Capital and the Paradox of Accumulation." *Monthly Review* 61, no. 5 (October 2009): 1–20.

Foucault, Michel. *The Birth of the Clinic: An Archeology of Medical Perception.* New York: Pantheon Books, 1973.

_____. *Discipline and Punish.* London: Allen Lane, 1977.

_____. *Foucault Live: Collected Interviews, 1961–1984.* Edited by Sylvere Lotringer. New York: Semiotext(e), 1996.

_____. *The History of Sexuality, Volume One.* Harmondsworth: Penguin Books, 1981.

_____. *Madness and Civilization: A History of Insanity in the Age of Reason.* New York: New American Library, 1971.

_____. *The Order of Things: An Archeology of the Human Sciences.* New York: Random House, 1970.

Fukuyama, Francis. *Trust: The Social Virtues and the Creation of Prosperity.* New York: The Free Press, 1995.

Galilei, Galileo. *On Motion and On Mechanics.* Translated by I.D. Drabkin and S. Drake. Madison: University of Wisconsin Press, 1960.

Gibson, William, and Bruce Sterling. *The Difference Engine.* London: Victor Gollancz Ltd., 1990.

Gillespie, Charles. *The Edge of Objectivity.* Princeton: Princeton University Press, 1960.

Gorz, Andre. *Farewell to the Proletariat.* Boston: South End Press, 1983.

_____. *Paths to Paradise: On the Liberation from Work.* Boston: South End Press, 1985.

Granovetter, Mark. "Economic Action and Social Structure: The Problem of Embeddedness." In *The Sociology of Economic Life*, edited by Mark Granovetter and Richard Swedberg. Boulder: Westview Press, 1992.

Greenleaf, William, ed. *American Economic Development Since 1860.* New York: Harper and Row, 1968.

Guattari, Felix, and Antonio Negri. *Communists Like Us.* New York: Semiotext(e), 1990. Republished as *New Lines of Alliance, New Spaces of Liberty.* Brooklyn: Minor Compositions/Autonomedia, 2010.

Habermas, Jürgen. *Legitimation Crisis.* Boston: Beacon Press, 1975.

Haraway, Donna. *Simians, Cyborgs, and Women: The Reinvention of Nature*. New York: Routledge, 1991.

Hardt, Michael, and Antonio Negri. *Empire*. Cambridge, MA: Harvard University Press, 2000.

_____. *The Labor of Dionysius: A Critique of the State Form*. Minneapolis: University of Minnesota Press, 1994.

_____. *Multitude: War and Democracy in the Age of Empire*. Cambridge, MA: Harvard University Press, 2004.

Hayek, Friedrich A. *Individualism and the Economic Order*. London: Routledge and Kegan Paul, 1949.

Heckscher, Eli. *Mercantilism. Volume Two*. 2nd revised edition. London: George Allen & Unwin Ltd., 1955.

Hobbes, Thomas. *Leviathan*. Indianapolis: Hackett Publishing Co., 1994.

Hodges, Andrew. *Alan Turing: The Enigma*. New York: Simon and Schuster, 1983.

Hofstadter, D. *Gödel, Escher, Bach: The Eternal Golden Braid*. New York: Random House, 1980.

Hollander, Samuel. *The Economics of John Stuart Mill, Vol. 1: Theory of Method*. Toronto: University of Toronto Press, 1985.

Hyman, Anthony. *Charles Babbage: Pioneer of the Computer*. Oxford: Oxford University Press, 1982.

Illich, Ivan. *Shadow Work*. London: Marion Boyers, 1981.

James, Selma. "Wageless of the World." In *Sex, Race, and Class—The Perspective of Winning: A Selection of Writings 1952–2011*. Oakland: PM Press/Common Notions, 2011. Originally in *All Work and No Pay*, edited by Wendy Edmonds and Suzie Fleming. Bristol: Falling Wall Press, 1975.

Johnson, Richard D., and Charles H. Holbrow, eds. *Space Settlements: A Design Study*. Washington, DC: NASA, Scientific and Technical Information Office, 1975.

Joint Committee on Defense Production. *Economic and Social Consequences of Nuclear Attacks on the United States*. Washington, DC: U.S. Government Printing Office, 1979.

Kalecki, Michal. *Selected Essays on the Dynamics of the Capitalist Economy, 1933–1970*. Cambridge: Cambridge University Press, 1971.

Kemeny, John G. *Report of the President's Commission on the Accident at Three Mile Island*. Washington, DC: U.S. Government Printing Office, 1979.

Keynes, John Maynard. *Essays in Persuasion*. Vol. 9 of *The Collected Writings of John Maynard Keynes*. London: The Macmillan Press, 1972.

_____. *The General Theory of Employment, Interest and Money*. New York: Classic Books America, 2009.

Kisch, Herbert. *From Domestic Manufacture to Industrial Revolution: The Case of the Rhineland Textile Districts*. New York: Oxford University Press, 1989.

Kriedte, Peter. *Peasants, Landlords and Merchant Capitalists: Europe and the World Economy, 1500–1800*. Cambridge: Cambridge University Press, 1983.

Kurzweil, Ray. *The Age of Spiritual Machines: When Computers Exceed Human Intelligence*. New York: Penguin, 2000.

Laslett, Barbara, and Johanna Brenner. "Gender and Social Reproduction." *Annual Review of Sociology* 15 (1989): 381–404.

Latouche, Serge. *In the Wake of the Affluent Society: An Exploration of Post-Development*. London: Zed Books, 1993.

Lenin, V.I. "Imperialism: The Highest Stage of Capitalism." In *Selected Works*, Vol. I. New York: International Publishers, 1967.

Leventon, Jacob Clavner. *The Mind & Art of Henry Adams.* Boston: Houghton Mifflin Co., 1957.

Linebaugh, Peter. *The Magna Carta Manifesto: Liberties and Commons for All.* Berkeley: University of California Press, 2007.

Linebaugh, Peter, and Bruno Ramirez. "Crisis in the Auto Sector." In *Midnight Oil: Work, Energy, War, 1973–1992.* Brooklyn: Autonomedia, 1992. Originally published in *Zerowork I* in 1975.

Lippi, Marco. *Value and Naturalism in Marx.* London: New Left Books, 1979.

Locke, Gary. "National Export Initiative Remarks." February 4, 2010. http://www.commerce.gov/news/secretary-speeches/2010/02/04/national-exports-initiative-remarks.

Lucas, J.R. "Minds, Machines and Gödel." *Philosophy* 36, no. 137 (April–July 1961): 112–27.

Luxemburg, Rosa. *The Accumulation of Capital.* New York: Monthly Review Press, 1968.

Machlup, Fritz. *The Production and Distribution of Knowledge in the United States.* Princeton: Princeton University Press, 1962.

Macrae, Joanna, and Anthony Zwi, eds. *War and Hunger: Rethinking International Responses to Complex Emergencies.* London: Zed Books and Save the Children (UK), 1994.

Malos, Ellen, ed. *The Politics of Housework.* London: Allison and Busby, 1982.

Mao Tse-Tung. *Selected Works of Mao Tse-Tung Vol. IV.* Peking: Foreign Languages Press, 1969.

Marazzi, Christian. *Capital and Language: From the New Economy to the War Economy.* Cambridge, MA: MIT Press/Semiotext(e), 2008.

_____. *The Violence of Financial Capitalism.* Los Angeles: Semiotext(e), 2010.

Marx, Karl. "British Incomes in India." In *Karl Marx on Colonialism and Modernization: His Dispatches and Other Writings on China, India, Mexico, the Middle East and North Africa,* edited by Shlomo Avineri. New York: Doubleday and Company, 1968.

_____. *Capital: Volume I: A Critique of Political Economy.* London: Penguin, 1976.

_____. *Capital: Volume II: A Critique of Political Economy.* London: Penguin, 1978.

_____. *Capital: Volume III: A Critique of Political Economy.* London: Penguin, 1981.

_____. *A Contribution to the Critique of Political Economy.* New York: International Publishers, 1970.

_____. *Grundrisse: Foundations of the Critique of Political Economy.* Harmondsworth: Penguin, 1973.

_____. *Pre-capitalist Economic Formations.* New York: International Publishers, 1964.

_____. *Theories of Surplus Value, Part I.* Moscow: Progress Publishers, 1963.

_____. *Theories of Surplus Value, Part II.* Moscow: Progress Publishers, 1968.

_____. *Value, Price and Profit.* New York: International Publishers, 1935.

Marx, Karl, and Friedrich Engels. *Selected Correspondences, 1846–1895.* London: Lawrence & Wishart, 1936.

Mathieu, Deborah. *Organ Substitution Technology: Ethical, Legal, and Public Policy Issues.* Boulder: Westview Press, 1988.

Mattick, Paul. *Marx and Keynes: The Limits of a Mixed Economy.* Boston: F. Porter Sargent, 1969.

McKenzie, Richard, and Gordon Tullock. *The New World of Economics: Explorations into the Human Experience*. Homewood, IL: Richard D. Irwin Inc., 1978.

Meillassoux, Claude. *Maidens, Meal and Money: Capitalism and the Domestic Community*. Cambridge: Cambridge University Press, 1988.

Menzel, Paul. *Strong Medicine: The Ethical Rationing of Health Care*. New York: Oxford University Press, 1990.

Midnight Notes Collective, eds. *Auroras of the Zapatistas: Local and Global Struggles in the Fourth World War*. Brooklyn: Autonomedia, 2001.

_____. *Midnight Oil: Work, Energy, War, 1973–1992*. Brooklyn: Autonomedia, 1992.

_____. *The New Enclosures*. Brooklyn: Autonomedia, 1990.

_____. *One No, Many Yeses*. Brooklyn: Autonomedia, 1998.

_____. *Outlaw Notes*. Brooklyn: Midnight Notes, 1985.

_____. *Strange Victories: The Anti-nuclear Movement in the U.S. & Europe*. Jamaica Plain, MA: Midnight Notes, 1979.

_____. "The Working Class Waves Bye-Bye: A Proletarian Response to Andre Gorz." *Lemming Notes*. Special issue of *Midnight Notes* 7 (1984): 12–16.

Midnight Notes Collective and Friends. *Promissory Notes: From Crisis to Commons*. Brooklyn: Autonomedia, 2009.

Mirowski, Philip. *More Heat than Light: Economics as Social Physics, Physics as Nature's Economics*. Cambridge: Cambridge University Press, 1989.

Negri, Antonio. *Marx Beyond Marx: Lessons on the Grundrisse*. Brooklyn: Autonomedia, 1991.

New York Times, The Downsizing of America. New York: Times Books/Random House, 1996.

Nordhaus, William D. "The Falling Share of Profits." *Brookings Institute Papers*. Washington, DC: Brookings Institute Press, 1975.

Novalis. *Henry von Ofterdingen: A Novel*. New York: Frederick Ungar Pub. Co., 1964.

O'Connor, James. *The Fiscal Crisis of the State*. New York: St. Martin's Press, 1973.

Odum, Howard T., and Elisabeth C. Odum. *Energy Basis for Man and Nature*. New York: McGraw-Hill, 1976.

O'Neill, Gerard, ed. *Space Colonies*. New York: Penguin, 1977.

Organization for Economic Cooperation and Development. *Education Policy Analysis: Education and Skills*. Paris: OECD, 2001.

_____. *The OECD Jobs Study: Evidence and Explanations*. Paris: OECD, 1994.

Ord-Hume, Arthur W.J.G. *Perpetual Motion: The History of an Obsession*. New York: St. Martin's Press, 1977.

Pack, Spenser J. *Reconstructing Marxian Economics: Marx Based upon a Sraffian Commodity Theory of Value*. New York: Praeger, 1986.

Palloix, Christian. *Les firmes multinationales et le procès d'internationalisation*. Paris: Francois Maspero, 1973.

Picchio, Antonella. *The Political Economy of Social Reproduction*. Cambridge: Cambridge University Press, 1992.

Polanyi, Karl. "The Economy as Instituted Process." In *The Sociology of Economic Life*, edited by Mark Granovetter and Richard Swedberg. Boulder: Westview Press, 1992.

_____. *The Great Transformation: The Political and Economic Origins of Our Times*. Boston: Beacon Press, 1944 [1957].

_____. *Primitive, Archaic and Modern Economies: The Essays of Karl Polanyi*. Edited by George Dalton. Boston: Beacon Press, 1968.

Posner, Richard. *Sex and Reason*. Cambridge Mass.: Harvard University Press, 1992.

Post, Emil. "Finite Combinatory Processes: Formulation 1." *Journal of Symbolic Logic* 1, no. 3 (1936): 103–5.

p.m. *bolo'bolo*. Brooklyn: Autonomedia, 2011 [1985].

Rediker, Marcus. *Villains of All Nations: Atlantic Pirates in the Golden Age*. Boston: Beacon Press, 2004.

Reich, Robert. *The Work of Nations*. New York: Random House, 1992.

Ricardo, David. *Principles of Political Economy and Taxation*. New York: Macmillan Co., 1914.

Rifkin, Jeremy. *The End of Work: The Decline of the Global Labor Force and the Dawn of the Post-market Era*. New York: G.P. Putnam's Sons, 1995.

Savio, Mario. "An End to History." In *The New Left: A Documentary History*, edited by Massimo Teodori. Indianapolis: Bobbs-Merrill, 1969.

Say, Jean-Baptiste. *A Treatise on Political Economy or the Production, Distribution and Consumption of Wealth*. New York: Augustus M. Kelly Reprints of Economic Classics, 1964.

Schlumbohm, Jürgen. "Relations of Production—Productive Forces—Crises." In *Industrialization before Industrialization: Rural Industry in the Genesis of Capitalism*, edited by Peter Kriedte, Hans Medick, and Jürgen Schlumbohm. Cambridge: Cambridge University Press, 1981.

Schor, Juliet B. *The Overworked American: The Unexpected Decline of Leisure*. New York: Basic Books, 1991.

Schrodinger, Erwin. *What Is Life?* Cambridge: Cambridge University Press, 1944.

Schumpeter, Joseph. *Economic Doctrine and Method*. New York: Oxford University Press, 1967.

Sen, Amartya K. *Poverty and Famines: An Essay on Entitlement and Deprivation*, Oxford: Clarendon Press, 1981.

Seneca, Lucius Annaeus. *Moral Epistles*. Translated by Richard M. Gummere. Cambridge, MA: Harvard University Press, 1917.

Sensat, Julius, Jr. *Habermas and Marxism: An Appraisal*. Beverly Hills, CA: Sage, 1979.

Serafini, Alessandro, ed. *L'operaio multinazionale in Europa*. Milan: Feltrinelli, 1974.

Shaikh, Anwar. "Marx's Theory of Value and the 'Transformation Problem.'" In *The Subtle Anatomy of Capitalism*, edited by Jesse Schwartz. Santa Monica: Goodyear Pub. Co., 1977.

Sharlet, Jeff. "Inside America's Most Powerful Megachurch." *Harper's* (May 2005): 41–54.

Sheppard, Harold L., and Neal Q. Herrick, *Where Have All the Robots Gone? Worker Dissatisfaction in the '70s*. New York: The Free Press, 1972.

Simmel, Georg. *The Philosophy of Money*. London: Routledge, 2002.

Smart, Barry. *Foucault, Marxism and Critique*. London: Routledge and Kegan Paul, 1983.

Smelser, Neil J., and Richard Swedberg. "The Sociological Perspective on the Economy." In *The Handbook of Economic Sociology*, edited by Neil J. Smelser and Richard Swedberg. Princeton: Princeton University Press, 1994.

Smith, Adam. *Wealth of Nations*. Amherst, NY: Prometheus Books, 1991 [1776].

Sohn-Rethel, Alfred. *Intellectual and Manual Labour: A Critique of Epistemology*. London: Macmillan, 1978.

Special Task Force to the Secretary of Health, Education, and Welfare. *Work in America*.

Cambridge, MA: The MIT Press, 1973.

Spinoza, Benedict de. *On the Improvement of the Understanding. The Ethics. Correspondence*. New York: Dover, 1955.

Sraffa, Piero. *Production of Commodities by Means of Commodities*. Cambridge: Cambridge University Press, 1960.

Steedman, Ian, et al. *The Value Controversy*. London: Verso, 1981.

Steele, David Ramsay. *From Marx to Mises: Post-capitalist Society and the Challenge of Economic Calculation*. La Salle, IL: Open Court, 1992.

Stewart-McDougall, Mark Lynn. *The Artisan Republic: Revolution, Reaction, and Resistance in Lyon, 1848–1851*. Kingston: McGill-Queens University Press, 1984.

Swedberg, Richard, ed. "Economic Sociology: Past and Present." *Current Sociology* 35 (1987): 1–221.

_____. *Economics and Sociology: Redefining Their Boundaries, Conversations with Economists and Sociologists*. Princeton: Princeton University Press, 1990.

_____. "Major Traditions of Economic Sociology." *Annual Review of Sociology* 17 (1991): 251–76.

Sweezy, Paul. *The Theory of Capitalist Development*. New York: Monthly Review Press, 1942.

Taton, Rene, ed. *Science in the Nineteenth Century*. New York: Basic Books, 1965.

Taussig, Michael T. *The Devil and Commodity Fetishism in South America*. Chapel Hill, NC: University of North Carolina Press, 1980.

Teller, Edward. "Energy: A Plan for Action." In *Power & Security*, edited by Edward Teller, Hans Mark, and John S. Foster Jr., 1–82. Lexington, MA: Lexington Books, 1976.

Thomas, J.J. *Informal Economic Activity*. Ann Arbor: University of Michigan Press, 1992.

Thompson, E.P. *Customs in Common*. New York: The New Press, 1991.

_____. "Notes on Exterminism: The Last Stage of Civilization." In *Peace Studies: Critical Concepts in Political Scienc*e, edited by Mathew Evangelista, 186–214. New York: Routledge, 2005.

Thomson, George. *The First Philosophers*. London: Lawrence and Wishart, 1955.

Tronti, Mario. "Workers and Capital." *Telos* 14 (1972): 25–62. Subsequently published as "Capitale Sociale." *Telos* 17 (1973): 98–121.

Truesdell, C.A. *The Tragicomical History of Thermodynamics, 1822–1854*. New York: Springer-Verlag, 1980.

Tullock, Gordon. "Economic Imperialism." In *The Theory of Public Choice*, edited by James M. Buchanan and Robert D. Tollison. Ann Arbor: University of Michigan Press, 1972.

Turing, Alan. "Computing Machinery and Intelligence." *Mind* 59, no. 236 (May 1950): 433–60.

_____. "On Computable Numbers." In *The Undecidable*, edited by Martin Davis. Hewlett, NY: Raven Press, 1965.

_____. "On Computable Numbers with an Application to the Entscheidungsproblem." In *The Essential Turing: Seminal Writings in Computing, Logic, Philosophy, Artificial Intelligence, and Artificial Life, Plus: The Secrets of Enigma*, edited by Jack Copeland. Oxford: Clarendon Press, 2004 [1936]: 58–90.

Ure, Andrew. *The Philosophy of Manufactures*. New York: Augustus M. Kelley, 1967.

Vercellone, Carlo. "Cognitive Capitalism and Models for the Regulation of Wages." In *Towards a Global Autonomous University: Cognitive Labor, the Production of Knowledge, and Exodus from the Education Factory*, edited by the Edu-factory Collective. Brooklyn: Autonomedia, 2009.

_____. "From Formal Subsumption to General Intellect: Elements for a Marxist Reading to the Thesis of Cognitive Capitalism." *Historical Materialism* 15 (2007): 13–36.

_____. "The Hypothesis of Cognitive Capitalism." Paper presented at the Historical Materialism annual conference, London, November 4–5, 2005.

_____. "The New Articulation of Wages, Rent and Profit in Cognitive Capitalism." Paper presented at the conference "The Art of Rent." Queen Mary University School of Business and Management, London, 2008.

Virno, Paolo. *A Grammar of the Multitude.* New York: Semiotext(e), 2004.

von Böhm-Bawerk, Eugene. "Control or Economic Law." In *Shorter Classics of E. Von Böhm-Bawerk*. South Holland, IL: Libertarian Press, 1962

_____. *Karl Marx and the Close of His System.* London: Porcupine Press, 2006.

von Neumann, John. "The General and Logical Theory of Automata." In *The World of Mathematics*, edited by James Newman. New York: Simon and Schuster, 1956.

Weber, Max. *The Protestant Ethic and the "Spirit" of Capitalism.* Translated by Peter Baehr and Gordon C. Wells. London: Penguin Books, 2002.

Weiner, Norbert. *Cybernetics; or, Control and Communication in the Animal and the Machine.* Cambridge, MA: MIT Press, 1965.

White, Luise. *Speaking with Vampires: Rumor and History in Colonial Africa.* Berkeley: University of California Press, 2000.

Widick. B.J. "Work in Auto Plants: Then and Now." In *Auto Work and Its Discontents*, edited by B.J. Widick. Baltimore: John Hopkins University Press, 1976.

Wild, Larry. "Film Production." http://www3.northern.edu/wild/th100/flmprod.htm.

Williams, Jeffrey. "The Pedagogy of Debt." In *Towards a Global Autonomous University: Cognitive labor, the Production of Knowledge, and Exodus from the Education Factory*, edited by the Edu-factory Collective. Brooklyn: Autonomedia, 2009.

Williamson, Oliver. "Transaction Cost Economics and Organization Theory." In *The Handbook of Economic Sociology*, edited by Neil J. Smelser and Richard Swedberg. Princeton: Princeton University Press, 1994.

World Bank. *Constructing Knowledge Societies: New Challenges for Tertiary Education.* Washington, DC: World Bank, 2002.

_____. *Higher Education: The Lessons of Experience. Development in Practice Series.* Washington, DC: World Bank, 1994.

_____. *The World Bank and the Environment.* Washington, DC: World Bank, 1992.

Youmans, Edward L. *The Correlation and Conservation of Forces: A Series of Expositions.* New York: Appleton & Co., 1872.

Zinn, Howard. *A People's History of the United States.* New York: HarperCollins, 2003.

INDEX

George Caffentzis is a philosopher of money and a leading thinker in the development of autonomist thought. He has been a participant in numerous movements since the civil rights period, when he was first arrested in sit-ins during the early 1960s. He continued his political activism, especially in the antinuclear power movement, throughout the 1970s and early 1980s. In 1974, he coedited the first issue of *Zerowork* and in 1978 cofounded the Midnight Notes Collective, publishing the journal of the collective over the next thirty years.

Starting in 1983, Caffentzis taught logic, philosophy, and the history of science in the Department of Philosophy and Religious Studies at the University of Calabar, near the oil center of Nigeria. It was here that he first learned of the "new enclosures" implicit in the World Bank's structural adjustment programs and the politics of oil from the ground level. He returned to the United States to teach at the University of Southern Maine, where he is now a professor in the Philosophy Department and the Honors Program.

Caffentzis has published many books and articles on issues ranging from the death penalty, self-reproducing automata, peak oil, the enclosure of knowledge in Africa, and the philosophy of money. His writing has been consistently motivated by his political engagements in the anti-nuclear, anti-war, anti–capital punishment, alter-globalization, pro-Zapatista, and pro-commons movements. Over the years, his original and powerful contributions to international anti-capitalist movements have stemmed from his stretching and developing of autonomist concepts steeped in the insights from feminist experiences of Wages for Housework, operaist thinkers and militants in Italy, and historical studies of class struggle inspired by E.P. Thompson and his comrades.

George Caffentzis is also cofounder of the Committee for Academic Freedom in Africa. He has taught and lectured in colleges and universities throughout the world and his work has been translated into many languages. His books include *Clipped Coins, Abused Words, and Civil Government: John Locke's Philosophy of Money*, and *Exciting the Industry of Mankind: George Berkeley's Philosophy of Money*. His coedited books include: *Midnight Oil: Work, Energy, War, 1973–1992*; *Auroras of the Zapatistas: Local and Global Struggles in the Fourth World War*; and *A Thousand Flowers: Social Struggles Against Structural Adjustment in African Universities*.

BECOME A FRIEND OF

These are indisputably momentous times—
the financial system is melting down globally
and the Empire is stumbling. Now more than
ever there is a vital need for radical ideas.

In the six years since its founding—and on a mere shoestring—
PM Press has risen to the formidable challenge of publishing and
distributing knowledge and entertainment for the struggles ahead.
With over 250 releases to date, we have published an impressive and
stimulating array of literature, art, music, politics, and culture. Using
every available medium, we've succeeded in connecting those hungry
for ideas and information to those putting them into practice.

Friends of PM allows you to directly help impact, amplify, and
revitalize the discourse and actions of radical writers, filmmakers, and
artists. It provides us with a stable foundation from which we can
build upon our early successes and provides a much-needed subsidy
for the materials that can't necessarily pay their own way. You can
help make that happen—and receive every new title automatically
delivered to your door once a month—by joining as a Friend of PM
Press. And, we'll throw in a free T-Shirt when you sign up.

Here are your options:
- $25 a month: Get all books and pamphlets plus 50% discount
  on all webstore purchases
- $40 a month: Get all PM Press releases (including CDs and
  DVDs) plus 50% discount on all webstore purchases
- $100 a month: Superstar—Everything plus PM merchandise,
  free downloads, and 50% discount on all webstore purchases

For those who can't afford $25 or more a month, we're introducing
Sustainer Rates at $15, $10 and $5. Sustainers get a free PM Press
t-shirt and a 50% discount on all purchases from our website.

Your Visa or Mastercard will be billed once a month, until you tell us
to stop. Or until our efforts succeed in bringing the revolution around.
Or the financial meltdown of Capital makes plastic redundant.
Whichever comes first.

PM PRESS was founded at the end of 2007 by a small collection of folks with decades of publishing, media, and organizing experience. PM Press co-conspirators have published and distributed hundreds of books, pamphlets, CDs, and DVDs. Members of PM have founded enduring book fairs, spearheaded victorious tenant organizing campaigns, and worked closely with bookstores, academic conferences, and even rock bands to deliver political and challenging ideas to all walks of life. We're old enough to know what we're doing and young enough to know what's at stake.

We seek to create radical and stimulating fiction and non-fiction books, pamphlets, t-shirts, visual and audio materials to entertain, educate and inspire you. We aim to distribute these through every available channel with every available technology—whether that means you are seeing anarchist classics at our bookfair stalls; reading our latest vegan cookbook at the café; downloading geeky fiction e-books; or digging new music and timely videos from our website.

PM Press is always on the lookout for talented and skilled volunteers, artists, activists and writers to work with. If you have a great idea for a project or can contribute in some way, please get in touch.

PM PRESS
PO Box 23912
Oakland CA 94623
510-658-3906
www.pmpress.org

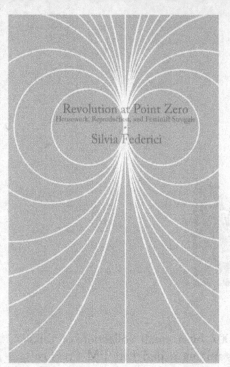

Revolution at Point Zero: Housework, Reproduction, and Feminist Struggle
by Silvia Federici
ISBN: 978-1-60486-333-8
$15.95

Written between 1974 and the present, *Revolution at Point Zero* collects forty years of research and theorizing on the nature of housework, social reproduction, and women's struggles on this terrain—to escape it, to better its conditions, to reconstruct it in ways that provide an alternative to capitalist relations.

Indeed, as Federici reveals, behind the capitalist organization of work and the contradictions inherent in "alienated labor" is an explosive ground zero for revolutionary practice upon which are decided the daily realities of our collective reproduction.

Beginning with Federici's organizational work in the Wages for Housework movement, the essays collected here unravel the power and politics of wide but related issues including the international restructuring of reproductive work and its effects on the sexual division of labor, the globalization of care work and sex work, the crisis of elder care, the development of affective labor, and the politics of the commons.

Praise:

"Finally we have a volume that collects the many essays that over a period of four decades Silvia Federici has written on the question of social reproduction and women's struggles on this terrain. While providing a powerful history of the changes in the organization of reproductive labor, *Revolution at Point Zero* documents the development of Federici's thought on some of the most important questions of our time: globalization, gender relations, the construction of new commons."
—Mariarosa Dalla Costa, coauthor of *The Power of Women and the Subversion of the Community* and *Our Mother Ocean*

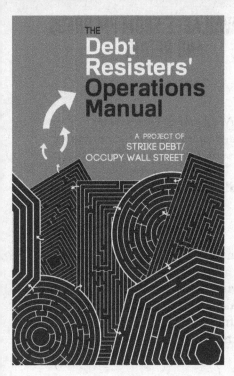

Ned Ludd & Queen Mab:
Machine-Breaking, Romanticism, and the
Several Commons of 1811-12
by Peter Linebaugh
ISBN: 978-1-60486-704-6
$6.95

Peter Linebaugh, in an extraordinary historical and literary *tour de force*, enlists the anonymous and scorned 19th century loom-breakers of the English midlands into the front ranks of an international, polyglot, many-colored crew of commoners resisting dispossession in the dawn of capitalist modernity.

Praise:

"Sneering at the Luddites is still the order of the day. Peter Linebaugh's great act of historical imagination stops the scoffers in their tracks. It takes the cliche of 'globalization' and makes it live: the Yorkshire machine-breakers are put right back in the violent world economy of 1811-12, in touch with the Atlantic slave trade, Mediterranean agri-business, the Tecumseh rebellion, the brutal racism of London dockland. The local and the global are once again shown to be inseparable—as they are, at present, for the machine-breakers of the new world crisis."
—T.J. Clark, author of *The Absolute Bourgeois and Image of the People*

"My benediction" —E.J. Hobsbawm, author of *Primitive Rebels* and *Captain Swing*

"E.P. Thompson, you may rest now. Linebaugh restores the dignity of the despised luddites with a poetic grace worthy of the master. By a stunning piece of re-casting we see them here not as rebels against the future but among the avant-garde of a planetary resistance movement against capitalist enclosures in the long struggle for a different future. Byron, Shelley, listen up! Peter Linebaugh's *Ned Ludd & Queen Mab* does for 'technology' what his London Hanged did for 'crime.' Where was I that day in Bloomsbury when he delivered this commonist manifesto for the 21st century? The Retort Pamphet series is off to a brilliant start." —Mike Davis, author of *Planet of Slums* and *Buda's Wagon*